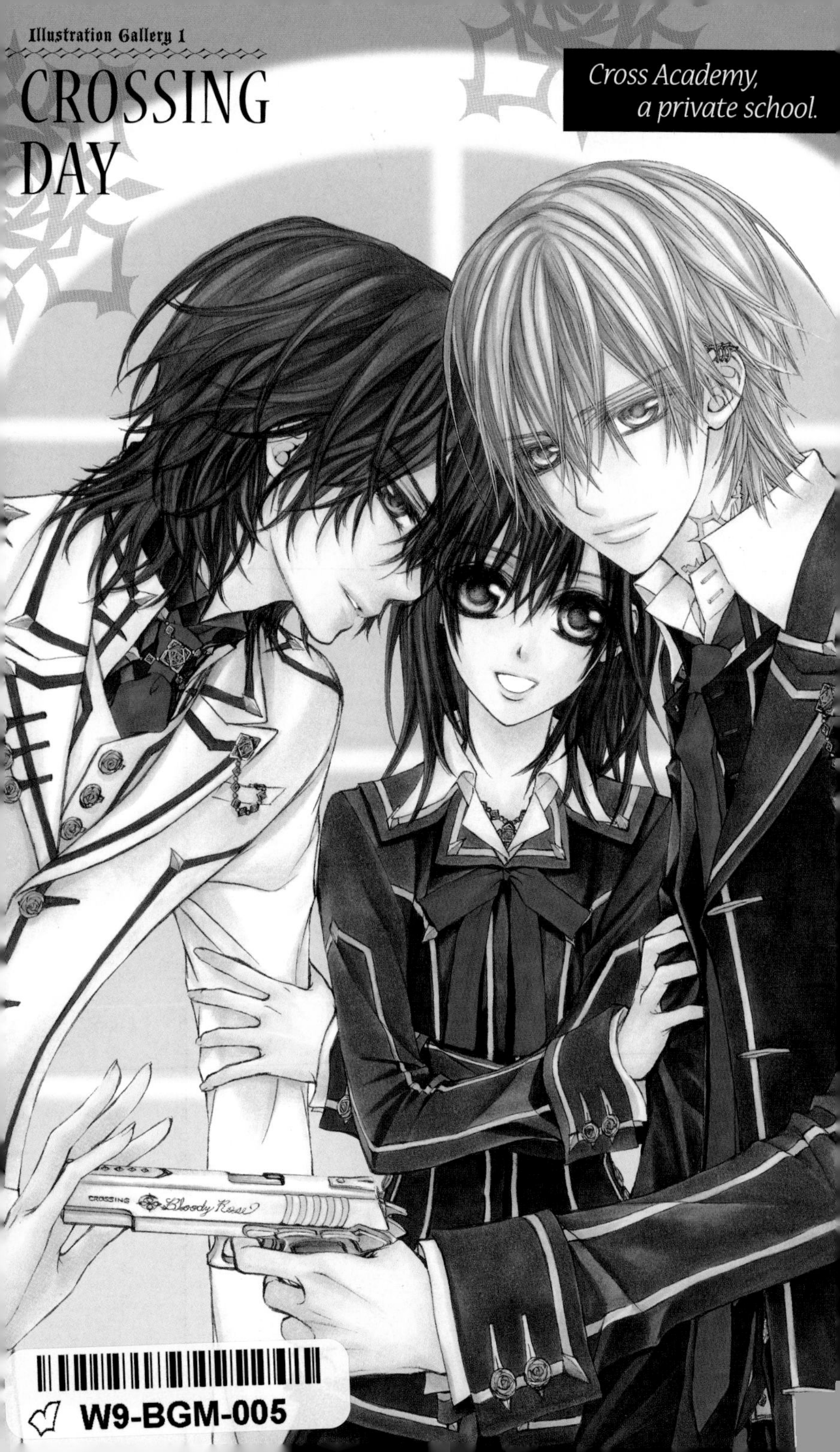
Illustration Gallery 1
CROSSING DAY
Cross Academy, a private school.
CROSSING Bloody Rose

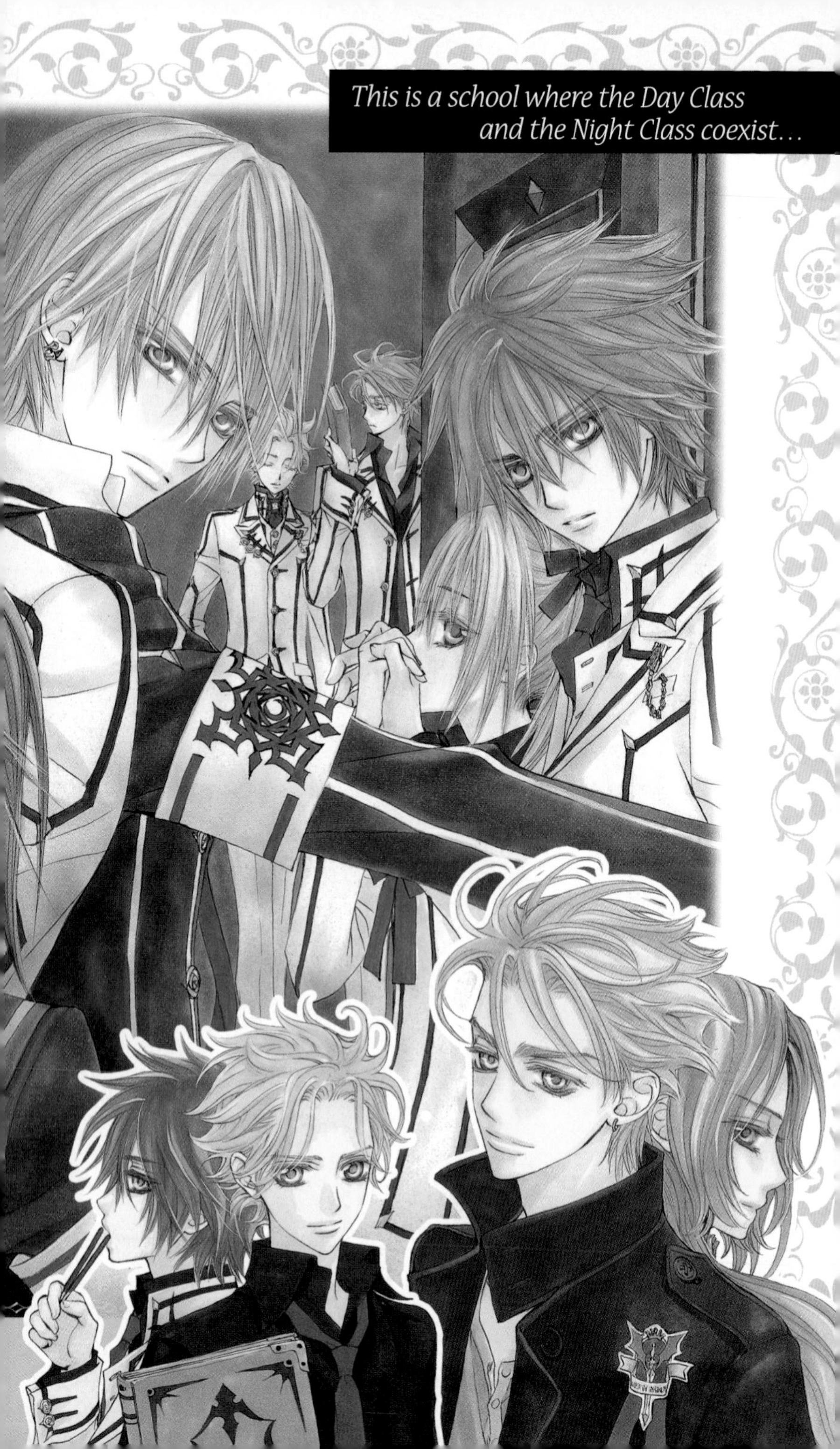
This is a school where the Day Class
and the Night Class coexist...

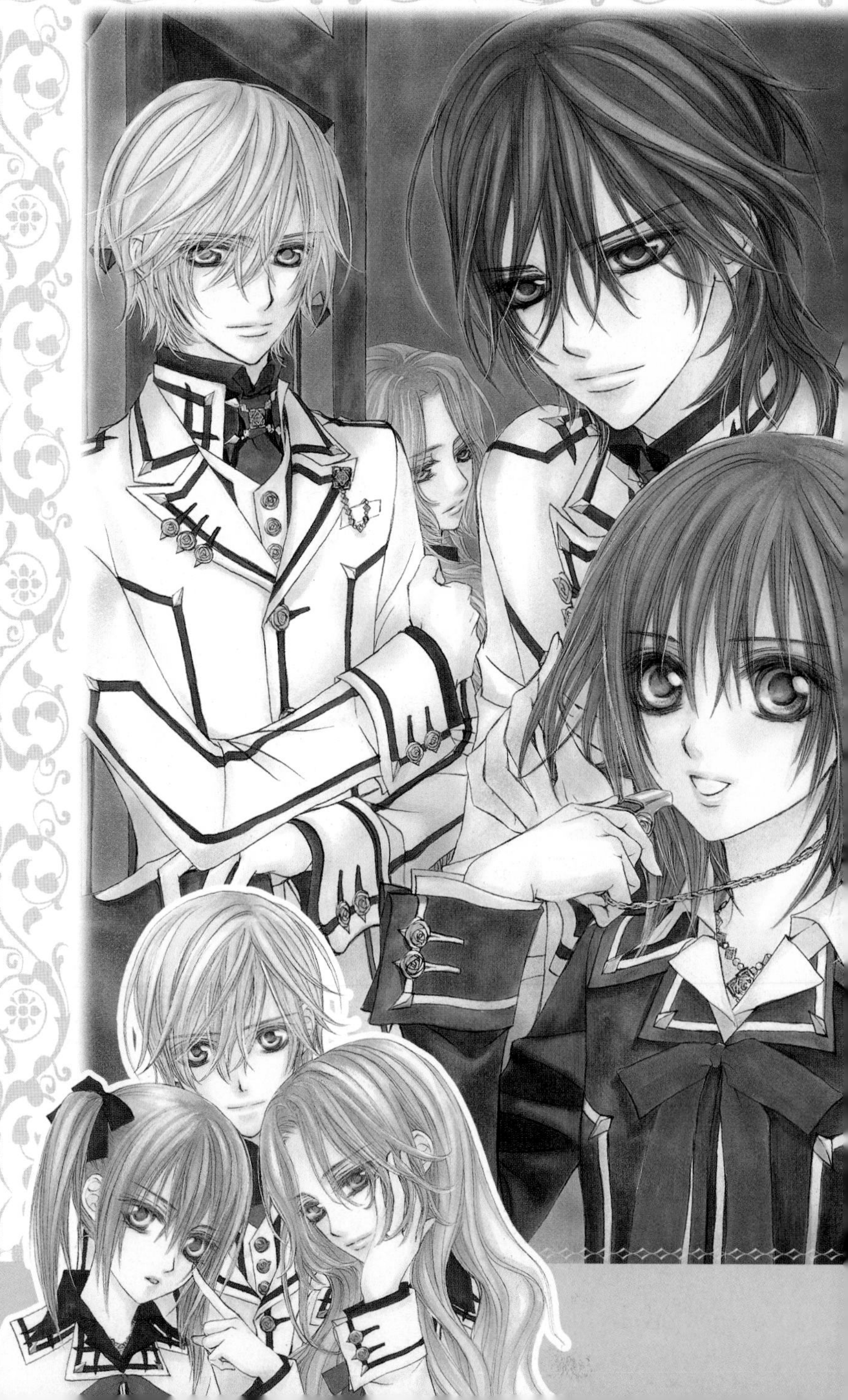

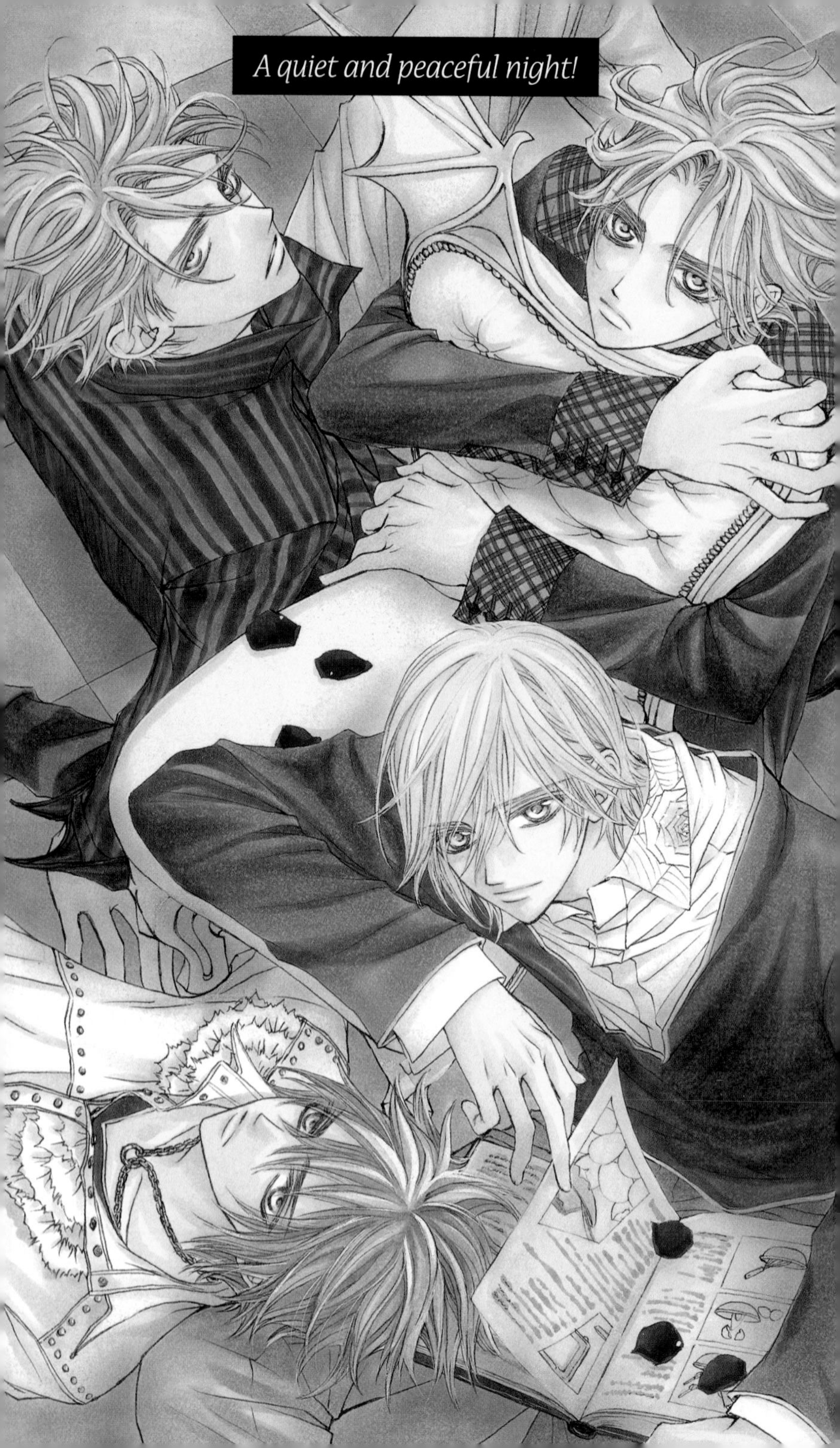
A quiet and peaceful night!

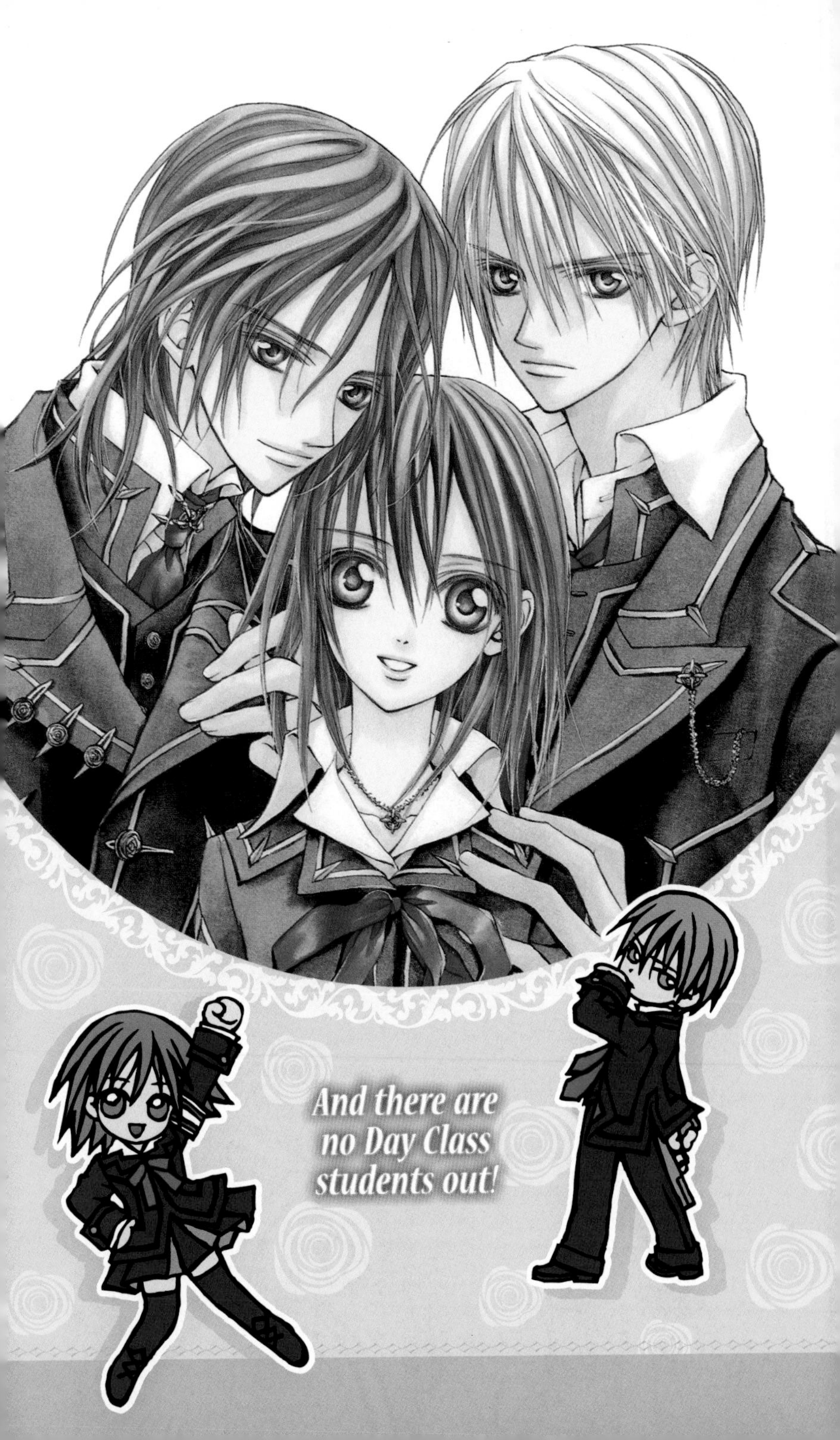
And there are no Day Class students out!

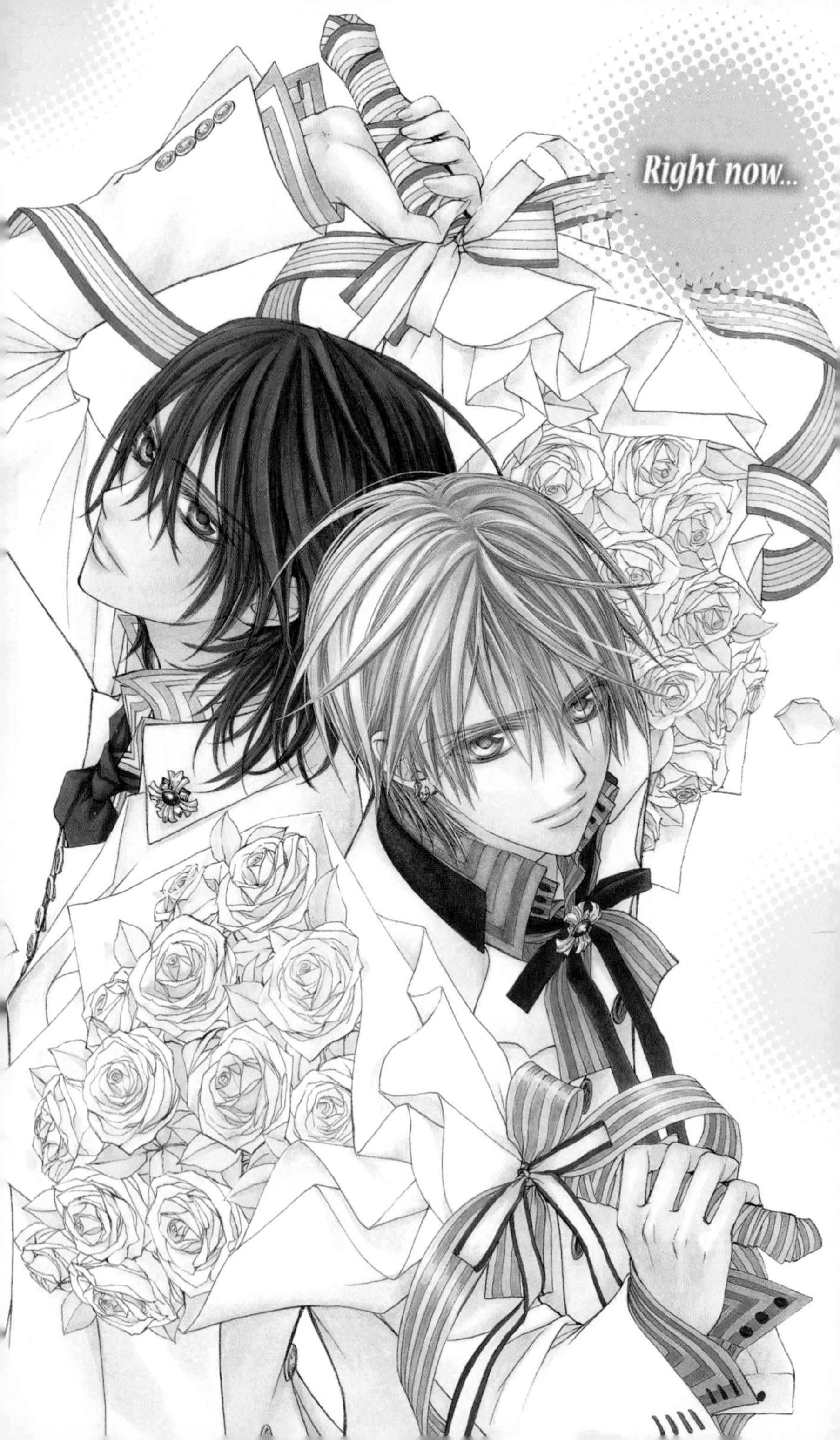
Right now...

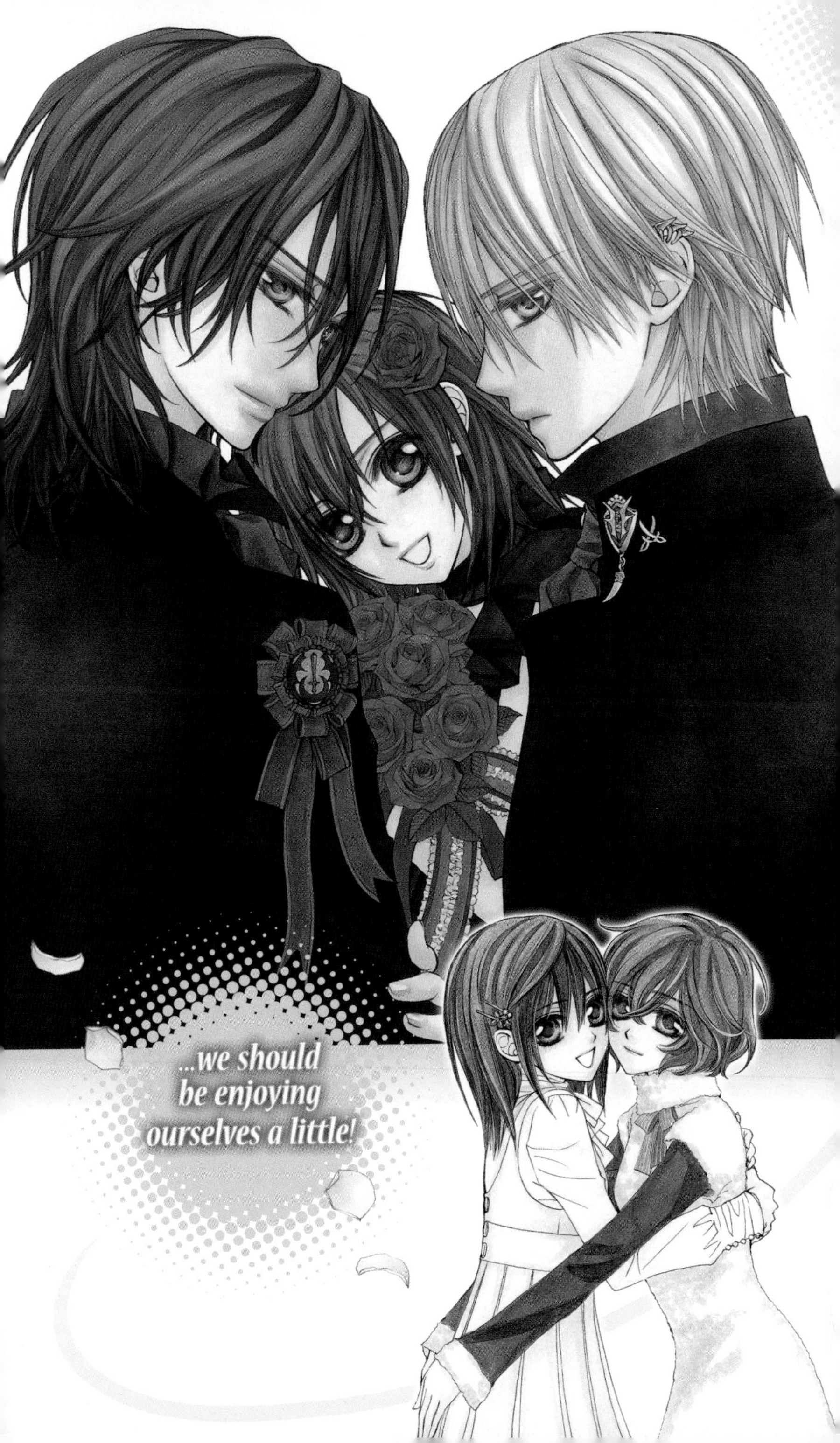
...we should be enjoying ourselves a little!

Welcome back,
Night Class.

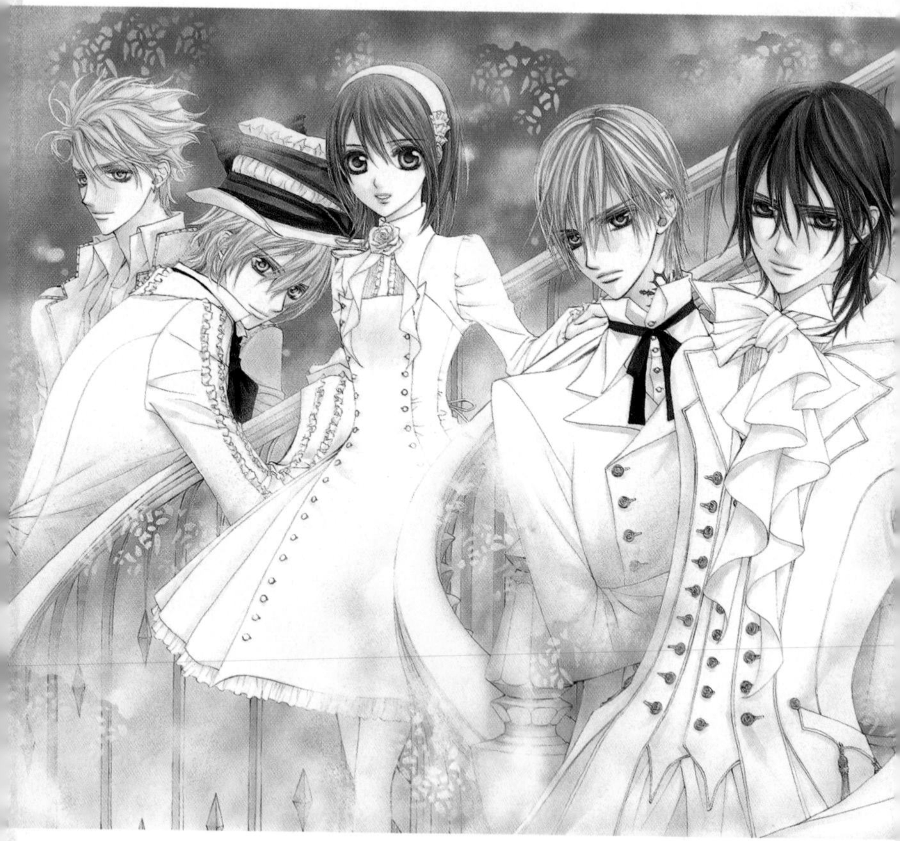

Thank you,
Miss Disciplinary Committee.

VAMPIRE KNIGHT

OFFICIAL FANBOOK

MATSURI HINO

Contents

Prologue
Cross Academy

A Peaceful Sandbox Where Humans and Vampires Coexist

A quiet, idyllic place where two species, humans and vampires, manage to coexist under the Headmaster's proud ideology…

We introduce the student life of the two classes, the Day Class and the Night Class, using illustrations that are being made public for the first time!!

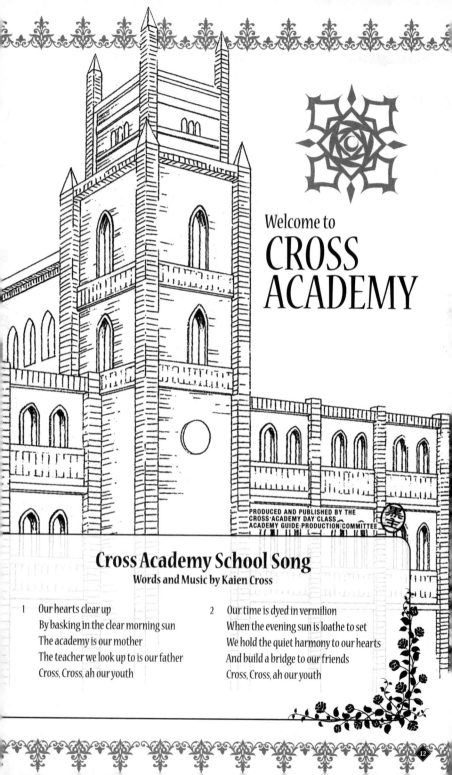

Welcome to
CROSS ACADEMY

PRODUCED AND PUBLISHED BY THE
CROSS·ACADEMY DAY CLASS
ACADEMY GUIDE PRODUCTION COMMITTEE

Cross Academy School Song
Words and Music by Kaien Cross

1. Our hearts clear up
   By basking in the clear morning sun
   The academy is our mother
   The teacher we look up to is our father
   Cross, Cross, ah our youth

2. Our time is dyed in vermilion
   When the evening sun is loathe to set
   We hold the quiet harmony to our hearts
   And build a bridge to our friends
   Cross, Cross, ah our youth

GREETINGS — WELCOME

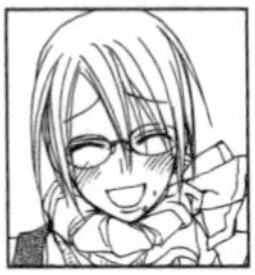

We teach and foster harmony through cross-cultural interaction.

HEADMASTER, CROSS ACADEMY
Kaien Cross

Welcome to my wonderful academy! Pay attention to the school song first. ♥ I took the trouble of writing it, but the Night Class students won't sing it. Oh, the theme is cross-cultural interaction. Think of the Day Class and the Night Class as the sun and the moon… Hm? No more space?

MESSAGES — FROM THE STUDENTS

I welcome cute girls!

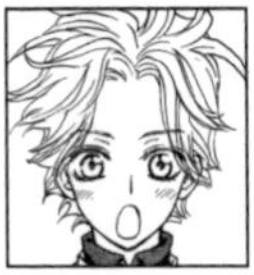

You're lucky you get to meet me. ♥ If you want to give me a gift, give me your delicious ■※▲×.
(CENSORED BY THE DISCIPLINARY COMMITTEE)

—Hanabusa Aido, Night Class

I'll make you cry if you won't listen to me.

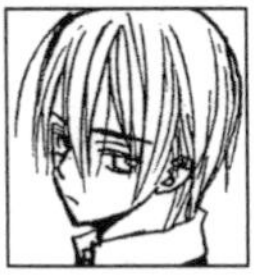

I'll punish you if you make a fuss and interfere with my duties when the Night Class comes out. This is an order from the Disciplinary Committee.

—Zero Kiryu, Day Class

Zero, don't make threats!

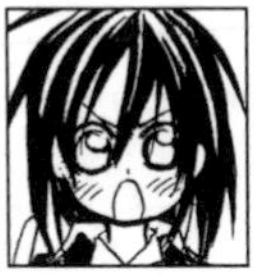

C'mon, you're going to scare everyone! And Headmaster! Choose your photo carefully! There's rice around your mouth!

—Yuki Cross, Day Class

A place for learning, located in a quiet forest…
Students who nurture intelligence and education, noble personalities and the spirit of fellowship…
This guide is an introduction to the academy for the new student. We hope your three years here will be fruitful…

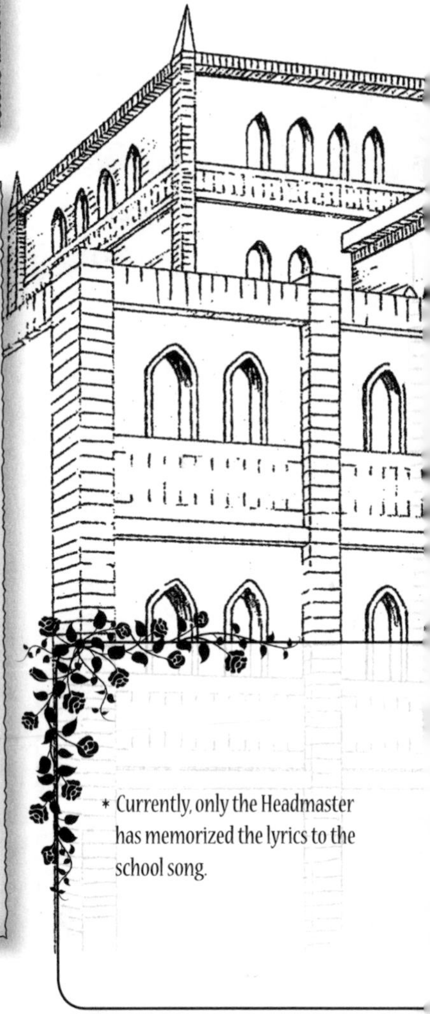

* Currently, only the Headmaster has memorized the lyrics to the school song.

A system that educates students a notch above the others

The academy produces excellent talents through its thorough entrance and promotion system. There are two classes—a Day Class and a Night Class—that consist of superior students. Both classes have their own dormitory.

PROMOTION SYSTEM

Night Class	Day Class
	Grade School
	↓
Integrated School System	Junior High School
	↓
	High School
	↓
	College

ENTRY SYSTEM

Night Class	Day Class
Those who've never attended school can recommend themselves or have someone else recommend them.	Recommendation from designated schools and sister schools
↓	↓
Headmaster interview	Written exam
Pass	Pass
Night Class dorm president interview	Interview
Pass	Pass
Entry procedures for the academy and the dormitory	Entry procedures for the academy and the dormitory

NIGHT CLASS

Exterior of the Moon Dormitory (the male dorm)

◇❖◇‹From the male Moon Dormitory dorm president›◇❖◇

I'm Kaname Kuran, president of the Night Class and dorm president. Students of the Moon Dormitory take classes from early evening through the night, so a lot of them are sleepy in the mornings. If you keep the noise level down near the Moon Dormitory during the morning, I'd appreciate it… Thanks.

➡ The Day Class and the Night Class school rules differ a little. Fighting and drinking blood are prohibited… Huh?! Drinking blood?

FIGHTING IS PROHIBITED!

IT SAYS SO IN THE STUDENT HANDBOOK!

DAY CLASS

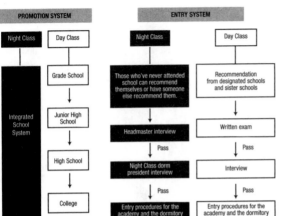

Exterior of the Sun Dormitory (the male dorm)

◇❖◇‹From the male Sun Dormitory dorm president›◇❖◇

The dorm is lively and fun. Even if the Night Class steals the show…

◇❖◇‹From the female Sun Dormitory dorm president›◇❖◇

I'm having trouble dealing with fans of the Night Class who create a fuss every evening and break curfew.

WHY DON'T YOU SET UP A HIDDEN CAMERA IN THE MOON DORM? NO ONE WOULD BE THERE DURING THE HOLIDAYS.

HEY.

UM.

EH?!

SHH, SHH.

⬆ Even if you're interested in the Night Class, no hidden cameras are allowed.

UNIFORMS

A noble look with rose designs

Jackets have rose-shaped buttons, vinelike stitches and thornlike studs. The stitching on the Day Class and Night Class uniforms differs a bit.

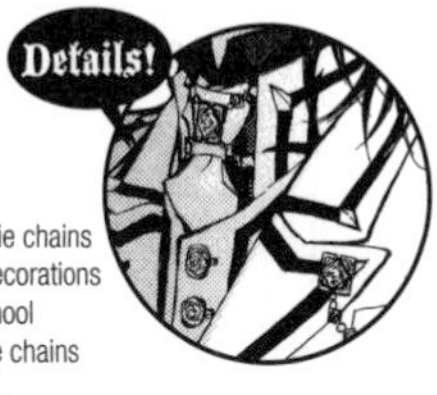
Details!

Boys wear tie chains and lapel decorations with the school emblem. Tie chains are optional.

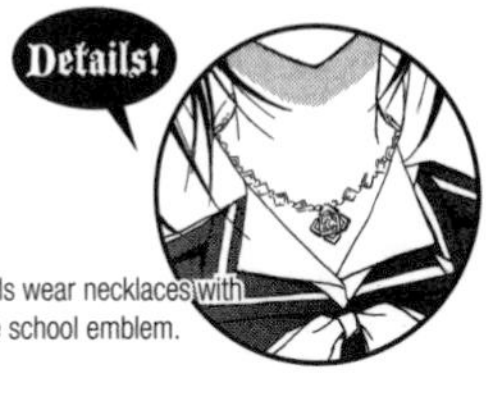
Details!

Girls wear necklaces with the school emblem.

Boys

Girls

Both boys and girls wear pure white shirts.

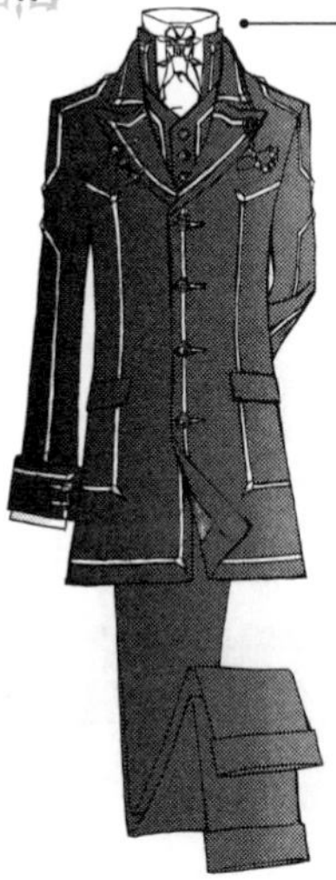

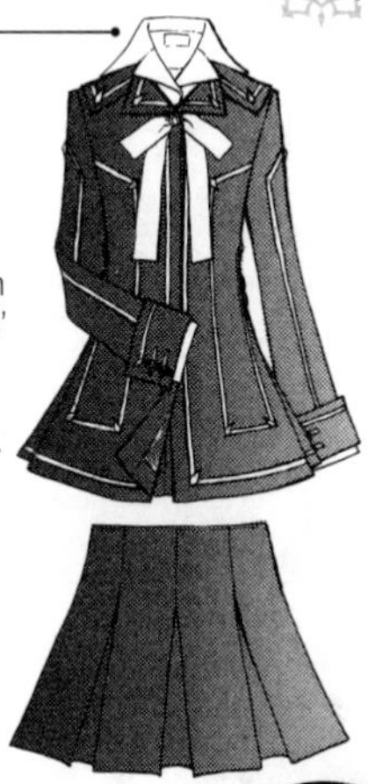

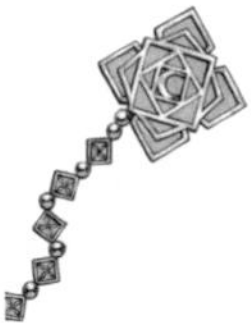

Day Class

At least 10 cm of the skirt must show from underneath the jacket. The cuffs of boys' pants must be 4–4.5 cm wide. Buttons and school badges must be pure silver.

Shoes must be school-specified ones. Socks must be black.

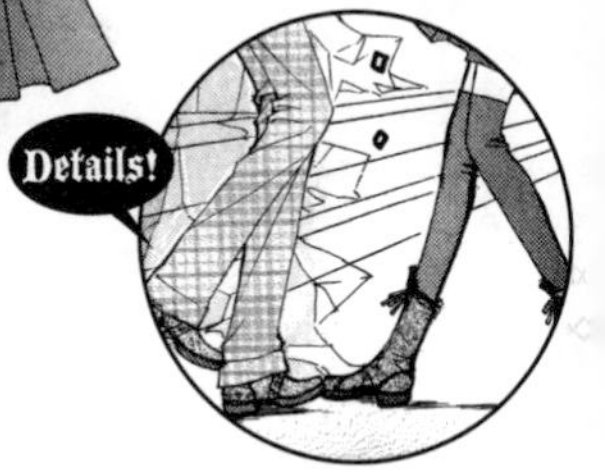
Details!

Night Class

Night Class uniforms are all pure white. The shirts are black.

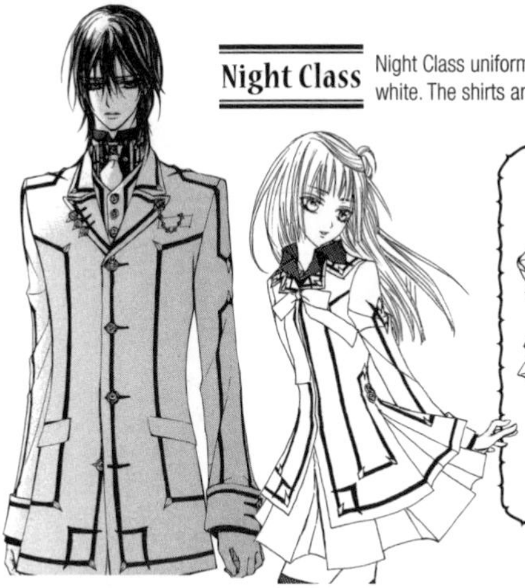

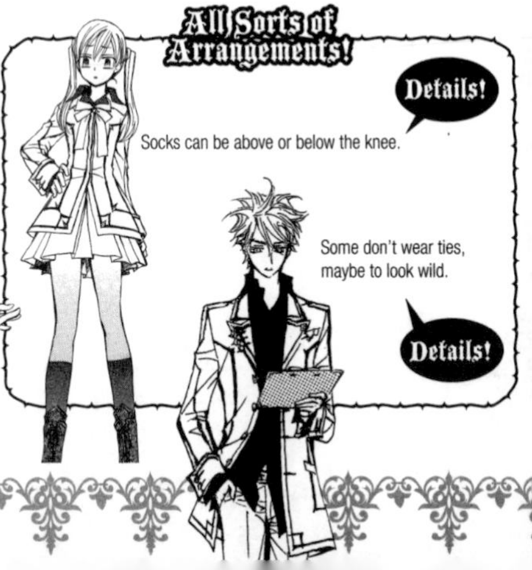
All Sorts of Arrangements!
Details!
Details!

Socks can be above or below the knee.

Some don't wear ties, maybe to look wild.

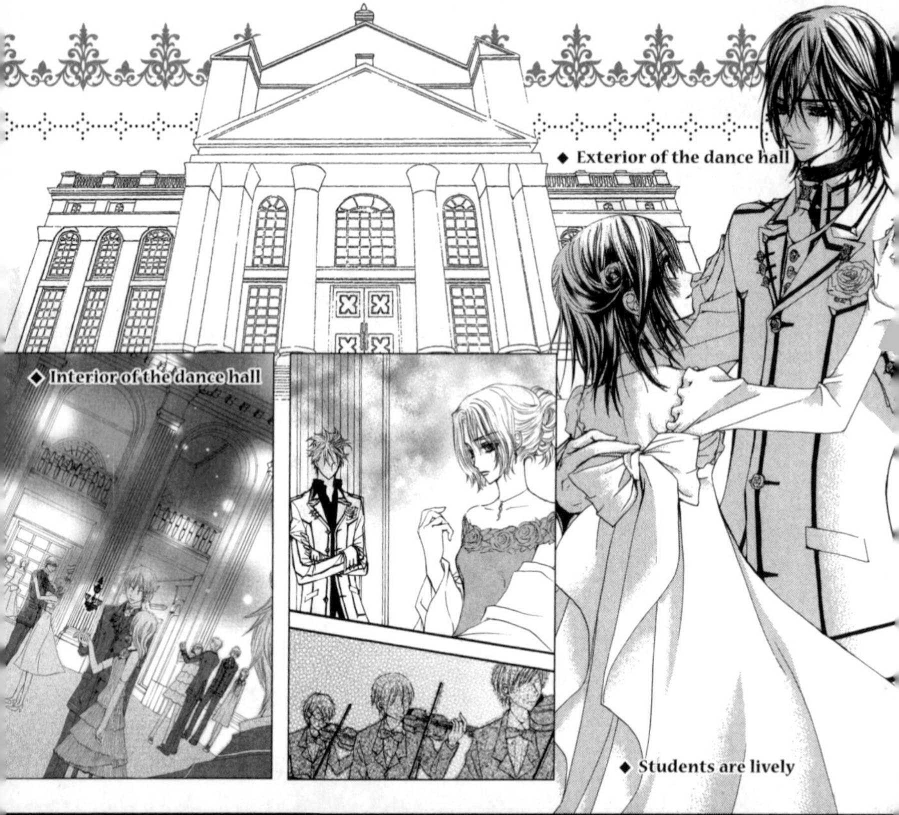
◆ Exterior of the dance hall
◆ Interior of the dance hall
◆ Students are lively

Like a Celebrity

The academy holds many fun events where the two classes can get close to each other! Let's check them out. ★

A grand love race where you wait to run!

St. Xocolatl's Day

The day when girls fight!! It's an event when you can give chocolates to the boy you like (mostly Night Class students) and tell them you like them. There are rules to make sure no one gets hurt.

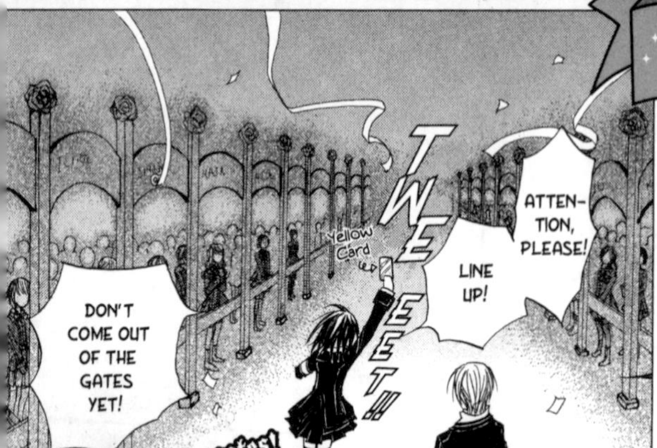
ATTEN-TION, PLEASE!
LINE UP!
TWEEET!!
Yellow Card
DON'T COME OUT OF THE GATES YET!
Everyone enter the gates!

⬆ Night Class students receive chocolates in front of their gates.

A traditional place for social interaction in the academy

The Ball

HUH?
ISN'T IT CURFEW ALREADY?
OH, THE FIRST-YEAR STUDENTS DON'T KNOW...

The entrance is decorated as well ♪

⬆⬅ The class that works on the ball decorates the hall that's used for various purposes.

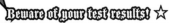

Beware of your test results! ☆

⬇ If you don't get good results, the class rep may hate you?!

SO IF I DON'T GET TO DANCE WITH RUKA...
...I'LL HOLD A GRUDGE AGAINST YOU FOR LIFE.
RRMB
RRMB
RRMB

One typical event is the traditional ball. It is an opportunity to dance and really get close ♥ to the beautiful, graceful, and somehow mysterious students of the Night Class that you adore!!

Er, excuse me. I got too excited. Unfortunately, the class that comes in last in the school exams held right before the ball must work at the ball. You can't enjoy the event unless you practice dancing and study hard.

Heart-fluttering incidents may occur?! ☆

KIRYU?
...
WOULD YOU DANCE WITH ME?

Gorgeous Events That Make You Feel

Every day is a battle!!

When the Night Class Comes Out

Every day, the girls eagerly wait for the Night Class to attend classes in the early evening. The female students get excited to the mega MAX!

KURAN, PLEASE ACCEPT MY CHOCOLATE!
KURAN
OH...
glance
...

What's gonna happen at the final turn?!

⬆ The event is over when the boys cannot receive any more chocolates. You have an advantage if you get in line early.

IF WE WEREN'T AROUND, PEOPLE WOULD GET HURT!
KYAAAAAAAH
DOMP
TMP
ACK!
TMP

The girls are hyper every day!

SCENES OF CLASSES

Graceful and Strict— A helping hand to the bad students

Our academy provides classes in liberal arts as well as special and high-level classes like riding lessons. Even if there are those with failing grades, the teachers are eager to give supplementary classes, so no need to worry. ♪

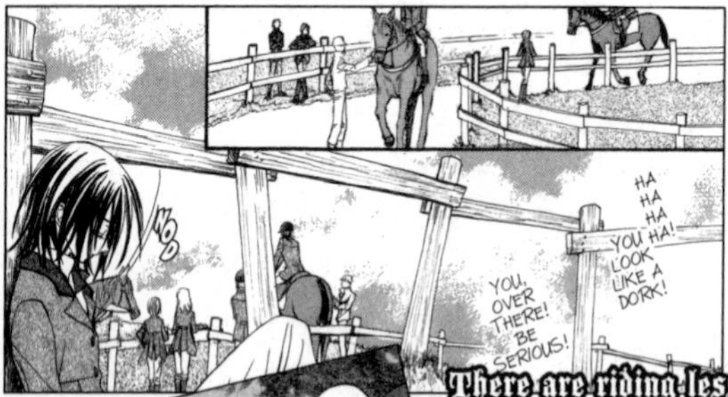
NOD
HA HA HA HA!
YOU LOOK LIKE A DORK!
YOU, OVER THERE! BE SERIOUS!

There are riding lessons...

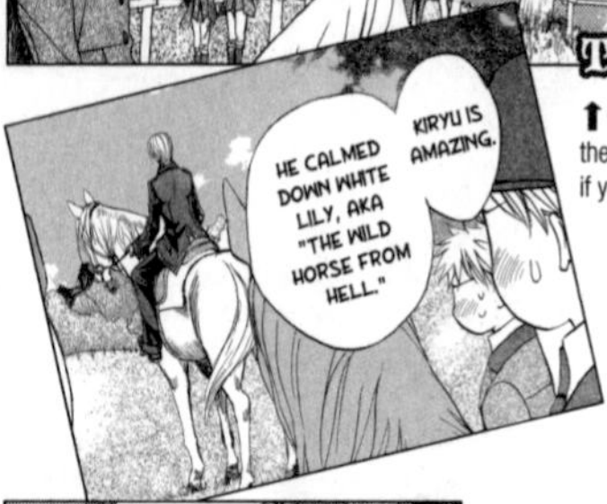
KIRYU IS AMAZING.
HE CALMED DOWN WHITE LILY, AKA "THE WILD HORSE FROM HELL."

⬆⬅These lessons can be given because of the academy's vast property. You'll be a hero if you can manage to ride a wild horse!

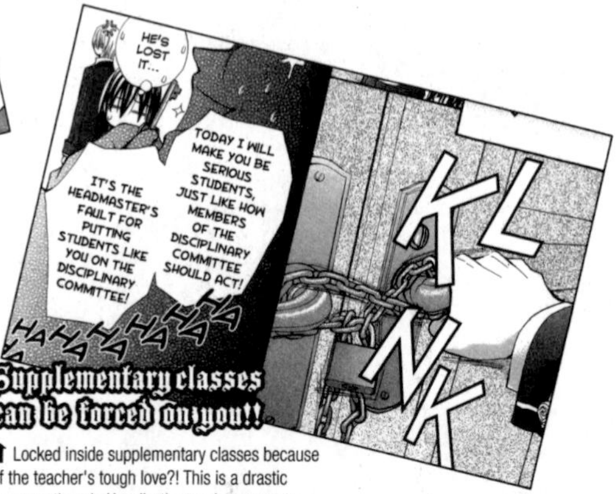
HE'S LOST IT...
TODAY I WILL MAKE YOU BE SERIOUS STUDENTS, JUST LIKE HOW MEMBERS OF THE DISCIPLINARY COMMITTEE SHOULD ACT!
IT'S THE HEADMASTER'S FAULT FOR PUTTING STUDENTS LIKE YOU ON THE DISCIPLINARY COMMITTEE!
HA HA HA HA HA HA
KL NK

Supplementary classes can be forced on you!!

⬆ Locked inside supplementary classes because of the teacher's tough love?! This is a drastic measure though. Usually, the teacher respects the students' autonomy.

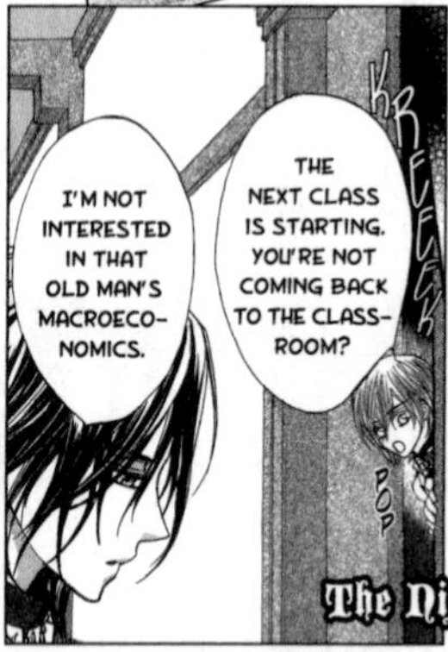
THE NEXT CLASS IS STARTING. YOU'RE NOT COMING BACK TO THE CLASSROOM?
I'M NOT INTERESTED IN THAT OLD MAN'S MACROECONOMICS.
POP

The Night Class is special! ⬅The Night Class consists of super excellent students. They can choose the classes they want to take.

Gatekeeper

The gatekeeper is at the rear gate of the Moon Dormitory, and Day Class students are prohibited from entering. To tell the truth, the gatekeeper's sex is unknown…

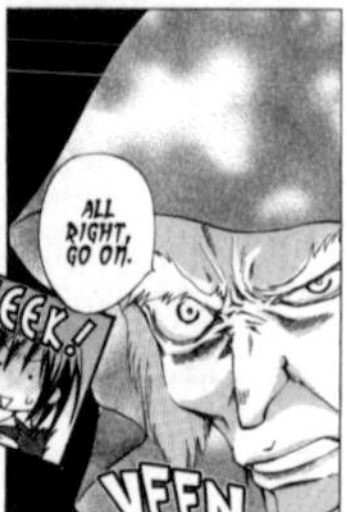
ALL RIGHT, GO ON.
EEEK!
VEEN

The maid and the people in black

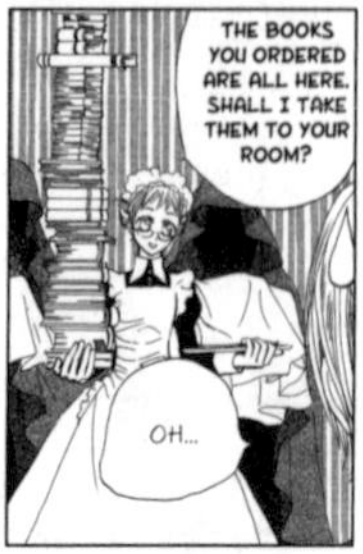
THE BOOKS YOU ORDERED ARE ALL HERE. SHALL I TAKE THEM TO YOUR ROOM?
OH...

They take care of students in the Moon Dormitory. Don't you want to know what the people wearing the cloaks look like?

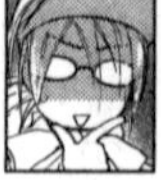

The Headmaster tells you a secret ♥

CROSS ACADEMY'S SPECIAL SECRET CHARACTERS

There are people in the academy that the Day Class students don't get to see.

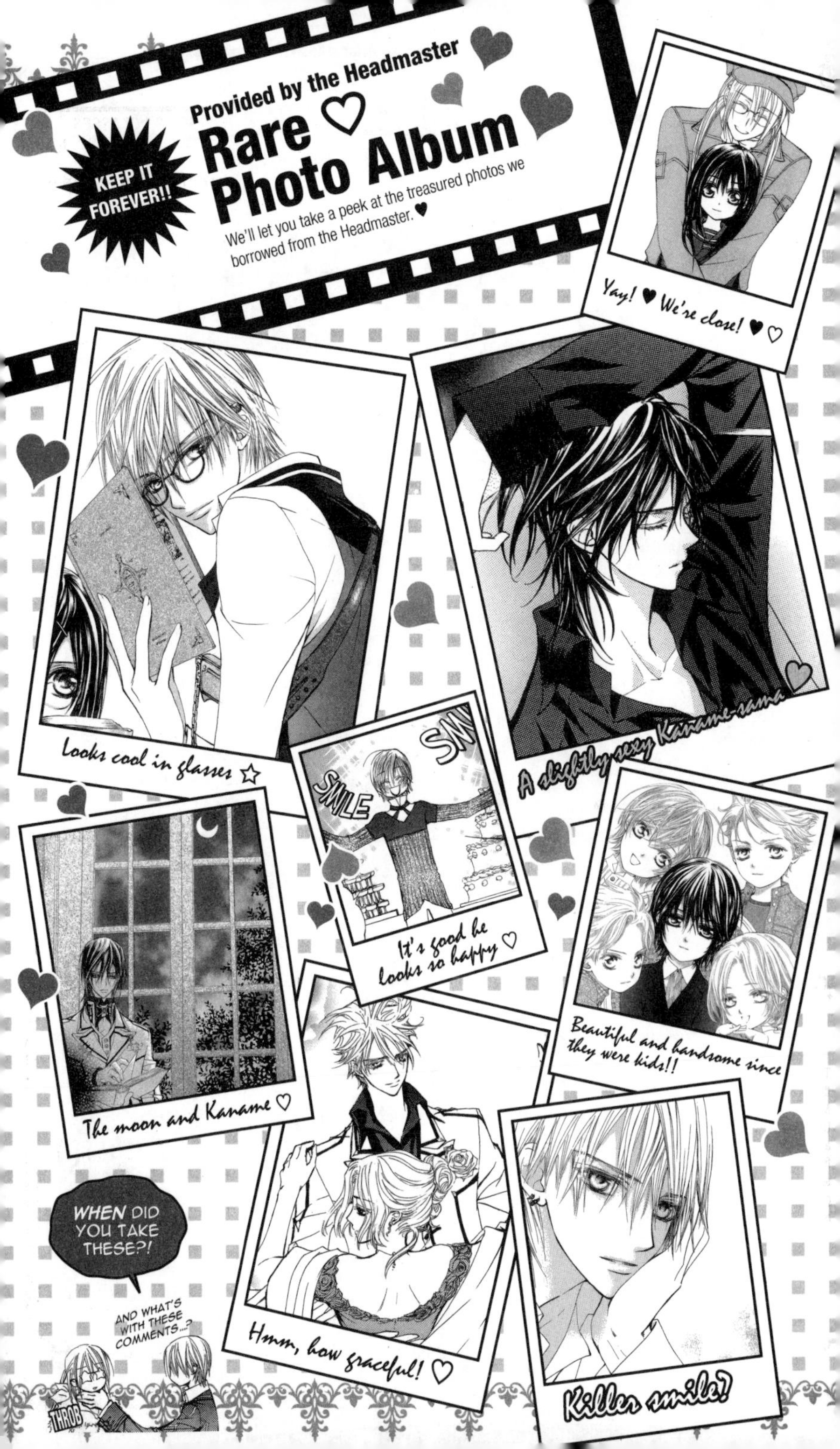
KEEP IT FOREVER!!
Provided by the Headmaster
Rare ♡ Photo Album
We'll let you take a peek at the treasured photos we borrowed from the Headmaster. ♥
Yay! ♥ We're close! ♥ ♡
A slightly sexy Kaname-sama ♡
Looks cool in glasses ☆
SMILE
It's good he looks so happy ♡
Beautiful and handsome since they were kids!!
The moon and Kaname ♡
Killer smile?
Hmm, how graceful! ♡
WHEN DID YOU TAKE THESE?!
AND WHAT'S WITH THESE COMMENTS...?
THROB

The Headmaster's SECRET Notebook

We took a peek at the notebook where the Headmaster keeps strange notes!

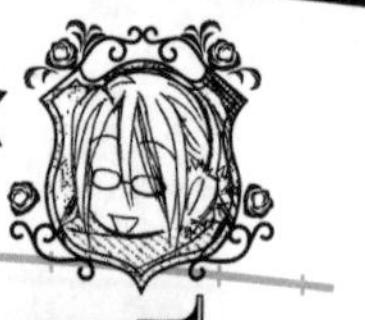

You want a peek?

Under consideration?!

Possible New Menus in the School Cafeteria

The cafeteria menu gets changed a lot every season to make Yuki happy, but these are good too.

Yuki Parfait! It's a parfait that Yuki makes.♥ It's yummy. Fruits, caramel, ice cream... A miracle parfait that uses lots of ingredients. Aido loves it too.♥

—Hyakka Yoshida, Nara Prefecture

← Yuki Parfait, hm. I'm sure it'll look cute, but how big is it going to be?!

↓This will make the vampires feel refreshed all the time!

When blood tablets aren't enough, there's artificial blood!! For everyone! For Kaname-sama too!! Because it's artificial, it's safe!! You can buy it from the vending machine, and it's 150 yen a pack!! (200 ml) What does it taste like...?? It's both sour and bitter.

–Shi-chan ★, Hokkaido

Specially Made by the Headmaster

Lunch, My Style
Lunch Set, My Style

—Kaori Yamamoto, Fukuoka Prefecture

← Daily lunches and lunch sets! You'll find out what it is after you order it. ♥

Oops, you saw it...

Extremely Inappropriate Words Coming from a Father

"Yuki! Let's wear *matching pajamas* forever!! Yuki! I love you!"
—Cho, Nagano Prefecture

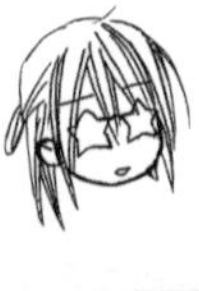

"Let's read your *diary* together later."
—Sou, Ehime Prefecture

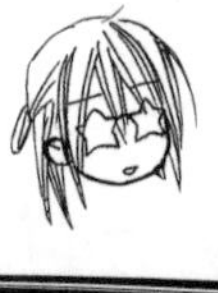

If I say these things, will Yuki hate me?

MEMO

Aido's Special Shaved Ice!!!! Only available in the summertime! It's super good. ❤ He provides the ice!

—Funfun Moffu, Tokyo

⬅ It might melt before you eat it because you're so excited!

Lunches that Night Class students make during COOKING CLASSES are available on the Day Class CAFETERIA MENU. (You can't get more than one lunch made by a particular Night Class student per day.)

—ANA, Tokyo

⬆ I can imagine the girls fighting over them at lunchtime…

Zero's Special Shio Ramen

—Dona dona, Kumamoto Prefecture

⬆ A prudent hit!

Red-Themed Lunch

A lunch full of red! Red curry, tomato soup, carrot salad, stuff marinated in red paprika, cranberry jelly…

–Puchikyu, Nagasaki Prefecture

⬅ Red vegetables are good for your health! They might taste better than blood!

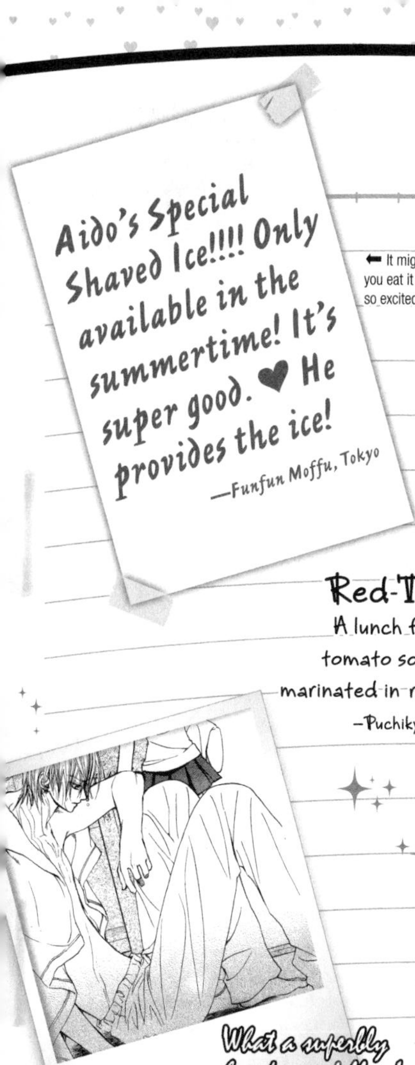

What a superbly handsome fellow!

Sheesh, these students are such delinquents. Should I create a club like this?

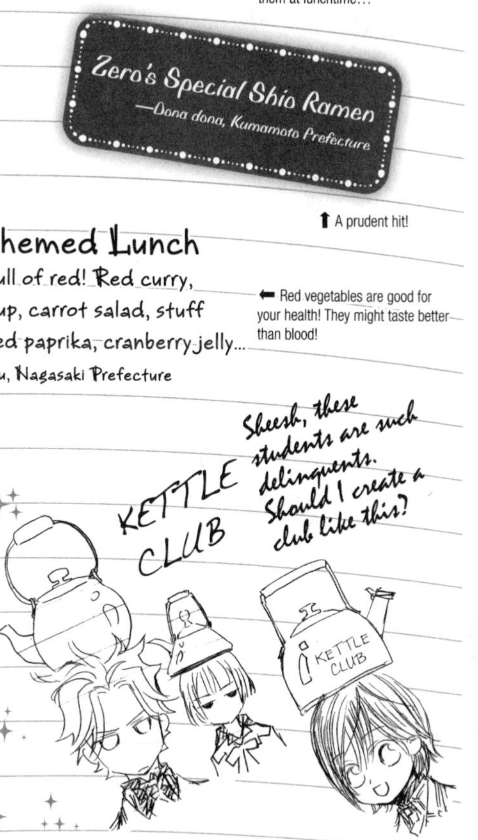
KETTLE CLUB
KETTLE CLUB

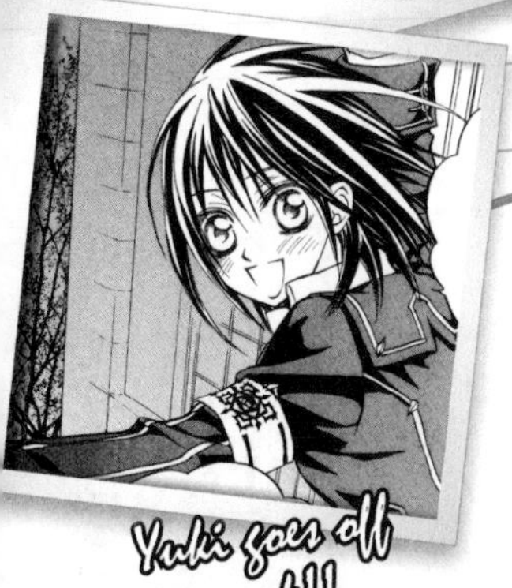

Yuki goes off to work!!

"Yuki… ♥ Because Yuki won't sleep beside me, I made this… ♥ A pillow that's the same size as Yuki."

—Panda Mama, Hyogo Prefecture

Okay! ❤ When shall I say this?

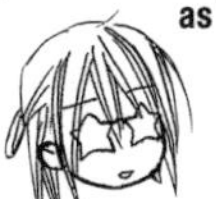

I hope everyone becomes closer! ♥

Possible New School Events

I feel like there aren't enough events for letting off steam… So should I sponsor some of these? ♪

The Annual Night Class Chess Tournament

Day Class students can leave their dorm at night and cheer for the participants. There's a chess set in Kaname-sama's room because he's practicing for it…

—Aya, Fukuoka Prefecture

⬆ Kaname is probably the only one who'll practice every day… ♥

Night Class students become lecturers! ♡ Once a year (on a rainy day), Night Class students come to teach the Day Class, but the Day Class students need to follow these rules.

RULES

1. *If you ask something not related to the class, the class ends right there.*
2. *Don't go "kyah kyah."*
3. *Don't ask questions you already know the answers to.*

—Sara, Shiga Prefecture

⬅ I think Aido will be the only one addressed as "teacher." And he'll be happy about it.

Have school rules like these! ♥

Rule 1: Girls must dress up as boys, boys must dress up as girls! ♥

Rule 2: You must tell a silly joke once a day!!

Rule 3: Switch the Day Class and Night Class uniforms. ♥

—Shiori Hashimoto, Fukuoka Prefecture

⬆ Kaname, Zero… It's the school rules. Now say something funny!

Did you picture this in your mind? Did you?! I think their photos would sell… ⬊

The Night Class Students' Night Pool

They'd swim wearing swimsuits… The water would be lit up… Because of their wet hair, they might look even more beautiful…

–Rika Nagai, Kagoshima Prefecture

"There's apparently a secret school rule—*anyone who hits on Yuki* is summoned to the *Headmaster's office.*"
—Tsumugi Yokoi, Osaka

"The Moon Dormitory has a *confession room* (aka "punishment room") for students who break the school rules. It's hardly ever used, but *Kaname-sama summoned Aido, so Aido set foot in there*…supposedly."
—Jane, Chiba Prefecture ♪

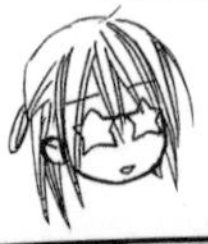

This is what people are saying!

Rumors of the Academy?!

Rumors that sound like the truth. Are they true or not?

MEMO

A MIDNIGHT SCHOOL FESTIVAL

It would be held from evening to late night. ☆ The Day Class and the Night Class dorms don't have curfew that day! Each class provides entertainment (like a café or a haunted house), but the main event is... the DRESS-IN-DRAG CONTEST!! The one who wins gets a "RIGHT TO SPEND A DAY OUTSIDE THE ACADEMY WITH ONE PERSON OF THEIR CHOICE" prize, so Aido will really try hard... (Hee.)

—Ringorira, Aomori Prefecture

⬆ And Aido would, of course, choose Kaname.

Have a Grand Sports Festival!

It'd be fun if you have Night Class students participate in the Day Class classes instead of having the Day Class and the Night Class compete! And I want to see the Night Class students wear P.E. uniforms...!! Especially Kaname-sama!!

—Rei, Aichi Prefecture

⬆ I want to see the Night Class students wear P.E. uniforms! Accepted!!

School Song

CROSS ACADEMY SCHOOL SONG

Verse 1: Two chains intersect where
the sun and moon cross each other.
The chain of the sun and the
chain of the moon...
They cross, pass each other and
become one.
Cross Academy

Verse 2: Red chains intersect where
dreams and reality cross each other.
The chain of dreams and the
chain of reality...
They link, come apart and
become two.
Cross Academy

I made up a school song. Just the lyrics though. I want Zero to sing it in an embarrassed way.

—Satomi Wagatsuma, Aichi Prefecture

⬅ Ah! This might be better than the one I wrote?!

The Moon Dormitory Tour

A tour held to go around the Moon Dormitory when it is empty during vacation. You must make a reservation in advance, and the tour is limited to five people a day.

– Risa Sasaki, Aichi Prefecture

⬆ Yuki and Zero will be the tour guides, of course, since there are places that are off-limits...

The next two pages contain information about the Cross Academy Fan Club!! Those who want to join must read it!!

Heh heh heh... You knew about this, huh... It's true, I set up a fan club!

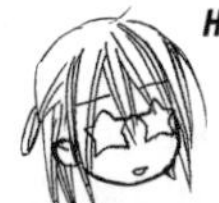

"There's a suspicious-looking mailbox that is located between the Day Class and the Night Class. You can put *fan letters* for the Night Class students in here. You can ask things and have your wishes made true as well. The one who's behind this is *the Headmaster*...maybe?!"

—Mei Kachora, Tochigi Prefecture

Membership Rules - To all members -

How to Use Your Membership Card

1 First, use scissors to cut out the card carefully.

2 Fill out the following:

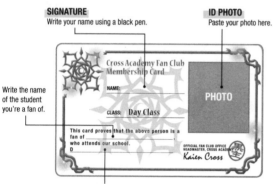

SIGNATURE
Write your name using a black pen.

ID PHOTO
Paste your photo here.

Write the name of the student you're a fan of.

Cross Academy Fan Club
Membership Card
NAME:
PHOTO
CLASS: Day Class
This card proves that the above person is a fan of ________, who attends our school.
D
OFFICIAL FAN CLUB OFFICE
HEADMASTER, CROSS ACADEMY
Kaien Cross

MEMBERSHIP NUMBER
Write down the initials of the Cross Academy student you're a fan of, a dash, and any 4-digit number. For example, if you're a Kaname fan, your membership number could be "KK-0101." If you're a Zero fan, something like "ZK-0000" would work, and so on.

3 When you've filled out everything, always carry the card with you as proof that you're a member.

GREETINGS

Welcome to the Cross Academy Fan Club! The fan club exists because of everybody's passion. Let's carry out club activities without overdoing things so that we don't inconvenience the students we're fans of.

THE DISCIPLINARY COMMITTEE WILL DO OUR BEST TO PROTECT EVERYONE'S SAFETY TOO!

Cross Academy
Student ID Card
Kaname Kuran
Night Class
Kaien Cross

Questions and Answers

Q If I find a membership card or an ID card, what do I do?

A If you find an ID card of a Cross Academy student, please notify the student affairs office right away. If someone loses their ID card, it becomes invalid in just one day. Therefore, the student who lost their card has to apply to have a new card issued immediately. If you find an ID card, it has probably been reissued already, so you may secretly just keep it for yourself.

Q What happens if I lose my membership card?

A The fan club membership card is like the soul of the fan. You only have one soul. So if you lose it, it cannot be reissued. If you really want a new one, we recommend that you buy another copy of this book.

WHAT?! YOU LOST IT?!

Q What happens if my family finds out about the membership card?

A You'll cause more trouble if you try to lie about it. Explain to your family that this fan club is a wholesome club. If any trouble occurs, however, we cannot take responsibility for it. We hope you understand.

Cross Academy Fan Club

CERTIFIED BY THE HEADMASTER

Membership Rules

Section 1: Registering as a Member
A member is one who agrees to the membership rules and registers as a member according to the procedures determined by the fan club. Member registration is complete when you fill out your name on the membership card. If there are duplicate membership numbers, we cannot take responsibility for it. We hope you understand.

Section 2: Membership Guidelines
A member must be able to fulfill all of the following conditions:
1. Vow that you **love** the student you're a fan of **forever**.
2. Eat **three bowls of rice** while thinking about the student you're a fan of.
3. Write the name of the student you're a fan of **in kanji**. (The kanji for the names can be found in the back of the manga volumes.)
4. Think about the student you're a fan of **three times a day**.
5. Make an effort to see the student you're a fan of **in your dreams** (by putting his/her photograph underneath your pillow, for example).
6. Refrain from disputes, strife and taking advantage of others.

Section 3: Membership Termination
In principle, we do not terminate membership. However, if trouble occurs because you refuse to compromise or if you violate Section 2, your membership will be terminated.

Section 4: Membership Card
Please keep the following in mind:
1. Members take responsibility for carrying and storing their membership cards.
2. The membership card must be shown when asked for.
3. The membership card must not be loaned or given to anyone else.
4. Membership cards will not be reissued. If a membership card is lost, it is recommended that you buy another copy of this book.
5. You cannot return membership cards. If you don't need your membership card anymore, dispose of it yourself.
6. The membership card is valid for as long as you're a fan.

This is the Night Class Student Handbook!!
Benefits for Fan Club Members!!
The right to see a little bit of the Night Class Student Handbook.
SCHOOL SONG
Our hearts clear up
By basking in the
clear morning sun
NIGHT CLASS RULES
If you cannot follow these rules so be careful.
SECTION 1: PROHIBITED ACTIONS
1. DRINKING BLOOD
Drinking blood on campus is strictly forbidden. Take blood tablets instead.
2. LEAVING THE SCHOOL GROUNDS WITHOUT PERMISSION
Leaving the school grounds is prohibited in principle. If you submit an application to go out and it is approved, you may leave the school.
3. FIGHTING
Disputes and fighting on school grounds are prohibited. Deal with everything in a spirit of peace.
4. INTERACTING WITH THE DAY CLASS
The only facilities shared with the Day Class are the classrooms after early evening. Going to the classrooms during the day and going to the Sun Dormitory at any time is prohibited.
IT'S A PRIVILEGE!
THAT'S IT?!

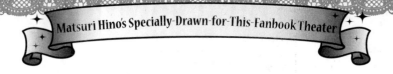

The mangaka's brain always welcomes vampires covered in blood!!

① And so, the inside of the mangaka's brain is made public. ↓

GRRR
SNAP
GRRR
KRAK
Die, fool.
Die, you piece of poop.
I hate you. I hate you.
I like dogs but I hate you.
I like cats but I hate you.

It's always like this. For background music,
I want Krauser from *Detroit Metal City*.

② This is a fanbook, so the mangaka interviews the characters as well.

Q: Are you a masochist? Or a sadist?

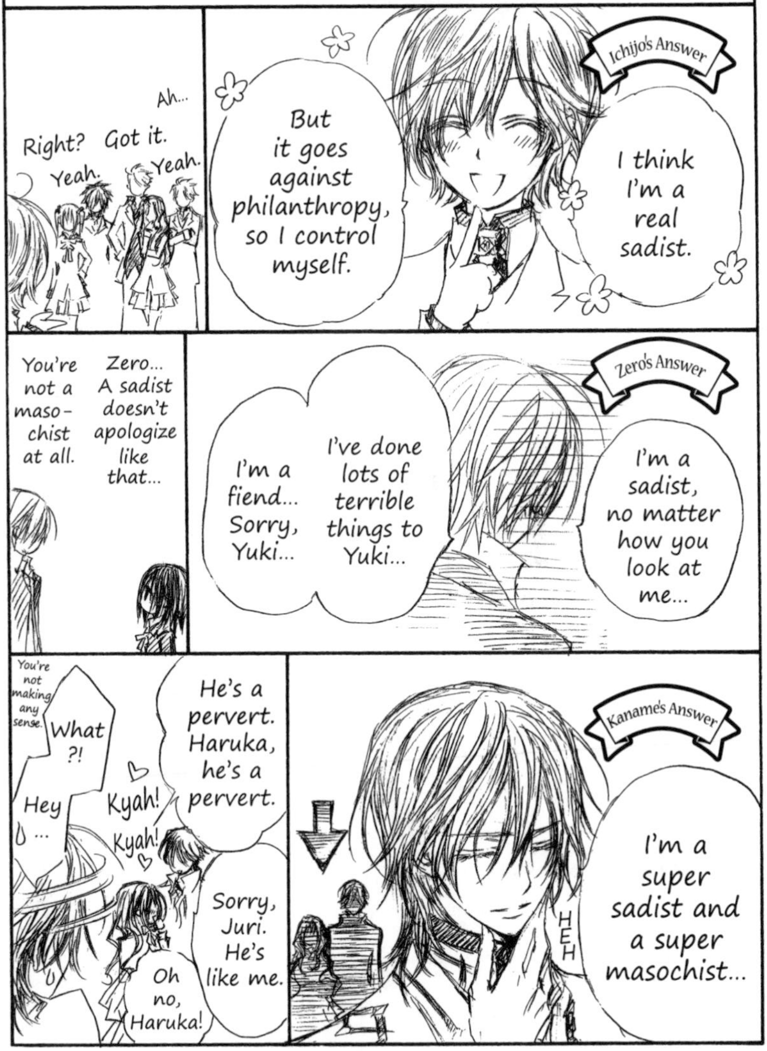
Ichijo's Answer
I think I'm a real sadist.
But it goes against philanthropy, so I control myself.
Ah...
Yeah.
Got it.
Right?
Yeah.
Zero's Answer
I'm a sadist, no matter how you look at me...
I've done lots of terrible things to Yuki...
I'm a fiend... Sorry, Yuki...
Zero... A sadist doesn't apologize like that...
You're not a masochist at all.
Kaname's Answer
I'm a super sadist and a super masochist...
HEH
He's a pervert. Haruka, he's a pervert.
What?!
You're not making any sense.
Kyah!
Kyah!
Hey...
Sorry, Juri. He's like me.
Oh no, Haruka!

③ I try out things irresponsibly.

I feel that I'll be forgiven since this is a fanbook.

I want to eat rare steak that's dripping blood...
Gurgle
Sob
She pleads with him.
...
So how are you going to treat me?
In charge of cooking

No way would this ever happen.

This is from my doodling notebook.

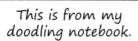

Kaname

The End

To all the readers who participated... To all the voice actors who sent in comments... To everyone at Caramel Mama who did the editing... And to my editor... Thank you so much!!

樋野まつり
Matsuri Hino

Chapter1
Day Class

And the Guardians Who Support Coexistence with Vampires

We get very close to Yuki Cross and Zero Kiryu, the Guardians who hold the key to coexistence with the Night Class and work really hard at their duties. We also present you the distinctive lineup of ordinary students of the Day Class who enjoy the peaceful school life!!

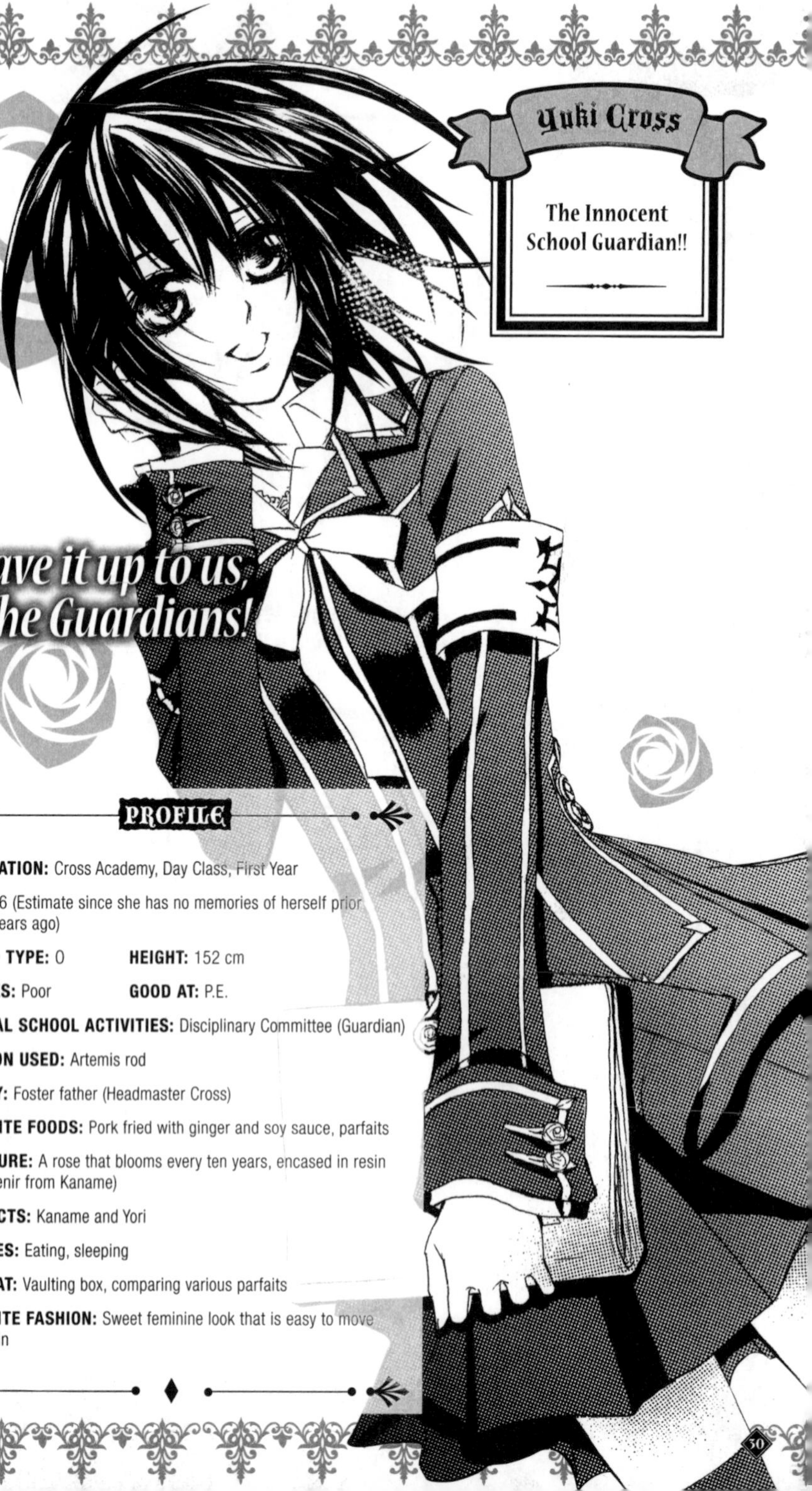

Yuki Cross

The Innocent School Guardian!!

Leave it up to us, the Guardians!

PROFILE

AFFILIATION: Cross Academy, Day Class, First Year

AGE: 16 (Estimate since she has no memories of herself prior to ten years ago)

BLOOD TYPE: O **HEIGHT:** 152 cm

GRADES: Poor **GOOD AT:** P.E.

SPECIAL SCHOOL ACTIVITIES: Disciplinary Committee (Guardian)

WEAPON USED: Artemis rod

FAMILY: Foster father (Headmaster Cross)

FAVORITE FOODS: Pork fried with ginger and soy sauce, parfaits

TREASURE: A rose that blooms every ten years, encased in resin (a souvenir from Kaname)

RESPECTS: Kaname and Yori

HOBBIES: Eating, sleeping

GOOD AT: Vaulting box, comparing various parfaits

FAVORITE FASHION: Sweet feminine look that is easy to move around in

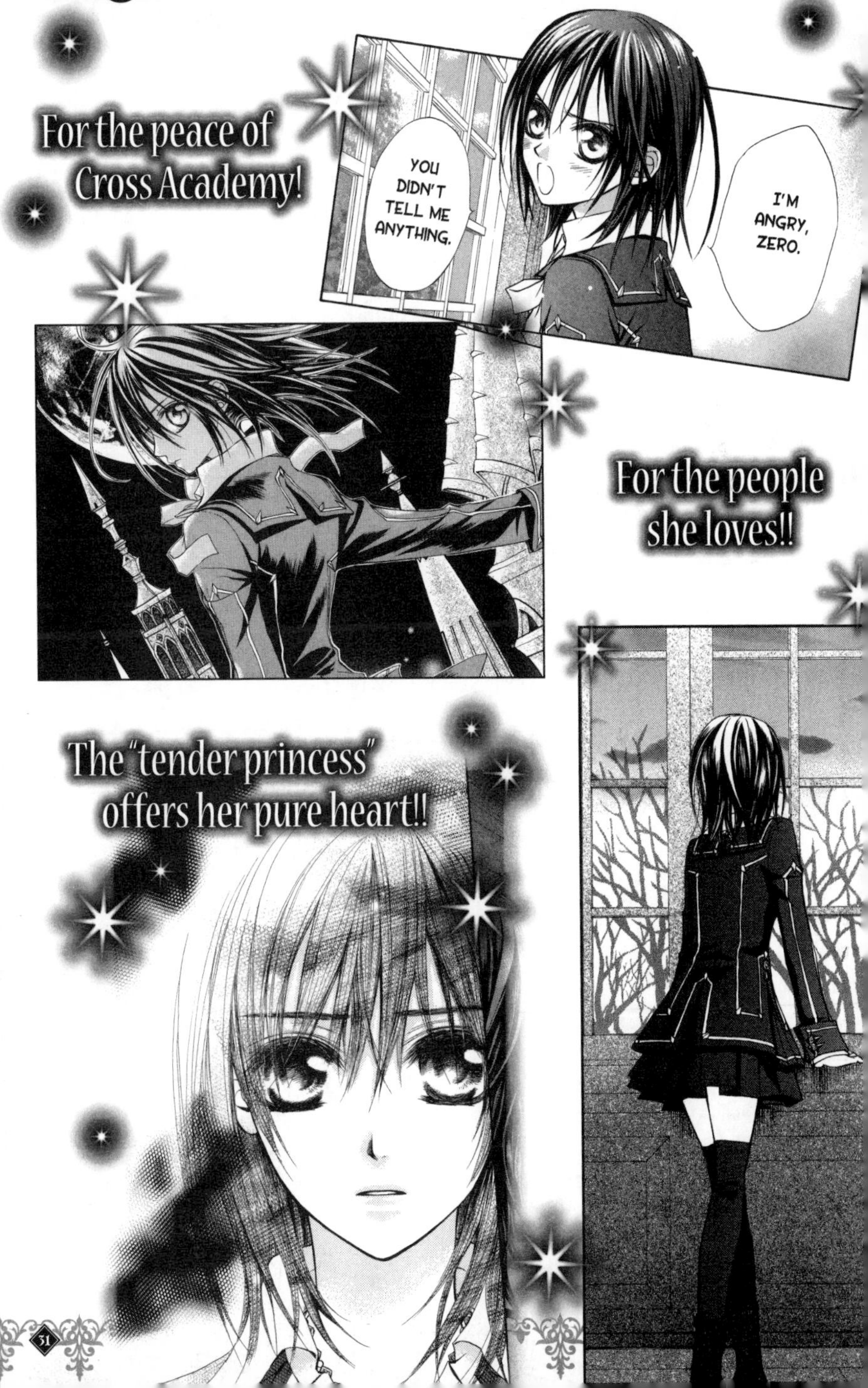
I'M ANGRY, ZERO.
YOU DIDN'T TELL ME ANYTHING.
For the peace of Cross Academy!
For the people she loves!!
The "tender princess" offers her pure heart!!

CHARACTER ANALYSIS

This is what Yuki Cross is like!

Hobbies + Favorites

OH!
SHE TOOK HIM TO A CAFÉ WITHOUT ASKING.

She loves sweet and cute desserts! ♡

She's a jock who eats the ginger-fried pork set at the school cafeteria. But like lots of girls, she loves sweets too.

...
ZERO, YOU EAT SOME-THING TOO.

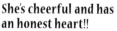

⬆ Yuki is invincible when she has her sweets…?!

Personality

She's cheerful and has an honest heart!!

She is happy-go-lucky and shows wonderful smiles to the one she loves!! Her true strength comes from her pure feelings.

GOOD NIGHT...
...KANAME.
BUT I ALWAYS GET TOO NERVOUS.

⬆ She smiles broadly in front of Kaname, whom she adores. ♥

Fighting Ability

Wields the special weapon Artemis!!

Yuki uses a weapon to protect the other school students. She fights using the extensible Artemis, which she keeps tucked underneath her skirt.

The Headmaster trained her on how to use her weapon. ➡

CHIK

WHO'S THERE?
KATAH
KATAH
KATAH

Her Past

She lost her memories… Then the Headmaster adopted her!!

TEN YEARS AGO...
...THAT MAN WAS THERE...

Ten years ago on a snowy night, a vampire attacked her, and she lost all her memories. With no one to depend on, she was put in the Headmaster's care.

⬅ Kaname saved the powerless little Yuki and took her to Headmaster Cross.

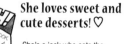

SCHOOLTIME

Her activities at school!

KYAAH KYAAH
IT'S MORNING...
PRESSS
...BUT THEY'RE ALREADY WAITING FOR THE NIGHT CLASS?!
TWEEET!

Extracurricular Activities

Busy days as a Disciplinary Committee member!

Yuki and Zero run around trying to prevent the Day Class girls who swarm the Night Class from going berserk!! They're called "Disciplinary Committee members," but they're actually "Guardians," security personnel who protect the secrets of the Night Class. Headmaster Cross completely trusts Yuki and Zero to handle this important duty.

⬅ Even though she's small, she bravely volunteers for the academy.

Sports

She loves P.E.! An outstanding athlete!!

Yuki's poor at her studies, and the only thing she's good at is P.E.!! Her everyday energetic actions prove her athletic abilities.

I'LL BE ON PATROL!
TAK

⬆ She's a tomboy who goes outside by jumping out of a window!!

Schoolwork

Keeps flunking her tests and attending supplementary classes

The biggest weakness of the cheerful Yuki is that she's really poor at her studies. She is a busy Guardian, but Zero gets excellent grades. Yuki can't make any excuses!!

Yuki and Zero are regulars in supplementary classes...!! ⬇

I CAN'T TAKE IT ANYMORE! CROSS! KIRYU!
YOU'VE GOT SUPPLE-MENTARY CLASSES UNTIL LATE!
I DON'T CARE ABOUT YOUR DISCI-PLINARY COMMITTEE DUTIES!
DOOM
...
...

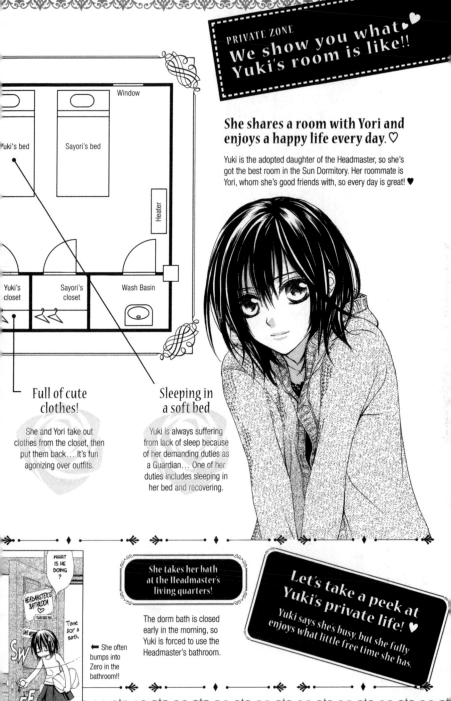

PRIVATE ZONE

We show you what Yuki's room is like!! ♥

Window
uki's bed
Sayori's bed
Heater
Yuki's closet
Sayori's closet
Wash Basin

Full of cute clothes!

She and Yori take out clothes from the closet, then put them back… It's fun agonizing over outfits.

Sleeping in a soft bed

Yuki is always suffering from lack of sleep because of her demanding duties as a Guardian… One of her duties includes sleeping in her bed and recovering.

She shares a room with Yori and enjoys a happy life every day. ♡

Yuki is the adopted daughter of the Headmaster, so she's got the best room in the Sun Dormitory. Her roommate is Yori, whom she's good friends with, so every day is great! ♥

WHAT IS HE DOING ?
HEADMASTER'S BATHROOM
Time for a Bath
SW
EE

⬅ She often bumps into Zero in the bathroom!!

She takes her bath at the Headmaster's living quarters!

The dorm bath is closed early in the morning, so Yuki is forced to use the Headmaster's bathroom.

Let's take a peek at Yuki's private life! ♥

Yuki says she's busy, but she fully enjoys what little free time she has.

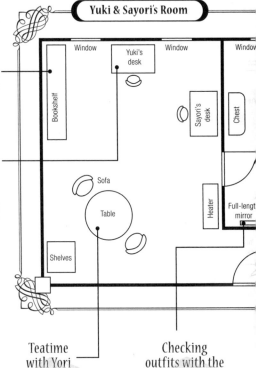

Yuki & Sayori's Room

Window
Yuki's desk
Window
Window
Bookshelf
Sayori's desk
Chest
Sofa
Table
Heater
Full-lengt
mirror
Shelves

There're books for making sweets too!

There're lots of books about making sweets and fashion!! Maybe she reads these books more than she reads her textbooks?

No sign of studying?

Even Yori has never seen Yuki studying at her desk...!! It's a waste of this splendid desk.

Teatime with Yori

When Yuki and Yori sit at the round table, they talk about things best friends can't discuss in the classroom!! Yori makes all sorts of tea, and they enjoy a time of supreme bliss.♥

Checking outfits with the big mirror

Both Yuki and Yori must have their hairstyles and ribbons done perfectly.♥ That's why a full-length mirror is a must.

⬅ She checks her appearance before going to school. She's off to work as a Guardian, all pumped up!!

HM. THE HEADMASTER ASKED US TO GET... LET'S SEE...
...
OH.
HE'S COOKING FOR US.
BEEF LIVER, BOK CHOY...

⬆ Rules restrict leaving school grounds. But there are lucky days when they can go out to run the Headmaster's errands!!

Sometimes she goes out to town!!

Yuki gets really excited when she occasionally goes out to town. She can't go out alone, so she goes with Zero or Yori.

Her number-one treasure is her best friend Yori.♡

Yuki has precious treasures in various parts of her room... But her number-one treasure in this room is her precious best friend, Yori.♥

Let's do a playback of her fluttering heart!! We inspect Yuki's racing heart rate!!

The pure Yuki is very busy with her heart-fluttering ♥ experiences every day!!

#2 Racing Heart Rate ♥ 150

GULK
HUFF

ZERO...

The forbidden act of drinking blood while the other students are preparing for the ball!!

Zero secretly drinks Yuki's blood while the other students are preparing for the ball in the dance hall. This is a time when her whole body was burning.

#3 Racing Heart Rate ♥ 30

Aido whispers sexy words to her…

When Yuki visits the Moon Dormitory, Aido says provocative things to her!! His saying, "You'd be in ecstasy" is too much…!!

IF YOU HEARD THE SOUND OF KANAME-SAMA TAKING IN YOUR BLOOD...
...YOU'D BE IN ECSTASY, YUKI.
BLUSH

...WILL GENTLY BRUSH YOUR NECK...
...AND HIS FANGS WILL SINK SLOWLY INTO YOU...

AH!
I WANT HER HEART TO FLUTTER FOR ME TOO...

#1 Racing Heart Rate ♥ 200

The moment when Kaname was on top of her…!!

The two beautiful ones look at each other… This incident occurred right after Yuki felt she could not come between Kaname and Sara Shirabuki…!! Kaname carried her, and the moment they were on the sofa together, Yuki's heart fluttered to the max!!

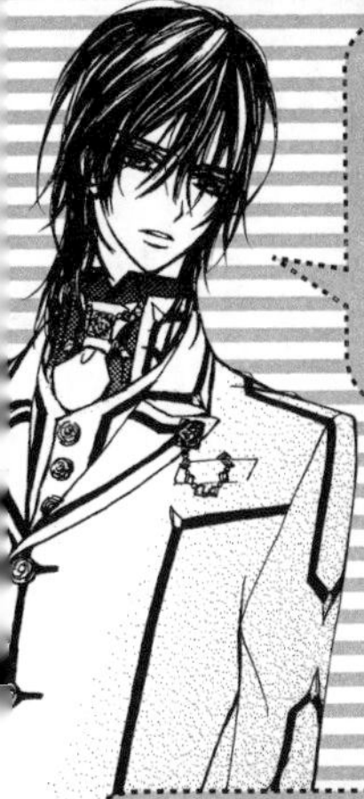

From Kaname Kuran

Yuki, you're cute today too. Heh, I'm not lying. You're blushing... And that makes you even more lovely. I find your carefree smile dazzling. I don't want you to change...

From Takuma Ichijo

I find it amusing that Kaname obviously acts differently when things involve Yuki. I have fun watching him.

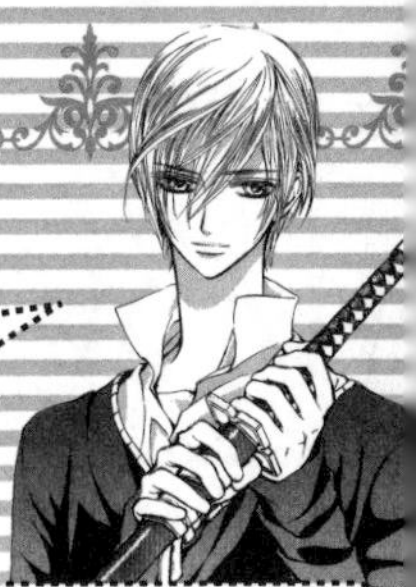

From Zero Kiryu

Her height hasn't increased, and her brain hasn't matured yet, but she treats me like a younger brother... That's why I have to watch her. (*Mumble*...)

Special messages to Yuki

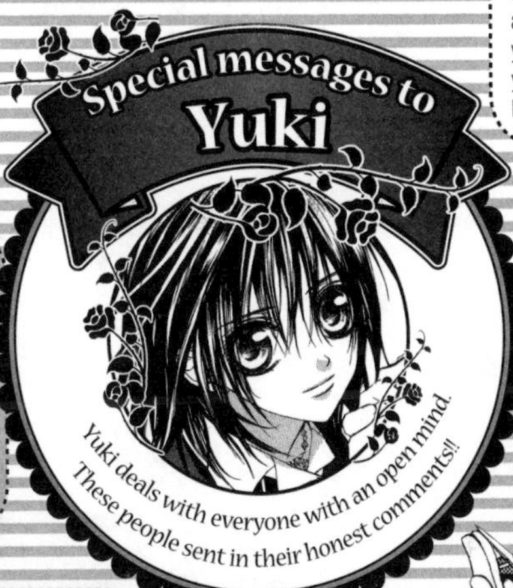

Yuki deals with everyone with an open mind. These people sent in their honest comments!!

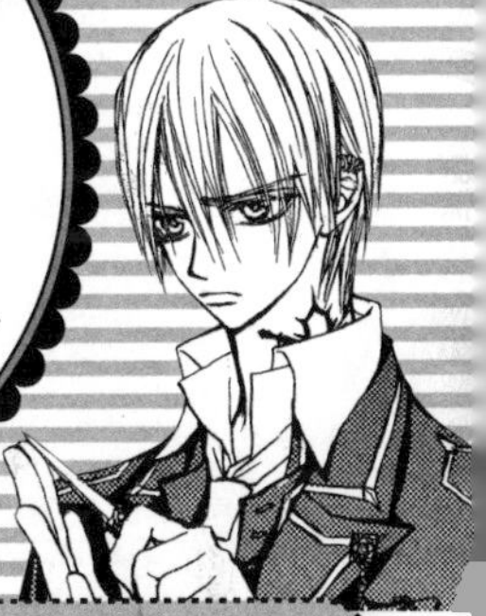

From Shiki Senri

The small female Disciplinary Committee member, huh... The President will probably scold me for saying this, but she reminds me of a rat that was in the garden once.

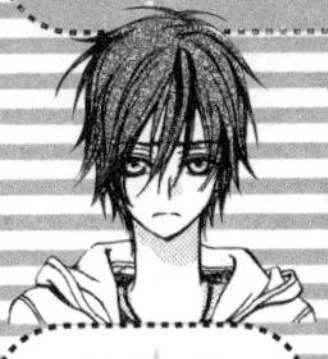

From Sayori Wakaba

I support Yuki's duties as a Disciplinary Committee member, but I'm worried about her health...!! She needs her sleep.

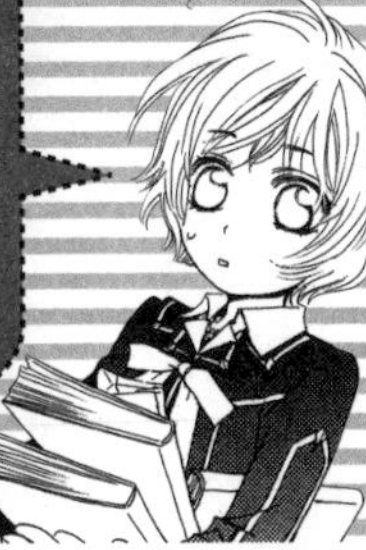

From Kasumi Kageyama

Cross, if you get terrible grades on your tests again, I'll hold a grudge against you for eternity!!

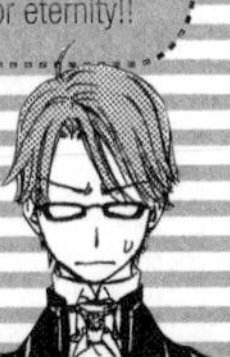

From Hanabusa Aido

Yuki, you're lively and look delicious today... ♥ Hm, the only thing good about you is the taste of your blood!!

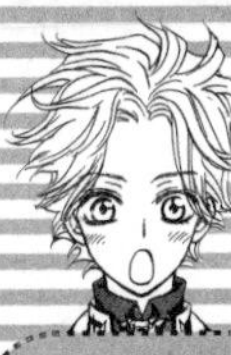

From Akatsuki Kain

She's doing things for the academy, but she's in a difficult position. Well, do your best, Disciplinary Committee member.

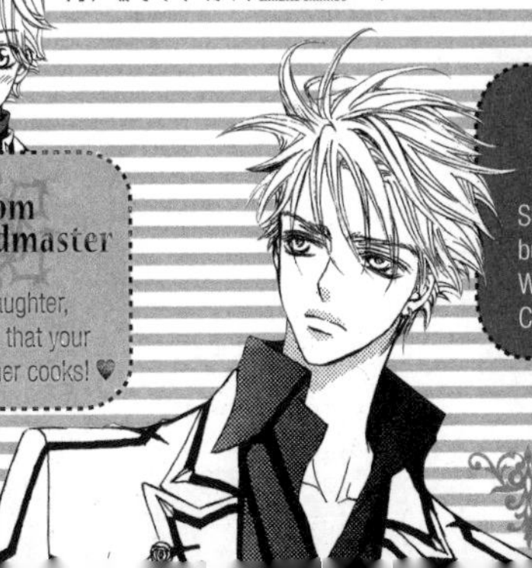

From the Headmaster

My lovely daughter, eat the food that your beloved father cooks! ♥

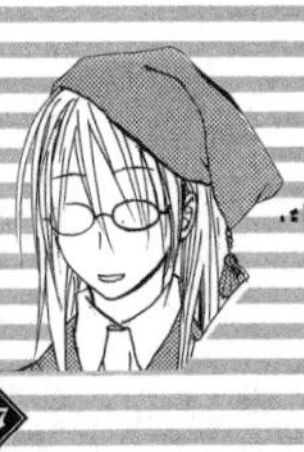

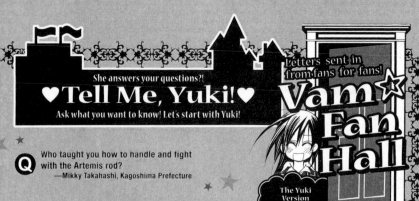

Letters sent in from fans for fans!

Vam☆Fan Hall

The Yuki Version

She answers your questions?!

♥Tell Me, Yuki!♥

Ask what you want to know! Let's start with Yuki!

Q Who taught you how to handle and fight with the Artemis rod?

—Mikky Takahashi, Kagoshima Prefecture

A Finally, a normal question! The Headmaster taught me how. I've been doing his "love training menu" every day, but I'm only grateful *now* because it's *useful*. Don't tell him that though.

Q If you started living in the Moon Dormitory, who would you like to be your roommate?

—Sekai no Gamakatsu, Nagasaki Prefecture

A Someone from the Night Class?! Hmm, I think that would always make me nervous. Ah, the maid?

Q If you had to call Zero and Kaname by nicknames, what would you call them?

—Tago Takako, Hyogo Prefecture

A Calling Kaname by a nickname?! No way!! Zero is brusque, so if I call him "Zero-pyon," the cute nickname might make him more popular… It… It's a joke, so don't glare at me, Zero!

Q So who do you like better, Kaname-sama or Zero?

—Ekaterina, Okinawa

A Wh…? Whaat?! …Oh!! It's time for the Night Class to attend class now!! Sorry, another time! ♣

Q Yuki, are you ever serious about your classes?

—I'm "Yuki" too, Aichi Prefecture

A *Ack*… Th… This is a difficult question to start off with… Of course I take them seriously…when I somehow manage to stay awake.

Q Are you not good at cooking?

—Julietta, Akita Prefecture

A Uh… Well, I might not be good, but *I do my best* when I cook. And surprisingly, it tastes pretty good… Right, Zero? What… *No*?

Q Please call the Headmaster "father"!!

—Kanamen, Tokyo

A This is not a question but a request. And it's easy to do… F… Fa… It looks like I *can't* do it after all…

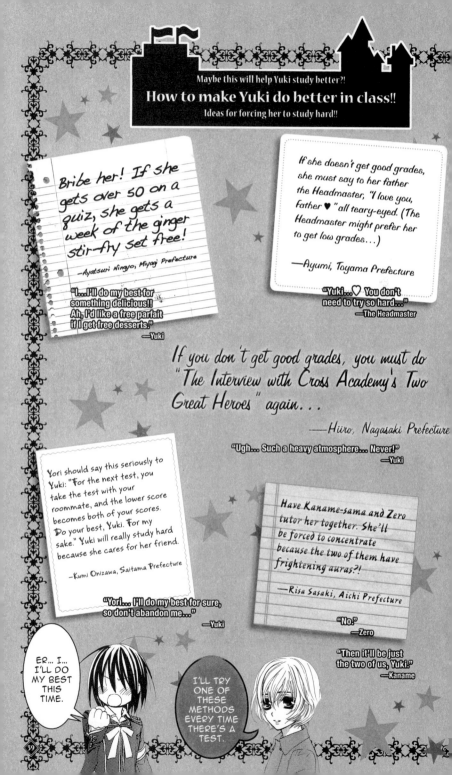

Maybe this will help Yuki study better?!

How to make Yuki do better in class!!

Ideas for forcing her to study hard!!

Bribe her! If she gets over 50 on a quiz, she gets a week of the ginger stir-fry set free!

—Ayatsuri Ningyo, Miyagi Prefecture

"I...I'll do my best for something delicious!! Ah, I'd like a free parfait if I get free desserts."

—Yuki

If she doesn't get good grades, she must say to her father the Headmaster, "I love you, father ♥" all teary-eyed. (The Headmaster might prefer her to get low grades...)

—Ayumi, Toyama Prefecture

"Yuki...♡ You don't need to try so hard..."

—The Headmaster

If you don't get good grades, you must do "The Interview with Cross Academy's Two Great Heroes" again...

—Hiiro, Nagasaki Prefecture

"Ugh... Such a heavy atmosphere... Never!"

—Yuki

Yori should say this seriously to Yuki: "For the next test, you take the test with your roommate, and the lower score becomes both of your scores. Do your best, Yuki. For my sake." Yuki will really study hard because she cares for her friend.

—Kumi Onizawa, Saitama Prefecture

"Yori... I'll do my best for sure, so don't abandon me..."

—Yuki

Have Kaname-sama and Zero tutor her together. She'll be forced to concentrate because the two of them have frightening auras?!

—Risa Sasaki, Aichi Prefecture

"No."

—Zero

"Then it'll be just the two of us, Yuki."

—Kaname

I'LL TRY ONE OF THESE METHODS EVERY TIME THERE'S A TEST.
ER... I... I'LL DO MY BEST THIS TIME.

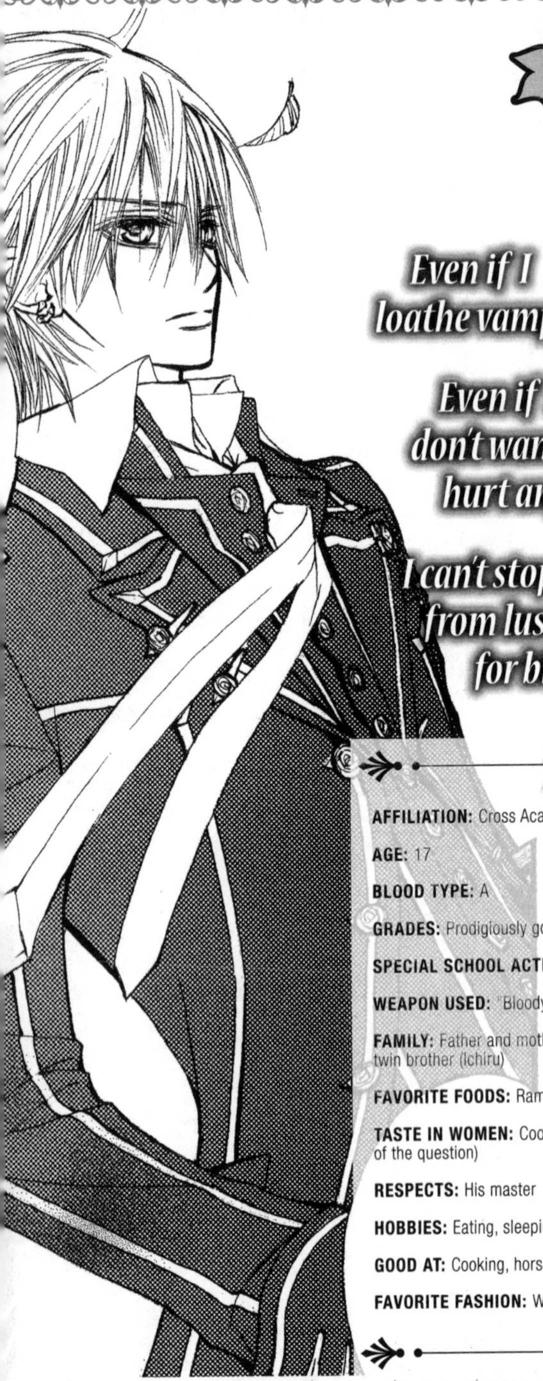

Zero Kiryu

The Guardian Who's Tormented in Many Ways!

Even if I loathe the vampires...

Even if I don't want to hurt anyone...

I can't stop myself from lusting for blood.

PROFILE

AFFILIATION: Cross Academy, Day Class, First Year

AGE: 17

BLOOD TYPE: A **HEIGHT:** 181 cm

GRADES: Prodigiously good **GOOD AT:** Sciences

SPECIAL SCHOOL ACTIVITIES: Disciplinary Committee (Guardian)

WEAPON USED: "Bloody Rose" gun

FAMILY: Father and mother (both vampire hunters and deceased), twin brother (Ichiru)

FAVORITE FOODS: Ramen with salt broth

TASTE IN WOMEN: Cool older women (flat-chested women are out of the question)

RESPECTS: His master

HOBBIES: Eating, sleeping

GOOD AT: Cooking, horseback riding, marksmanship

FAVORITE FASHION: Whatever (like what Yuki chooses for him)

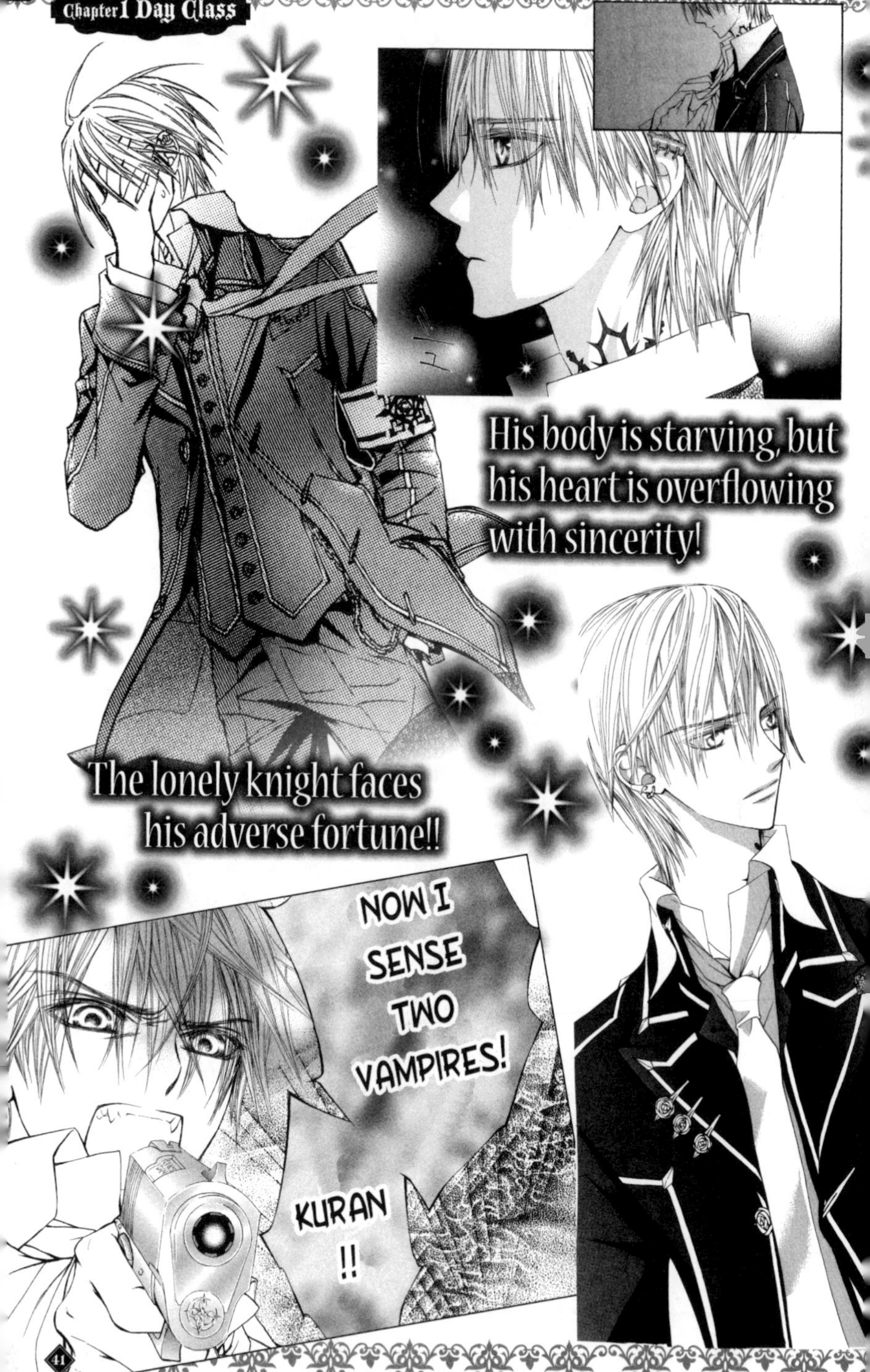
His body is starving, but his heart is overflowing with sincerity!
The lonely knight faces his adverse fortune!!
NOW I SENSE TWO VAMPIRES!
KURAN !!

CHARACTER ANALYSIS

This is what Zero Kiryu is like!

His Past

A horrible tragedy where a vampire robbed him of his parents…!!

The Kiryu family is a distinguished vampire hunter family. Four years ago, the pureblood vampire Shizuka Hio suddenly attacked them. She killed Zero's parents, and his younger brother Ichiru disappeared. Zero himself was bitten by Shizuka and suffers as he turns into a vampire.

YOU KILLED HIM...
...SO NOW I WILL PUNISH YOU.

⬆ The Kiryu family hunted Shizuka's lover, and she attacked them out of revenge.

Personality

He appears unemotional, but he's actually serious and kind!!

He's brusque and seems to keep his distance from the other students, but this is because of his complicated background. He's kind and is very serious. He has enough of a sense of responsibility as well.

He's determined to sacrifice himself for Yuki. ➡

THAT'S WHY I DON'T MIND USING WHAT'S LEFT OF MY LIFE FOR YOU.

Fighting Ability

Only effective against vampires! He shoots with the "Bloody Rose" gun!

As a Guardian, he carries a large anti-vampire handgun under his uniform. The bullets have special spells cast on them by vampire hunters, and they can seriously wound vampires. His marksmanship is first-class even among the hunters!!

Bloody Rose

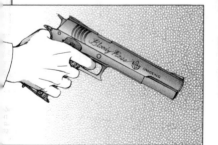

His Fate

He's from a vampire hunter family, yet he's turning into a vampire…!

YUKI...
A BEAST IN HUMAN FORM...

He suffers because he's turning into a vampire. He cannot control his thirst and desires human blood even though he knows it's forbidden…!! He cannot forgive himself for turning into the vampire he detests, so he agonizes in despair!

SCHOOLTIME

His activities at school!

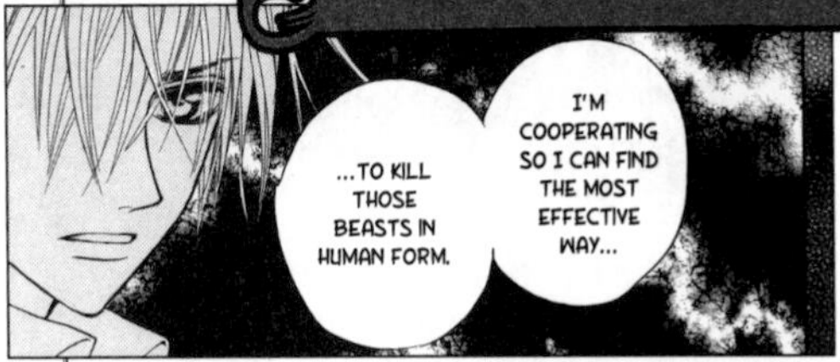
I'M COOPERATING SO I CAN FIND THE MOST EFFECTIVE WAY...
...TO KILL THOSE BEASTS IN HUMAN FORM.

⬆ Hatred of vampires is always at the bottom of his heart.

Zero likes to fight, Yuki doesn't. Their combination is perfect!! ➡

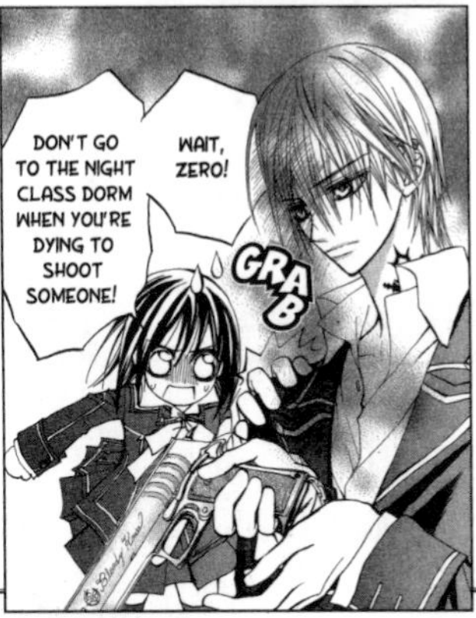
WAIT, ZERO!
DON'T GO TO THE NIGHT CLASS DORM WHEN YOU'RE DYING TO SHOOT SOMEONE!
GRAB

Extracurricular Activities

He hates vampires but fulfills his duties as a Guardian!!

He believes that his duty as a Guardian is a shortcut to defeating vampires, and he works hard at a job that no one wants to do. It's difficult for the petite Yuki to make the squealing Day Class girls shut up and the Night Class elites behave all by herself. Because Zero can glare in a way that even Kaname calls scary, the peace of the academy is maintained…!

Sports

The male students consider him the Day Class's rising star!!!

Although there are many male students in the Day Class, only Zero is a match for Kaname, who rules the Night Class!! Zero is not friendly at all, but the guys acknowledge him.

Only Zero can ride the wild horse White Lily. Here, the guys look at him with respect too!! ➡

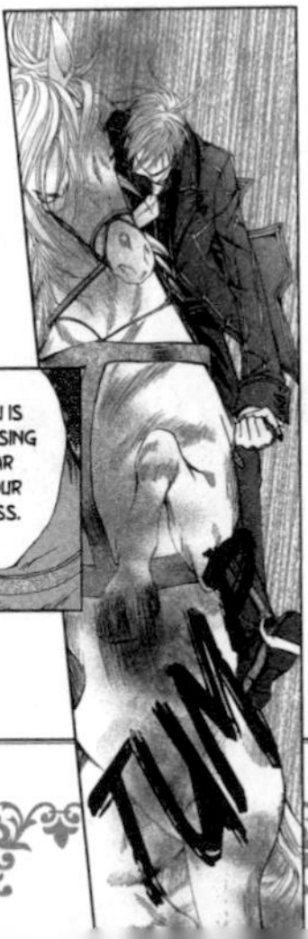
TUM

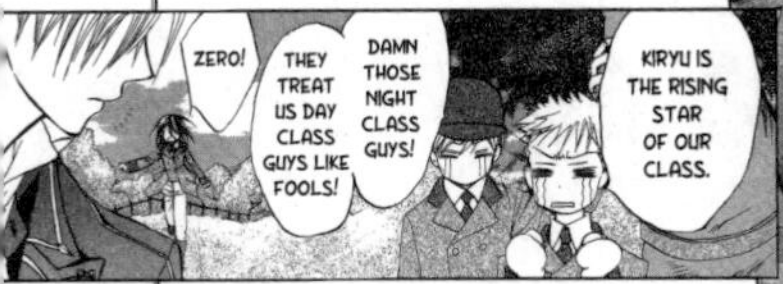
KIRYU IS THE RISING STAR OF OUR CLASS.
DAMN THOSE NIGHT CLASS GUYS!
THEY TREAT US DAY CLASS GUYS LIKE FOOLS!
ZERO!

Schoolwork

No problem at all! He's a genius who doesn't need to study hard!!

He's a genius who can understand everything by just listening in class. But because he's always late for class, he's forced to take supplementary classes.

He's a regular at the supplementary classes along with Yuki. ⬇

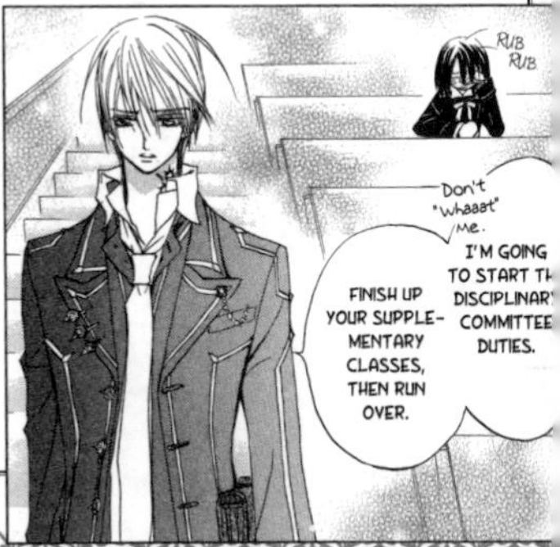
RUB RUB
Don't "Whaaat" me.
I'M GOING TO START TH DISCIPLINAR COMMITTEE DUTIES.
FINISH UP YOUR SUPPLE-MENTARY CLASSES, THEN RUN OVER.

He's so busy he has no time to study?

He has no time to study, but he doesn't need to study at his desk. When he wants to think, he leaves his desk and goes to where Lily is...

Where he secretly keeps his souvenir photo...

What's inside his closet is very simple. The Headmaster is managing the Kiryu family's belongings, so the only special item he has is the souvenir photo Yuki forced on him...

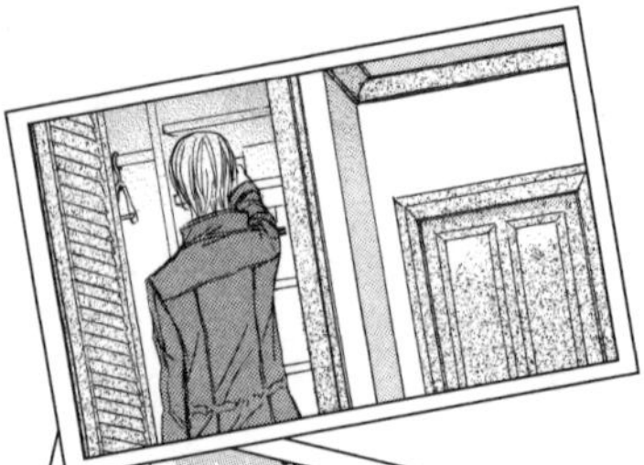

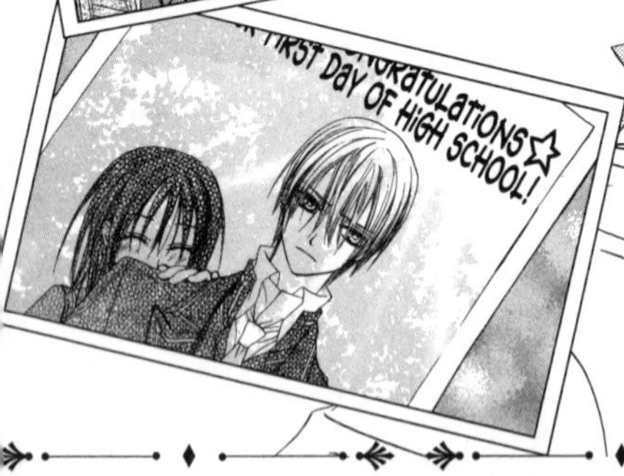
FIRST DAY OF HIGH SCHOOL!

PRIVATE ZONE

We show you what Zero's room is like!! ♥

A simple life in his own bare room where no one messes with him

When he entered the dormitory, Yuki recommended that he become roommates with someone cheerful, but Zero refused! He got his own room as requested, but it's small.

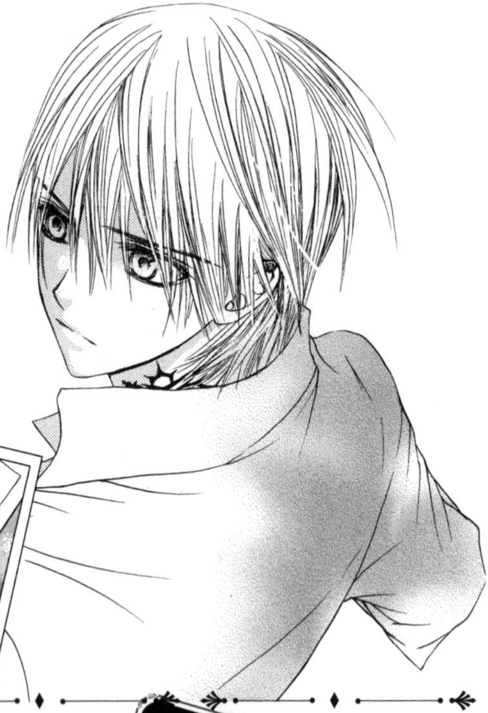

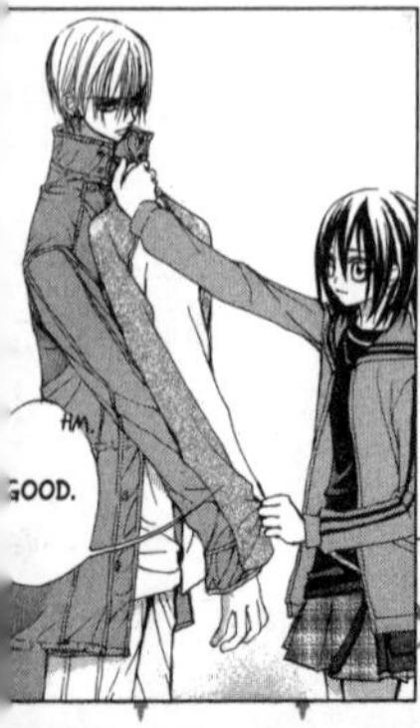
HM.
GOOD.

No interest in shopping? Yuki chooses his clothes!

Sometimes Yuki drags Zero to town, but he doesn't seem to be interested in shopping himself?

⬅ Yuki chooses his clothes.

Let's take a peek at Zero's private life! ♥

The only thing he really does on the weekends is eat with the Headmaster. The one thing he's particular about is that he's not particular about anything...?

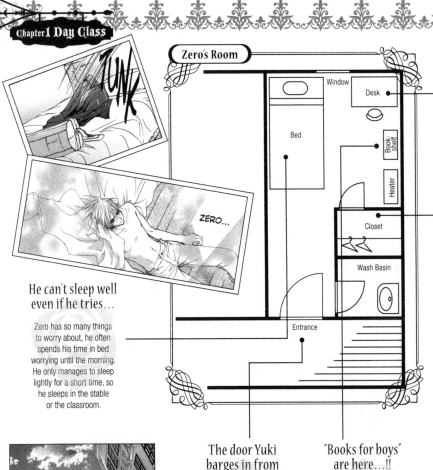

Zero's Room

Window

Desk

Bed

Book-shelf

Heater

ZERO...

Closet

Wash Basin

Entrance

He can't sleep well even if he tries...

Zero has so many things to worry about, he often spends his time in bed worrying until the morning. He only manages to sleep lightly for a short time, so he sleeps in the stable or the classroom.

The door Yuki barges in from

Zero lives in the male dormitory. But as a habit from when they were little, Yuki often sneaks in when she's worried about him.

"Books for boys" are here...!!

Apparently when Zero was away, the Headmaster put books here that teenage boys are supposed to enjoy reading... Zero, of course, completely ignores them...!!

I WONDER WHERE HE'S OFF TO? HE'S CUTTING HIS AFTERNOON CLASSES!

COULD HE BE RUNNING AWAY?!

↑→ Zero's suspected of running away from home because he goes out without saying where he's going.

He's suspected of running away from home every time he goes out alone...!!

Zero's belongings have been exactly the same since he entered the dormitory. He lives so simply, he could just leave without taking anything with him. Therefore it seems he's not attached to living in the dormitory at all.

Surprisingly, he's on good terms with the dorm president!!

He and the Sun Dormitory president seem to trust each other, based on the unspoken rule that they don't interfere with each other too much.

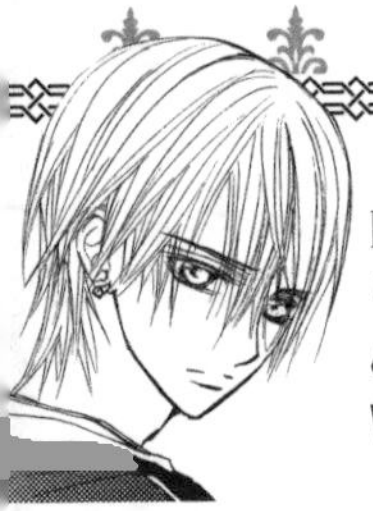

Let's hope he finds as much happiness as he has misfortune!!!

Zero's dark theater of life!!

Was he born under an unlucky star? No, that's not true!!

When he was a boy, a vampire attacked him, and his peaceful life changed forever!!

The Headmaster was really annoying when he was trying to cheer up Zero, who was turning into a vampire.

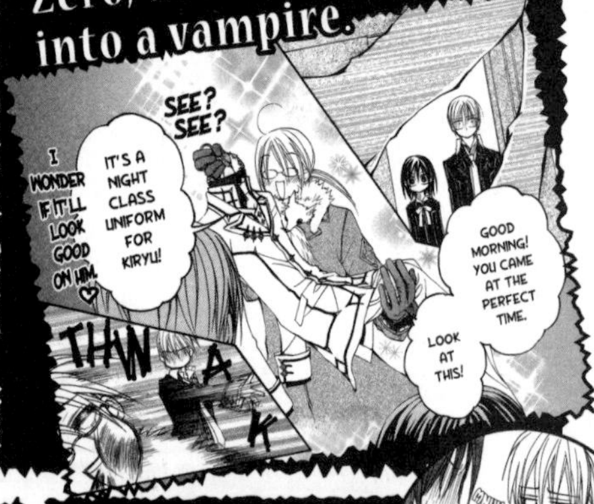
GOOD MORNING! YOU CAME AT THE PERFECT TIME.
LOOK AT THIS!
SEE? SEE?
IT'S A NIGHT CLASS UNIFORM FOR KIRYU!
I WONDER IF IT'LL LOOK GOOD ON HIM.
THWAK

The more he tries his best as a Disciplinary Committee member, the more girls and the Night Class students find him annoying...!!

HIS MASTER FOUND OUT THAT HE REPEATED A YEAR!!

Kaname gave him a souvenir designed to annoy him...!!

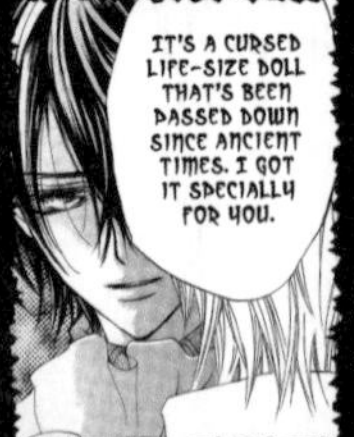
IT'S A CURSED LIFE-SIZE DOLL THAT'S BEEN PASSED DOWN SINCE ANCIENT TIMES. I GOT IT SPECIALLY FOR YOU.

Yuki's handmade chocolate tasted...

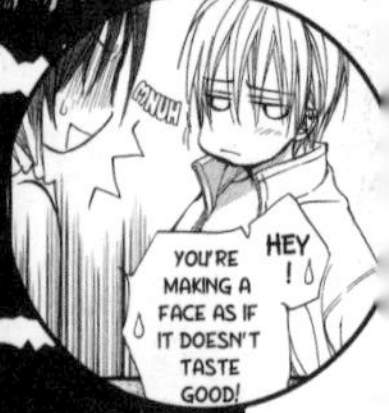
MNUH
HEY!
YOU'RE MAKING A FACE AS IF IT DOESN'T TASTE GOOD!

When he was napping outside, White Lily the wild horse woke him up!

It's useless teaching Yuki how to study...!!

The Headmaster calls him "son" without his permission!!

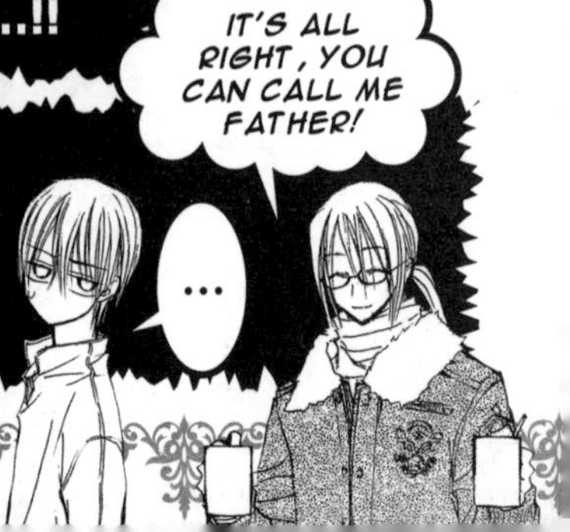
IT'S ALL RIGHT, YOU CAN CALL ME FATHER!
...

Special messages to Zero

Zero is always cranky, so no matter what you tell him, he can't get more cranky?!

From Yuki Cross

Zero's always scolding me, he's particular about details, he says I'm flat chested, he takes his clothes off in front of me…!! You just don't think I'm female, do you! Hmph!! But even though you always act that way, there must be times when you're suffering… You can depend on me more…

From Sayori Wakaba

In spite of everything, Zero and Yuki are a good pair. I don't think anybody except Yuki can understand him.…

From the Headmaster

Stop looking at me as if you're looking at a pervert. Yuki tells me what happens at school, but why won't you? Hit me with your youth and passion.

From Nadeshiko Shindo

K…Kiryu, thank you for rescuing me the other day. I'd like to give you a thank-you gift…

From Hanabusa Aido

Do not talk rudely to Kaname-sama… You're turning more into a vampire. You all right?

From Takuma Ichijo

Kiryu, you're always having a hard time. I'm sorry our Kaname always makes nasty comments. Disciplinary Committee member, do your best. ♥

From Akatsuki Kain

Kiryu, I understand the position you're in, but please don't fight with our Hanabusa…

From Senri Shiki

The male Disciplinary Committee member, huh… I'd like to know how strong he really is when he gets serious…

From Kaname Kuran

I protect Yuki. But Kiryu… You understand, don't you? You must become Yuki's shield and fulfill your duties…

He answers your questions?!

Questions for Kiryu

Let's be brave and ask Kiryu questions since he's usually hard to approach.

Letters sent in from fans for fans!

Vam☆ Fan Hall

The Zero Version

Q Have you ever had a fight with Ichiru?
—Sayamame, Hokkaido

A I don't think we've had any fights... When we were kids, Ichiru's health was frail. Even if he pouted, he'd be in a good mood shortly thereafter.

Q You seem to hate purebloods. Who do you hate more, Kaname or Shizuka?
—Yukki, Fukushima Prefecture

A *What kind of question is this?! This is stupid.* It's not a question of which. I hate *all* vampires.

Q Why do you always look cranky?
—Yumi Haketa, Nagano Prefecture

A That's *the way I am...* Hey! You *stupid-looking father and daughter!* Don't worry about the lines between my brows becoming permanent!

Q So do you like Yuki?
—Narumi, Oita Prefecture

A (Glare)......... You wanna cry?

Q When did you become a juvenile delinquent?
—Sayu ★, Kanagawa Prefecture

A So I'm doing this Q&A feature as well? And what do you mean, "juvenile delinquent"? Hey, this question better not be from that *stupid Headmaster!*

Q You said that you don't mind cooking. When did you start cooking?
—Maiko Ueda, Tokyo

A It was my job to cook when my parents were away...and when I trained under my master, he trained me to cook as well.

Q If the Night Class students weren't vampires, who would be your friend?
—Michiko Watanabe, Saitama Prefecture

A *No one, of course...* What, I have to choose? Well, that Kain guy could be someone I *might* manage to talk with...

How should we have the brusque Zero smile…?

Please… Smile, Zero!!

We'll do anything and everything to make Zero smile!!

The way she's wearing her clothes is wrong, but show Zero a photo of when Yuki wore her clothes all by herself (Eleventh Night).

—★Emi★, Shiga Prefecture

"This is one of my memories. I don't want to share it so easily…"
—Kaname

Lock him up in a room with Kain!! Maybe friendship will bloom between the two who are always having a hard time. (I want to see it, but I also don't want to see it.)

—Mini Chiroru, Iwate Prefecture

"We might be able to see the smiling faces of two people who understand each other, huh!!"
—Ichijo

If he plays with a very cute puppy, Zero will be forced to smile… I look forward to it 100 percent.

—Hiromi Ishizuka, Tokyo

"Zero has always been kind to animals."
—Yuki

Give him a photo book that contains photos of Yuki smiling. He'll take a peek at it when he's alone and will smile! (And when the Headmaster finds out, tragedy will occur?!)

—Yuri, Miyagi Prefecture

"Yuki's smile would melt anyone's heart."
—Sayori

Have Kaname-sama say a really bad pun in front of Zero, looking all serious. Even Zero will be forced to smile…

—cape★, Tokushima

"Kuran… Try it and see if I smile."
—Zero

Show him Yuki's funny and strange answers. He'll think, "That's not possible!!" and will smile?!

—Sayaka Ota, Kanagawa Prefecture

"Yuki's tests are always full of strange answers. So even if you show them to me now…"
—Zero

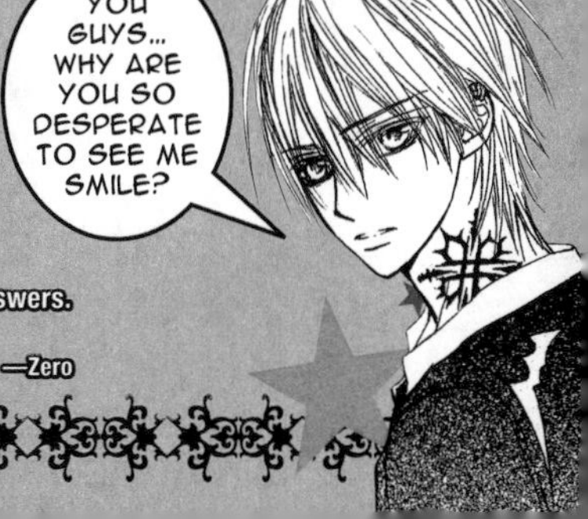
YOU GUYS… WHY ARE YOU SO DESPERATE TO SEE ME SMILE?

I've been waiting for Yuki to come back safely.

Sayori Wakaba

Yuki's Best Friend and Roommate

PROFILE

AFFILIATION: Cross Academy, Day Class, First Year **AGE:** 16

TASTE IN MEN: "Someone I get when I add Yuki and Zero, then divide by two." **FAVORITE FOODS:** Everything

FAMILY: Father and mother (She comes from a pretty old and distinguished family. Apparently she has a fiancé, but she doesn't know his name or what he looks like.)

GOOD AT: Staying calm **DOESN'T LIKE:** Kaname Kuran

FAVORITE FASHION: Classy clothes that don't make her look improper

YAWN
WHAT A HARD LIFE. EVERY DAY YOU RETURN TO THE DORM IN THE EARLY MORNING, YOU TAKE NAPS DURING CLASSES...
SUPPLE-MENTARY CLASSES AGAIN?
AWWW...

⬅ Makes a sharp comment to Yuki, who's sleepy because of her Disciplinary Committee duties.

CHARACTER ANALYSIS

This is what Sayori Wakaba is like!

Personality

She's a kind, ordinary girl who really cares about her friend.

She's serious and low-key, but she has a steadfast kindness to her. She's worried that Yuki is seriously bothered by something, but she doesn't pry too much and waits for the time when she can do something for Yuki. No matter what sort of secrets Yuki has, her feelings of really liking Yuki will not waver.

YUKI...
YOU'VE HAD SOMETHING ON YOUR MIND RECENTLY.
IS THERE ANYTHING I CAN DO TO HELP?

⬅ She looks straight at Yuki's eyes and asks her a question. Because she wants to do something for Yuki...

Nadeshiko Shindo

The Girl in the Sun Dormitory Who's in Love

She doesn't look it, but she acts when necessary, and she's not afraid of anything.

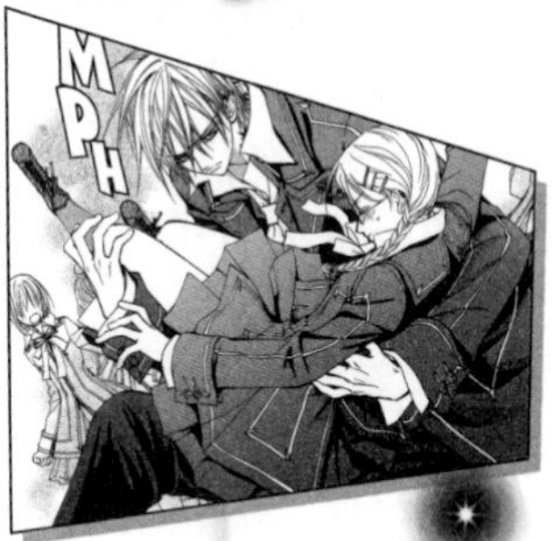
MPH

With her glasses and braids, she may look like a quiet girl, but she's active when she's in love. She tried to climb over the Moon Dormitory wall, and she asked Zero for a dance when everybody else is afraid of him... Is she actually brave?

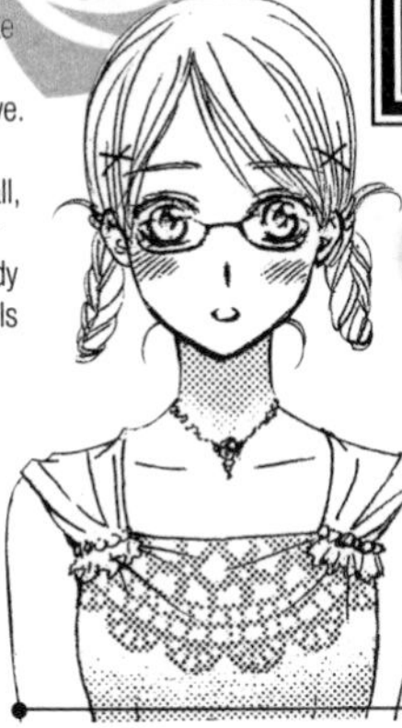

⬆ She tried to climb over the Moon Dormitory wall and fell. Zero caught her. This was the moment when her heart melted...?

⬅ She dressed up the best she could and summoned all her courage to talk to Zero...

The Moon Dormitory Maid

Takes Care of the Night Class

She does her work promptly, even when the demands are unreasonable.

A competent maid who works in the Moon Dormitory that is full of capricious aristocrats. She smiles and handles everyone's chores.

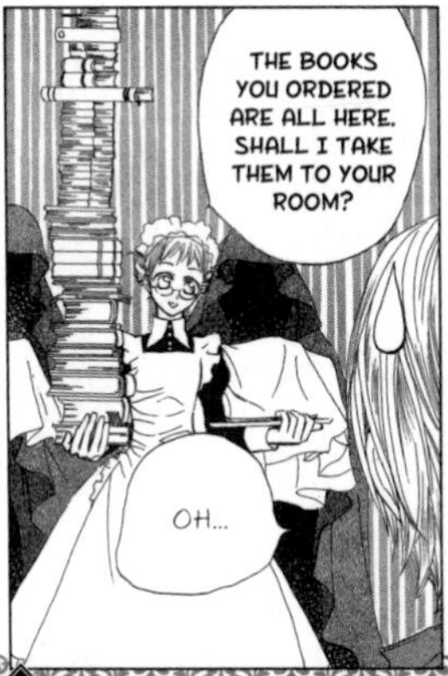
THE BOOKS YOU ORDERED ARE ALL HERE. SHALL I TAKE THEM TO YOUR ROOM?
OH...

⬅ Ichijo asked for a whole lot of books, but she delivered them as if they were nothing. Behind her are the ones in black who hold things like the phone.

Kasumi Kageyama

The Class Rep of the Day Class

He does his best, but he's not rewarded.

He's serious and does his best to interact more with the Night Class (especially Ruka). He's irritated at Yuki, who lowers the class average...

⬇ He gets really close to Ruka?! But he's instantly rejected.

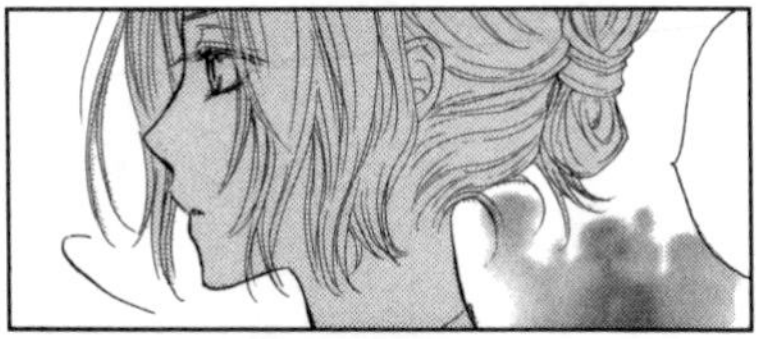

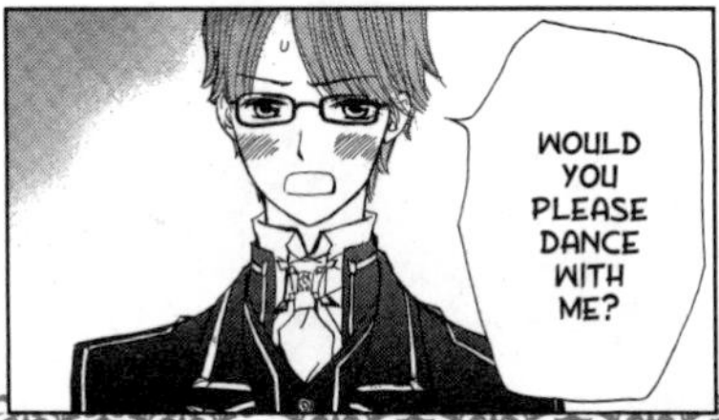
WOULD YOU PLEASE DANCE WITH ME?

From the Day Class

Fun Ways to Approach the Night Class

How do you meet the students of the Night Class?!
Even if the Disciplinary Committee cracks down on you...!!
We tell you how to get close to them!!

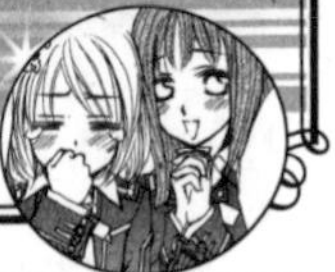

1 A surprise attack!!

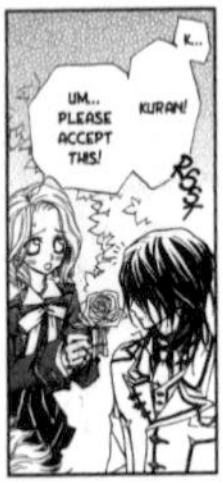
K...
UM... PLEASE ACCEPT THIS!
KURAN!
RUSTLE

Hide in the bushes and jump out when he passes by. Even the Disciplinary Committee won't be able to stop you.

2 Get in the very first row!

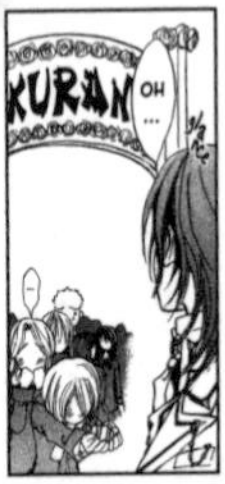
KURAN
OH...

When it's necessary to get in line, get in the very first row. Your opportunity decreases drastically if you're in the second row or further behind.

Tip

Hold your camera in one hand!!

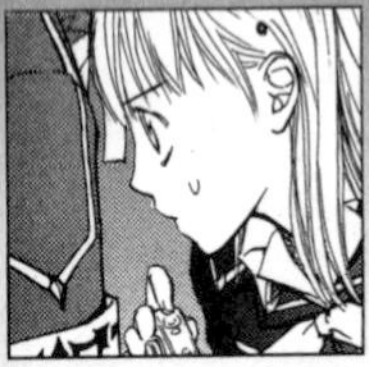

You must take photos fast with one hand so you don't miss any photo opportunities!!

3 Make a Disciplinary Committee Member your ally!!

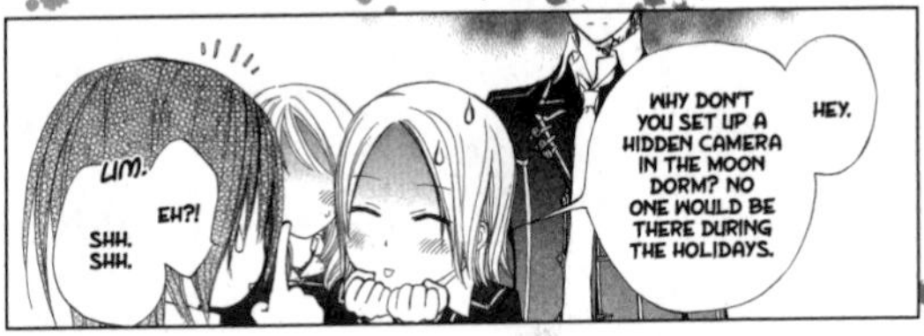
HEY.
WHY DON'T YOU SET UP A HIDDEN CAMERA IN THE MOON DORM? NO ONE WOULD BE THERE DURING THE HOLIDAYS.
EH?!
UM.
SHH. SHH.

The Disciplinary Committee has contact with the Night Class and can enter the Moon Dormitory freely. If you can make them your ally, things will be much easier!! It is important to get close to them even if you have to bribe them.

4 Walk around the corridor!!

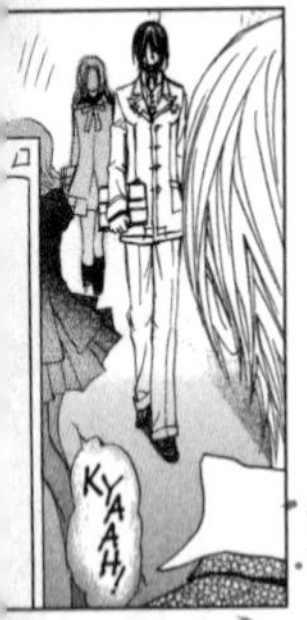
KYAAAH!

Occasionally, the Night Class students appear at school during the day!! Keep walking around the school to increase your opportunities for chance encounters.

5 Have a Strong Heart!!

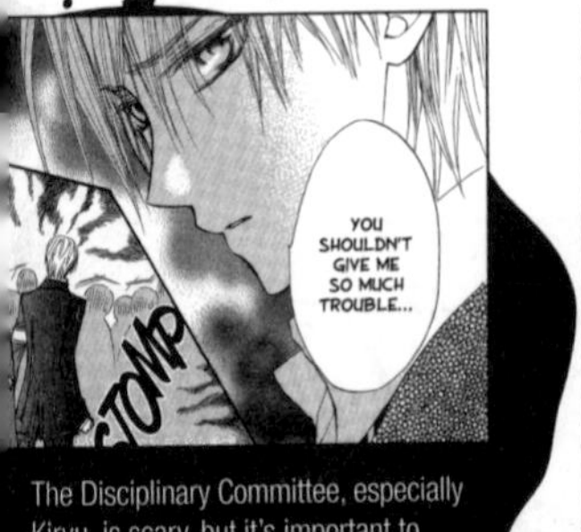
YOU SHOULDN'T GIVE ME SO MUCH TROUBLE...
STOMP

The Disciplinary Committee, especially Kiryu, is scary, but it's important to have the courage to step forward...

Reference

1 How to Climb Up Walls

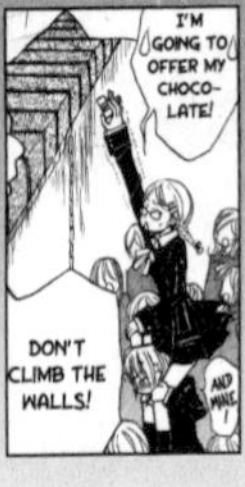
I'M GOING TO OFFER MY CHOCOLATE!
DON'T CLIMB THE WALLS!
AND MINE!

Get on someone's shoulders and reach up.

2 How to Climb Down Walls

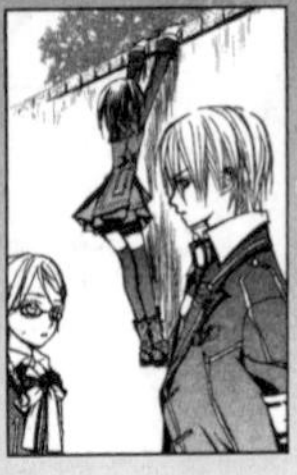

Put your hands on the top of the wall and descend slowly using your legs.

Chapter 2
Night Class

The Beautiful Elite Vampires

We get close to the charms of the elite vampires who hide their true selves and attend and live in Cross Academy! This is the first time the rooms of the Moon Dormitory (which is off-limits to the Day Class students) are revealed.

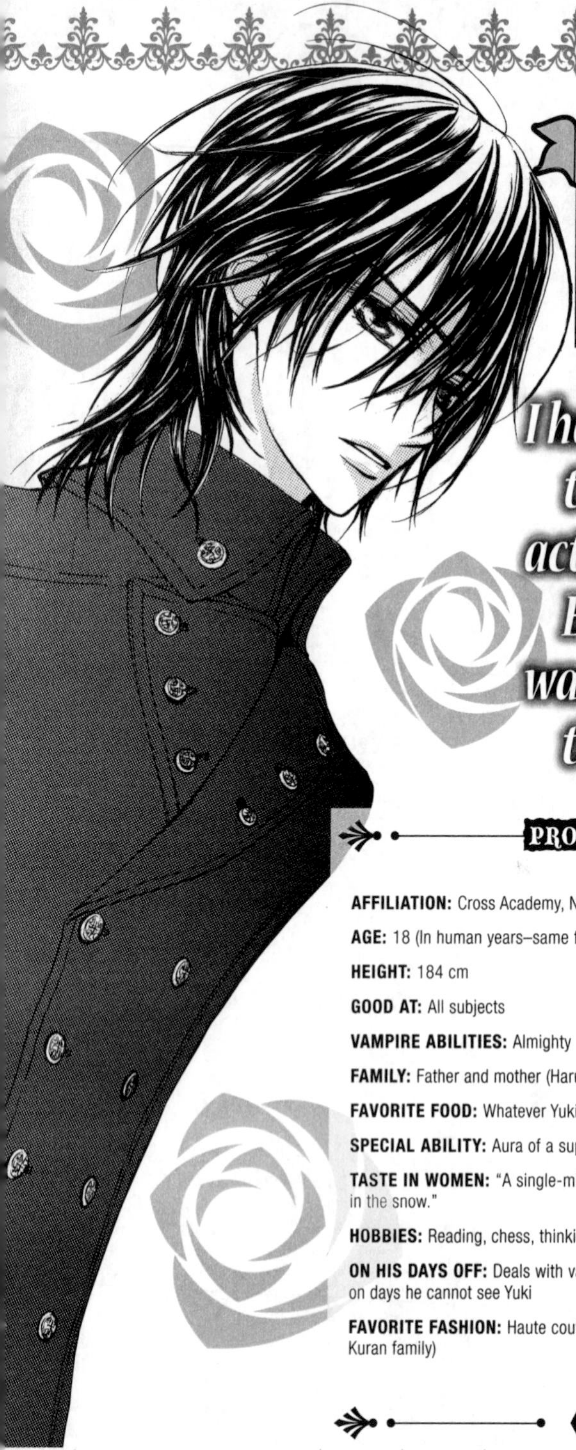

Kaname Kuran

The Proud "Head of the Night"!!

I have let the forbidden acts pass… Everything was done for this day.

PROFILE

AFFILIATION: Cross Academy, Night Class

AGE: 18 (In human years–same for the other vampires)

HEIGHT: 184 cm

GOOD AT: All subjects

VAMPIRE ABILITIES: Almighty **VAMPIRE LEVEL:** Pureblood

FAMILY: Father and mother (Haruka and Juri, both deceased)

FAVORITE FOOD: Whatever Yuki makes

SPECIAL ABILITY: Aura of a supreme ruler ←Aido added this in

TASTE IN WOMEN: "A single-minded girl who keeps waiting for me in the snow."

HOBBIES: Reading, chess, thinking about Yuki

ON HIS DAYS OFF: Deals with various work and sulks in bed on days he cannot see Yuki

FAVORITE FASHION: Haute couture (Tailored by a purveyor to the Kuran family)

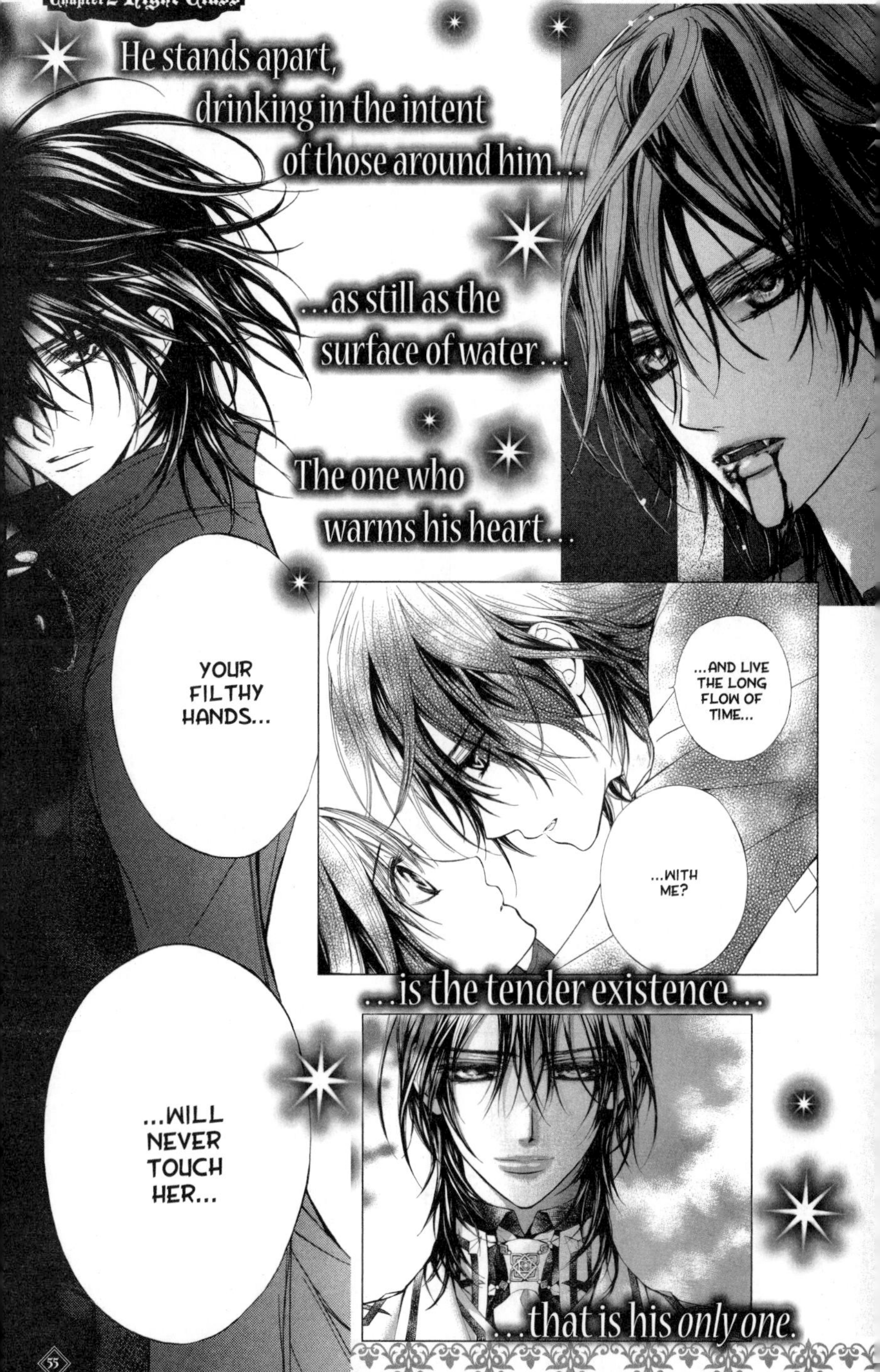
He stands apart, drinking in the intent of those around him...
...as still as the surface of water...
The one who warms his heart...
...and live the long flow of time...
...with me?
Your filthy hands...
...is the tender existence...
...will never touch her...
...that is his *only one*.

CHARACTER ANALYSIS

This is what Kaname Kuran is like!

His Past

For ten years he watched over his loved one…!!

The days he spent with Yuki as the son of Juri and Haruka Kuran end with Rido's attack. Kaname himself is kept under the Senate's watch. He thinks about Yuki, who survived, and hopes to create a place where she can live happily.

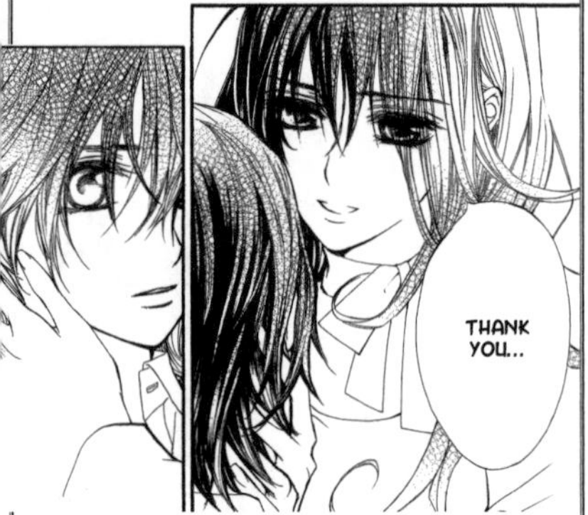
THANK YOU…

⬆ Juri kisses Kaname goodbye and leaves Yuki in his care. After this, Kaname's only reason for living is Yuki's existence.

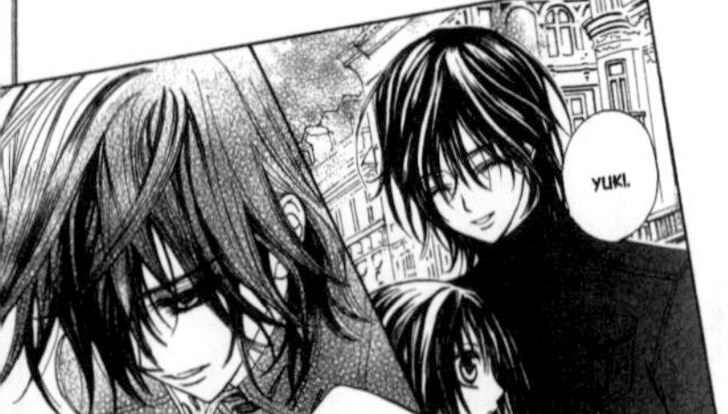
YUKI.
KANAME-SAMA!

⬆ He evades his guards and spends happy times with Yuki.

Personality

He hides his sharp fangs with his elegant smile…!!

He stands out even in the Night Class, which is full of graceful and attractive elites! The students support and think of him as a perfect "prince." However, he is capable of using cold-blooded measures to protect Yuki, who is more important to him than anyone else.

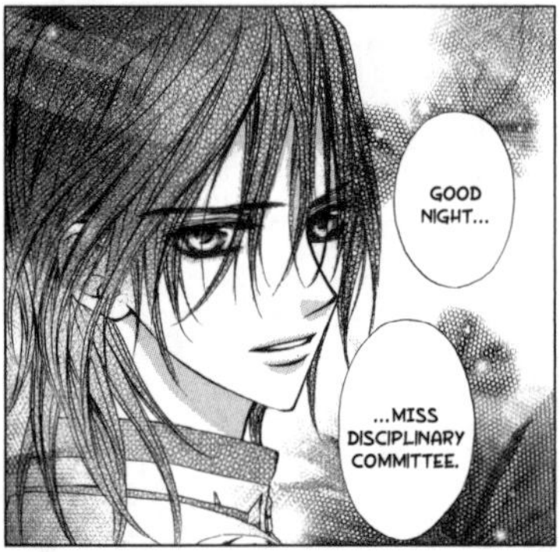
GOOD NIGHT…
…MISS DISCIPLINARY COMMITTEE.

⬆ He smiles charmingly at Yuki. We're lured in too.♥

➡ He expresses his true feelings to Zero and warns him… A moment when you see Kaname's merciless side!

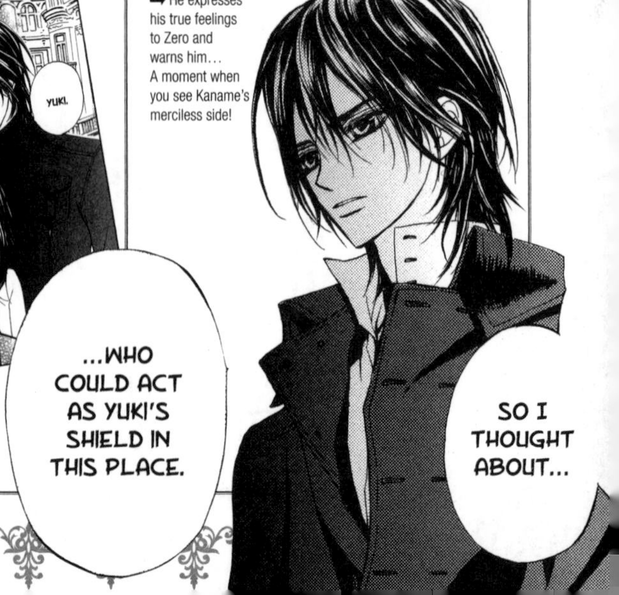
SO I THOUGHT ABOUT…
…WHO COULD ACT AS YUKI'S SHIELD IN THIS PLACE.

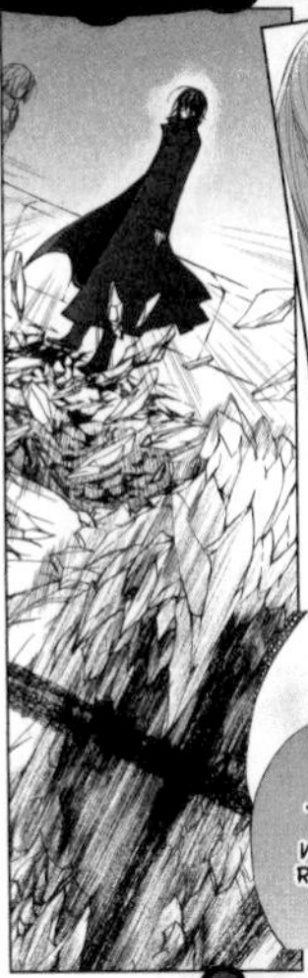

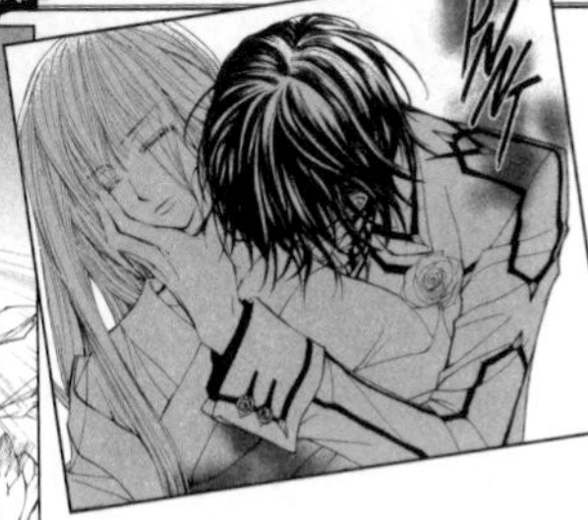

⬆ By drinking Shizuka's blood, Kaname gains even stronger powers!!

Fighting Ability

An almighty pureblood with an overwhelming presence!!

As a pureblood, a supreme existence among vampires, he has abilities that surpass human understanding! Kaname himself still holds secrets, so his full abilities are unknown.

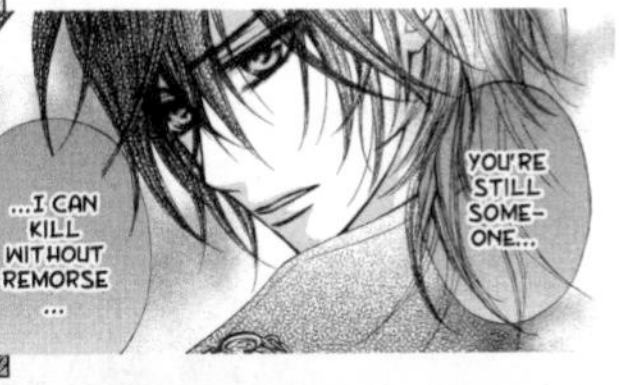
YOU'RE STILL SOME-ONE...
...I CAN KILL WITHOUT REMORSE ...

⬅ When Kaname bares his intent to kill... The aura and shock waves that radiate are beyond imagination!!

SCHOOLTIME

His activities at school!

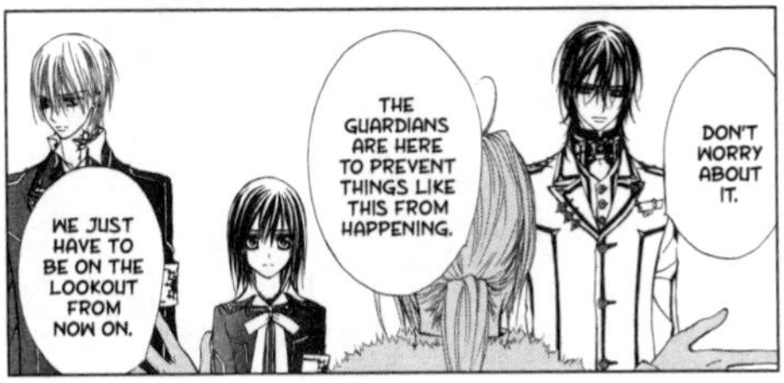
DON'T WORRY ABOUT IT.
THE GUARDIANS ARE HERE TO PREVENT THINGS LIKE THIS FROM HAPPENING.
WE JUST HAVE TO BE ON THE LOOKOUT FROM NOW ON.

⬆ Kaname takes part in resolving the incident in which a vampire drank blood from a Day Class student...

Classes & Extracurricular Activities

The president of the Night Class who supports pacifism!!

Kaname worked with Headmaster Cross to set up the Night Class because he supports the Headmaster's ideology of educating those who can become bridges between humans and vampires. Peace in the academy is maintained because Kaname, who is the president of the Night Class and a pureblood, demonstrates that he values coexistence with humans!

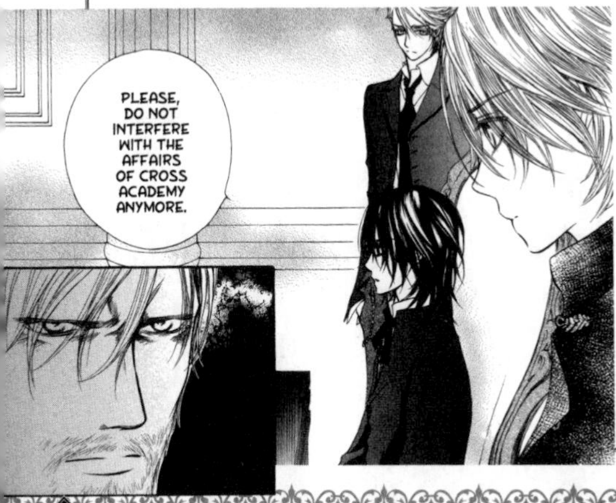
PLEASE, DO NOT INTERFERE WITH THE AFFAIRS OF CROSS ACADEMY ANYMORE.

⬅ He restrains the Senate, who tries to meddle with the academy after Shizuka is killed.

PRIVATE ZONE

We show you what Kaname's room is like!! ♥

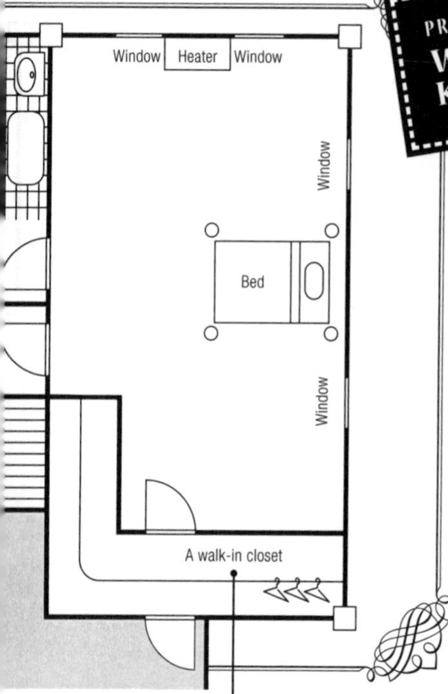
Window
Heater
Window
Window
Bed
Window
A walk-in closet

A gorgeous room provided only for the dorm president

A single room that is the largest room in the Moon Dormitory! The furniture is gorgeous, but he doesn't have many belongings (according to Kaname, it's because they break easily as a result of his stress as dorm president), so the room doesn't really look as if anybody lives there. There is also space that isn't used…

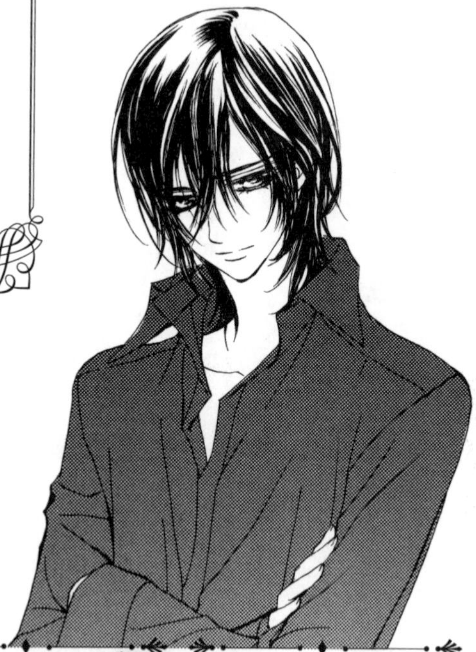

Contains secret photos!!

He files and treasures photos of Yuki growing up that Headmaster Cross periodically sent him. (Rumor has it Kaname agreed to cooperate with the Headmaster when setting up the Night Class because of these photos…) Kaname probably knows more about Yuki's memorable moments than she does!

Let's take a peek at Kaname's private life! ♥

His private life is full of mystery. But basically, other than being with Yuki, he spends his time lazily?

Intelligent hobby time

He passes time playing chess, reading or thinking about Yuki… These are Kaname's hobbies.♥

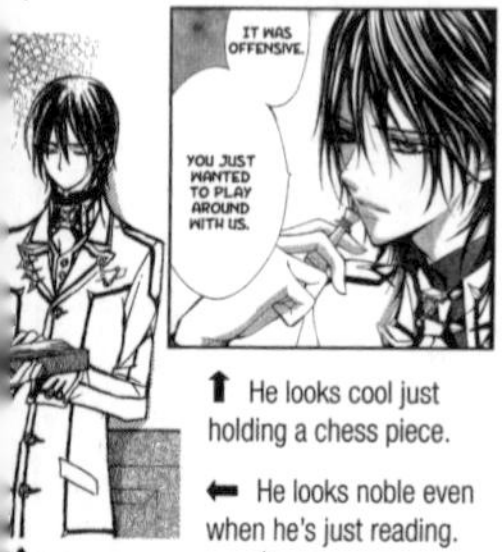
IT WAS OFFENSIVE.
YOU JUST WANTED TO PLAY AROUND WITH US.

⬆ He looks cool just holding a chess piece.

⬅ He looks noble even when he's just reading.

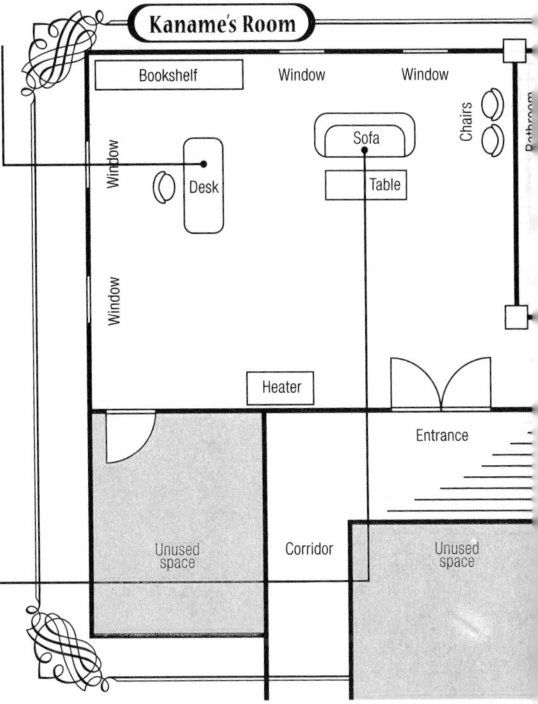
Kaname's Room
Bookshelf
Window
Window
Chairs
Sofa
Table
Window
Desk
Window
Heater
Entrance
Unused space
Corridor
Unused space

Writing reports is part of the dorm president's job

The dorm president has various chores to do, including writing reports to the Senate! This is why he has a large business desk.

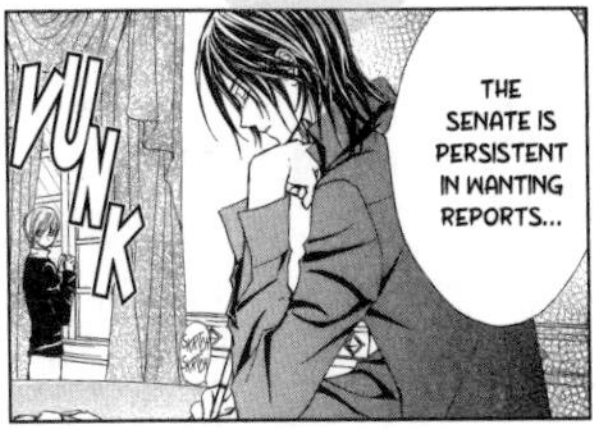
VUNK
THE SENATE IS PERSISTENT IN WANTING REPORTS...

⬆ He has work to do on his days off too! You can see the riding grounds from the window where Ichijo is standing.

He likes the big sofa ♥

A sofa and a low table are placed in front of the desk. The elegant and massive furniture is perfect for Kaname's noble demeanor.

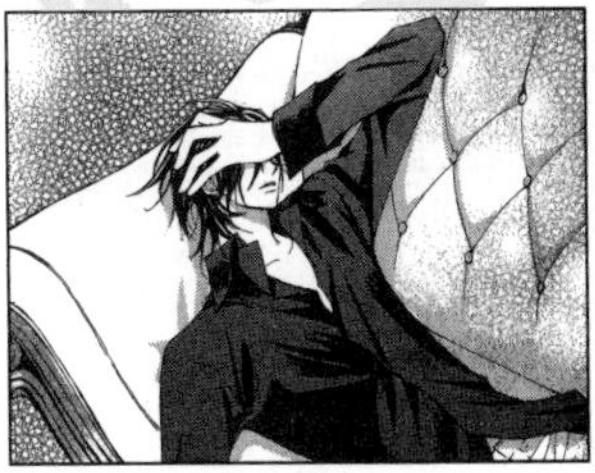

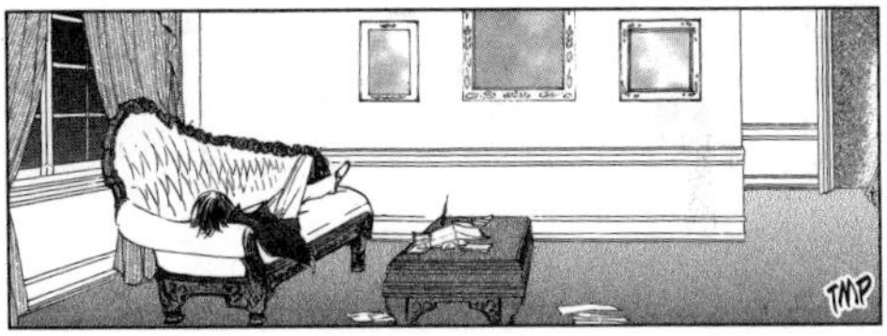
TMP

⬅ ⬆ He lies down and rests on the sofa when he's tired from doing his chores. Kaname uses it often. Is it because it's comfortable or just because it's nearby?

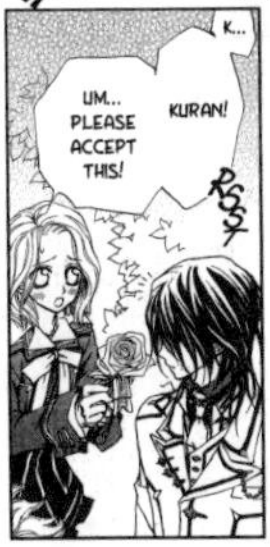
K...
KURAN!
UM... PLEASE ACCEPT THIS!
RSSL

⬅ A female student gives him a rose. ♥ Usually, it's the guy who gives flowers...

⬇ The girls blush and stare at Kaname...

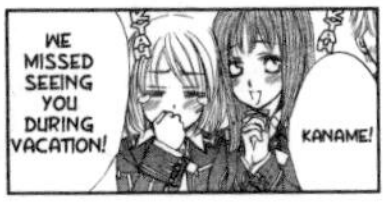
KANAME!
WE MISSED SEEING YOU DURING VACATION!

Days of girls loving his elegance

Kaname is so noble, people find it difficult to approach him. But because he's that way, he has lots of passionate fans!!

He takes care of his chores during the day, but...!!

Even if he's lazily working, he quickly acts when he senses Yuki nearby!!

Let's learn from Kaname-sama! ♥

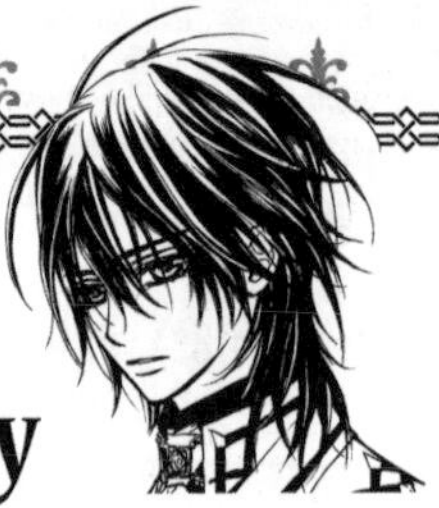

Ways to be popular with girls, in order of difficulty

As a pureblood, Kaname-sama has superior abilities! Take a look at his supreme powers and skills (mainly used against Yuki)!!

Step 1 Help out like a gentleman!

Difficulty: ★★

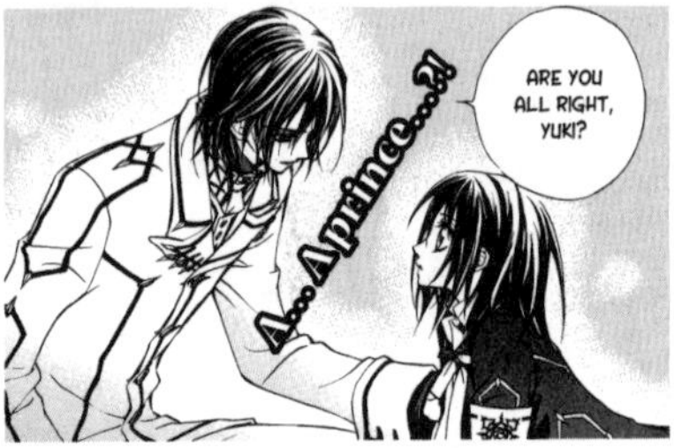
ARE YOU ALL RIGHT, YUKI?
A... A prince...?!

If a lady falls down in front of you, kneel elegantly and extend your hand. You should look into her eyes when you do this.

Step 2 Dance smartly

Difficulty: ★★★

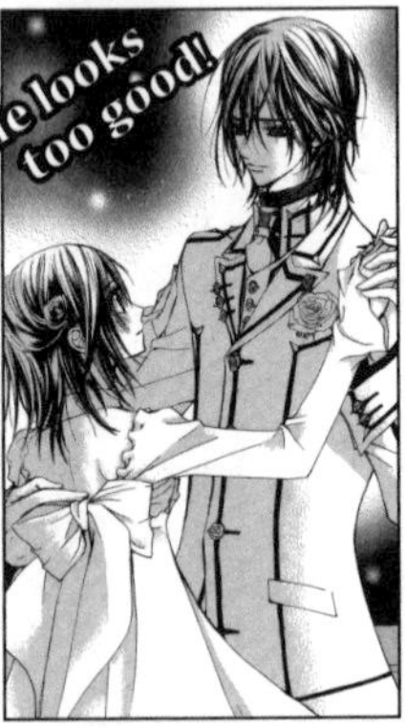
He looks too good!

Skills such as ballroom dancing are a must if you want ladies to love you. Lead the lady with confidence if she's not used to dancing. You'll be able to get close to her.

Step 3 Be scary on occasion...?!

Difficulty: ★★★★

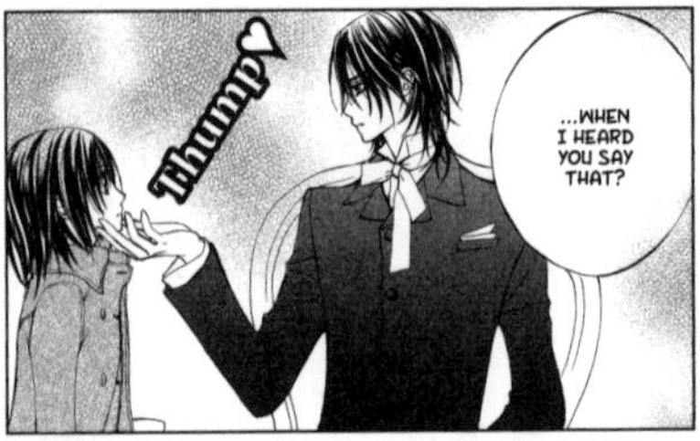
...WHEN I HEARD YOU SAY THAT?
Thump♥

Simply being nice will only make the lady see you as a friend. You'll score high points if you show a side that's different from usual. ♥ How about being bold and punishing her?

Step 4 Whisper in her ear ♥

Difficulty: ★★★★★

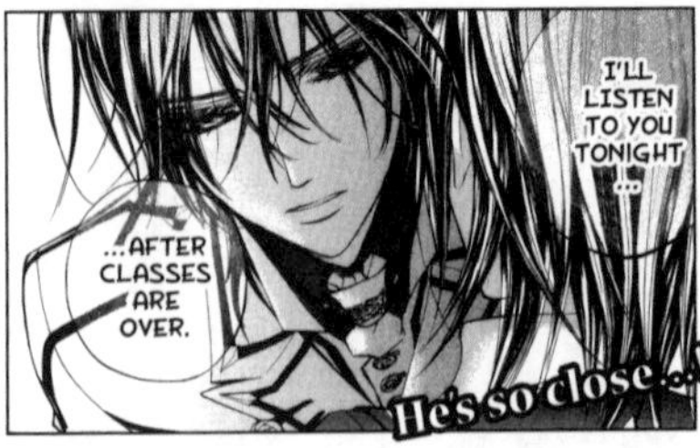
I'LL LISTEN TO YOU TONIGHT...
...AFTER CLASSES ARE OVER.
He's so close...!!

Whisper so close that she can feel your breath... ♥ Even an ordinary promise will sound like an important secret then. This is the ultimate technique!!

COMMENTS

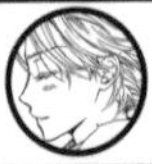

Aido: I surrender, Kaname-sama!!

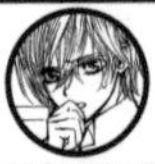

Ichijo: Kaname is sort of indecent!

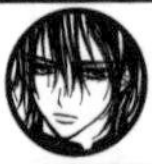

Kaname: ... ...

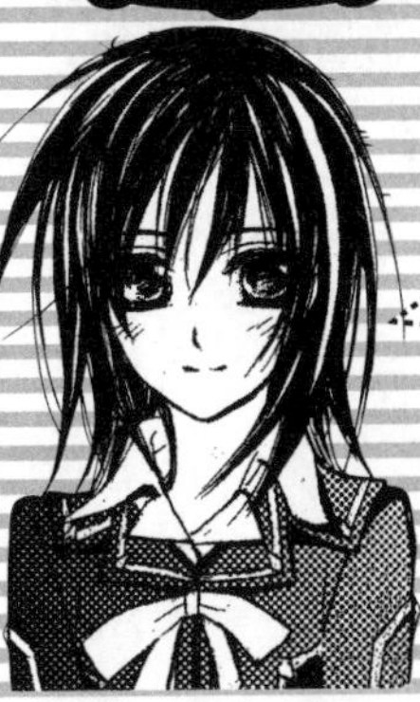

From Yuki Cross

Thanks for all your work, Kaname. It must be difficult being the Moon Dormitory president and the Night Class president, so please take care of yourself!

From the Headmaster

I'm glad Kaname grew up wonderfully! But I won't give Yuki to him. ♥

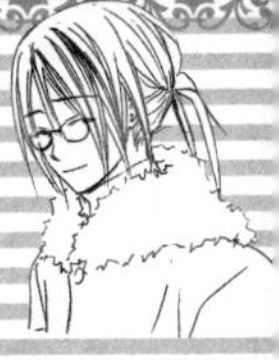

From Ruka Souen

I will always go wherever Kaname-sama goes… I'll handle Aido as well!!

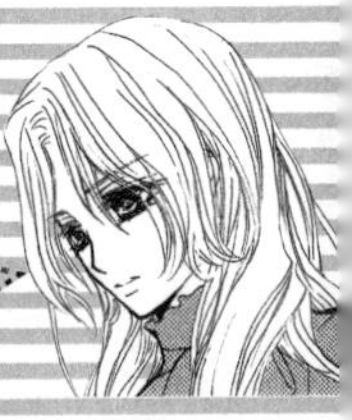

Special messages to Kaname

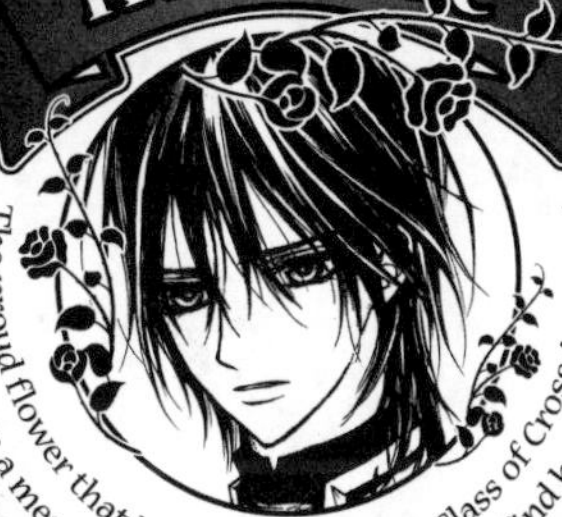

The proud flower that blooms in the Night Class of Cross Academy! Give him a message, even if it's something you find hard to say.

From Zero Kiryu

From me? What do you want me to say? This is inane.

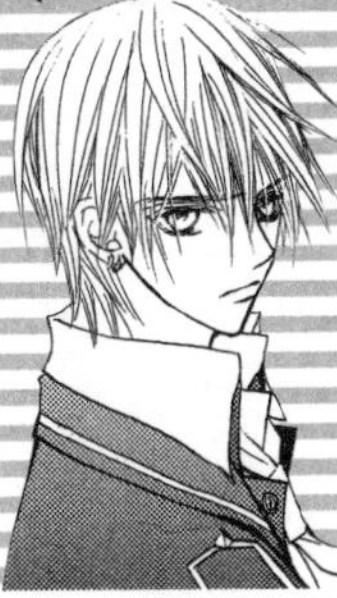

From Rima Toya

I feel like he's always having a hard time…

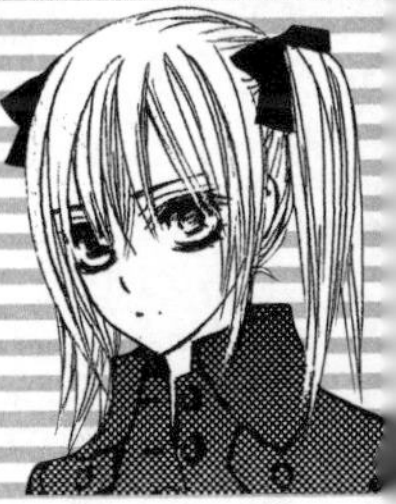

From Hanabusa Aido

My feelings for Kaname-sama cannot be expressed here… (Cut)

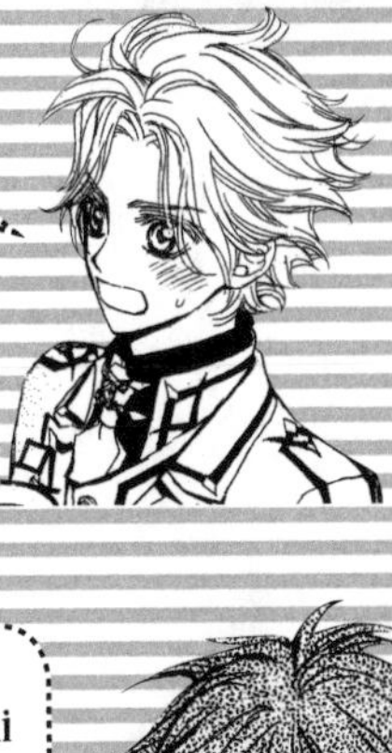

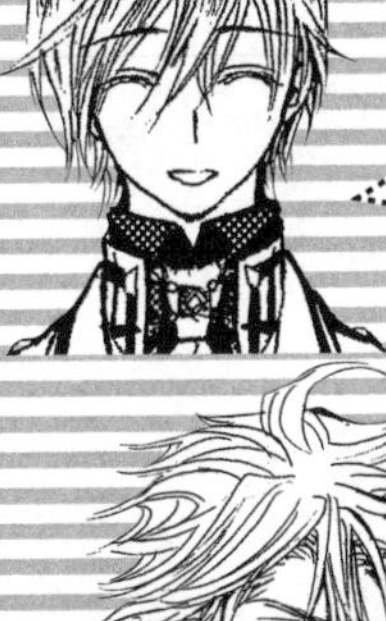

From Takuma Ichijo

Kaname is a worrier, so I must take care of him. ♥ I'll give you a rakugo DVD next time. ♪

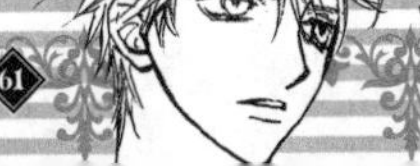

From Akatsuki Kain

I apologize for Hanabusa causing you trouble.

From Senri Shiki

I get the feeling he's always having a hard time…

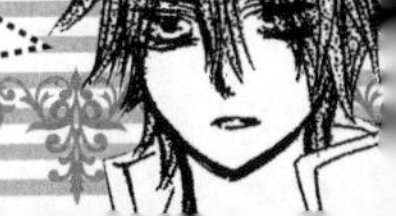

Letters sent in from fans for fans!

Vam☆Fan Hall

The Kaname Version

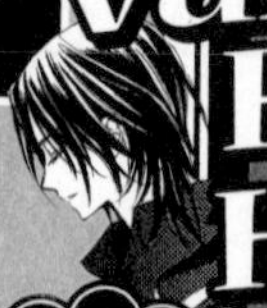

He answers your questions?!

Please tell us, Kaname-sama...

Even Kaname-sama, the head of the Night Class, cooperated!!

Q **If Yuki said, "I hate you, Kaname!!" what would you do?**

—Asuka Ijuin, Hokkaido

A Heh... What amusing words... So you *want* me to imagine that...?

Q **What sort of cake do you like?**

—Rina Matsumoto, Tokyo

A However clumsily made, a cake someone did her best to make for me...

Q **Will you ever fall in love with someone other than Yuki? (Please fall in love with me!! [Hee.])**

—Matsurina Kaname, Toyama Prefecture

A My arms exist to hold only one person. I can't hold anyone else... Sorry...

Q **How do you feel about Zero?**

—Erina Matsuoka, Aichi Prefecture

A I don't feel anything... Ah, sorry. I hope he'll be fine. Because otherwise, he won't be able to act as a shield. And I have no need for weak shields. ♣

Q **Do you wear glasses? I think you'd look really good in them.**

—Shion Natsumeki, Kanagawa Prefecture

A Thank you, but I don't need them... I'll wear them if *Yuki* wants me to though.

Q **What are you going to do about Aido?**

—Mieko Matsui, Hyogo Prefecture

A What am I going to do? Nothing, because it'd be a bother.

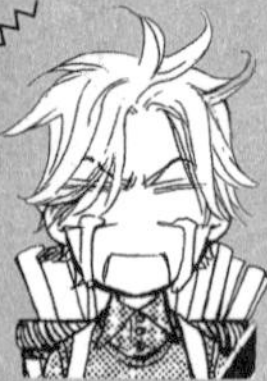

Q **If you could go on a date with the one you like for just one day, where would you go?**

—Gin Usagi, Tokyo

A Well... I'd like to go somewhere *Y*...the one I like wants to go. I'm happy if I'm able to see *Y*...the one I like happy.

Even Kaname-sama has weaknesses?!

Look for the weaknesses of Mr. Perfect Kaname-sama

If you discover a surprising weakness, you'll be even more fascinated by Kaname-sama...?!

He wants a more macho body, so he watches what Kain does. And only Ichijo knows about this.
—Tomomi Sekiguchi, Tokyo

"Yes! But a macho Kaname would be weird!!"
—Ichijo

The many treasured pictures of the cute little Yuki that Headmaster Cross secretly took. Kaname-sama hides them in the books he reads...
—Junko Okada, Nara Prefecture

"It becomes a weakness because he hides photos he doesn't need to hide."
—Headmaster

He's not good at cat's cradle. They were playing when Yuki was a child, and when he got the strings tangled up, she innocently said, "Kaname-sama is not good at playing cat's cradle!"
—Nana, Aichi Prefecture

"What...?! I said something like that to Kaname when I was a kid?"
—Yuki

The St. Xocolatl's Day chocolates he received from Yuki these past several years were never eaten and are stored securely.
—Chameleon, Yamagata Prefecture

"I'm happy about it, but I want him to eat them."
—Yuki

When he was a child, his mother Juri forced him to drink five liters of milk a day so he would grow, so he hates milk even now.
—Rena Ejiri, Hyogo Prefecture

"It's not that I can't drink it. I've already drunk a lifetime's worth of milk, so I don't feel like drinking it anymore."
—Kaname

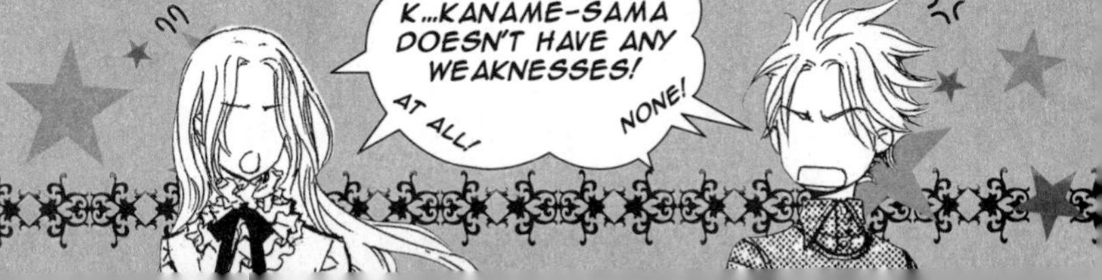
K...KANAME-SAMA DOESN'T HAVE ANY WEAKNESSES!
NONE!
AT ALL!

Hanabusa Aido

The Proud Right-Hand Man!!

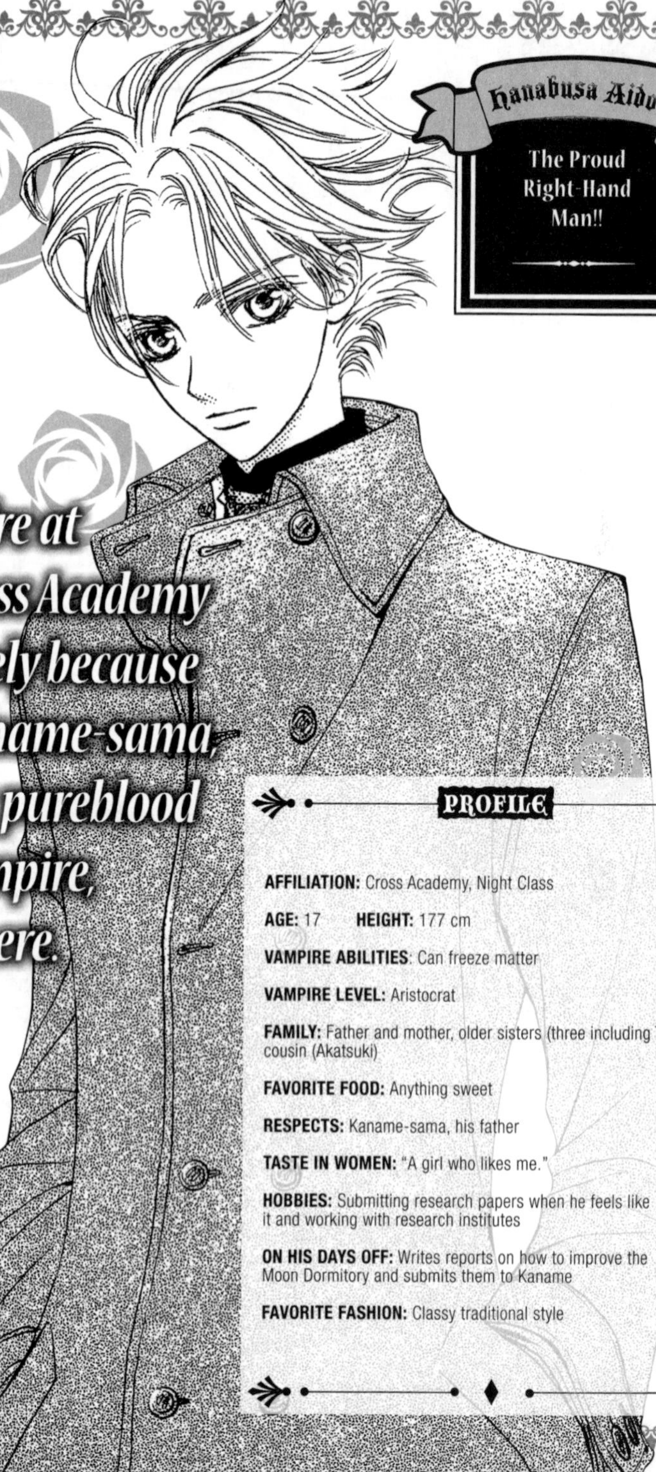

We're at Cross Academy solely because Kaname-sama, the pureblood vampire, is here.

PROFILE

AFFILIATION: Cross Academy, Night Class

AGE: 17 **HEIGHT:** 177 cm

VAMPIRE ABILITIES: Can freeze matter

VAMPIRE LEVEL: Aristocrat

FAMILY: Father and mother, older sisters (three including Tsukiko), cousin (Akatsuki)

FAVORITE FOOD: Anything sweet

RESPECTS: Kaname-sama, his father

TASTE IN WOMEN: "A girl who likes me."

HOBBIES: Submitting research papers when he feels like it and working with research institutes

ON HIS DAYS OFF: Writes reports on how to improve the Moon Dormitory and submits them to Kaname

FAVORITE FASHION: Classy traditional style

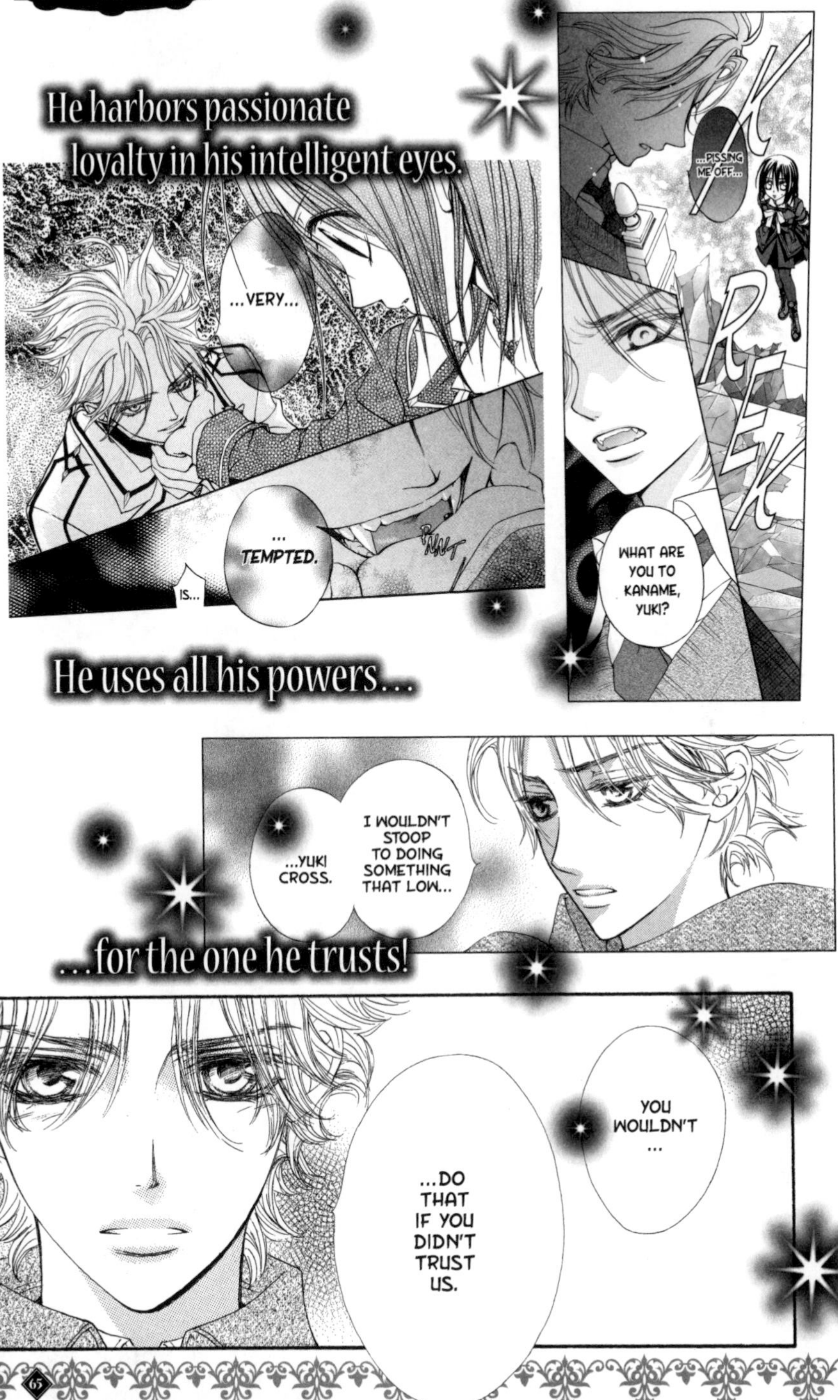
He harbors passionate loyalty in his intelligent eyes.
...PISSING ME OFF...
KREEK
WHAT ARE YOU TO KANAME, YUKI?
...VERY...
IS...
... TEMPTED.
He uses all his powers...
I WOULDN'T STOOP TO DOING SOMETHING THAT LOW...
...YUKI CROSS.
...for the one he trusts!
YOU WOULDN'T ...
...DO THAT IF YOU DIDN'T TRUST US.

CHARACTER ANALYSIS

This is what Hanabusa Aido is like!

His Past

The fated meeting that determined his way of living!

To Aido, Kaname was the first person who seemed superior to himself. Aido couldn't be honest with himself at first, but he felt emotions like tenderness and sympathy because of Kaname… It turns out he is attracted to Kaname (not simply because he's a pureblood), and he decides to follow him.

FROM THE FIRST MOMENT I SAW HIM...
...I KNEW HE WAS SPECIAL.
...
UM...
OH

⬆ Love at first sight?! He feels the force of Kaname's presence even as a child, but his pride interferes…!

I LOVE YOU, KANAME-SAMA.

⬆ Kaname somehow changed after his parents' death. Aido hopes to protect Kaname's heart.

Personality

His pride reaches the heavens

He's self-centered because he grew up pampered and surrounded by his three older sisters. His arrogant words and actions often put everyone in a tizzy, but he demonstrates strong loyalty towards Kaname and sees himself as Kaname's right-hand man along with his cousin Kain. His pride is supreme.

➡ When he "ran away from home" to the Sun Dormitory, he made various demands of Yuki and Zero as he pleased!

OH, AND IS THERE A BED I CAN SLEEP IN DURING THE DAY?
I PREFER SOFT BEDS.
THE LINEN MUST SMELL OF LAVENDER.
AND THE CURTAINS...

...BUT THIS INVOLVES OUR PRIDE AS ARISTOCRATS.

⬆➡ As the heir of a distinguished family, his words and actions in public are commanding. His sense of responsibility as an aristocrat is stronger than anyone else's.

OKAY.
YOU'RE EMBAR-RASSED?
THEN I'LL FREEZE YOU WITH MY ICE AND TAKE YOU TO HIM.
!!
KR
ESS
...
WHO ARE...
THAT'S WHY I NEED--
TH
NK

⬆ It is easy for him to generate enough ice to cover a target instantly.

⬅ An icicle can pierce an enemy's vitals like a sharp spear.

Fighting Ability

Absolute-zero ice that can catch anything!!

As an elite vampire, he has the ability to freeze matter. The target can be anything from the enemy's body to moisture in the air. Anything Aido touches instantly becomes pieces of ice!!

SCHOOLTIME

His activities at school!

WOOSH
YAY!!
I'VE GOT TO GET ALL THE CHOCOLATES!

⬅ St. Xocolatl's Day is one of his favorite events. He's merrier than usual.♥

Classes & Extracurricular Activities

The gifted genius is everyone's "idol."♥

Aido loves himself. He willingly participates in school events and stands out with his flashy actions!! That's why the female Day Class students call him "Idol" and love him. He's also a genius research scientist with numerous accomplishments. Thus, he has the most contact with the outside world.

THIS IS SOMETHING THAT WE CAN ASK ONLY OF YOU, THE "MIRACLE GENIUS"!
PLEASE HELP US WITH OUR RESEARCH INSTITUTE!
HUH?
BUT I DON'T HAVE ANY INTEREST IN DAY WORK.
SLEEPY
I'M TIRED, SO WILL YOU LEAVE NOW?
THE DOOR IS OVER THERE.
KREE

⬅ Research institutes all over the world want his genius brain!

PRIVATE ZONE

We show you what Aido's room is like!! ♥

Window
Window
Aido's Desk
Bookshelf
Bookshelf
Kain's Desk
Shelves
Heater
Table
Sofa

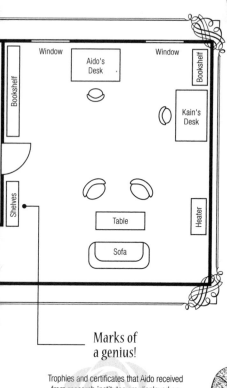

The room of a genius has strange rubbish (?) all over!

The room looks neat, but if you look carefully, there are various pieces of rubbish around! Torn cloth and a fountain pen with a crushed tip… Uh, is this the rumored "Kaname-sama Collection"?!

Marks of a genius!

Trophies and certificates that Aido received from research institutes are displayed on these shelves! Normally, people would cherish such things, but they're carelessly kept here…? He still submits research papers while attending school (when he feels like it), so things keep piling up here!

Let's take a peek at Aido's private life! ♥

He goes to bed at lights out and wakes up exactly one hour before classes begin. You can see that he is well bred.

KA-CHAK
UGH
IT'S BRIGHT.
I'M SLEEPY.
I'M GRUMPY.
IT'S ALL THEIR FAULT.

⬆ Guests disturb his sleep, and he's obviously not his usual self…

He's cranky during the day!!

Aido can't "stay up late" during the day! He tried once, but he fell asleep during classes and Kaname scolded him.

A gorgeous bed with a canopy!

He sleeps elegantly wearing silk pajamas in a soft bed. You wouldn't believe this is a dorm room. The pajamas are a gift from his sisters. ♥

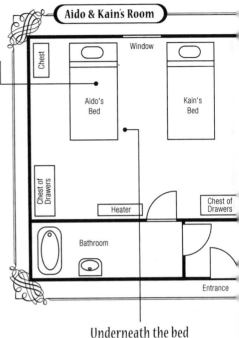

UNNGH...
MOOSH
I WAS JUST ABOUT TO FALL ASLEEP.

Aido & Kain's Room

Window
Chest
Aido's Bed
Kain's Bed
Chest of Drawers
Heater
Chest of Drawers
Bathroom
Entrance

Underneath the bed are photos... ♥

Underneath the bed is an album of photos of Kaname that Aido secretly took. Should we say "Oh my" or "I knew it"? According to Kain, Aido is sometimes lost in deep thought for four hours straight while looking at photos of young Kaname...

⬅ The thick canopy that blocks out sunlight is very important for protecting the delicate Aido's sleep!

TWEEEET
HEY!
IDOL--AIDO! WHAT ARE YOU DOING?! STOP!!
HEY BABY, WHAT'S YOUR BLOOD TYPE?
KYAAH

⬆ It looks as if he's elegantly coming on to a girl... But he's asking her blood type?! Which blood type does he prefer...?

A dangerous come-on...?!

While Yuki is doing her duties, he sometimes merrily hunts for blood. ♥ Hey, Kaname-sama will slap you again!!

Spends all his energy observing Kaname-sama ♪

His daily routine includes wandering around the floor where Kaname's room is, both on weekdays and on the weekends! Thus, his "Kaname Collection" keeps increasing...

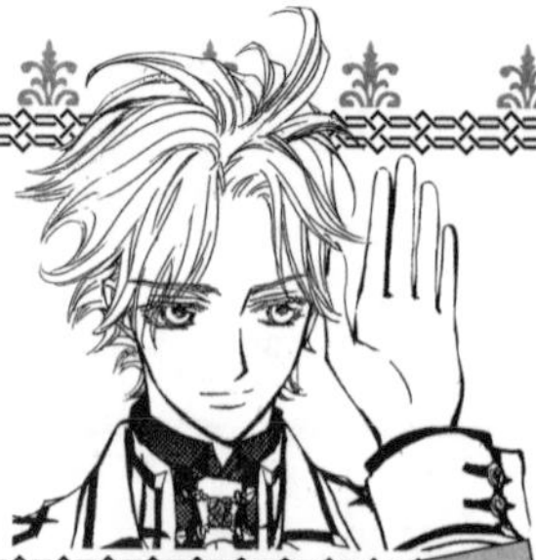

This is the ideal master-servant relationship...♥

I'll follow you, Kaname-sama!!

You can measure the strength of the bond between master and servant by the types of punishments handed out?! Here's the beautiful history!!

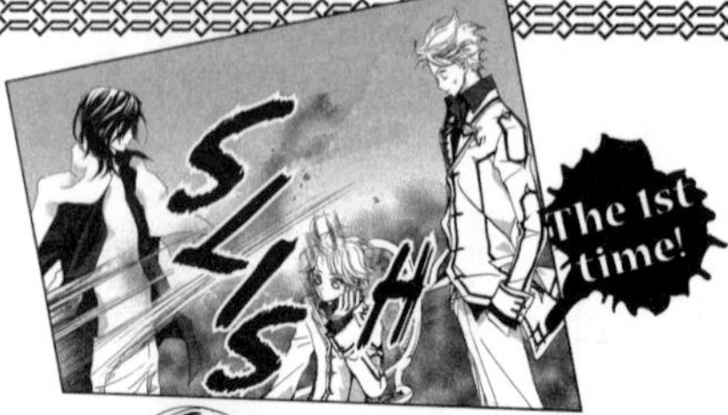
SLISH
The 1st time!

BOND 1 The Slap of Love ♥

Among all the numerous punishments, the right and proper slap was handed out the most. Kaname-sama might have chosen this because it sounds loud but doesn't hurt much. Plus, it's easy. The master and servant are perfectly synchronized.

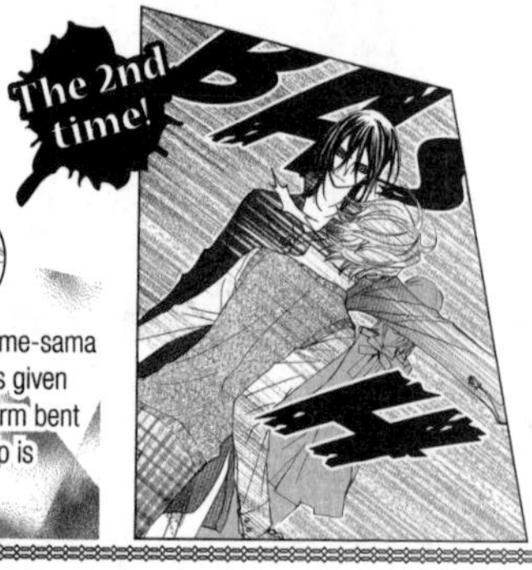
The 2nd time!

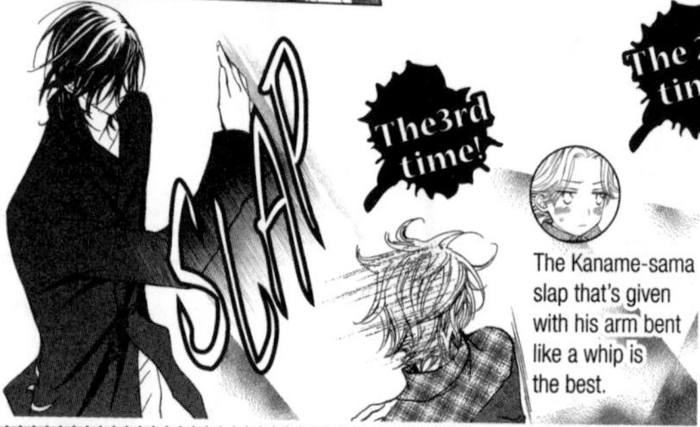
The3rd time!
SLAP

The Kaname-sama slap that's given with his arm bent like a whip is the best.

BOND 2 Bucket-holding ♥

The bucket that was put on Aido's head is truly icing on the cake. It clearly says "I must be a better Night Class student than anyone else."

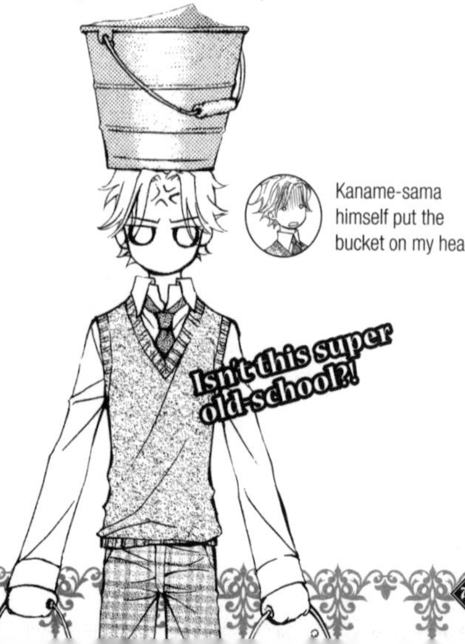
Isn't this super old-school?!

Kaname-sama himself put the bucket on my head...

BOND 3 I'm a "Kuran." ♥

Kaname-sama ripped Aido's handmade election poster! Even Kaname-sama found Aido really annoying, and he just couldn't help it.

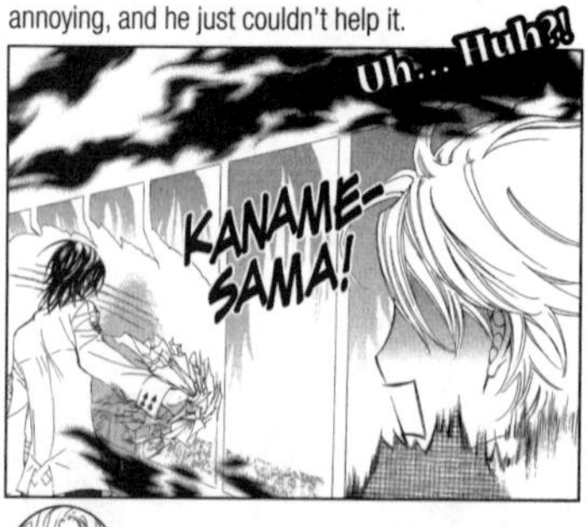
Uh... Huh?!
KANAME-SAMA!

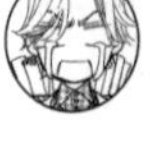

I was a fool for making a fuss in front of Kaname-sama. He prefers peace...!

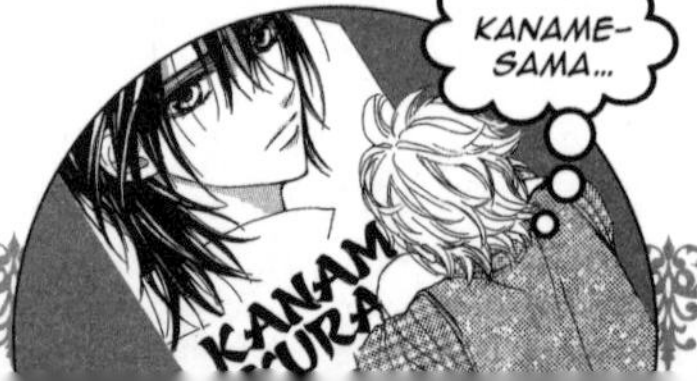
KANAME-SAMA...

Special messages to Aido

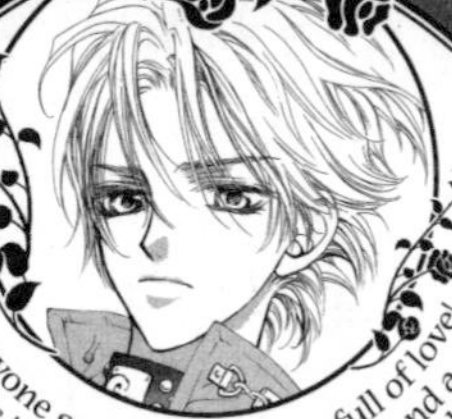

Everyone sent in comments full of love! This is all because he's a genius and a beautiful boy, and people love to mess with him?!

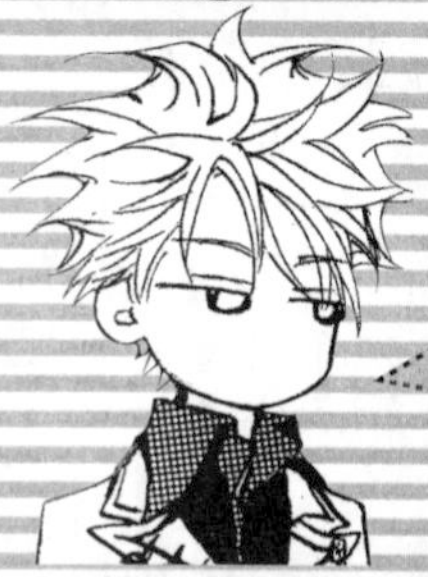

From Akatsuki Kain

I admire you for doing something thoroughly when you're into it… but I'd be happy if you also controlled yourself when necessary.

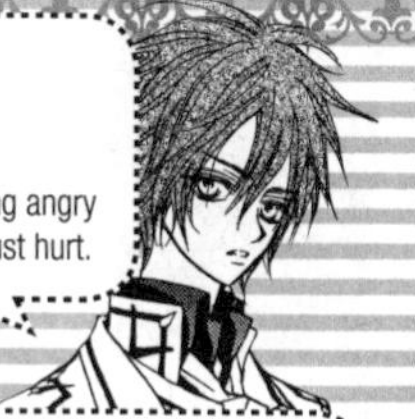

From Senri Shiki

Aido… He's always getting angry and frowning. His face must hurt.

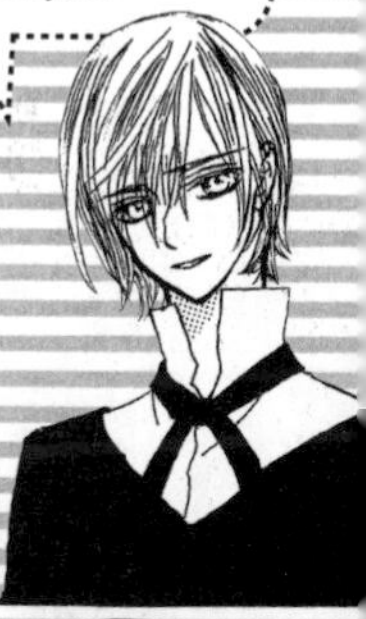

From Takuma Ichijo

As dorm vice president and Kaname's friend, I'm often impressed by Aido. And he's fun to tease… *Koff!* I'm counting on you!!

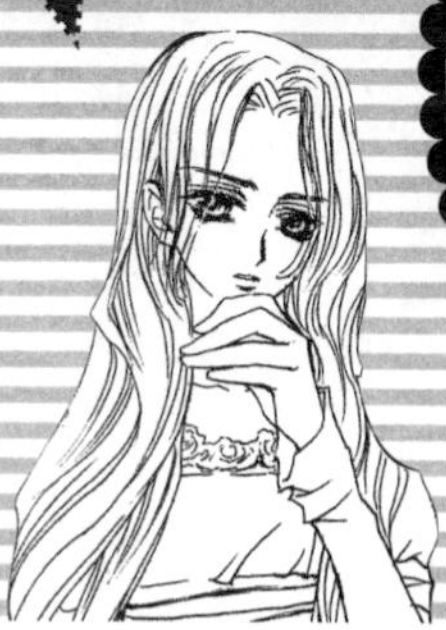

From Ruka Souen

If you want to call yourself "Kaname-sama's right-hand man," act like it!

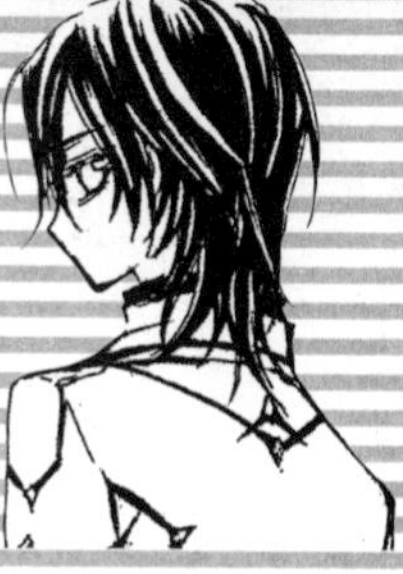

From Kaname Kuran

Aido… I know that you're not a bad person…

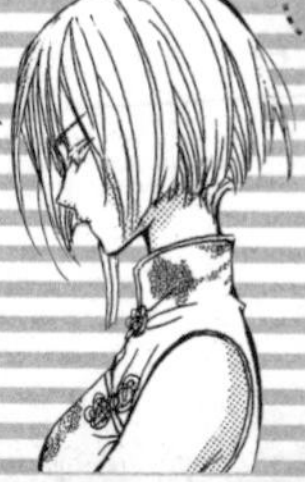

From Seiren

I think you should refrain from troubling Kaname-sama.

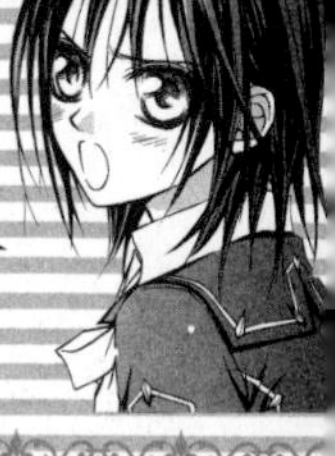

From Yuki Cross

Aido, no mischief, okay?!

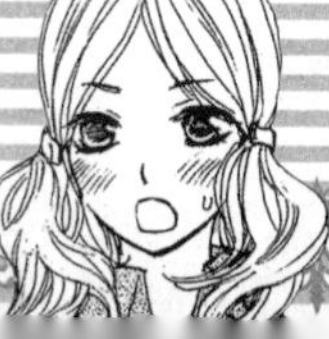

From a female student

Idol's smile is like a shining jewel or a pretty flower.♥

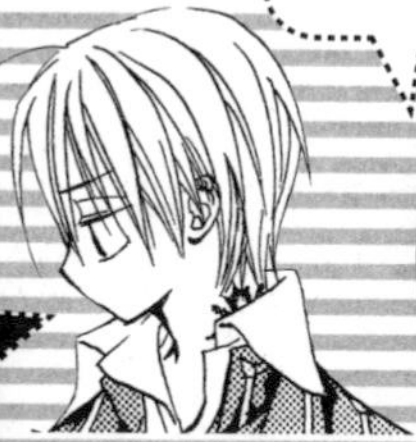

From Zero Kiryu

Stuff like "running away from home" to the Sun Dormitory… Please cut it out.

He answers your questions?!

♥ **Tell me, Idol!** ♥

Let's barrage the popular Idol with questions.♥

Letters sent in from fans for fans!

Vam☆Fan Hall

The Aido Version

Q You're always with Kain, so do you two ever get in fights with each other?? If you do, who's stronger?

–Uraha, Hokkaido

A Now that you mention it, we've never gotten into fights... Well, I'd win, of course. Akatsuki, why don't we fight and see? Uh, why are you sighing?!

Q Are you...a masochist?

–Miki Kitayama, Wakayama Prefecture

A What do you mean by "masochist"? Hey, Ichijo, tell me...
!! Absolutely not. Even if Kaname-sama slaps me... Slaps me... *B-bmp b-bmp...*

Q If you could be Kaname Kuran for a day, what would you do?

–Noriko Kato, Tokyo

A W-well, there'd be so many things I'd want to do, I'd panic... I'd like to stare in the mirror all day... Oh! K...Kaname-sama!! W-were you listening to what I was saying just now...?! (Unable to continue reply) ✤

Q Why are you so handsome? Plus you're smart, and you call yourself a "genius" in addition to "a frail, handsome boy." You're such a narcissist... No, you're just truthful!

–Junna, Tokyo

A Sorry to keep all my fans waiting! It's my turn! This is a good first question. Even if I hide it, the fact that I'm a genius and handsome shows through. Ah, but I can't compete against Kaname-sama at all!

Q What blood type do you prefer?

–Totsuki, Toyama Prefecture

A What, what? Do you want to offer blood to me? Asking ladies their blood type is my way of being polite. Any blood type is all right. So, my dear, what's yours?

Q What sort of women do you prefer?

–Kazuki, Iwate Prefecture

A Well... She must be as smart and beautiful as me so that we match. And her blood must be delicious!

He went this far because he loves Kaname-sama...

Overdoing it with love and respect...

Because he worships Kaname-sama, Aido overdoes things... But how exactly?

He secretly takes pictures of Kaname-sama and has a photo album called "LOVE ★ Kaname-sama, The Beautiful Days."
—Ayaka Yasuda, Saitama Prefecture

"Aido doesn't give up even if Kaname-sama finds out about the secret photos and scolds him."
—Shiki

He's written a song called "A song for the Kaname-sama I love" and practices it... Ruka saw him practicing, and the two of them ended up singing the song passionately together.
—Haruka Matsumoto, Tokyo

"Even Ruka knows about Hanabusa's daily singing..."
—Kain

He keeps Kaname's photos under his pillow so that he can see Kaname in his dreams.
—Sakuran, Tokyo

"The night before last, he had ten photos under his pillow..."
—Kain

He writes about how he's been punished by Kaname in his "Kaname-sama Notebook"
—Yuka Ringo, Chiba Prefecture

"It's full of details. How much does he like Kaname?"
—Ichijo

He made his own Kaname-sama doll! The doll can speak in Kaname-sama's voice too! Aido wakes up every day to Kaname-sama's voice saying, "Morning, Aido." ♥
—Mizuki Aikawa, Yamagata Prefecture

"I'd be thrilled if I could start every day hearing Kaname-sama's voice."
—Aido

Kaname-sama found Aido alone one night imitating him. Aido's depressed now thinking Kaname-sama hates him.
—Himeri, Kanagawa Prefecture

"Please don't do anything that hurts Kaname-sama's dignity."
—Ruka

AIDO...MAY I HAVE A WORD WITH YOU?
YES.
TREMBLE
SHIVER

Akatsuki Kain

The Sincere Master of Fire!

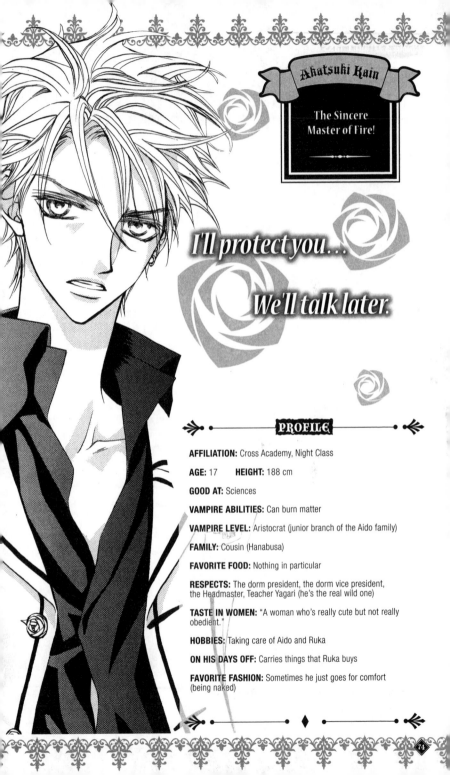

I'll protect you... We'll talk later.

PROFILE

AFFILIATION: Cross Academy, Night Class

AGE: 17 **HEIGHT:** 188 cm

GOOD AT: Sciences

VAMPIRE ABILITIES: Can burn matter

VAMPIRE LEVEL: Aristocrat (junior branch of the Aido family)

FAMILY: Cousin (Hanabusa)

FAVORITE FOOD: Nothing in particular

RESPECTS: The dorm president, the dorm vice president, the Headmaster, Teacher Yagari (he's the real wild one)

TASTE IN WOMEN: "A woman who's really cute but not really obedient."

HOBBIES: Taking care of Aido and Ruka

ON HIS DAYS OFF: Carries things that Ruka buys

FAVORITE FASHION: Sometimes he just goes for comfort (being naked)

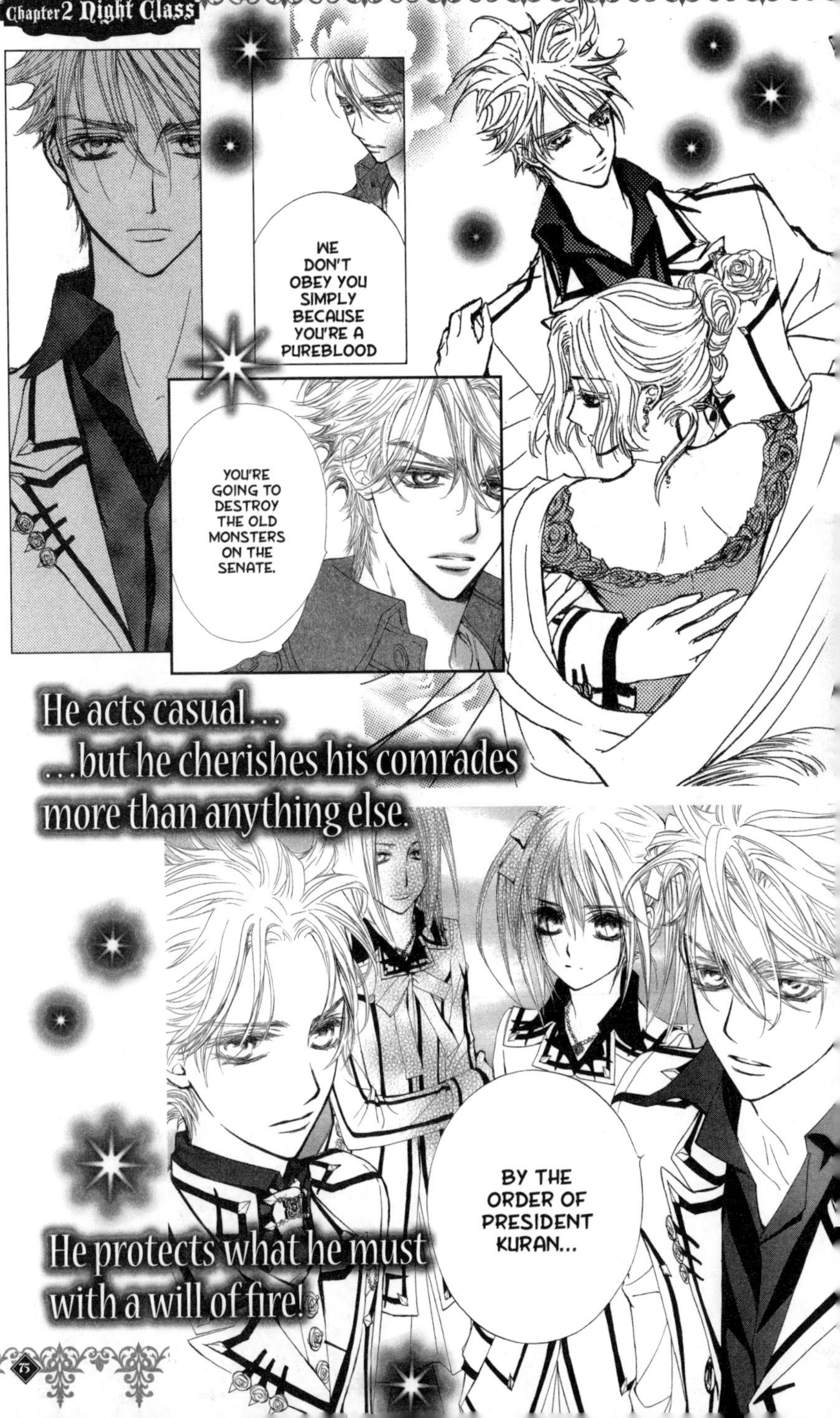
WE DON'T OBEY YOU SIMPLY BECAUSE YOU'RE A PUREBLOOD
YOU'RE GOING TO DESTROY THE OLD MONSTERS ON THE SENATE.
He acts casual...
...but he cherishes his comrades more than anything else.
BY THE ORDER OF PRESIDENT KURAN...
He protects what he must with a will of fire!

CHARACTER ANALYSIS

This is what Akatsuki Kain is like!

His Past

The inseparable (?) three!

Kain's family along with Ruka's Souen family are distinguished aristocrats, junior branches of the Aido family. Kain, Aido and Ruka are very close relatives, and the three of them grew up together. They act like siblings as they're closer than childhood friends. Kain cherishes the other two more than anything, and strong bonds link them all.

HUH?
?
I SHOULDN'T HAVE TOLD RUKA?
AKATSUKI TOLD ME THAT YOU MET KANAME-SAMA.
...
HEY! WHAT WAS HE LIKE?

⬆ Participates in the experiment to test the strength of sand materials (?) that Aido hosts. They get excited talking about Kaname!

Personality

From the outside, you wouldn't guess his thoughtfulness

He may look really wild, but he's one of the most mellow vampires in the Night Class. He's good at taking care of others, so Aido and everyone around him create trouble for him… He is always calm enough to take a step back and see the whole picture, so he always has a broad view of things!

I CAN TELL BY THE WAY YOU'RE ACTING...
...THAT SOMETHING IS BOTHER-ING YOU.

⬆ He's especially sensitive regarding his partner Aido! He notices Aido's slight changes right away.

He dodges Yuki's Artemis rod attack with a smile! ➡

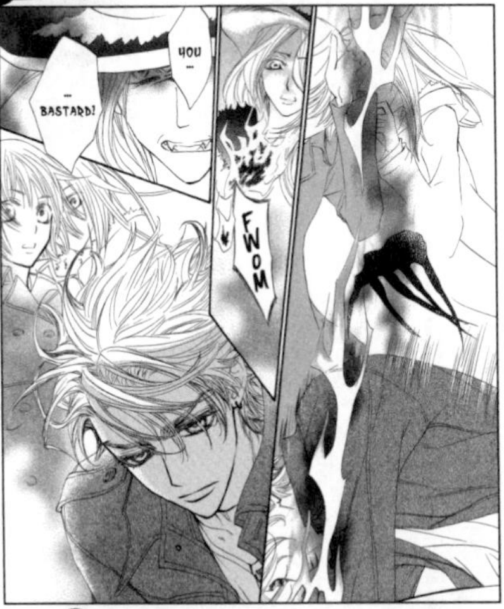
YOU ...
... BASTARD!
FWOM

Fighting Ability

Flames that silently destroy the enemy!!

He has the ability to use fire to burn matter. According to Ruka, the power of Kain's flames can easily stop the enemy from fighting even when he's going easy on them!!

⬅ Beautiful flames dance and repel those trying to attack Cross Academy. He never involves the frail students of the Day Class!

SCHOOLTIME

His activities at school!

He investigates the transfer student Maria Kurenai with Aido because they have their suspicions. ⬇

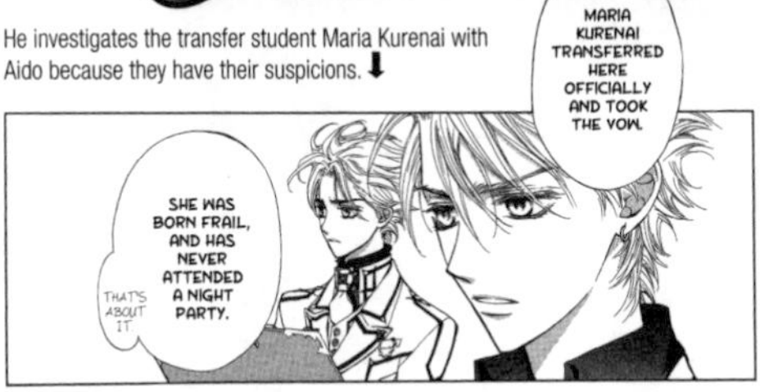
MARIA KURENAI TRANSFERRED HERE OFFICIALLY AND TOOK THE VOW.
SHE WAS BORN FRAIL, AND HAS NEVER ATTENDED A NIGHT PARTY.
THAT'S ABOUT IT.

Classes & Extracurricular Activities

He helps with everything, from investigation to protection!!

He respects Kaname and Ichijo as his seniors, but his original intent in attending Cross Academy was to take care of Aido and Ruka. However, Kaname trusts Kain because of his thoughtfulness and sincerity. He is considered to be Kaname-sama's right-hand man along with Aido, and the other Night Class students respect him.

He guards Yuki under Kaname's orders. The way he kneels is like a real knight…! ⬇

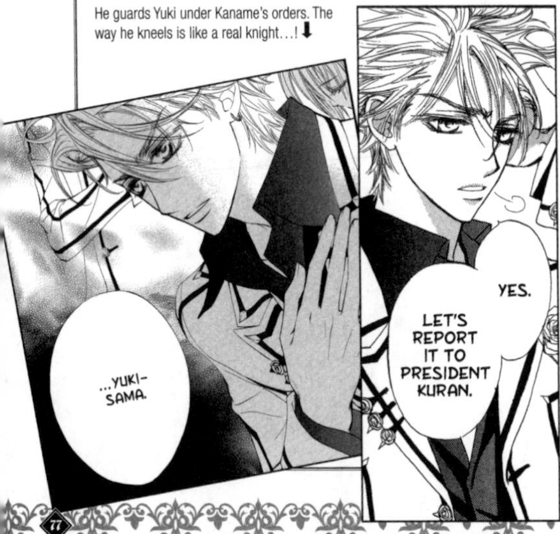
YES.
LET'S REPORT IT TO PRESIDENT KURAN.
...YUKI-SAMA.

⬅ Even when he found Shizuka Hio's corpse, he calmly dealt with it. He reports any strange occurrences to the dorm president first!

PRIVATE ZONE

We show you what Kain's room is like!! ♥

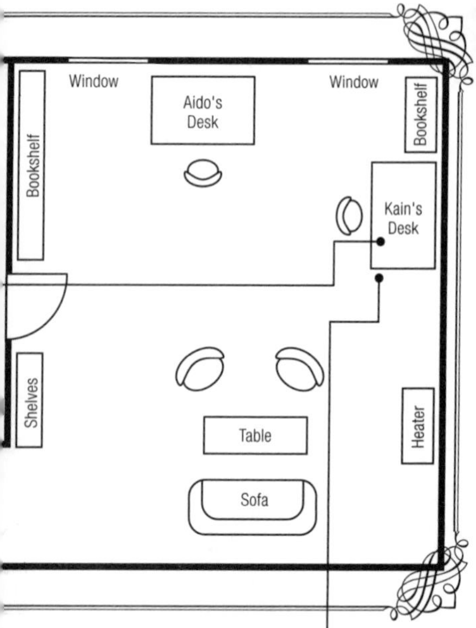
Window
Window
Bookshelf
Aido's Desk
Bookshelf
Kain's Desk
Shelves
Table
Heater
Sofa

They're cousins and roommates!

Being childhood friends, Kain and Aido are often together. They're also roommates! Aido has a terrible reputation for being selfish and self-centered. The only one who can be with him is Kain because he has a calm heart that's more expansive than the ocean…?!

The doll that's been abandoned…

What's shoved underneath Kain's desk is a creepy Kaname doll!! Aido started making it, but then he abandoned it… If Kaname ever finds this, something terrifying will happen for sure, but Kain's not too worried about it.

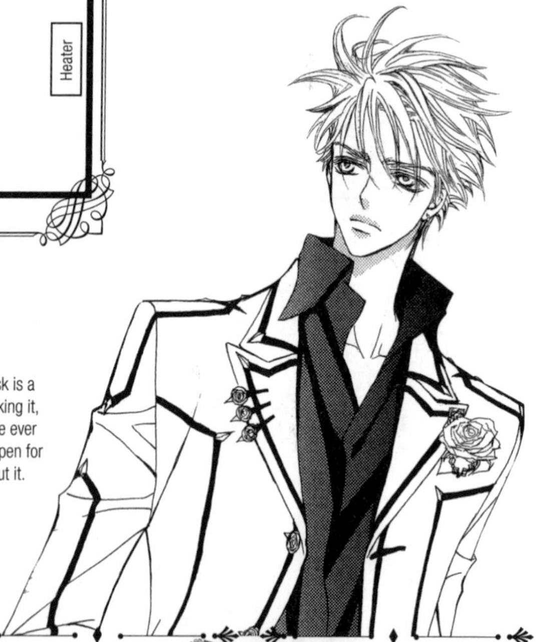

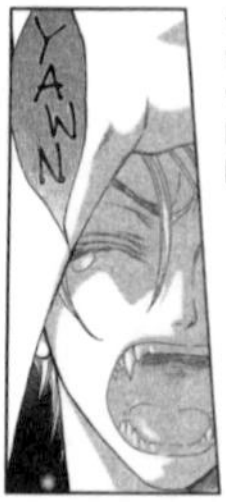
YAWN

⬅ He yawns when he's just woken up. His fangs are beautiful too. ♥

A (vampire's) regular lifestyle… Even his yawn is wild!★

He "stays up late" during the day when he has things he wants to do, but he wakes up when he's supposed to. But usually, being healthy is his first priority!

Let's take a peek at Kain's private life! ♥

He maintains a regular and healthy lifestyle that suits his nickname "Wild." Getting dragged into things is part of his daily routine.

Nice gifts from the vice president ♥

On the desk are "books for boys," souvenirs from Ichijo, who sometimes visits them. Ichijo leaves some books every time he visits, so Kain throws them away once they pile up. But first, he browses through them with a blank look… ♥

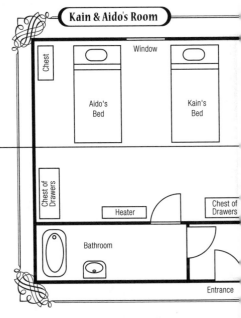

He's half naked in his room!

Either he's being wild or he simply doesn't care. Kain's motto is to be naked during the day! He generously bares his sexy top half. ♥ By daring to wear as little as possible, his wildness increases, plus he also succeeds in having a sturdy body…?!

Kain & Aido's Room
Window
Chest
Aido's Bed
Kain's Bed
Chest of Drawers
Heater
Chest of Drawers
Bathroom
Entrance

OH...
I KNOW WHAT IT IS. TODAY IS...
WHAT ?!

⬆ Kain is half naked, and Aido is wearing super-expensive silk pajamas. The two are friends. ♪

I'M NOT GOING.
YOU GO.
SIGH

⬅ He has trouble pacifying Aido! He takes care of Aido like an older brother and even like a mom (?) sometimes.

Taking care of Idol, who's high maintenance

Kain cleans the room when Aido's away. Because of this, Aido believes that rooms get tidy by themselves.

Spending his days off with his childhood friends

When school isn't in session, he accompanies Aido or Ruka to whatever they want to do. This sounds like a bother, but Kain actually enjoys doing this.

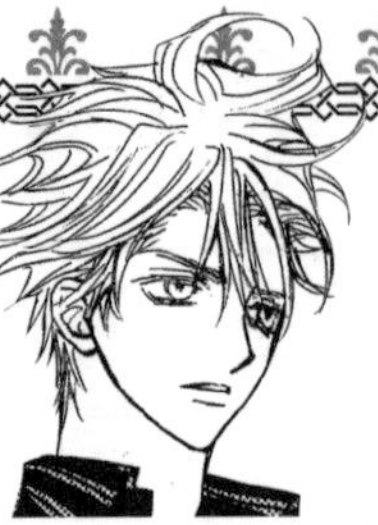

Ah, today as well…

The "Victim of Circumstances" Diary!

Is it the fate of being Aido's cousin or is it because he's just too nice?! Here's the diary of the slightly unfortunate Kain. ♪ Reading it will make you sad…

I tried to stop them from fighting.

MONTH △
DAY □

The Night Class students and the Disciplinary Committee member were glaring at each other. Fighting is prohibited, so I tried to stop them, but I was thrown beautifully as if we were at some sort of demonstration.

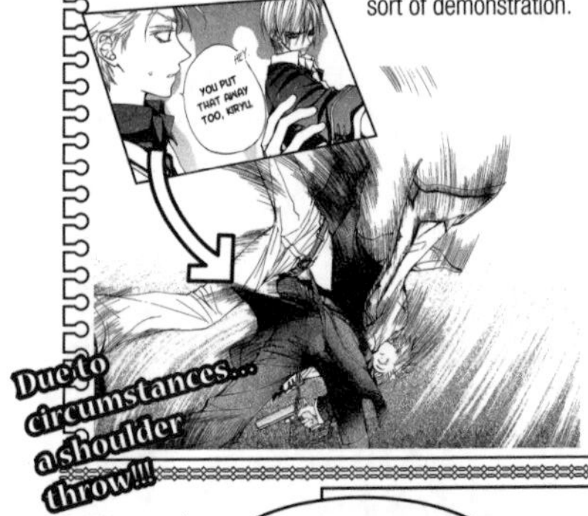
HEY
YOU PUT THAT AWAY TOO, KIRYU.
Due to circumstances… a shoulder throw!!!

My cousin bit the gang leader's dear one.

MONTH ○
DAY ×

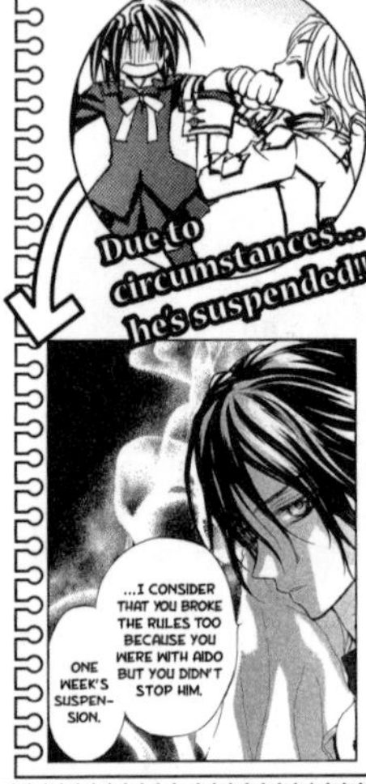
Due to circumstances… he's suspended!!
…I CONSIDER THAT YOU BROKE THE RULES TOO BECAUSE YOU WERE WITH AIDO BUT YOU DIDN'T STOP HIM.
ONE WEEK'S SUSPENSION.

Hanabusa angered the gang…I mean, the dorm president, and I was suspended as well. Is it my fault because I didn't stop him? I guess it is.

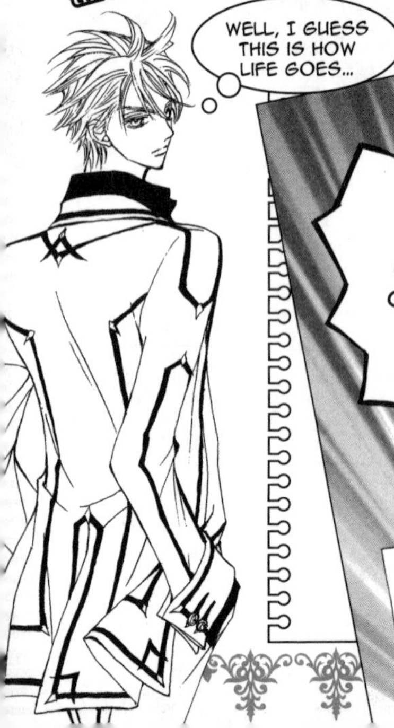
WELL, I GUESS THIS IS HOW LIFE GOES...

My cousin got a stupid-sounding nickname.

MONTH ◎
DAY ☆

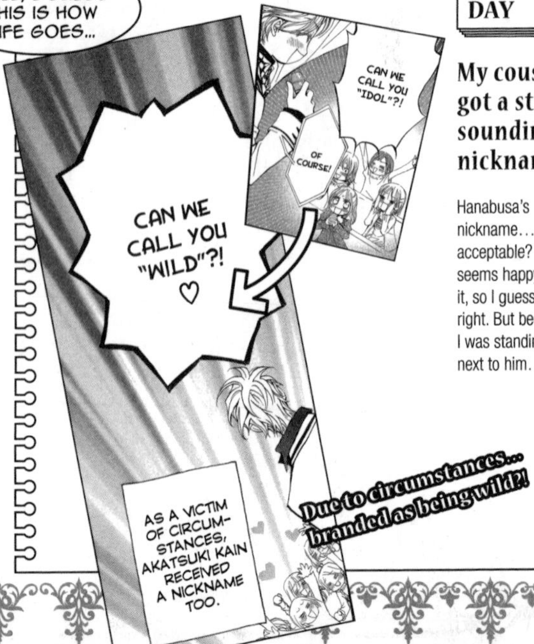
CAN WE CALL YOU "IDOL"?!
OF COURSE!
CAN WE CALL YOU "WILD"?! ♡
AS A VICTIM OF CIRCUMSTANCES, AKATSUKI KAIN RECEIVED A NICKNAME TOO.
Due to circumstances… branded as being wild?!

Hanabusa's nickname… Is it acceptable? Well, he seems happy about it, so I guess it's all right. But because I was standing next to him…

Special messages to Kain

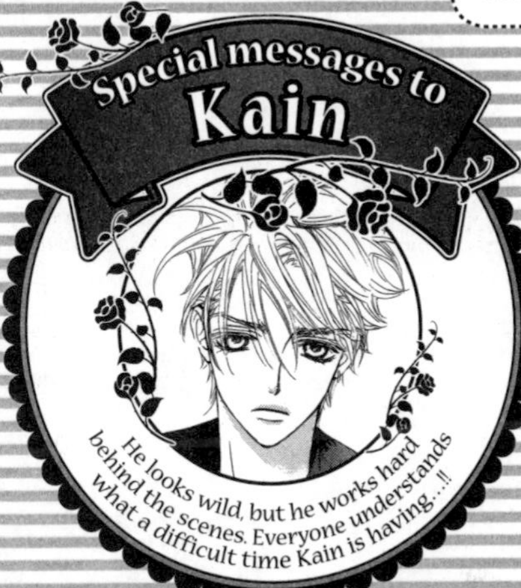

He looks wild, but he works hard behind the scenes. Everyone understands what a difficult time Kain is having...!!

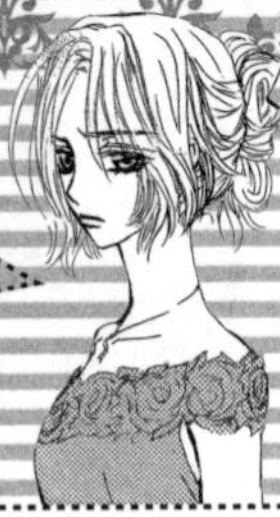

From Ruka Souen

I think Akatsuki helps me in many ways. I can't help depending on him... I hate to say it, but please continue looking after me.

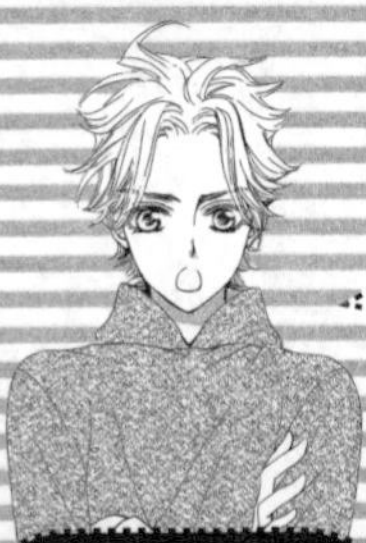

From Hanabusa Aido

Akatsuki understands things even if I don't say anything... I end up depending on him like that, and I absolutely need him.

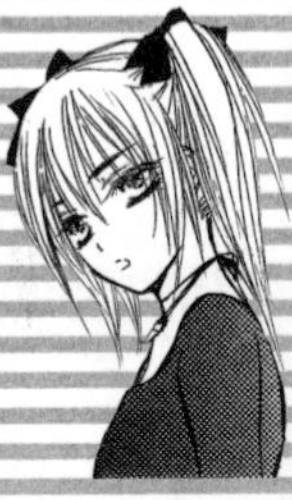

From Rima Toya

I feel like he's the hardest worker...

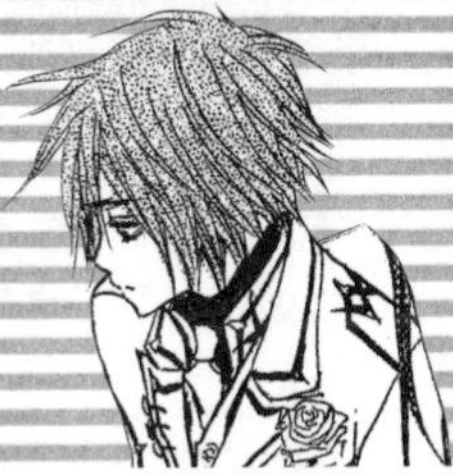

From Senri Shiki

I'm glad I'm not Aido's cousin...

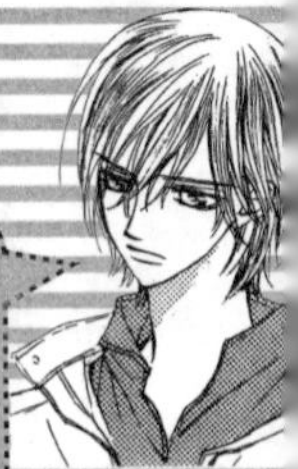

From Takuma Ichijo

Kain is indifferent to things, so he doesn't try to stand out. But I know that he's really capable!

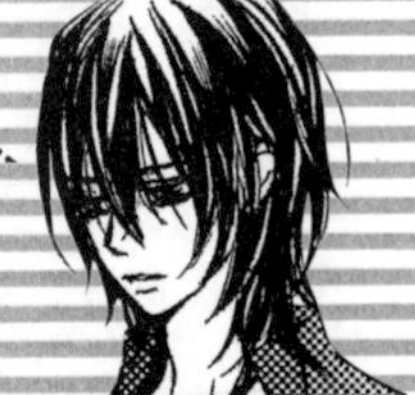

From Kaname Kuran

I always end up depending on you...

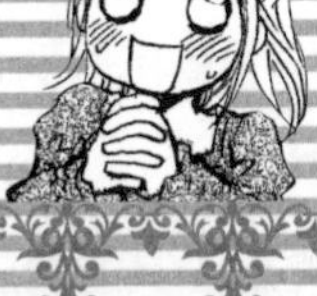

From a female student

I can't help wanting Wild to rescue me! ♥

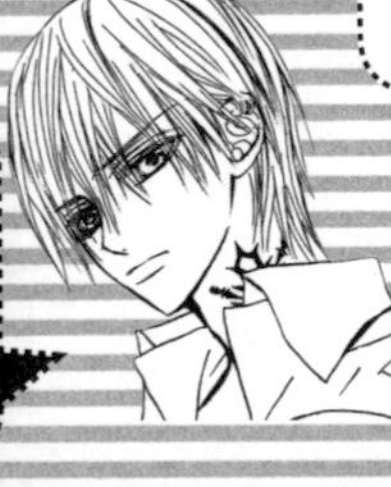

From Zero Kiryu

I guess you're having a hard time too... Sorry for throwing you.

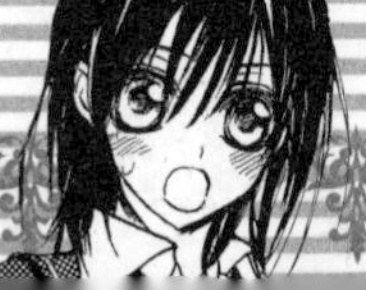

From Yuki Cross

The Moon Dormitory absolutely needs Kain!!

He answers your questions?!

♥ Tell me, Wild! ♥

We get to see a bit of the manly Wild's surprising real self...?

Letters sent in from fans for fans!

Vam☆Fan Hall

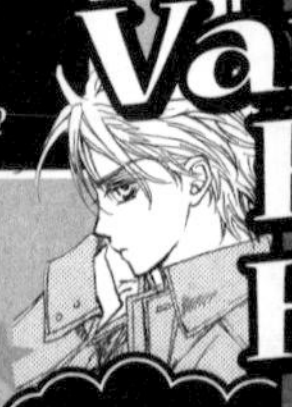

The Kain Version

Q **So Zero threw you easily...?**

—Yuki Usagi, Hiroshima

A Well... How do I put this? I was *caught off guard*... I was just impressed at how Kiryu could deftly throw me in that situation.

Q **Why are you always the victim of circumstances?**

—Fuko Shiratori, Mie Prefecture

A I wonder... I guess I was just born under that star.

Q **Aren't you tired of babysitting Aido?**

–Otome Kariage, Shimane Prefecture

A *Tired...?* Well, I don't think I'm babysitting him. We've been together since we were babies...

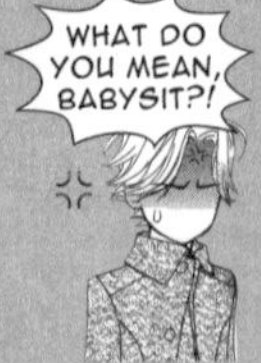
WHAT DO YOU MEAN, BABYSIT?!

Q **You are so cool! What's your dream?**

—Sayaka, Yamaguchi Prefecture

A If I have to pick something, I guess it's to live on the moon... I think I'd be able to live in peace out there... Just joking.

Q **Why don't you wear a tie?**

—Mitsuki Yoshino, Fukui Prefecture

A Cuz wearing one makes me feel cramped.

Q **Why are you always sleeping half naked? [Hee.]**

—Kyo, Osaka

A Cuz it's *comfortable*... Plus I don't always sleep that way.

Q **How long does it take to set your cool hair?**

—GT, Tottori Prefecture

A I don't do anything to it.

Q **How do you feel about being called "Wild"?**

—Kinakocchi, Aomori Prefecture

A I got used to it. I also gave up on it...

He takes care of people so well, he's always the victim of circumstances.

Legends of Wild's bad luck

Here are the funny incidents that everyone thought up...!!

Every time Aido and Ruka fight, the dorm president lectures Kain about not stopping the two of them.
—Sora Oto Iro, Nagasaki Prefecture

"Why do I get lectured each time?"
—Kain

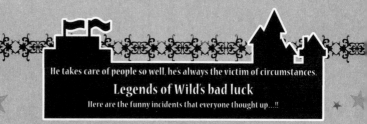

Because he cleans their room, it became a habit to clean up after Aido, so Aido skips his cleaning duties.
—Chie, Kyoto

"Hanabusa became self-centered because Akatsuki's too soft on him."
—Ruka

Among some female Day Class students, there's a rumor that says Wild is Aido's bodyguard and lover...
—Amenbo, Ehime Prefecture

"That's only a rumor...right?"
—Yuki

A part of Hanabusa's "Kaname-sama Collection" that was supposed to have been gotten rid of by the Disciplinary Committee was later found under Kain's bed.
—Monkey pod, Aichi Prefecture

"Kain, what is this?"
—Kaname
"It's not mine."
—Kain

After Hanabusa went on a rampage, Kain had to take care of him, and both of them were punished...
—Free, Tokyo

"Well, it may have been my fault for not being able to stop Hanabusa..."
—Kain

Aido and Kain were playing with fireworks when they were kids. Then the spinning fireworks all moved towards Kain...
—Yuki Nakagawa, Tokyo

"Akatsuki manipulates fire, so maybe fire is attracted to him."
—Aido

HE REALLY IS.
THE VICTIM OF CIRCUMSTANCES KING...

WELL, THINGS LIKE THIS ALWAYS HAPPEN.

Takuma Ichijo

The Gentle Vice President!

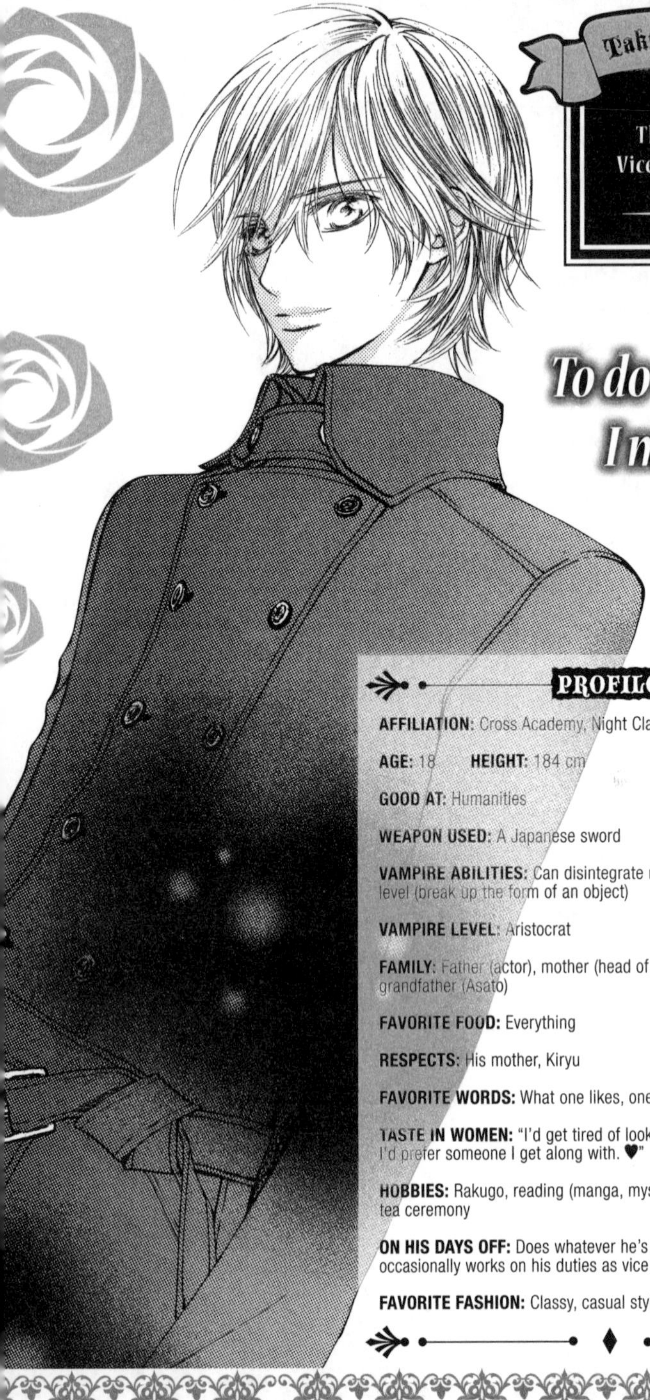

To do what I must...

PROFILE

AFFILIATION: Cross Academy, Night Class

AGE: 18 **HEIGHT:** 184 cm

GOOD AT: Humanities

WEAPON USED: A Japanese sword

VAMPIRE ABILITIES: Can disintegrate matter down to a molecular level (break up the form of an object)

VAMPIRE LEVEL: Aristocrat

FAMILY: Father (actor), mother (head of a flower-arranging school), grandfather (Asato)

FAVORITE FOOD: Everything

RESPECTS: His mother, Kiryu

FAVORITE WORDS: What one likes, one will do well.

TASTE IN WOMEN: "I'd get tired of looking at a beautiful woman, so I'd prefer someone I get along with. ♥"

HOBBIES: Rakugo, reading (manga, mysteries, dictionaries), tea ceremony

ON HIS DAYS OFF: Does whatever he's into for the entire day and occasionally works on his duties as vice president

FAVORITE FASHION: Classy, casual style

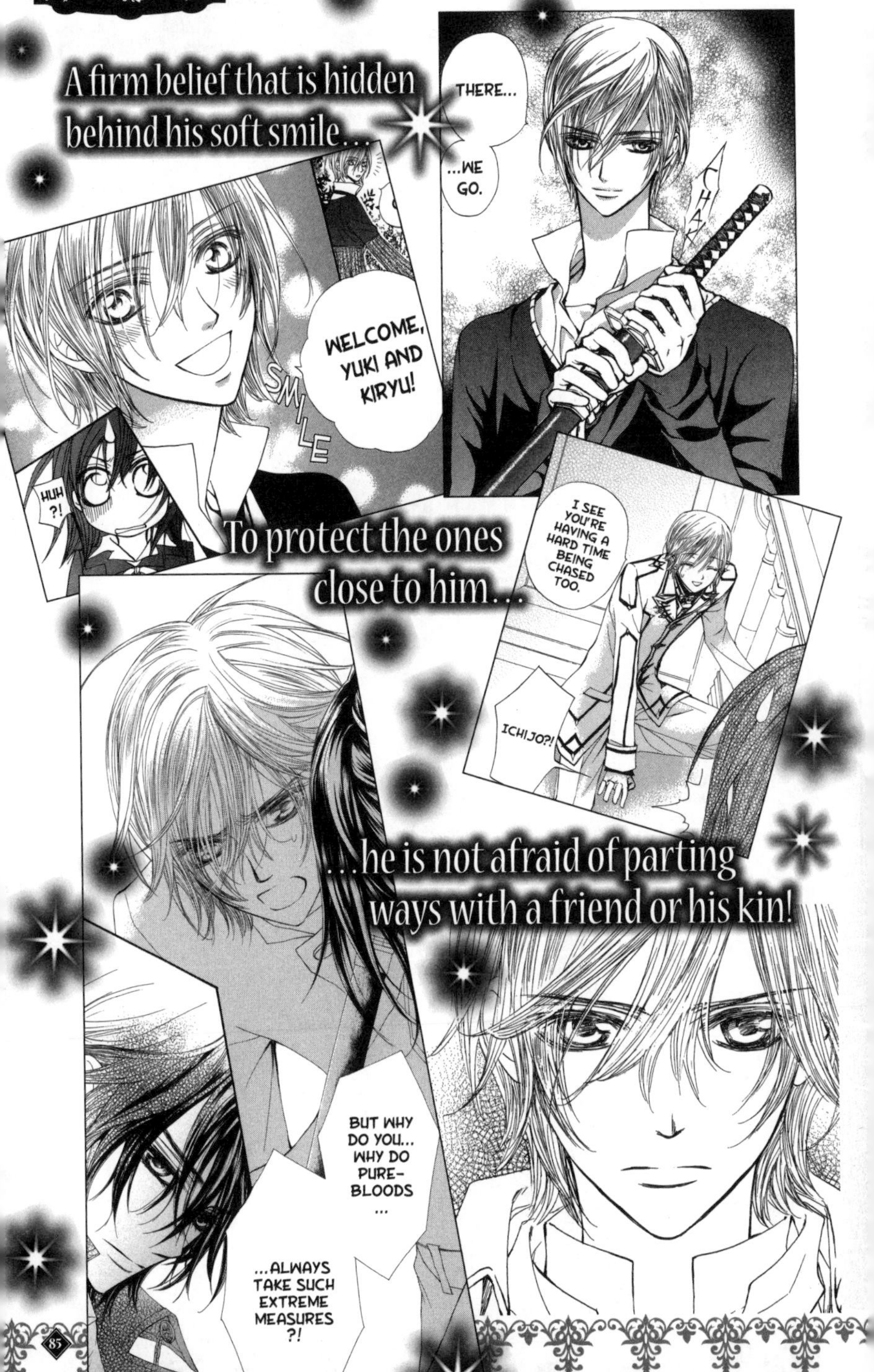
A firm belief that is hidden behind his soft smile...
THERE...
...WE GO.
CHAK
WELCOME, YUKI AND KIRYU!
SMILE
HUH?!
To protect the ones close to him...
I SEE YOU'RE HAVING A HARD TIME BEING CHASED TOO.
ICHIJO?!
...he is not afraid of parting ways with a friend or his kin!
BUT WHY DO YOU... WHY DO PURE-BLOODS ...
...ALWAYS TAKE SUCH EXTREME MEASURES?!

CHARACTER ANALYSIS
This is what Takuma Ichijo is like!!

His Past

His relationship of trust with Kaname, built on their shared past

He was born into the Ichijo family, the first family of the vampire aristocrats. He grew up with Kaname, who was under the guardianship of his grandfather Asato. While Asato's guardianship meant supervision, Ichijo cared for Kaname, and Kaname began to show his true self to Ichijo. Ichijo watches over Kaname as one of the few who know about his past.

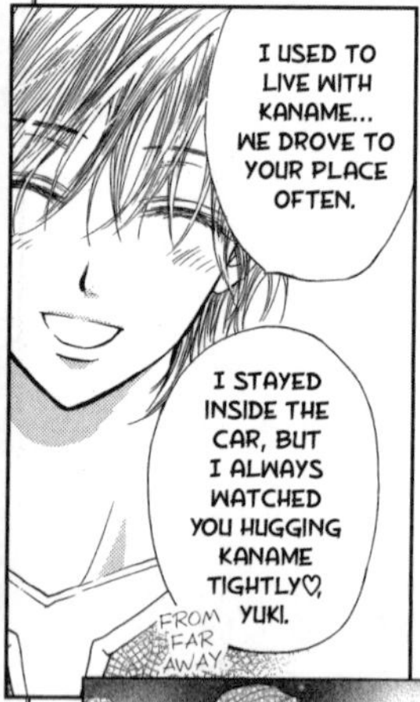
I USED TO LIVE WITH KANAME... WE DROVE TO YOUR PLACE OFTEN.
I STAYED INSIDE THE CAR, BUT I ALWAYS WATCHED YOU HUGGING KANAME TIGHTLY♡, YUKI.
FROM FAR AWAY

⬅⬇ Because he's been with Kaname since they were little, he understands the relationships between Kaname and the other vampire aristocrats.

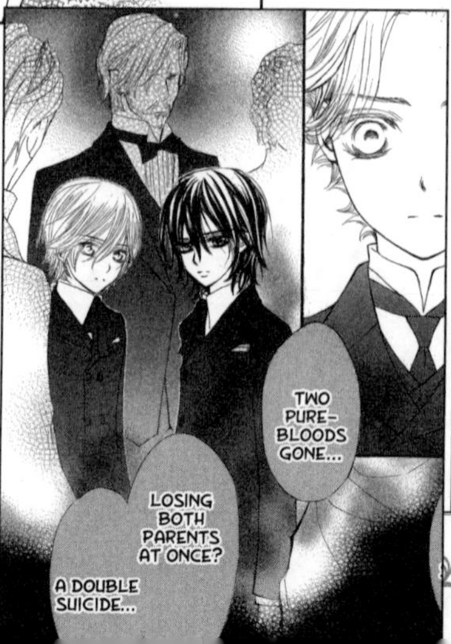
TWO PURE-BLOODS GONE...
LOSING BOTH PARENTS AT ONCE?
A DOUBLE SUICIDE...

Personality

He's friendly and has inner strength!

He's always smiling, loves manga and events, and is also fine during the day. He's a very humanlike vampire. He has a gentle personality, but he doesn't hesitate to fight to protect his friends and juniors—those who are precious to him!! He does not bow to any sort of pressure!

He loves joking around and is a prankster! Sometimes it's hard to tell whether he means what he says or not. ⬇

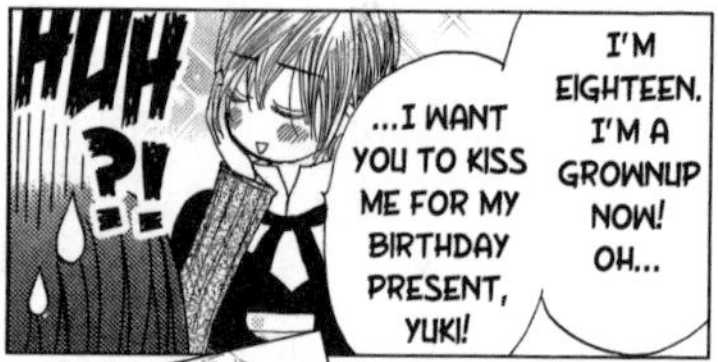
HUH ?!
I'M EIGHTEEN. I'M A GROWNUP NOW! OH...
...I WANT YOU TO KISS ME FOR MY BIRTHDAY PRESENT, YUKI!

⬅⬇ He confronts his grandfather, who tells him to keep an eye on Kaname, and he confronts Kaname when he tries to hurt Shiki's body!

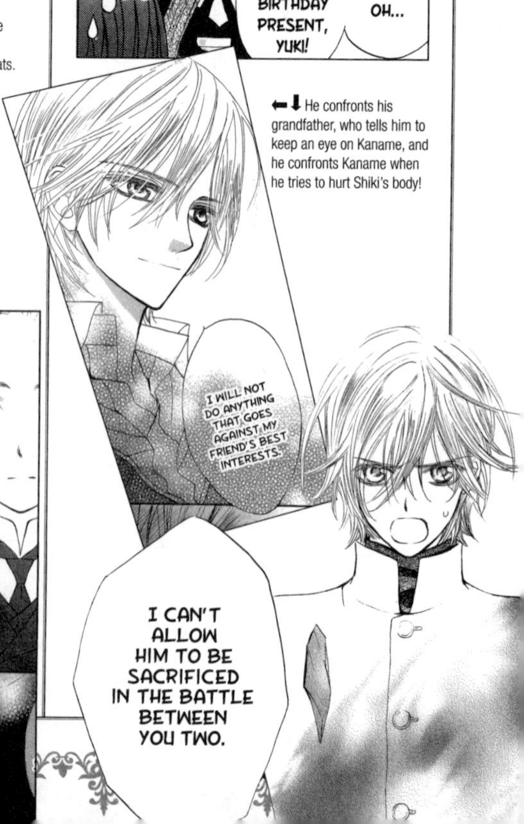
I WILL NOT DO ANYTHING THAT GOES AGAINST MY FRIEND'S BEST INTERESTS.
I CAN'T ALLOW HIM TO BE SACRIFICED IN THE BATTLE BETWEEN YOU TWO.

SHAA
WHAT?!
YOU'RE...

⬅⬇ A brilliant handling of the sword! He sliced a Level E vampire in two and rescued Yuki.

Fighting Ability

The sharp glint of a Japanese sword that turns everything to dust!!

He has the ability to disintegrate matter, and when he fights, he uses a Japanese sword as a medium for his power! A vampire that receives Ichijo's sword turns to ashes with no time to fight back!!

SCHOOLTIME

His activities at school!

KANAME IS BUSY RIGHT NOW...
...SO I'LL SIGN FOR HIM.
YES.

⬅ When he realizes Kaname isn't feeling too well, he acts on behalf of the dorm president by doing things such as permitting someone to enter the dorm.

Classes & Extracurricular Activities

A good go-between for the Day Class and the Night Class

As vice president of the Night Class and the Moon Dormitory, he spends his days supporting Kaname! The Night Class students are hard to approach mostly, but because Ichijo is gentle, he often helps them interact with the Day Class… In the Night Class, no one loves events more than Ichijo, and he hosts various parties. He's the life of the party?!

I'M SORRY FOR ASKING SO MANY QUESTIONS.
ARE YOU ALL RIGHT?
YES... I'M SORRY I COULDN'T BE OF ANY HELP.

⬅ He's gentle when he asks a Day Class student who was attacked by a vampire about what happened. He brings flowers to express his sympathy. ♥

PRIVATE ZONE

We show you what ♥ Ichijo's room is like!!

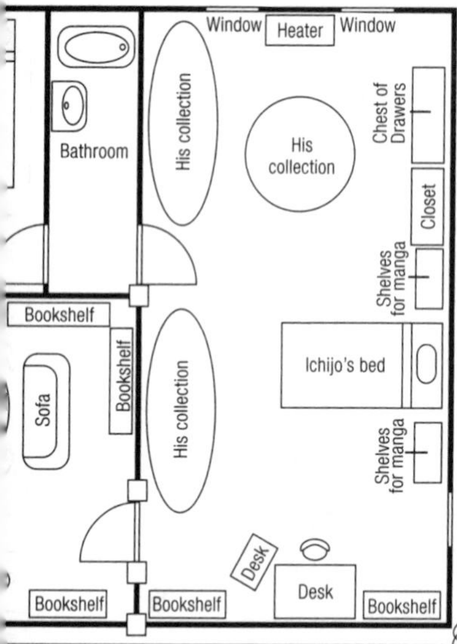

Window
Heater
Window
Bathroom
His collection
His collection
Chest of Drawers
Closet
Shelves for manga
Bookshelf
Bookshelf
Sofa
Ichijo's bed
His collection
Shelves for manga
Desk
Desk
Bookshelf
Bookshelf
Bookshelf

A mini-alternate dimension where huge collections reside

"He's got too many things..." Everyone who enters Ichijo's room makes this comment... From "some sort of object" to "something of something," the room is full of things... He even has Shiki in his room.

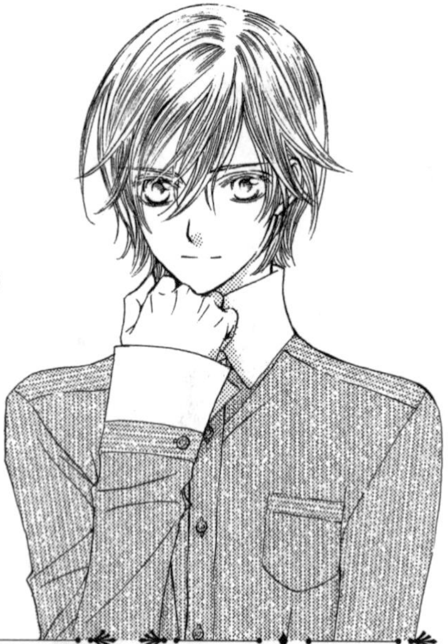

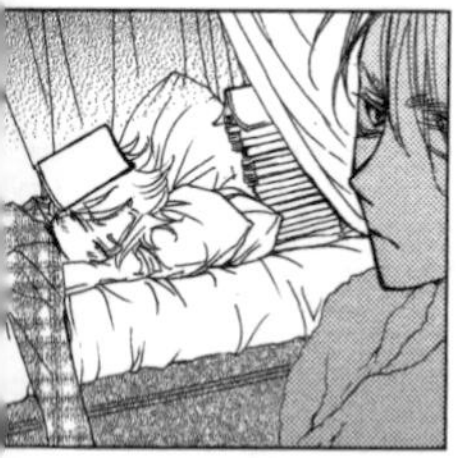

⬆ He forces manga on Aido too. And it's a vampire story...

You can borrow his manga anytime

He likes to recommend books that he found interesting to those around him. He freely lends out his books, but there are many complaints (?) like, "I wasn't interested, but he forced the books on me with a smile"...?!

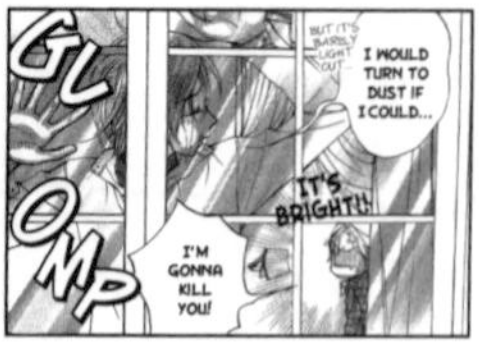

GLOMP
I WOULD TURN TO DUST IF I COULD...
IT'S BRIGHT!!
I'M GONNA KILL YOU!

⬆ He barges in during the day and opens the curtains. How annoying...!!

He doesn't mind sunlight ♪ (Vampirish) irregular hours!

Vampires don't like the day, but he's full of energy. He sometimes "stays up" all day while reading his favorite manga.

Let's take a peek at Ichijo's private life! ♥

He usually spends his time on his hobbies. To tell the truth, he only does his duties as vice president when he feels like it...

Mountains of books that keep increasing...!!

He collects books as he pleases, mainly manga, mysteries, and rakugo-related books. Ichijo's ambition is to put ten thousand manga in the Moon Dormitory library. ♪

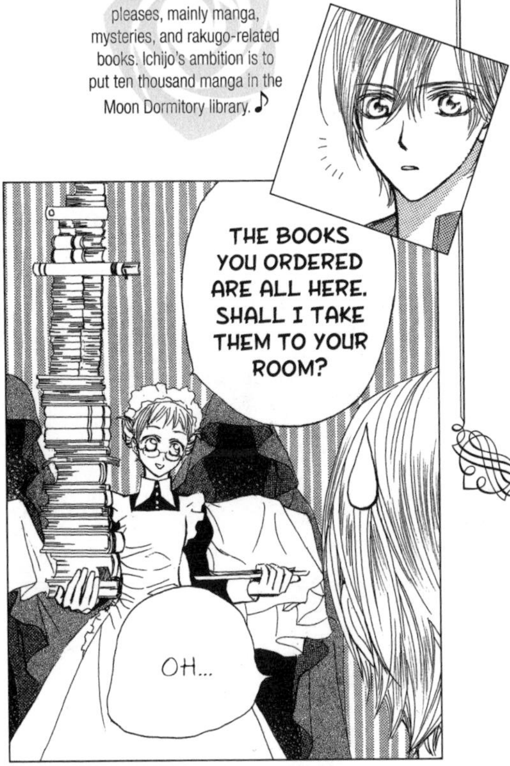
THE BOOKS YOU ORDERED ARE ALL HERE. SHALL I TAKE THEM TO YOUR ROOM?
OH...

⬆ He borrows so many books, you can make a tower out of them!! Soon he'll finish reading all the books in the library...?!

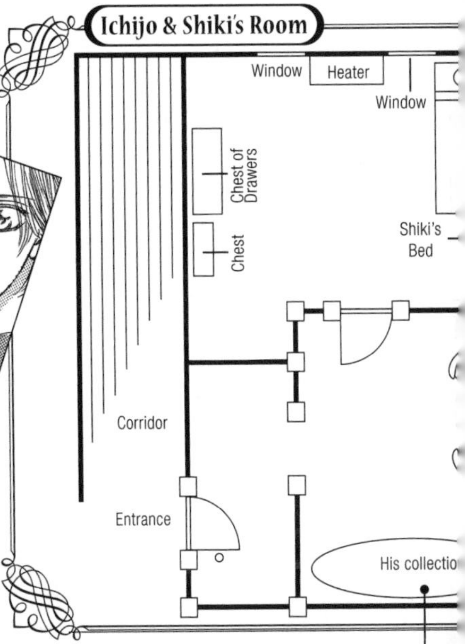
Ichijo & Shiki's Room
Window
Heater
Window
Chest of Drawers
Chest
Shiki's Bed
Corridor
Entrance
His collectio

Danger zone?! Mysterious collections

His hobbies keep changing. Anything he likes becomes a treasure! Therefore his room is full of things that cannot be described... Supposedly, Ichijo displays these things according to rules that he devises, but no one has ever understood them.

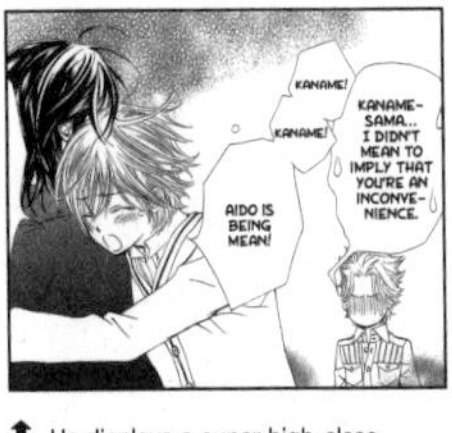
KANAME-SAMA... I DIDN'T MEAN TO IMPLY THAT YOU'RE AN INCONVENIENCE.
KANAME!
KANAME!
AIDO IS BEING MEAN!

⬆ He displays a super high-class technique, which is pleading with Kaname in front of Aido! And it works wonderfully!

He toys with Idol once a day ♥

Ichijo loves fun, and his favorite type of fun involves Aido. ♥ He loves to mess with Aido, who gives his all to Kaname-related matters.

Participates in the Day Class tea ceremony club

His mother, who's the head of a flower-arranging school, trained him in tea ceremony! Rumor has it that Ichijo occasionally shows up at the Day Class tea ceremony club.

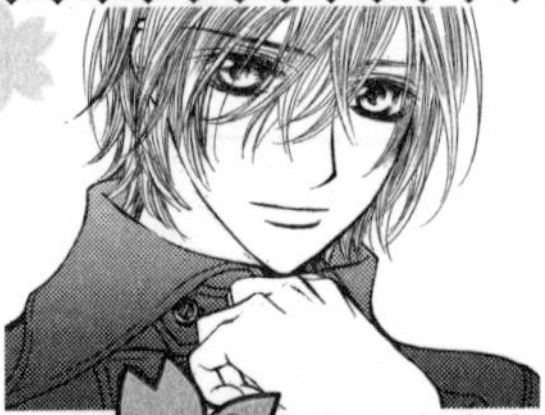

I know because I'm vice president. ♪

Tips for getting along with the dorm president ♥

The vice president, who's the closest to Kaname, gives you a secret lecture. ★

This is acceptable!

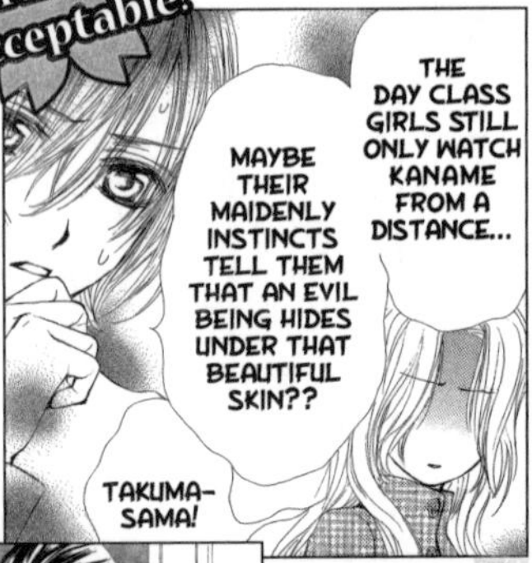
THE DAY CLASS GIRLS STILL ONLY WATCH KANAME FROM A DISTANCE...
MAYBE THEIR MAIDENLY INSTINCTS TELL THEM THAT AN EVIL BEING HIDES UNDER THAT BEAUTIFUL SKIN??
TAKUMA-SAMA!

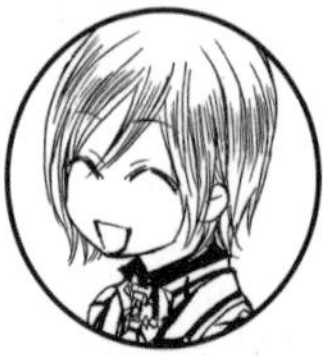

Hi! I'm Takuma Ichijo, the dorm vice president. ♥ Today, I'll secretly tell you how to get along with Kaname Kuran, our dorm president. ♪ Apparently, I can do this because I'm the only one who calls Kaname by name without honorifics… You don't need to be so scared! If you don't step on his landmines, Kaname won't get angry! But he has a short temper. (Heh.) First of all, Kaname doesn't get angry even if you speak ill of him. He's just not interested. I say what I want to, but I'm okay!

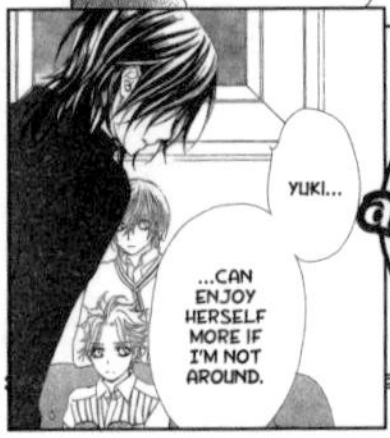
YUKI...
...CAN ENJOY HERSELF MORE IF I'M NOT AROUND.

Barely acceptable?

And no matter how much you like Kaname, it's dangerous to keep telling him that. Everything in moderation… All right, Aido?

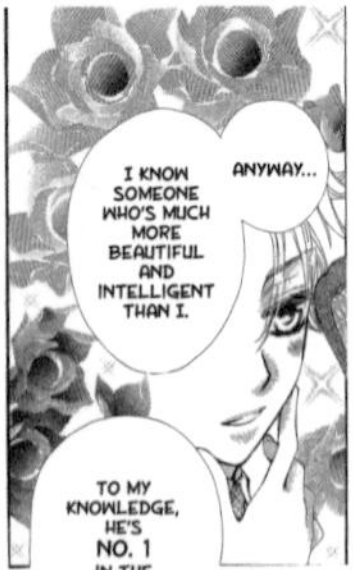
ANYWAY...
I KNOW SOMEONE WHO'S MUCH MORE BEAUTIFUL AND INTELLIGENT THAN I.
TO MY KNOWLEDGE, HE'S NO. 1 IN THE WORLD.

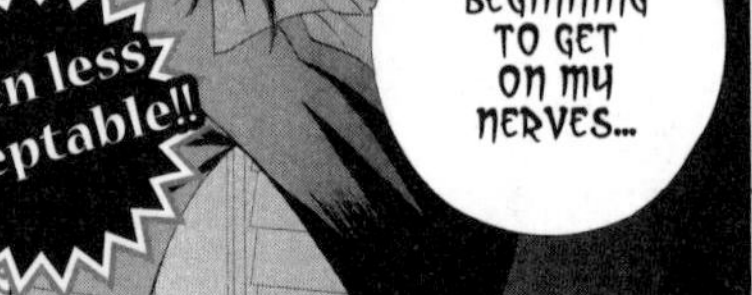
HE'S BEGINNING TO GET ON MY NERVES...

Even less acceptable!!

Second, do not do this… Don't tease him about Yuki!! Even teasing him lightly will make him cranky. If you seriously tease him, he'll glare at you with cold eyes that register absolute zero! Like Headmaster Cross here, see? Ha ha, he's reckless.

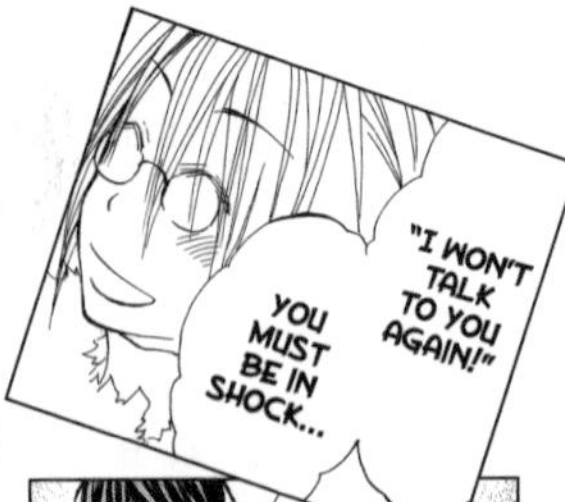
"I WON'T TALK TO YOU AGAIN!"
YOU MUST BE IN SHOCK...

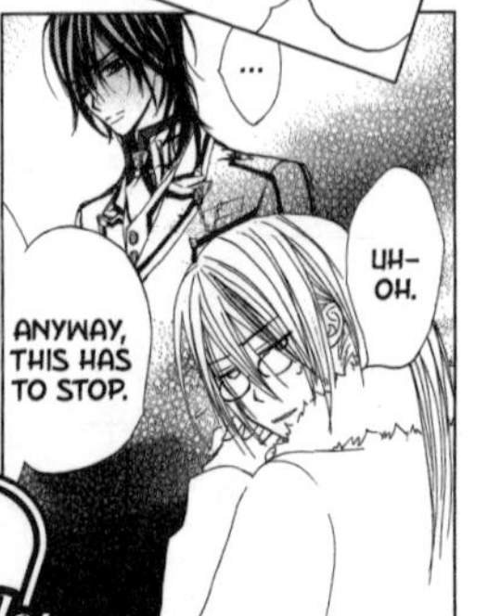
...
UH-OH.
ANYWAY, THIS HAS TO STOP.

Not acceptable!

Special messages to Ichijo

The vice president who's nice, friendly and has a wonderful smile... But people say that you can't take him lightly...?

From Senri Shiki

I like Ichijo because he's nice and kinda fun. The pickles he gave me the other day were delicious... But they smelled really bad...

From Kaname Kuran

For me, Ichijo is a very precious friend... I can act freely because Ichijo supports me... Will he be happy if I tell him that?

From the maid

Ichijo-sama's bright smile makes us happy too! ♥

From Hanabusa Aido

Stop teasing and playing with me!! And don't get too close to Kaname-sama!!

From Rima Toya

Please stop involving me when you drag Shiki into things...

From Akatsuki Kain

I think he's amazing because he's good at dealing with President Kuran and Hanabusa.

From Ruka Souen

Ichijo-sama's words and actions sometimes make me nervous.

From the Headmaster

The tea Ichijo made for me was superb.♥

From Yuki Cross

He's always cheerful and smiling, so he's approachable.

He answers your questions?!

Questions for Ichijo ♥

Ichijo's smile is lovely ♥, but he may have a different side?

Letters sent in from fans for fans!

Vam☆Fan Hall

The Ichijo Version

Q You seem to stay awake past the morning or afternoon. Don't you get sleepy?
—Kopperian, Kagawa Prefecture

A Some humans are night people, right? I'm the same. I get sleepy, but I just *can't stop* staying up all day. There are too many interesting manga! My recommendation right now is *MeruPuri.* ♥

Q Why do you use a Japanese sword as a weapon?
—Akibu, Kanagawa Prefecture

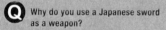

A Of course I can fight without one! But our family has been using Japanese swords for generations. My grandfather trained me to use one when I was a child, so I end up using them now. Moreover, I look more like *a hero* if I'm holding one, right? Heh, that was just a joke!

Q If Kaname didn't exist, who would have been the leader of the Night Class?
—Date Masamune, Miyagi Prefecture

A I don't think the Night Class would've *existed* then... Uh-oh... That's it for my questions? Isn't this fewer questions than the others? ♣

Q Hello, Ichijo! ♥ Your smile always makes me smile. ♥ What's the secret to keeping your smile?
—Snow White, Mie Prefecture

A Hello! Smiling is easy. You just need to keep thinking about fun things. Kain was just saying to Aido, "You haven't been taught any *manners*," so how about imagining Aido running around the garden with dog ears...? See? Doesn't that make you smile?

I DIDN'T SAY THAT.

Q Have you ever eaten natto?
—Suisui Pool No. 1, Tokushima Prefecture

A I *have*! I like how gooey it is. The strings keep coming at you! Hey, I know! Let's try to serve natto as *Kaname's breakfast*!!

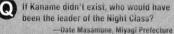

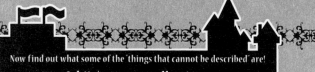

Now find out what some of the "things that cannot be described" are!

Ichijo's strange collections

What are some of the mysterious objects displayed in Ichijo's room...?

He discovered some strange mushrooms on the school grounds! He and Shiki took them and made them part of his collection.

—Jane ♪, Chiba Prefecture

"Shiki, those mushrooms looked delicious."

—Ichijo

The Kaname doll that Aido had. After Kaname confiscated it, it was passed to Ichijo and became part of his collection. ♪

—Northern Cross, Hyogo Prefecture

"Aido is good at handicrafts!!"

—Ichijo

"Ichijo... Will you please get rid of it?"

—Kaname

Secret photos of the Night Class students! Aido watching Kaname-sama from behind something, Shiki's sleeping face, photos of Kaname when he's going a little berserk... There's nothing in the Moon Dormitory that Ichijo doesn't know about?!

—Anzu, Tokyo

"Our vice president knows so much..."

—Kain

He collects antiques that are called "th cursed ______." He's experimenting to see whether he really will be cursed or not. (Only Kaname and Shiki know about this.)

—Tsukushinbo, Kochi Prefecture

"I won't be satisfied unless I try and see if I'll really be cursed."

—Ichijo

A blood-sucking rose. Kaname gave it to him as his 17th birthday gift. Ichijo left it alone because it was creepy, but one night it drank his blood. Sometimes Shiki plays around with it.

-Kumiko Kotake, Tochigi Prefecture

"Ichijo plays around with it too. He'll do things like put a ribbon on the rose."

—Shiki

HEY, SHIKI, THEY'RE NOT AS STRANGE AS PEOPLE SAY, RIGHT?
ACTUALLY, THE ITEMS ARE EVEN MORE INCREDIBLE...

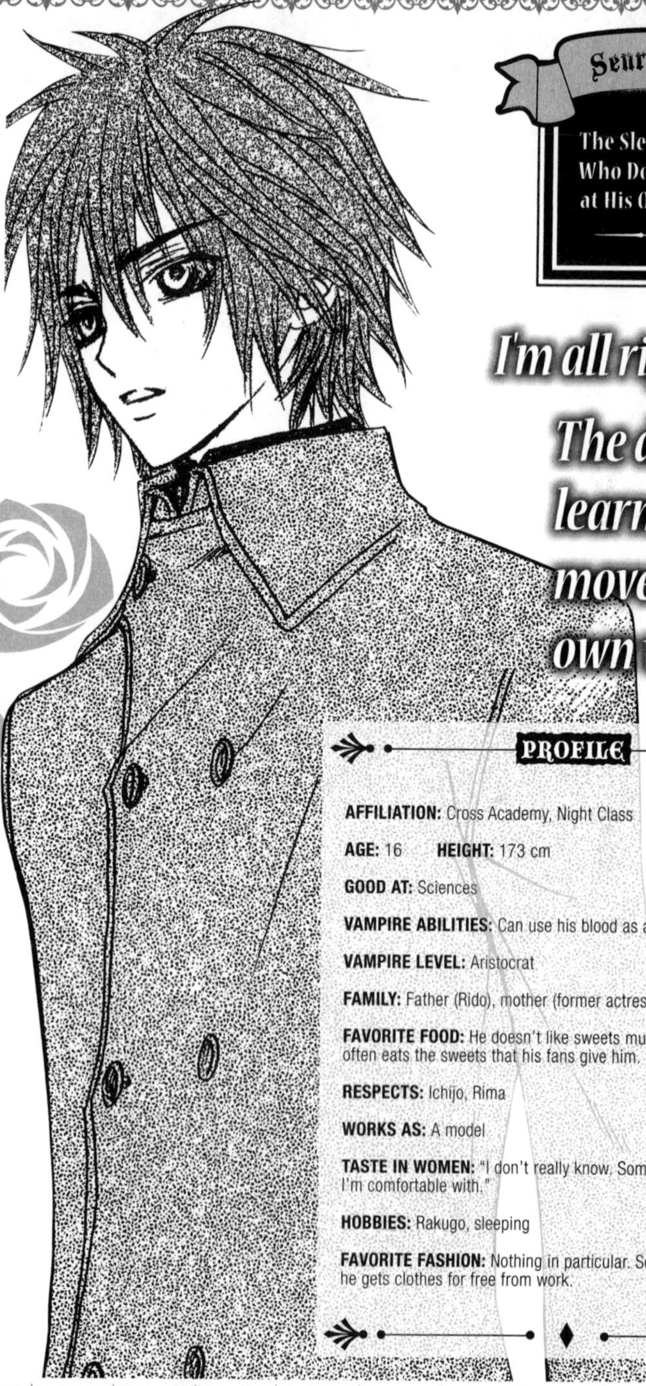

Senri Shiki

The Sleeping Boy Who Does Things at His Own Pace!!

I'm all right... The doll has learned to move by its own will.

PROFILE

AFFILIATION: Cross Academy, Night Class

AGE: 16 **HEIGHT:** 173 cm

GOOD AT: Sciences

VAMPIRE ABILITIES: Can use his blood as a physical weapon

VAMPIRE LEVEL: Aristocrat

FAMILY: Father (Rido), mother (former actress), great-uncle

FAVORITE FOOD: He doesn't like sweets much, but he often eats the sweets that his fans give him.

RESPECTS: Ichijo, Rima

WORKS AS: A model

TASTE IN WOMEN: "I don't really know. Someone I'm comfortable with."

HOBBIES: Rakugo, sleeping

FAVORITE FASHION: Nothing in particular. Sometimes he gets clothes for free from work.

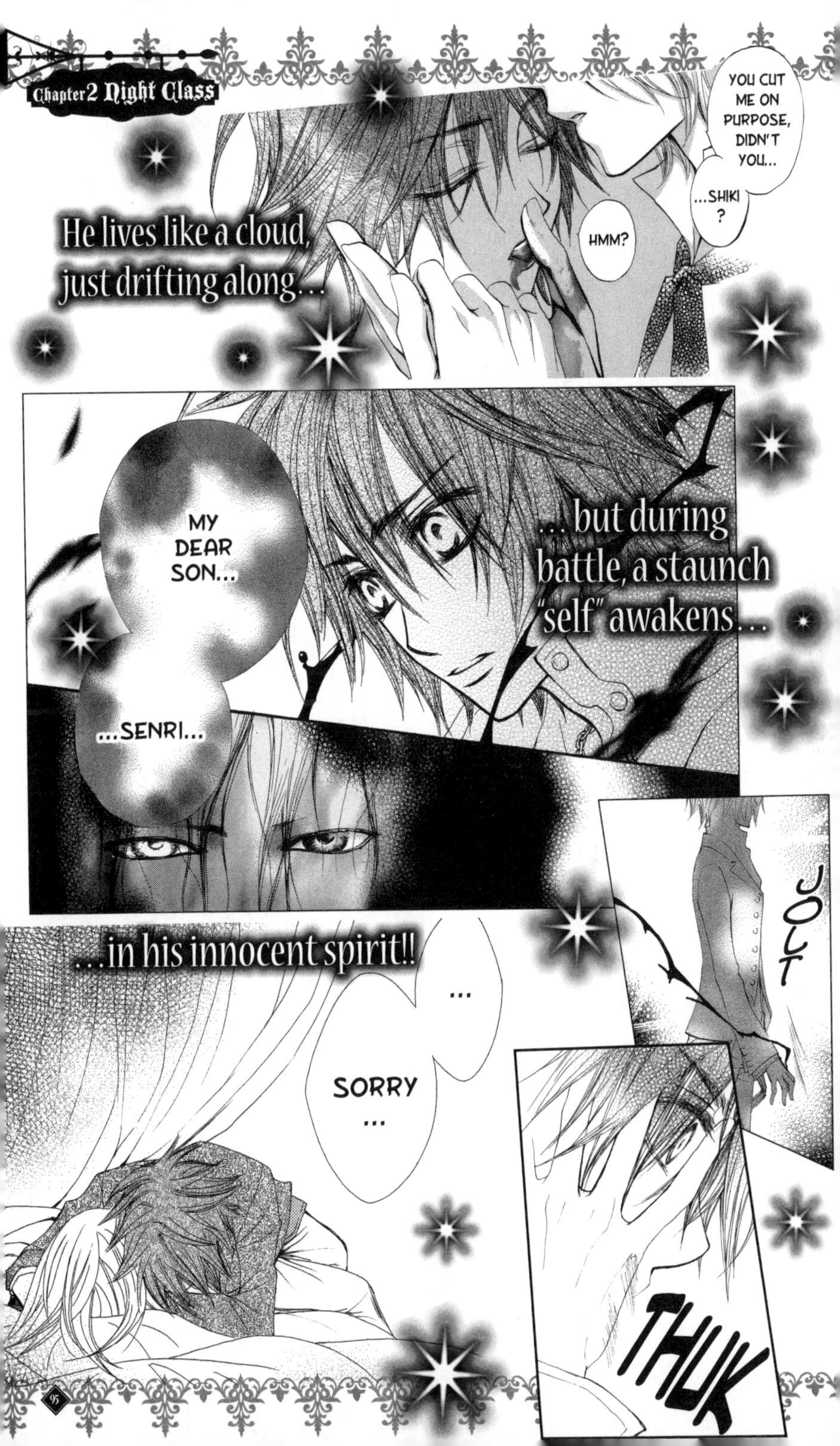
You cut me on purpose, didn't you...
...Shiki ?
Hmm?
He lives like a cloud, just drifting along...
...but during battle, a staunch "self" awakens...
My dear son...
...Senri...
...in his innocent spirit!!
JOLT
THUK
...
Sorry ...

CHARACTER ANALYSIS

This is what Senri Shiki is like!!

His Past

Like a doll... Days when he was passive

He was born into the Shiki family, but he didn't know who his father was and grew up alone with his mother. His mother gradually became mentally unstable and hurled her feelings at Shiki... The solution that little Shiki came up with was to suppress himself so that he didn't hurt his mother.

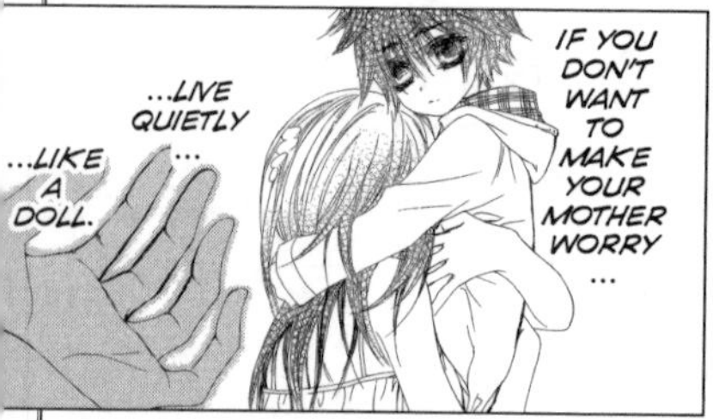
IF YOU DON'T WANT TO MAKE YOUR MOTHER WORRY...
...LIVE QUIETLY...
...LIKE A DOLL.

⬆ Shiki's mother clings to the young Shiki... He could only accept her as she was.

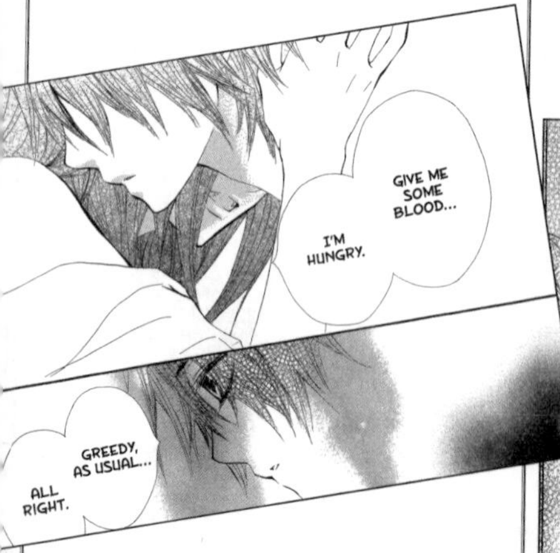
GIVE ME SOME BLOOD...
I'M HUNGRY.
GREEDY, AS USUAL...
ALL RIGHT.

⬆ He comes home from the academy after a long absence, but his home is the same as usual. Shiki goes along with his mother's capricious words and actions.

Personality

He's low-key, but he's got sharp senses!!

Except for a selected few like Ichijo and Rima, he's not very interested in things around him, and he does things at his own pace. He's very laid back, but he's got sharp senses that help him detect things he fears and doesn't like so that he can keep away from them!

He even ignores St. Xocolatl's Day even though the entire academy makes a fuss... ⬇

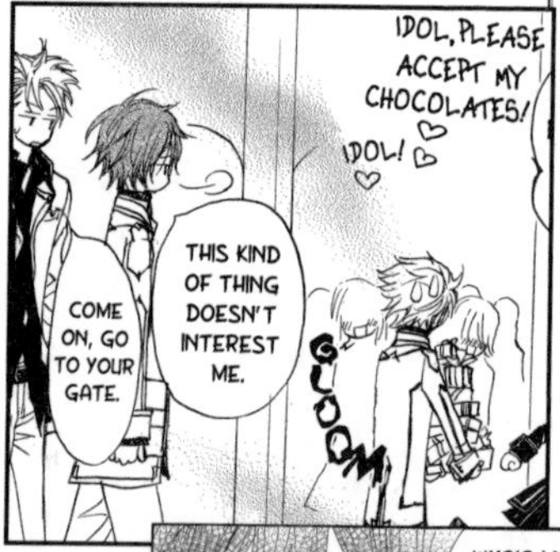
IDOL, PLEASE ACCEPT MY CHOCOLATES!
IDOL!
THIS KIND OF THING DOESN'T INTEREST ME.
COME ON, GO TO YOUR GATE.
GLOOM

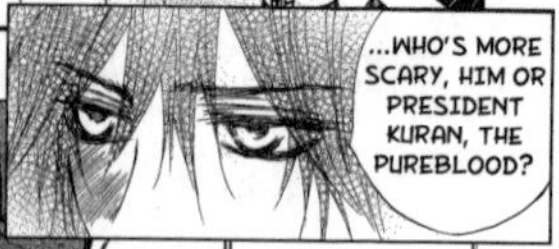
...WHO'S MORE SCARY, HIM OR PRESIDENT KURAN, THE PUREBLOOD?

⬆ He senses that Ichio and Kaname are terrifying.

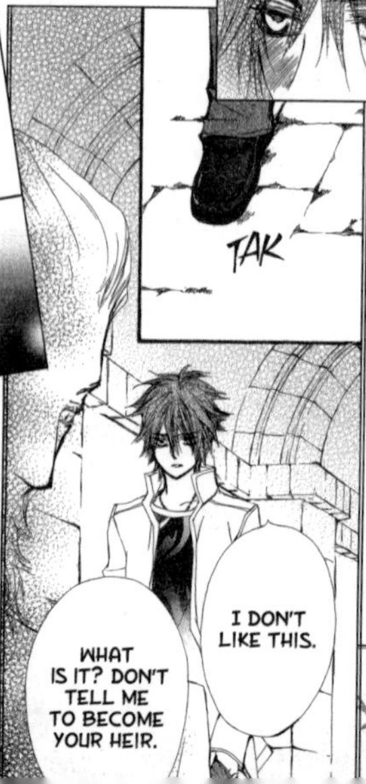
TAK
I DON'T LIKE THIS.
WHAT IS IT? DON'T TELL ME TO BECOME YOUR HEIR.

⬅ Shiki confronts his father, the ominous pureblood Rido Kuran, who was waiting for him at his great-uncle's mansion!

SHOVE
GET OUT OF THE WAY.
BAM BAM

Fighting Ability

He pierces and restrains the enemy with his blood!!

He can manipulate his own blood and use it as a powerful weapon!! Those who get attacked by his blood whip have nowhere to hide and are at a loss… Using his blood as a shooting weapon, he's good at fighting within an intermediate range. If he can pierce the vitals, his blood is so destructive that he can kill with one blow.

⬅ He shoots his blood at a Level E! It looks like thin ropes, but each strand is strong enough to penetrate the earth.

SCHOOLTIME

His activities at school!

He appears in an ad for a famous brand in the magazine Ichijo was holding!! Does your heart beat fast at his sexy demeanor, which is so different from usual? ⬇

Classes & Extracurricular Activities

He hides his true self and works as a model!

He's busy every day. At night, he's a student in the Night Class of Cross Academy. During the day, he's a popular model. He began modeling when he accompanied his actress mother to her workplace and was scouted there. He hides the fact that he's a vampire and has gotten used to the "day" world. He has a lot of fans in the Day Class…

His manager doesn't know, but he hunts Level E vampires while working as a model. ⬇

FINISH YOUR ERRAND QUICKLY OR YOU'LL BE LATE FOR THE PHOTO SHOOT!
AND SHIKI, YOU GET SUNBURNT EASILY, SO YOU GET UNDER RIMA'S PARASOL TOO!
YOU'RE A PROFESSIONAL MODEL!
WHY MINE?
OKAY.

PRIVATE ZONE

We show you what Shiki's room is like!! ♥

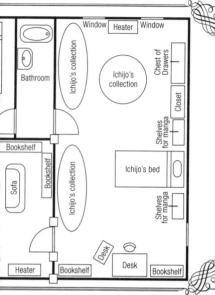

Window
Heater
Window
Ichijo's collection
Ichijo's collection
Chest of Drawers
Bathroom
Closet
Shelves for manga
Bookshelf
Bookshelf
Sofa
Ichijo's collection
Ichijo's bed
Shelves for manga
Desk
Desk
Heater
Bookshelf
Bookshelf

Lots of sweets that compete with Ichijo's collections ★

This room used to be vice president Ichijo's own room, but Shiki started crashing here (he got what used to be the living room). The bedroom is full of the smell of sweets…!

MY POKKIN CHOCO! I WANTED TO GIVE SOME TO DORM PRESIDENT KURAN!
NOOOO!
CHMF
CHMF

⬆ He even eats Aido's sweets! He ate them because they were there!!

He eats sweets if they're there!

Actually, Shiki doesn't like sweets all that much. But because he answered, "I like sweets" in a magazine interview without thinking, the sweets that his fans send him keep piling up.

Let's take a peek at Shiki's private life! ♥

He's low-key but busy. He studies hard and gets lots of sleep.

GOOD MORNING!
KANAME DOES MAKE PEOPLE DO INTERESTING THINGS.
YOU GETTING TIRED?

⬆ He ignores Aido because he's sleepy even though Aido's different from usual!

He's never late but has trouble getting up?!

Because school is his first priority, he gets up on time even if he's busy with his modeling job. But sometimes he walks around half asleep with no shoes on…

Lazy times for the gentle pair…

Shiki is attached to his roommate Ichijo. Ichijo has a lot of hobbies, so Shiki's been exploring new worlds such as getting familiar with rakugo and enjoying tea! Shiki and rakugo… They don't go together well, but he enjoys it?!

↓ An innocent sleeping face, just like a baby. He's relaxed and is leaning against Ichijo. ♥

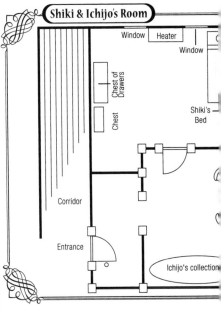

Shiki & Ichijo's Room

Window | Heater
Window
Chest of Drawers
Shiki's Bed
Chest
Corridor
Entrance
Ichijo's collection

Because he finds everything a bother…

He likes keeping things neat! Actually, he finds it a bother to mess up his room. Shiki's style is to keep the things that he put away and to pile things that keep piling up (like sweets and his clothes). ♪ Rima regularly takes care of managing these things.

GO AFTER IT!

DASH

I DON'T LIKE CHASING..

↑ You don't like chasing?! The enemy's running away!

Laid-back even when hunting!

Because he often leaves the academy for work, the Senate and Kaname often order him to hunt Level E vampires. But Shiki doesn't seem too eager about it…

A regular cycle

Sleep ➡ Wake up ➡ Eat ➡ Walk with Ichijo or Rima ➡ … Shiki's days are a repeat of this! He never gets tired of this routine.

Lots of damage with just a few words ★

Shiki's blunt comments

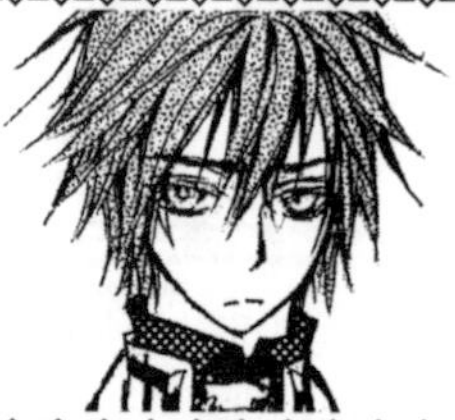

whispered

The silent, deadpan Shiki spins out words that can kill!

Phrase 1 To Kain, who was thrown

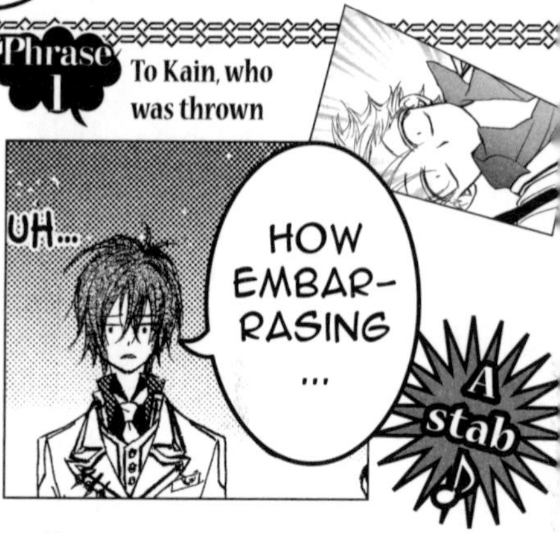
UH...
HOW EMBAR-RASING ...
A stab ♪

Effects

Kain stepped in when people were just about to start fighting. You can almost hear a harsh voice saying, "I admire your guts, but you should've thought things through." That's why Kain's the victim of circumstances!!

Phrase 2 To the Disciplinary Committee member who was called "nice"

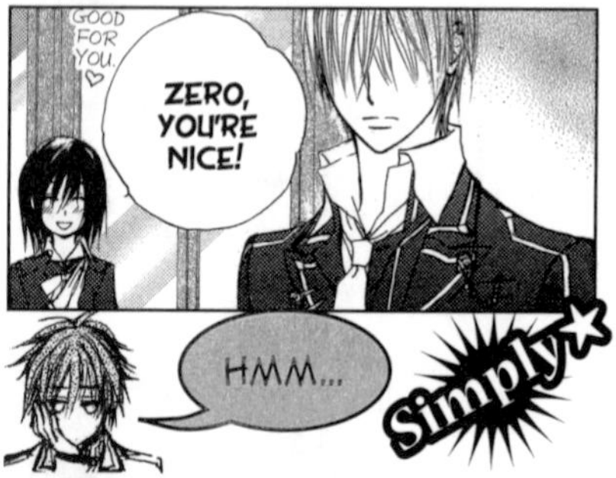
ZERO, YOU'RE NICE!
GOOD FOR YOU. ♡
HMM...
Simply★

Effects

A response that goes against the idea that Zero is actually nice despite looking scary. "If he looks scary, he's scary"... Shiki's "Hmm..." crushes girls' wishful thinking!!

Phrase 3 To Aido, who was suspected of drinking blood

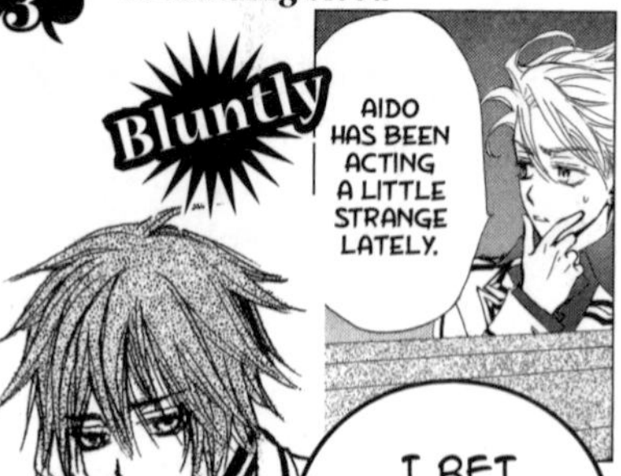
AIDO HAS BEEN ACTING A LITTLE STRANGE LATELY.
Bluntly
I BET AIDO DID IT.

Effects

Terrifying words that changed "Maybe Aido did it...?!" (everyone suspecting Aido 50%) to "So it was Aido...!!" (everyone suspecting Aido 99%) in an instant. But Shiki, you're not even interested in who did it!!

From his roommate Ichijo

Well... Shiki doesn't have any evil intentions. He's just not really eager to do things... Yeah...

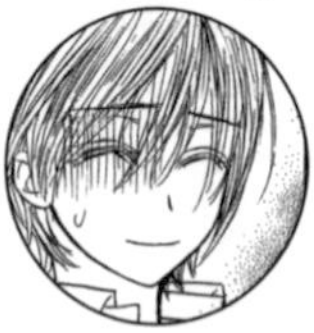

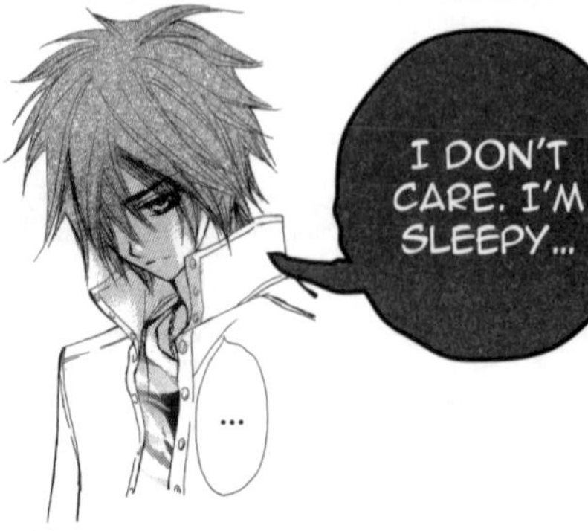
I DON'T CARE. I'M SLEEPY...
...

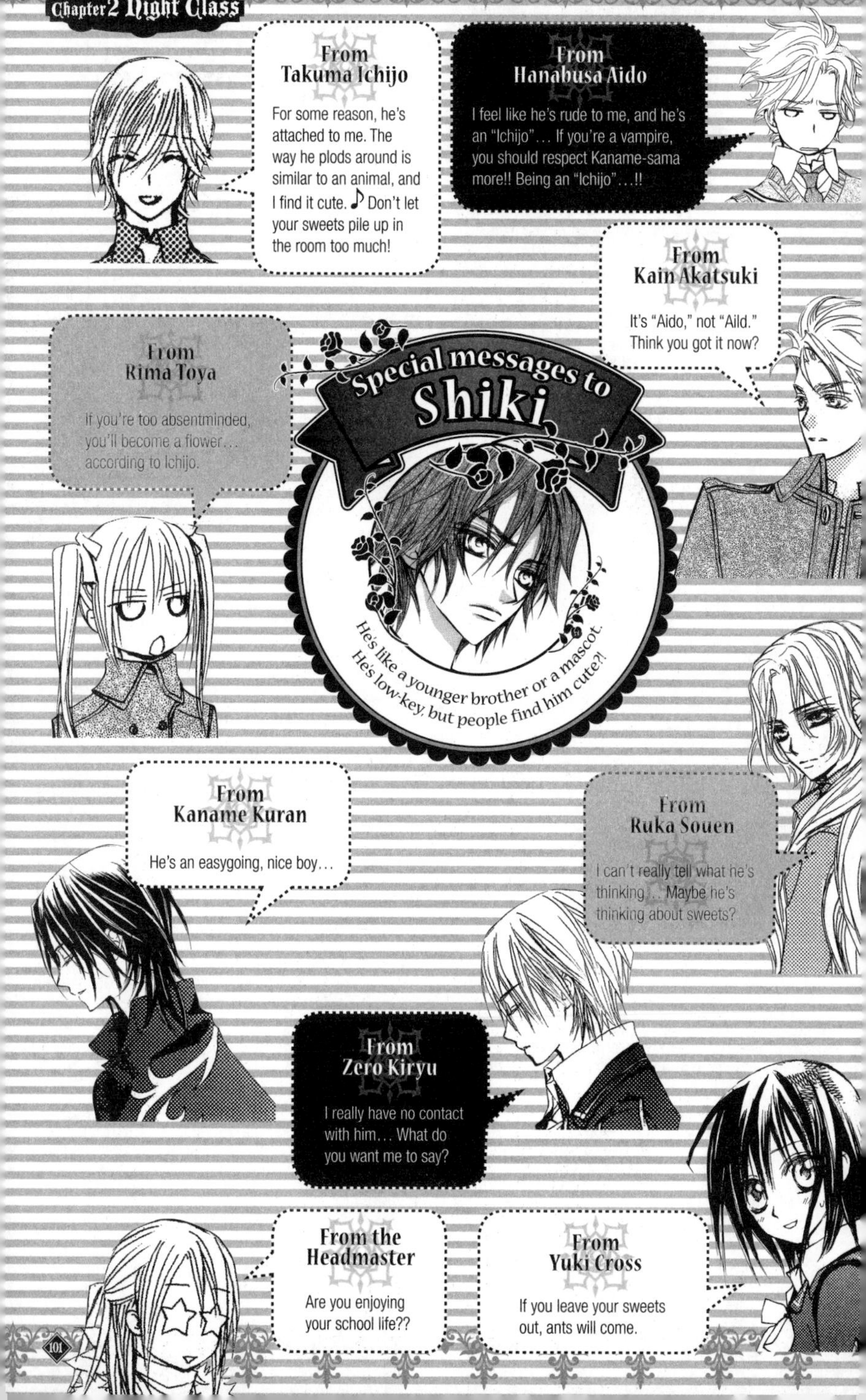
From Hanabusa Aido
I feel like he's rude to me, and he's an "Ichijo"… If you're a vampire, you should respect Kaname-sama more!! Being an "Ichijo"…!!
From Takuma Ichijo
For some reason, he's attached to me. The way he plods around is similar to an animal, and I find it cute. ♪ Don't let your sweets pile up in the room too much!
From Kain Akatsuki
It's "Aido," not "Aild." Think you got it now?
Special messages to Shiki
He's like a younger brother or a mascot. He's low-key, but people find him cute?!
From Rima Toya
If you're too absentminded, you'll become a flower… according to Ichijo.
From Ruka Souen
I can't really tell what he's thinking… Maybe he's thinking about sweets?
From Kaname Kuran
He's an easygoing, nice boy…
From Zero Kiryu
I really have no contact with him… What do you want me to say?
From Yuki Cross
If you leave your sweets out, ants will come.
From the Headmaster
Are you enjoying your school life??

Letters sent in from fans for fans!

Vam☆ Fan Hall

The Shiki Version

He answers your questions?!

Questions for Shiki!!

The quiet Shiki really talks this time ♥

Q How did you end up attending Cross Academy?

—Nopporin, Shizuoka Prefecture

A When Ichijo said he was going, my great-uncle said, "Senri, you go too"... Plus Rima, a fellow model, also said she'd attend.

Q How do you feel about Kaname?

—Eseru, Aichi Prefecture

A I respect President Kuran... But he's scary sometimes...

Q Why are you so attached to Ichijo?

—Makky, Osaka

A Cuz it's fun being with him.

I THINK ICHIJO IS JUST PLAYING WITH YOU.

Q You always look sleepy. Have you ever fallen asleep standing up?

—Ryoko Kishi, Aichi Prefecture

A I have. Ichijo supported me and stopped me from falling over. By the way... I'm sleepy right now... Can we end this? ♣

Q What interests you the most right now?

—Planaria, Kumamoto Prefecture

A Sleeping... And rakugo. I borrowed some DVDs from Ichijo, and they were fun to watch.

Q What's your favorite food?

—BLUE, Nara Prefecture

A When I said in a magazine interview that I like sweets, people started sending me more sweets than I could eat, so now I like spicy food...

Q When do you work at your modeling assignments?

—Rubii, Kagawa Prefecture

A I often go during the day, so I get sleepy during my evening classes... But if I don't do things properly, Rima scolds me.

Q Has anyone ever told you that you're like a cat?

—Kotatsu de mikan, Kyoto

A Cuz I'm always sleeping...?

Shiki, who finds doing things a bother, gets challenges from Ichijo!!!

Ichijo recommended this to me...

Shiki, who does things at his own pace, is influenced by Ichijo?!

Ichijo said, "Let's test our courage," so the two of them explored the academy. But they can see well, even in the dark, so it was useless...
—Megupon, Yamanashi Prefecture

"It wasn't scary, but we had a good walk."
—Shiki

Ichijo proposed that he and Shiki draw dojinshi about the Night Class students, and they sold their work at Comiket. All the copies sold out!! Shiki was pretty happy too?!
—Meirin Yuki, Tokyo

"Aido bought all the copies featuring the president."
—Ichijo

Ichijo encouraged Shiki to dress in drag. Rima saw Shiki and was shocked, thinking, "He's cuter than me..." Aido hit on Shiki, not realizing it was him, and was shocked later...
—Woodpecker, Hokkaido

"Let's show Kaname how cute you are!!"
—Ichijo

Shiki stayed up all day reading manga he borrowed from Ichijo, so he fell asleep during class.
—Gekka bijin, Tochigi Prefecture

"We're models, so we should be professional and get enough sleep to keep our skin in top shape."
—Rin

"Yeah, I'll be careful."
—Shiki

Ichijo said, "Why don't we play a dating sim game?" and Shiki really got into it. Rima saw him playing the game and slapped him, saying, "You suck!"
—Ayako Kubosawa, Chiba Prefecture

"Rima should play too. It's fun..."
—Shiki

The two decide to set up a giant domino chain in a room in the Moon Dormitory! But Shiki kicks the pieces by accident, so they have to keep setting it up.
—Rinne Shiratori, Okayama Prefecture

"Ichijo... I'm getting sleepy. When do we start knocking them over?"
—Shiki

HEY, SHIKI. WHICH ONE WOULD YOU LIKE TO TRY NEXT?
ANY OF THEM WILL DO.

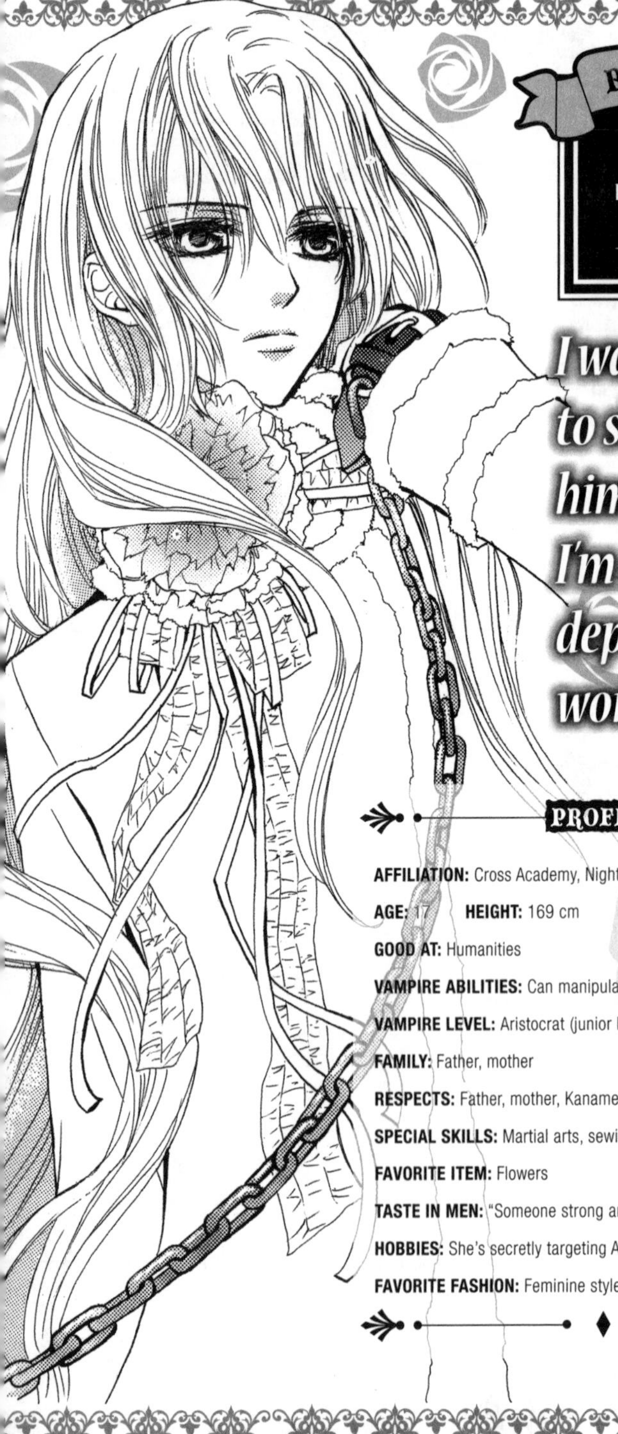

Ruka Souen

The Proud Flower That Blooms in the Night Class

I want to show him that I'm a cool, dependable woman.

PROFILE

AFFILIATION: Cross Academy, Night Class

AGE: 17 **HEIGHT:** 169 cm

GOOD AT: Humanities

VAMPIRE ABILITIES: Can manipulate the enemy through illusions

VAMPIRE LEVEL: Aristocrat (junior branch of the Aido family)

FAMILY: Father, mother

RESPECTS: Father, mother, Kaname-sama

SPECIAL SKILLS: Martial arts, sewing

FAVORITE ITEM: Flowers

TASTE IN MEN: "Someone strong and kind like Kaname-sama."

HOBBIES: She's secretly targeting Aido's Kaname-sama Collection

FAVORITE FASHION: Feminine style

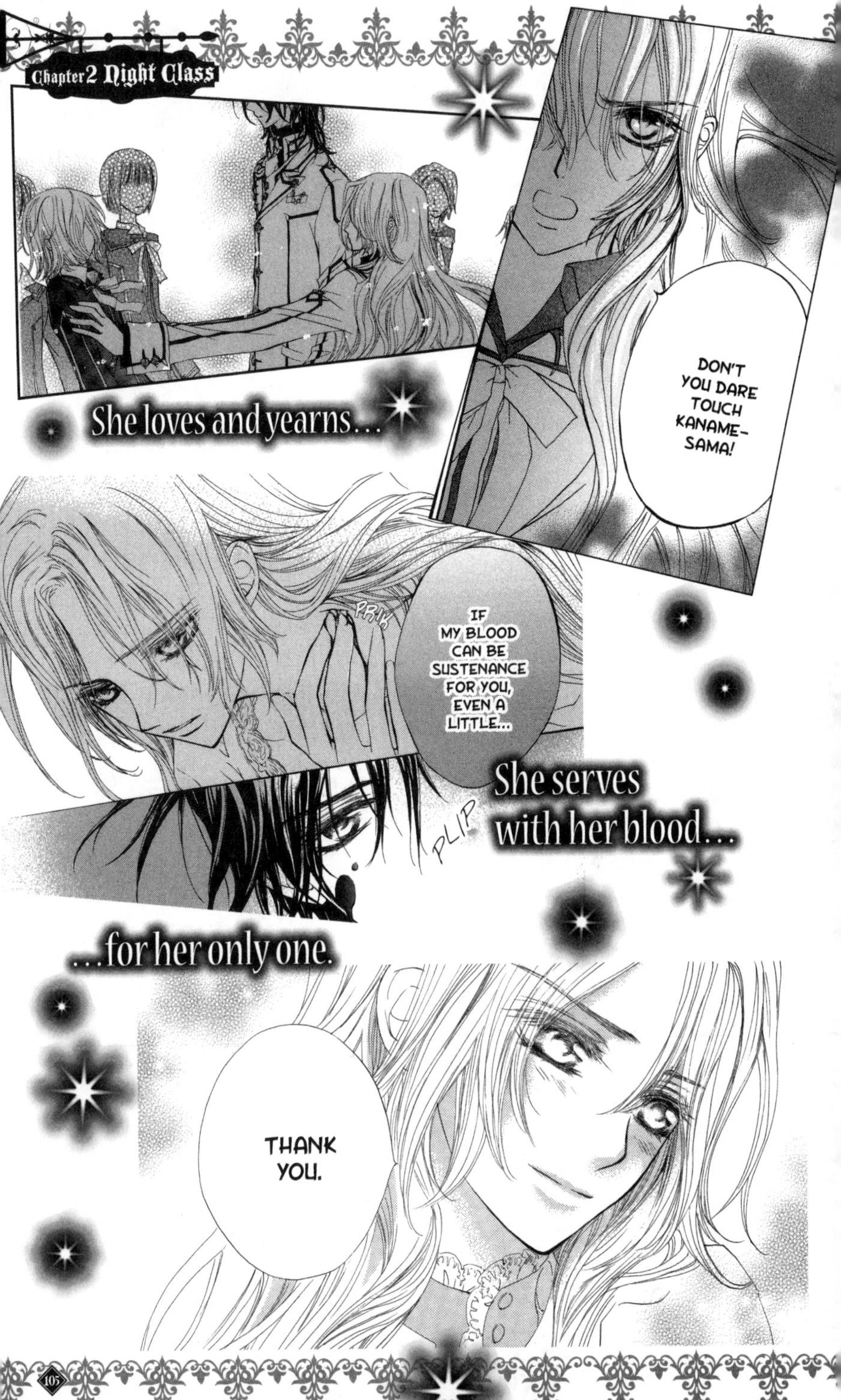
DON'T YOU DARE TOUCH KANAME-SAMA!
She loves and yearns...
PRIK
IF MY BLOOD CAN BE SUSTENANCE FOR YOU, EVEN A LITTLE...
She serves with her blood...
PLIP
...for her only one.
THANK YOU.

CHARACTER ANALYSIS

This is what Ruka Souen is like!!

Her Past

Longing... The lord whom she offered her blood to...

When Ruka was a child, she dreamingly admired the pureblood's handsome looks and superior abilities that she'd heard about. After she actually met Kaname himself, he became a supreme existence in her eyes, and to be able to offer her blood to him was bliss. But that only happened once...

When she was four in vampire years. She hears that Aido met Kaname-sama...⬇

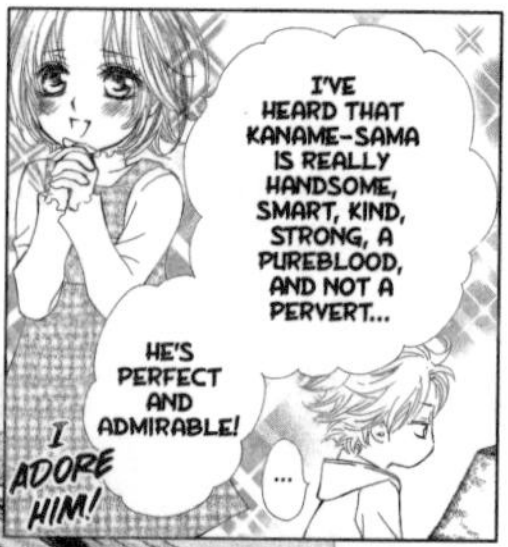
I'VE HEARD THAT KANAME-SAMA IS REALLY HANDSOME, SMART, KIND, STRONG, A PUREBLOOD, AND NOT A PERVERT...
HE'S PERFECT AND ADMIRABLE!
I ADORE HIM!
...

Once right after she came to Cross Academy, she offered her blood to Kaname, and he accepted. ⬇

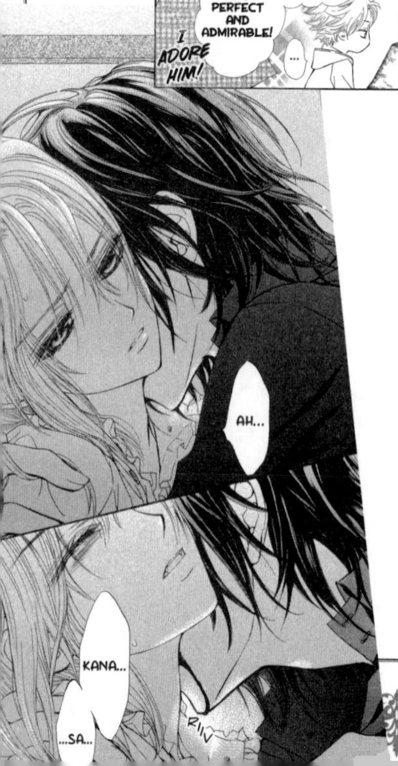
AH...
KANA...
...SA...
RIIV

Personality

Passion that's hidden beneath her noble exterior

She maintains grace and pride as an aristocrat and rarely loses her composure. However, things are different when it comes to Kaname. She is hostile to those who harm Kaname and becomes emotional when she sees women try to get close to him. The passion she hides beneath her graceful looks is incomparable.

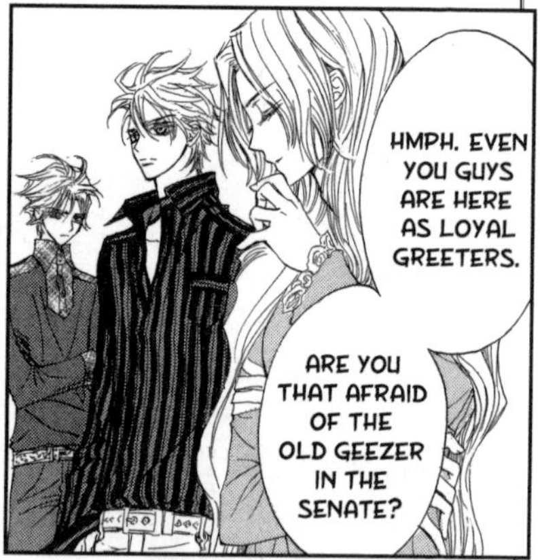
HMPH. EVEN YOU GUYS ARE HERE AS LOYAL GREETERS.
ARE YOU THAT AFRAID OF THE OLD GEEZER IN THE SENATE?

⬆ She bluntly cuts down those who stand ready for Ichio's visit. She's usually dauntless.

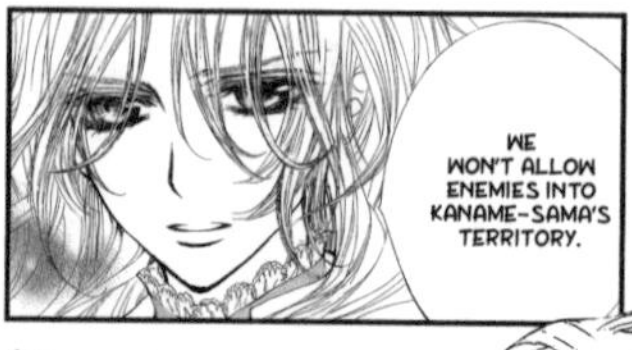
WE WON'T ALLOW ENEMIES INTO KANAME-SAMA'S TERRITORY.

⬆ She steps forward to protect the academy from the vampires' attack because she considers the academy to be Kaname's territory.

She confronts the rushing vampires and declares war against them. She's full of confidence and determination. ➡

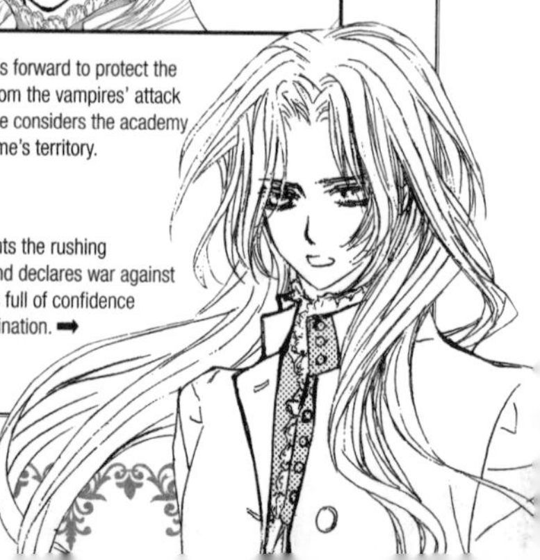

She's embarrassed she beat back an enemy with a kick. ➡

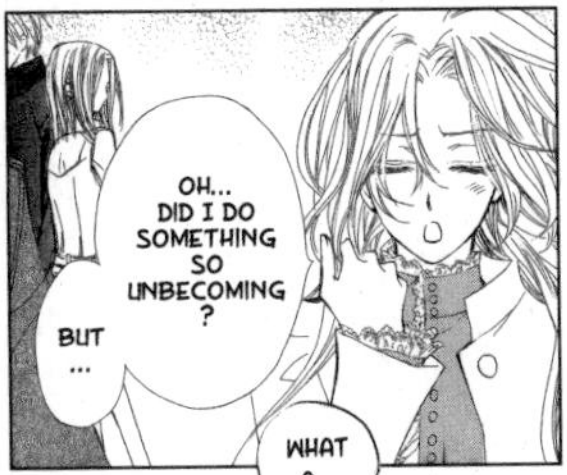
OH... DID I DO SOMETHING SO UNBECOMING?
BUT ...

She gives other Night Class students instructions so that they do exactly what Kaname wants them to do. ⬇

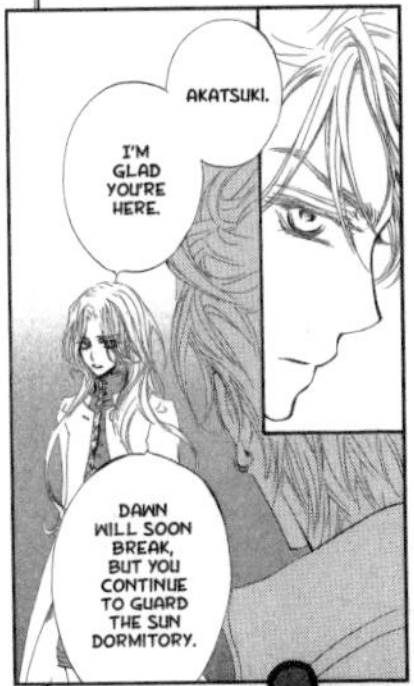
AKATSUKI.
I'M GLAD YOU'RE HERE.
DAWN WILL SOON BREAK, BUT YOU CONTINUE TO GUARD THE SUN DORMITORY.

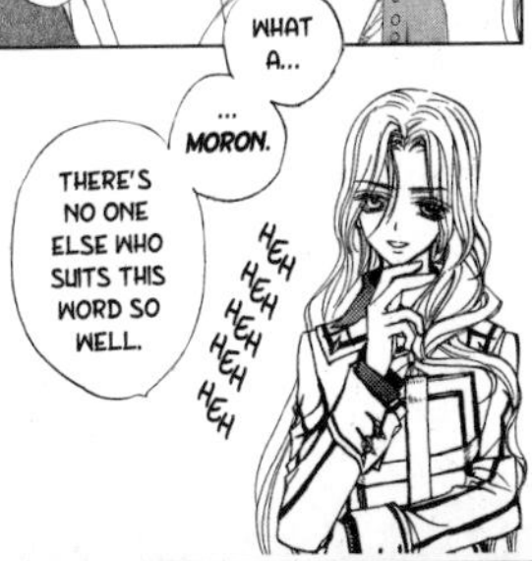
WHAT A...
... MORON.
THERE'S NO ONE ELSE WHO SUITS THIS WORD SO WELL.
HEH HEH HEH HEH HEH

Fighting Ability

A battle of wits using her calm judgment

As an elite vampire, she has the ability to show enemies illusions and manipulate them as she wishes. She can deal with emergencies using her superior analysis of situations and her good judgment.

⬅ She does not condone morons who cause trouble for Kaname-sama...

SCHOOLTIME

Her activities at school!

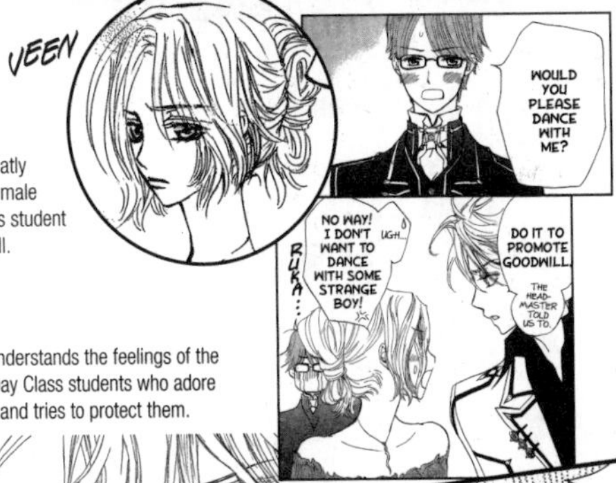
WOULD YOU PLEASE DANCE WITH ME?
VEEN
DO IT TO PROMOTE GOODWILL.
THE HEADMASTER TOLD US TO.
UGH...
NO WAY! I DON'T WANT TO DANCE WITH SOME STRANGE BOY!
RUKA...

➡ She flatly rejects a male Day Class student at the ball.

⬇ She understands the feelings of the female Day Class students who adore Kaname and tries to protect them.

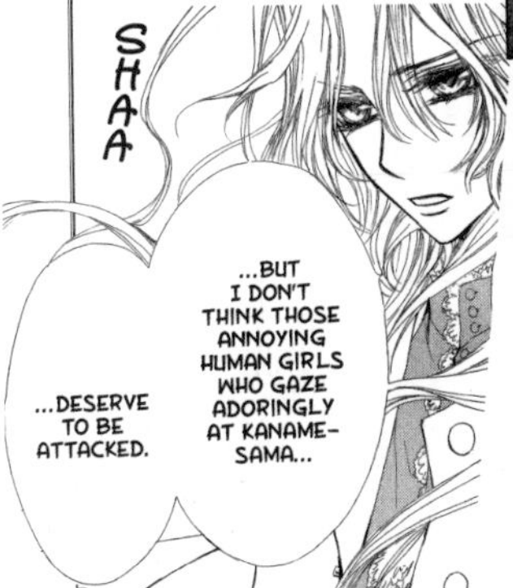
SHAA
...BUT I DON'T THINK THOSE ANNOYING HUMAN GIRLS WHO GAZE ADORINGLY AT KANAME-SAMA...
...DESERVE TO BE ATTACKED.

Classes & Extracurricular Activities

A strong and beautiful flower that's out of reach

A gorgeous look, a bold attitude... The male Day Class students adore Ruka. On the other hand, the female students are scared of her. Some of them do adore her passionately though.

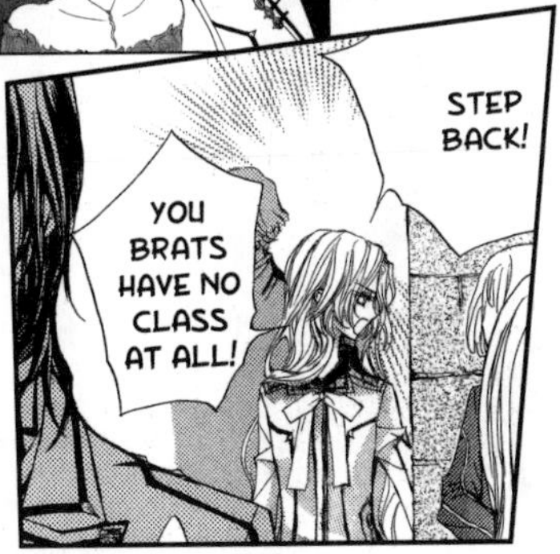
STEP BACK!
YOU BRATS HAVE NO CLASS AT ALL!

⬅ When the Disciplinary Committee isn't on duty, she yells at the female Day Class students who swarm around Kaname.

Rima Toya

The Cool, Bold and Beautiful Model

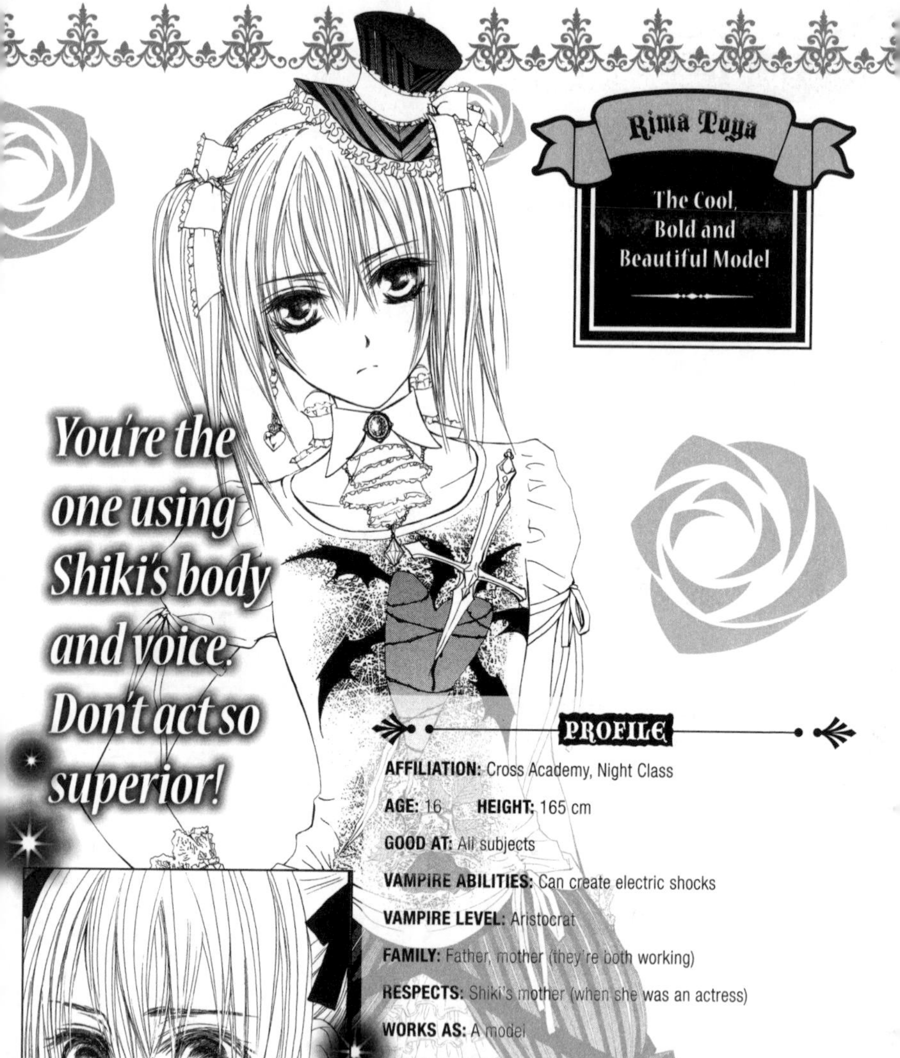
You're the one using Shiki's body and voice. Don't act so superior!

PROFILE

AFFILIATION: Cross Academy, Night Class

AGE: 16 **HEIGHT:** 165 cm

GOOD AT: All subjects

VAMPIRE ABILITIES: Can create electric shocks

VAMPIRE LEVEL: Aristocrat

FAMILY: Father, mother (they're both working)

RESPECTS: Shiki's mother (when she was an actress)

WORKS AS: A model

TASTE IN MEN: "Someone who doesn't make me feel tired."

FAVORITE FASHION: Casual gothic style

HOBBIES: Dressing up

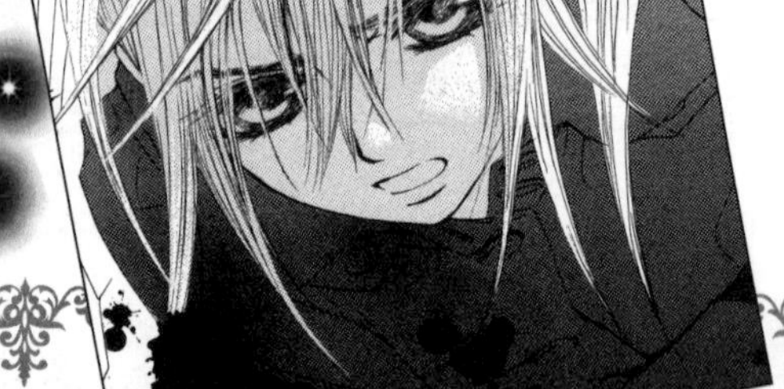

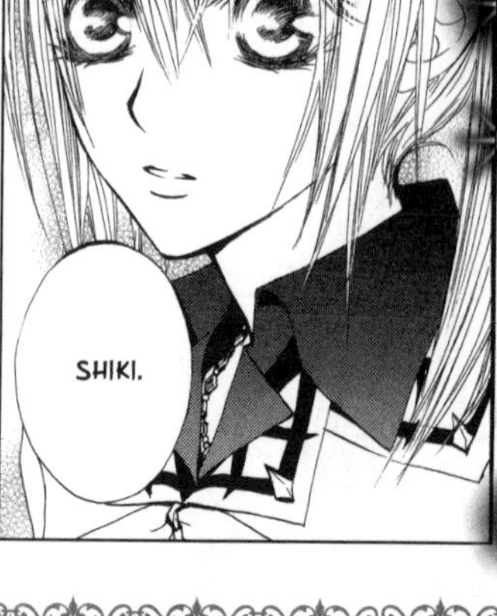
SHIKI.

CHARACTER ANALYSIS

This is what Rima Toya is like!!

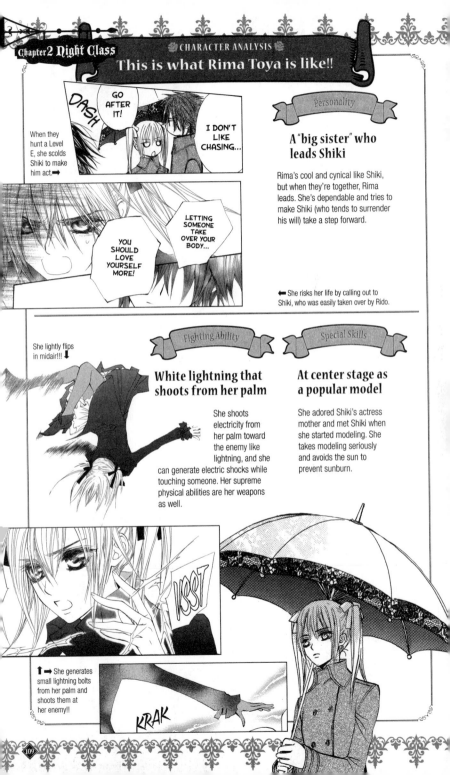

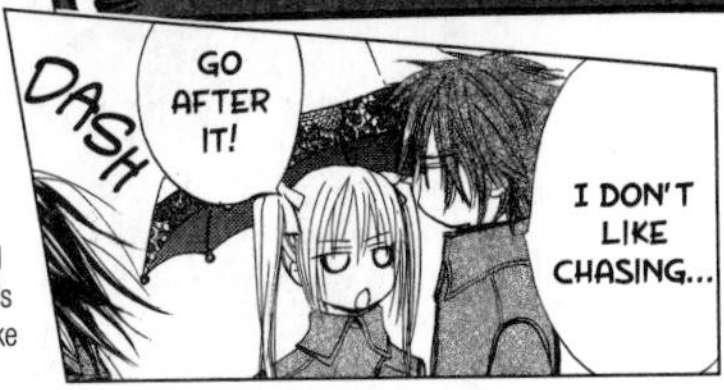
I DON'T LIKE CHASING...
GO AFTER IT!
DASH

When they hunt a Level E, she scolds Shiki to make him act.➡

Personality

A "big sister" who leads Shiki

Rima's cool and cynical like Shiki, but when they're together, Rima leads. She's dependable and tries to make Shiki (who tends to surrender his will) take a step forward.

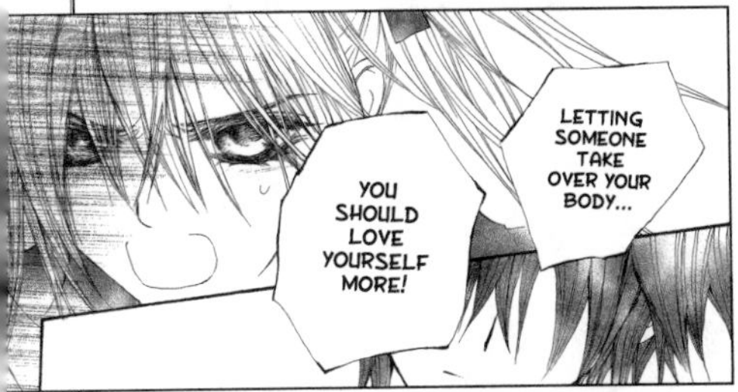
LETTING SOMEONE TAKE OVER YOUR BODY...
YOU SHOULD LOVE YOURSELF MORE!

⬅ She risks her life by calling out to Shiki, who was easily taken over by Rido.

Fighting Ability

White lightning that shoots from her palm

She lightly flips in midair!!! ⬇

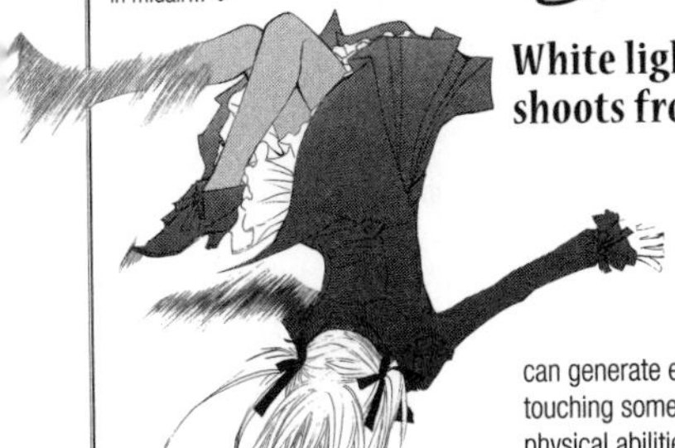

She shoots electricity from her palm toward the enemy like lightning, and she can generate electric shocks while touching someone. Her supreme physical abilities are her weapons as well.

Special Skills

At center stage as a popular model

She adored Shiki's actress mother and met Shiki when she started modeling. She takes modeling seriously and avoids the sun to prevent sunburn.

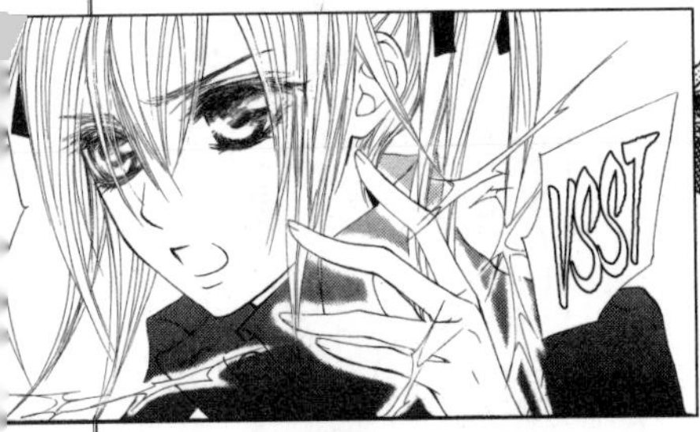
VSSST

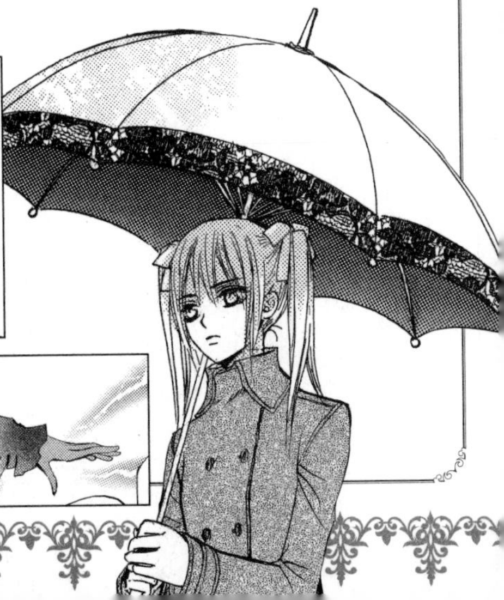

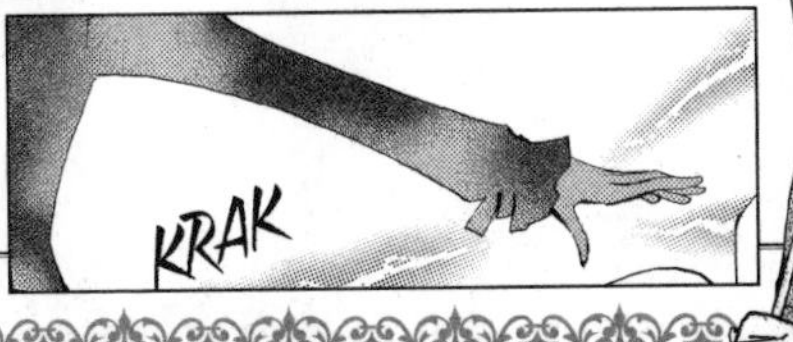
KRAK

⬆ ➡ She generates small lightning bolts from her palm and shoots them at her enemy!!

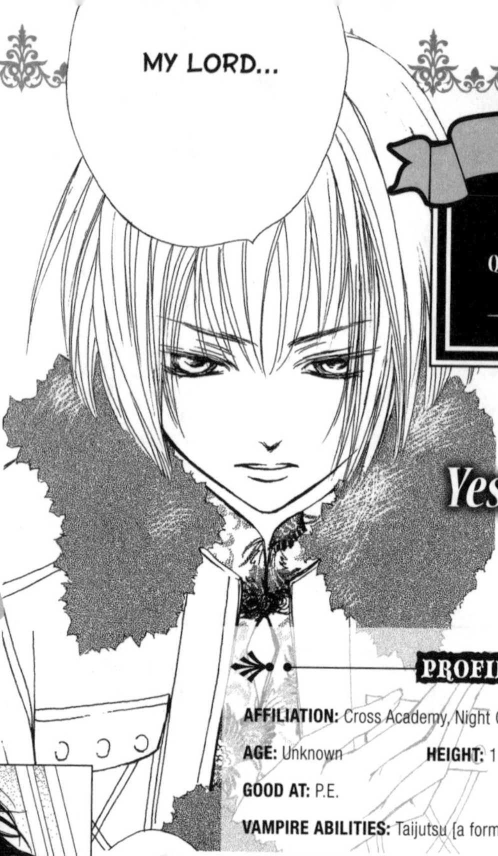
MY LORD...

Seiren

Kaname's Quiet Servant

Yes, my lord...

PROFILE

AFFILIATION: Cross Academy, Night Class

AGE: Unknown **HEIGHT:** 170 cm

GOOD AT: P.E.

VAMPIRE ABILITIES: Taijutsu [a form of mixed martial arts]

VAMPIRE LEVEL: Unknown

FAMILY: Unknown

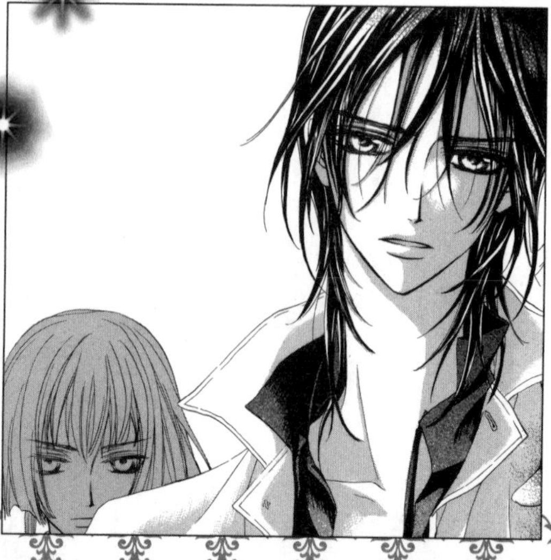

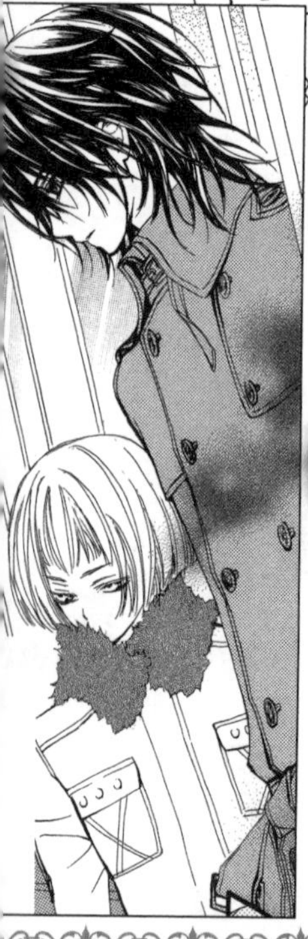

CHARACTER ANALYSIS

This is what Seiren is like!!

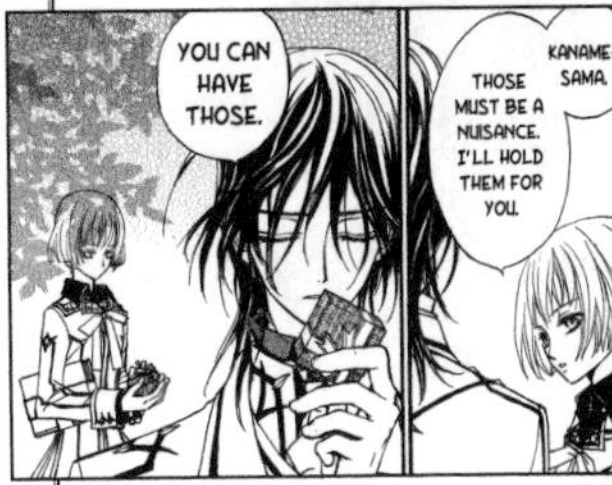
KANAME-SAMA.
THOSE MUST BE A NUISANCE. I'LL HOLD THEM FOR YOU.
YOU CAN HAVE THOSE.

⬆ She deals with Kaname's private life as well. Here, she carries the gifts from the female Day Class students.

⬇ She was investigating Rido's resurrection under Kaname's orders.

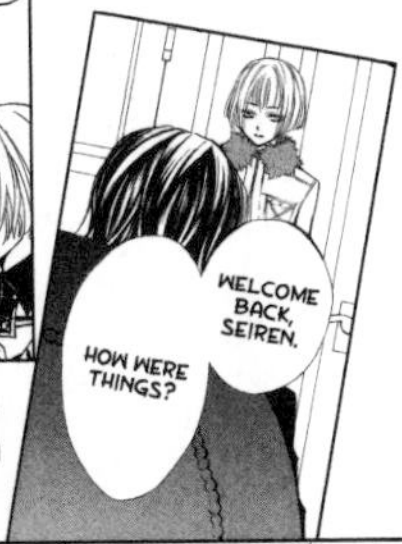
WELCOME BACK, SEIREN.
HOW WERE THINGS?

Personality

A loyal subject who serves Kaname both in public and in private

She waits by Kaname like a shadow and is always on guard. She acts instantly if necessary… Seiren acts only to fulfill Kaname's wishes. She takes pride in faithfully and selflessly fulfilling her missions.

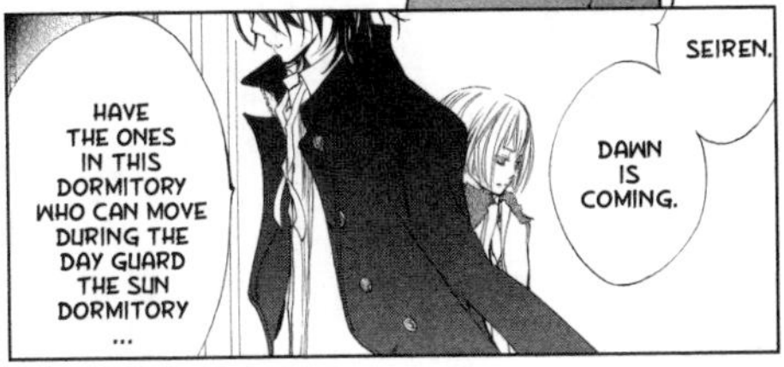
SEIREN.
DAWN IS COMING.
HAVE THE ONES IN THIS DORMITORY WHO CAN MOVE DURING THE DAY GUARD THE SUN DORMITORY …

⬅ When Cross Academy is in danger, she delivers Kaname's instructions to the other Night Class students.

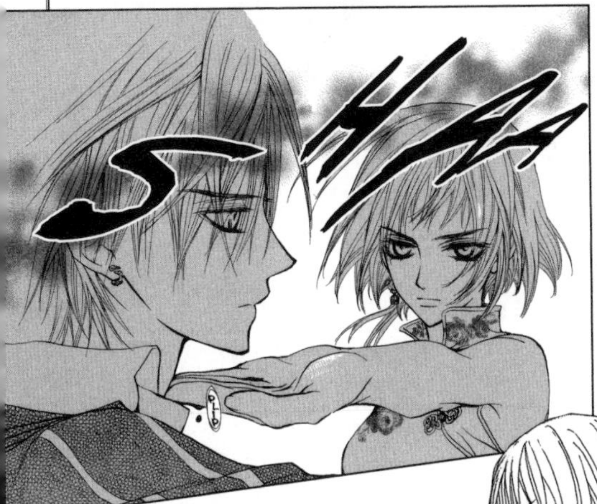
SHAA

⬆ When Zero points his gun at Kaname, she approaches him instantly and thrusts her hand at his throat like a sword.

Fighting Ability

A body that instantly becomes a weapon

She does not possess special powers, but she has superior physical strength that is particular to vampires. Her trained body itself is a powerful weapon. She can instantly get close to those who try to harm Kaname and can deal a fatal blow with her bare hand.

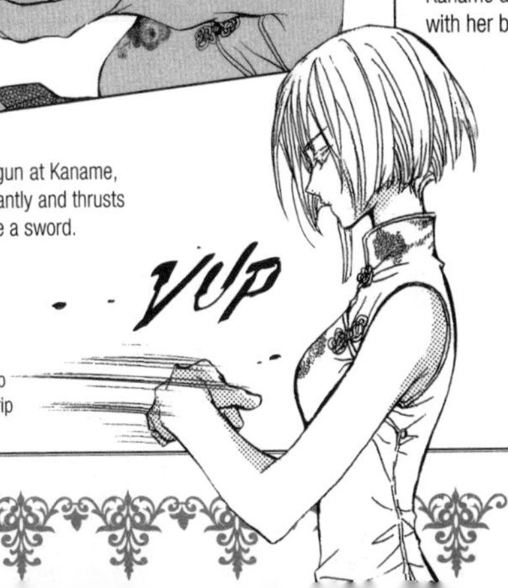
VUP

Her trained hands are sharp like a knife and can easily rip open human skin. ➡

Maria Kurenai

The Girl Who Offered Her Body to "Kuruizaki-Hime"

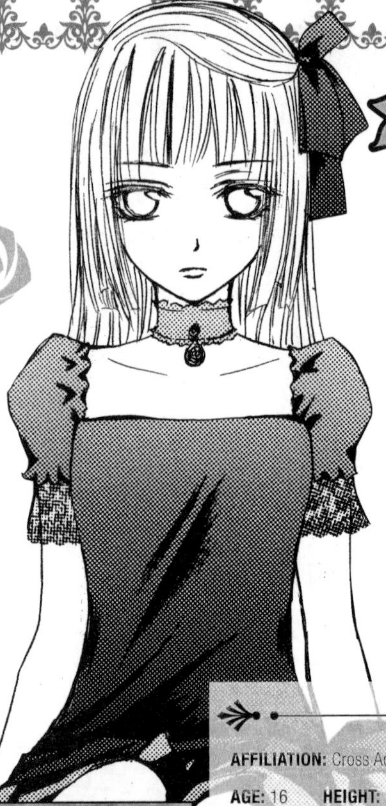

I want to tell you the truth...

PROFILE

AFFILIATION: Cross Academy, Night Class

AGE: 16 **HEIGHT:** 152 cm

GOOD AT: Home economics (making sweets)

VAMPIRE ABILITIES: Uses weapons to fight

VAMPIRE LEVEL: Aristocrat

FAMILY: Father (author), mother

TASTE IN MEN: "Ichiru"

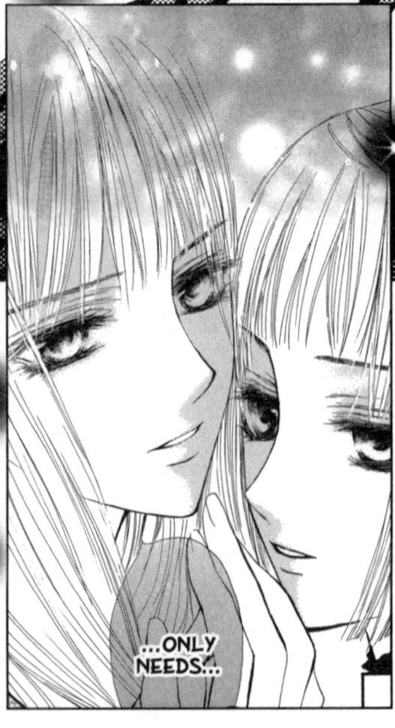
...ONLY NEEDS...

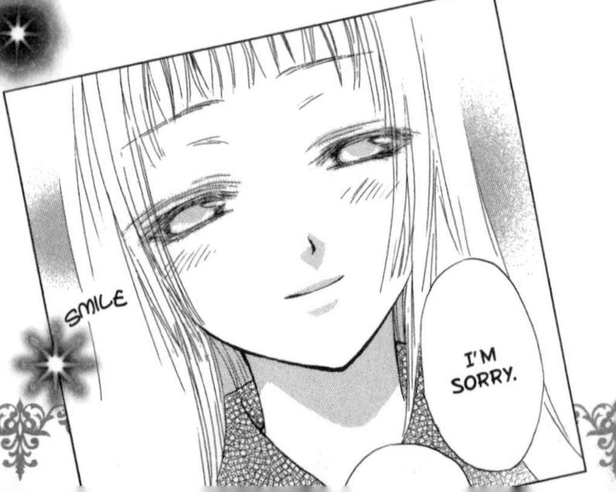
SMILE
I'M SORRY.

CHARACTER ANALYSIS

This is what Maria Kurenai is like!!

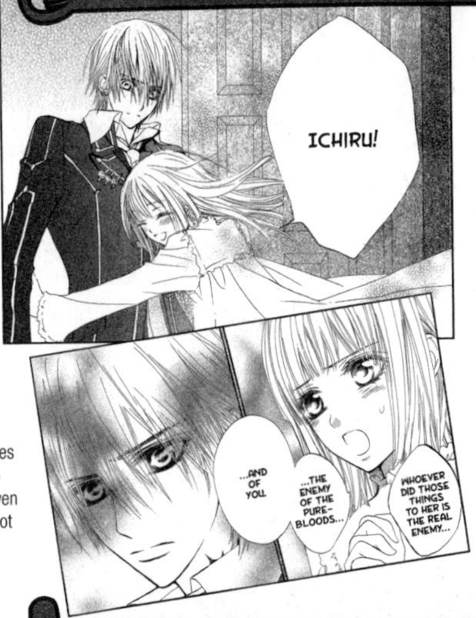
ICHIRU!
WHOEVER DID THOSE THINGS TO HER IS THE REAL ENEMY...
...THE ENEMY OF THE PURE-BLOODS...
...AND OF YOU.

She mistakes Zero for Ichiru. She spent time with Ichiru in the past and likes him.➡

When she wakes up, she tries to tell the truth even though she's not feeling well.➡

Personality

A pure and honest young lady

She is related to the Hio family, a distinguished pureblood family. Because she was frail, she was well taken care of. Her personality is honest and kind. She did not hesitate at all in offering her body to Shizuka and did not ask for anything in return. She is strong inside and tells Yuki and Zero about the existence of their true enemy.

SCHOOLTIME

Her activities at school!

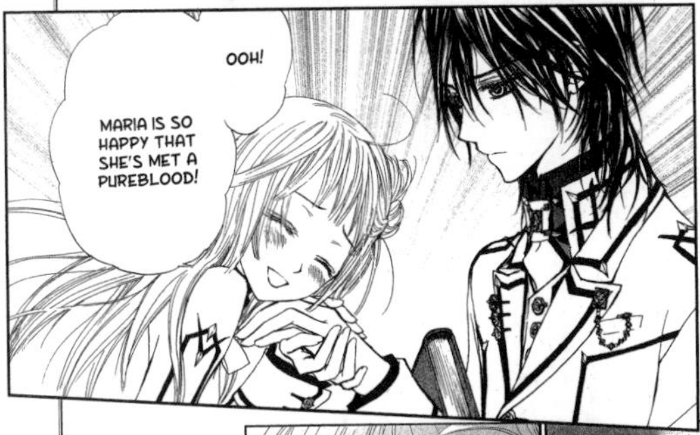
OOH!
MARIA IS SO HAPPY THAT SHE'S MET A PUREBLOOD!

A free and bold princess?!

The Maria that most Cross Academy students saw was the Maria taken over by Shizuka Hio. Therefore, she was bold and fearless at the academy. She was a mysterious girl who had a special aura. She approached the pureblood Kaname like a fan. She also ran to the café terrace where the Day Class students were. Her actions made the people around her nervous.

⬆ When she sees Kaname, she runs toward him and holds his hand. She's enjoying pretending to be an ordinary vampire.

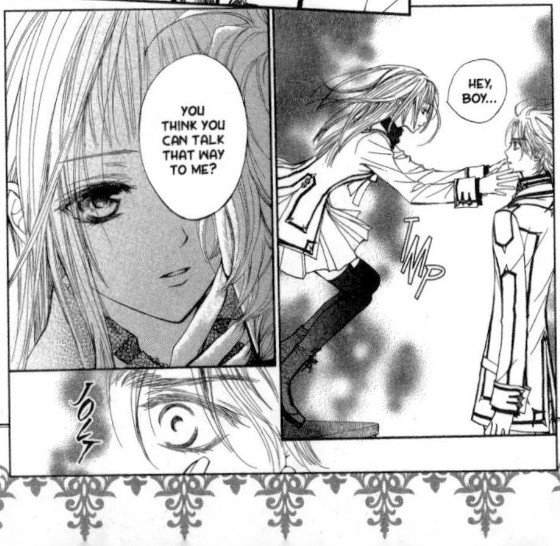
HEY, BOY...
TMP
YOU THINK YOU CAN TALK THAT WAY TO ME?
JOLT

⬅ She lightly warns Aido, who acted insolent. She displays her pureblood aura.

TAKE ME TO THE ~~MARTIAL ARTS TOURNAMENT~~ BALL!

Get Close to the Night Class... ♥ FEATURE 1

LET'S TAKE THE TEST WITH YUKI!

Heart-Racing Partner-Finding Test

The ball that makes your heart beat fast! Who's your perfect escort...?

START HERE!!

1 How was your homework today?

...

Ⓐ Finished it all, no problem. → to ④

Ⓑ I... I'll do it later. → to ②

2 To dance the waltz, the girl first...

Ⓐ Moves her left foot backward. → to ⑬

Ⓑ Moves her right foot backward. → to ⑩

WILL YOU DO ME THE HONOR OF DANCING WITH ME...

3 He made a bad joke! You...

Ⓐ S-Simply smile. → to ⑫

Ⓑ Drop your jaw. → to ④

4 Do you eat your favorite food first?

Ⓐ Yes. → to ⑤

Ⓑ No. → to ⑧

5 What is your blood type?

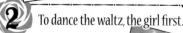

Ⓐ B or AB. → to ⑭

Ⓑ A or O. → to ⑥

HEY BABY, WHAT'S YOUR BLOOD TYPE?
Red Card
Um... type O. ♥

6 Can you endure a long silence?

Ⓐ Yes. → to ⑧

Ⓑ No. → to ⑦

...

7 Actually... Your childhood memories are hazy.

Ⓐ Yes. → TYPE A

Ⓑ No. → to ⑨

8 Animals like you.

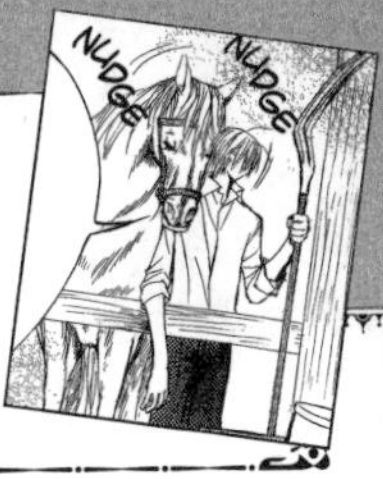
NUDGE
NUDGE

◆A Yes.
→ to ⑪

◆B No.
→ to ⑭

9 You don't catch colds easily.

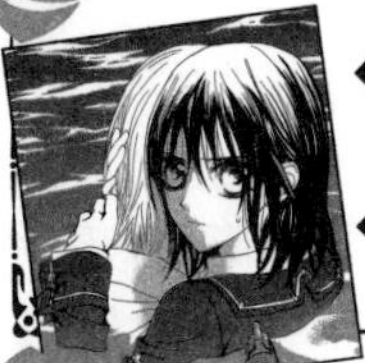

◆A Yes.
→ **TYPE D**

◆B No.
→ to ⑫

10 Which song is more appropriate for ballroom dancing?

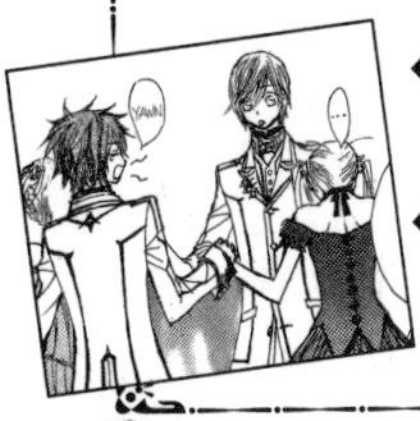
YAWN
...

◆A "Macarena"
→ to ③

◆B "I Kiss Your Hand, Madam"
→ to ④

11 You're pretty good at cooking.♥

◆A Yes.
→ to ⑮

◆B No.
→ to ⑭

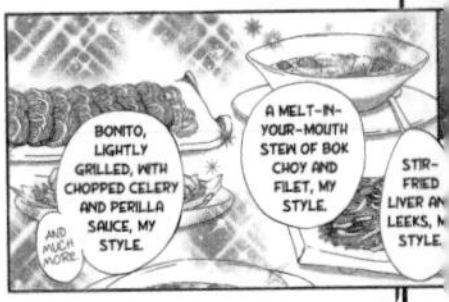
A MELT-IN-YOUR-MOUTH STEW OF BOK CHOY AND FILET, MY STYLE.
BONITO, LIGHTLY GRILLED, WITH CHOPPED CELERY AND PERILLA SAUCE, MY STYLE.
AND MUCH MORE
STIR-FRIED LIVER AN LEEKS, M STYLE

12 You visit the guys' room on your school trip! If a guy says, "Let's have a pillow fight," you...?

◆A Enjoy it.
→ **TYPE B**

◆B Something's not...quite right...
→ to ⑧

13 Ah!! Shoot... You stepped on his foot!! What do you do?

◆A Smile and quietly apologize.
→ to ③

◆B Run away because you're so embarrassed.
→ to ⑯

14 When a mosquito bites you...

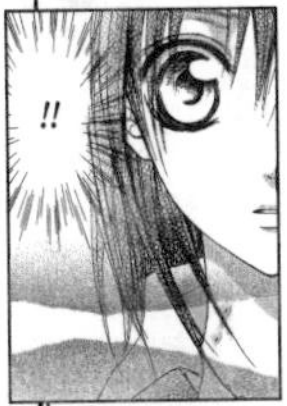
!!

◆A You notice it right away.
→ **TYPE E**

◆B You notice after it starts itching.
→ **TYPE C**

15 Is the top of your head slightly flat?

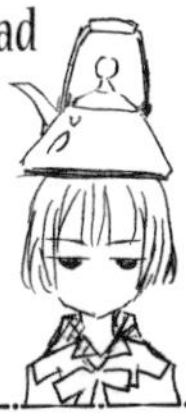

◆A Yes.
→ **TYPE C**

◆B No.
→ **TYPE D**

16 Perhaps you should just work behind the scenes.

*Why don't you take the test one more time?

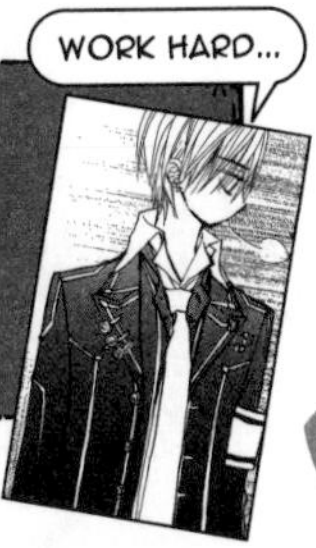
WORK HARD...

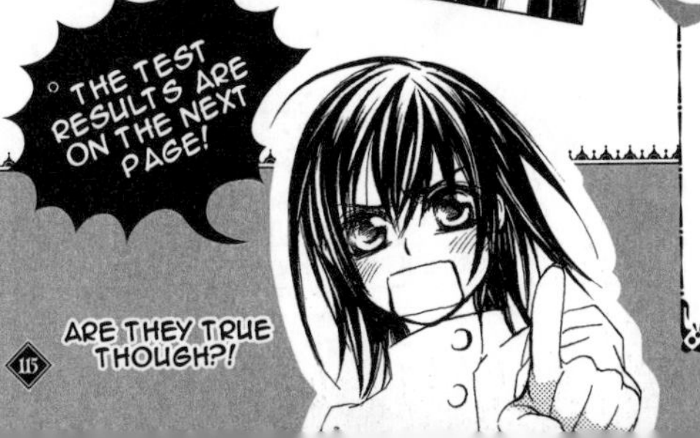
THE TEST RESULTS ARE ON THE NEXT PAGE!
ARE THEY TRUE THOUGH?!

Test Results for the Partner-Finding Test

Did you finish taking the test on the previous pages? Who will escort you to the ball?

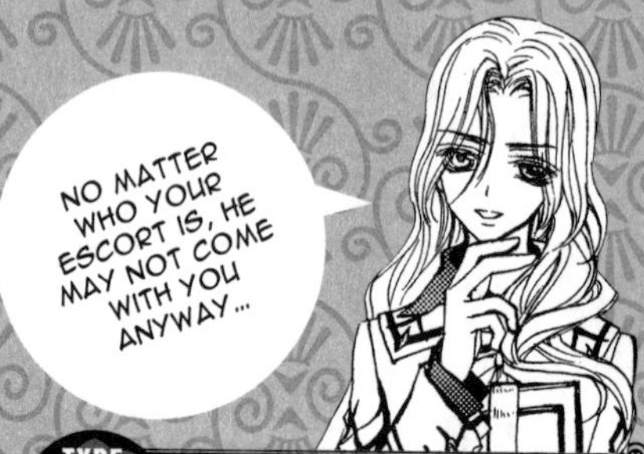
NO MATTER WHO YOUR ESCORT IS, HE MAY NOT COME WITH YOU ANYWAY...

TYPE A Kaname Kuran

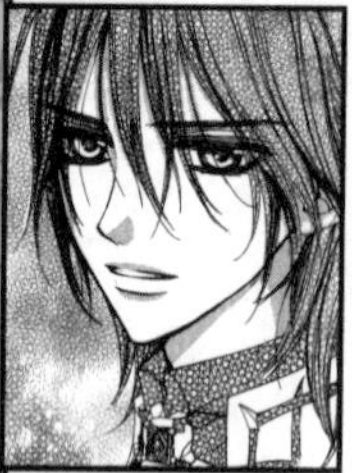

BASIC PERSONALITY

Your childhood memories are hazy... Wait... Isn't that me? You're a bit laid back, but you're good at dancing the waltz, so you'll be able to dance well with Kaname. Probably.

LUCKY ITEM: A rose corsage

LUCKY COLOR: Pale pink

TYPE B Takuma Ichijo

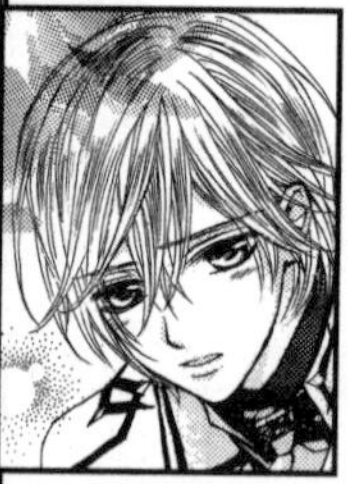

BASIC PERSONALITY

You're always smiling and cheerful, so Ichijo is perfect for you. You'll be able to spend some quiet time together. But if he starts dancing to "Macarena," tell him no quietly.

LUCKY ITEM: Fashion magazines

LUCKY COLOR: Sky blue

TYPE C Hanabusa Aido

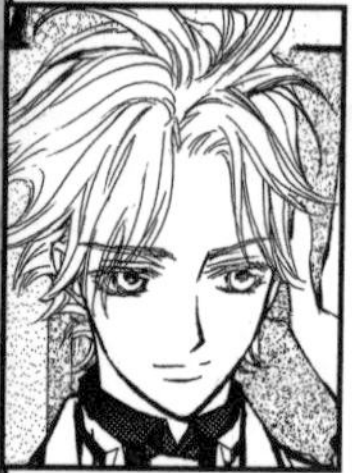

BASIC PERSONALITY

You'll be able to tame Aido by putting a bucket on your head too and by cooking for him. Compliment him well and have him escort you.★

LUCKY ITEM: Lavender perfume

LUCKY COLOR: Sunflower yellow

TYPE D Akatsuki Kain

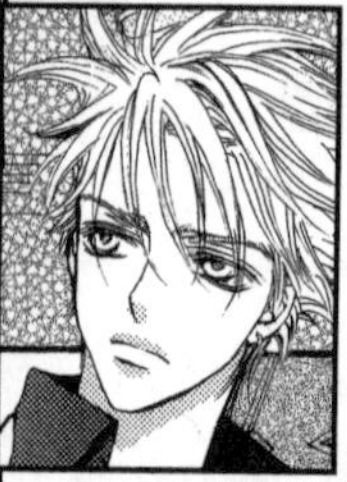

BASIC PERSONALITY

You have a mild and stable personality, so Kain, who has the most common sense, is perfect for you. If he becomes the victim of circumstances, console him with your tenderness.

LUCKY ITEM: Lace handkerchief

LUCKY COLOR: Dark green

TYPE E Senri Shiki

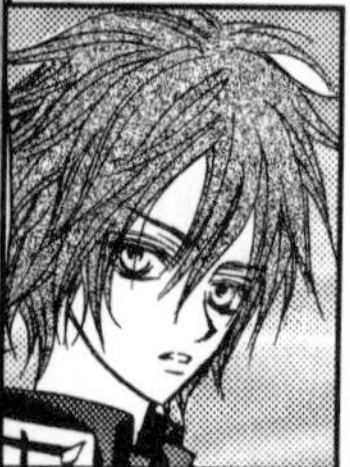

BASIC PERSONALITY

You're cool and mysterious and have a proud aura. Shiki will somehow listen to you. People will pay attention to your wonderful dancing?

LUCKY ITEM: Chocolate

LUCKY COLOR: Purple

Get Close to the Night Class... ♥ FEATURE 2

The Basics of Society Circles

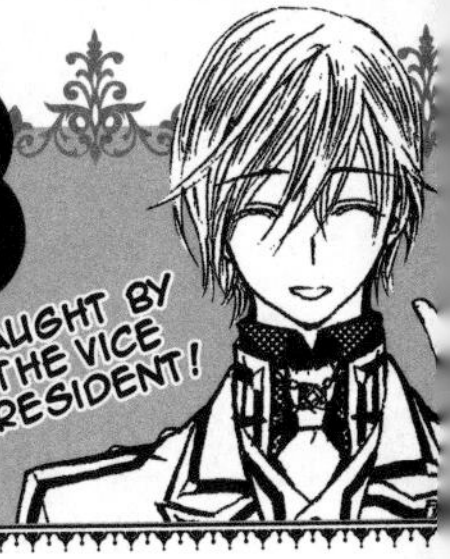
TAUGHT BY THE VICE PRESIDENT!

Of course, after the ball is...

The Soirée ♥ Before You Go...

Society circles have various strict rules. Please read the following before your debut.

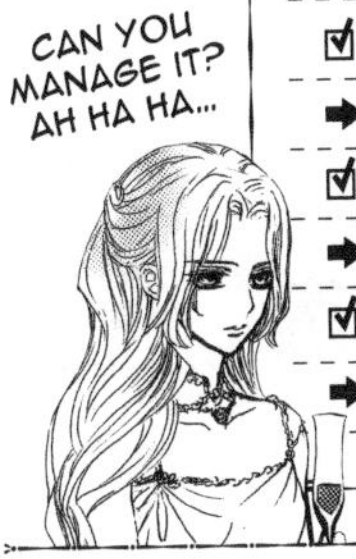
CAN YOU MANAGE IT? AH HA HA...

Let's Talk Like This

- ☑ You like it?
- ➡ How did you like it?
- ☑ They're here!
- ➡ They have arrived!
- ☑ Eat this.
- ➡ Please have some.

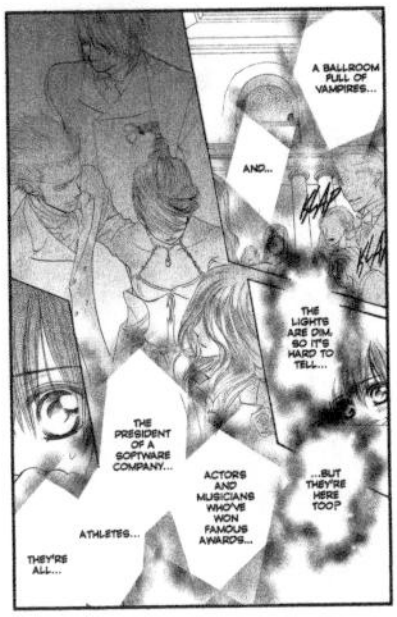
A BALLROOM FULL OF VAMPIRES...
AND...
THE LIGHTS ARE DIM, SO IT'S HARD TO TELL...
...BUT THEY'RE HERE TOO?
ACTORS AND MUSICIANS WHO'VE WON FAMOUS AWARDS...
THE PRESIDENT OF A SOFTWARE COMPANY...
ATHLETES...
THEY'RE ALL...

Use polite language when talking to your seniors ♥

The aristocrats who attend a soirée are all very proud. You'll be in trouble if you speak the wrong way. Use the proper honorific language.

⬅ Famous people from every walk of life are there.

GOOD

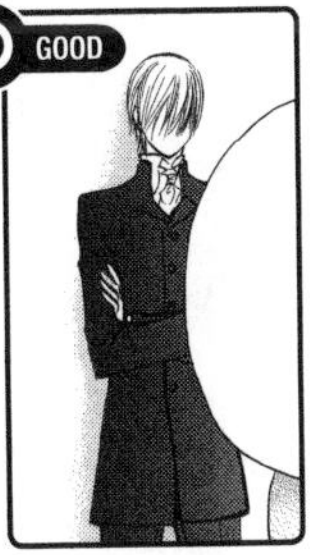

⬆ Kiryu's frock coat is acceptable.

NO GOOD

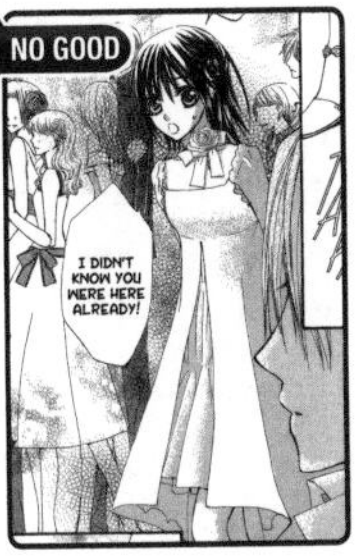
I DIDN'T KNOW YOU WERE HERE ALREADY!

⬆ Yuki's dress is for an afternoon party...

GOOD

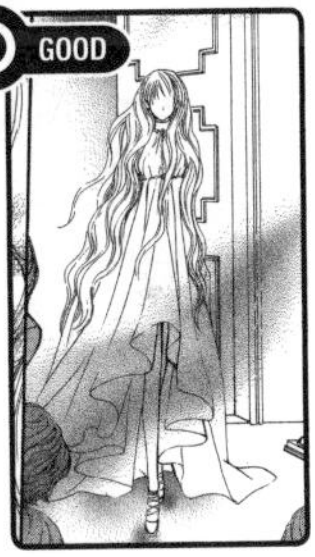

⬆ Sara-sama's dress is perfect. She's beautiful...

Men and women wear formal attire

At an evening party, women wear evening dresses, and men wear frock coats or tuxedos. Women's dresses must be long, and you must also wear gloves. A soirée is a little more high-class than the Cross Academy ball, so be careful.

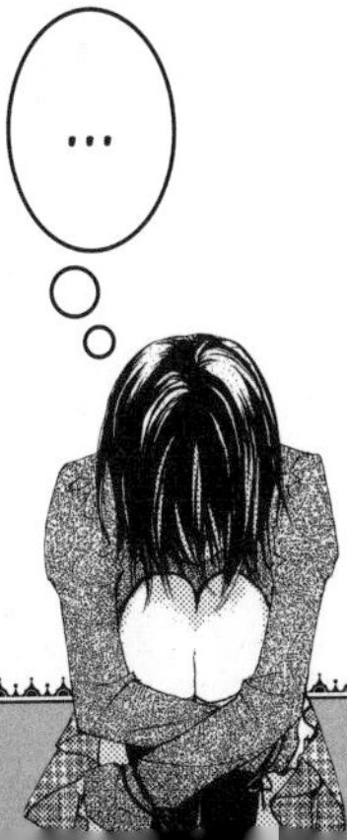
...

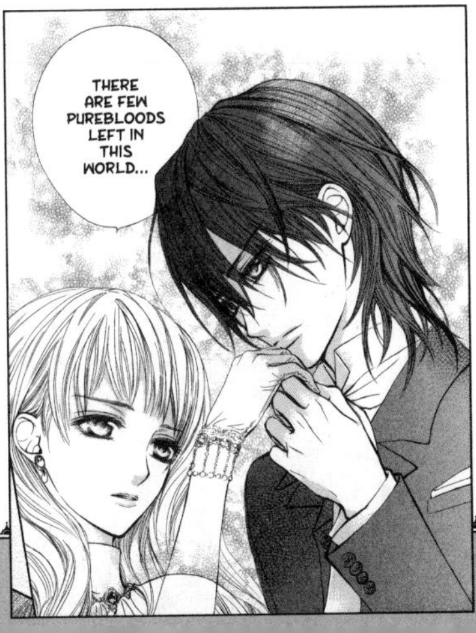
THERE ARE FEW PUREBLOODS LEFT IN THIS WORLD...

If you don't have a partner...

You're expected to attend a social party with a partner. A soirée is where vampires meet and get to know each other, so you might feel sad if you're forced to see a beautiful couple...

⬅ Kaname-sama looks wonderful kissing her hand.

Get Close to the Night Class...♥ FEATURE 3

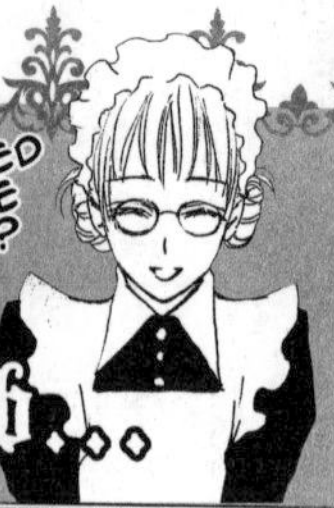
REVEALED BY THE MAID?

The maid witnessed it!!

The Truth About the Kettle Club...

Everyone in the Night Class claims they're noble aristocrats, but the truth about their hidden lives is...?

TRUTH 1 Fighting = Putting thumb tacks in shoes

They're supposed to have amazing super powers, but using thumb tacks...!! They must be fine even if they bleed.

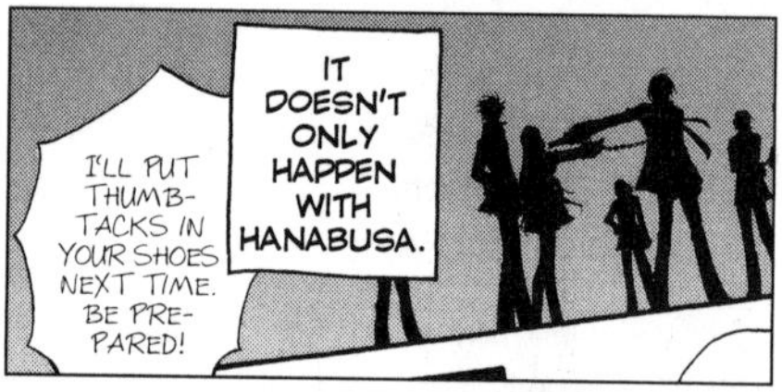
IT DOESN'T ONLY HAPPEN WITH HANABUSA.
I'LL PUT THUMB-TACKS IN YOUR SHOES NEXT TIME. BE PRE-PARED!

⬆ Ruka-sama's parting shot. She means it.

TRUTH 2 His backpack

Does Hanabusa-sama like picking edible wild plants or gathering firewood...??

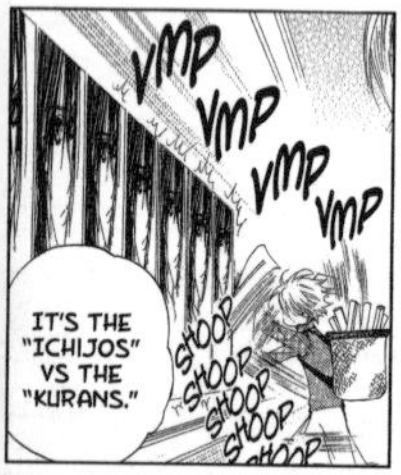
VMP VMP VMP VMP
IT'S THE "ICHIJOS" VS THE "KURANS."
SHOOP SHOOP SHOOP SHOOP SHOOP

⬅ During the election of the Ichijos vs. the Kurans. Hanabusa-sama puts up posters very quickly.

TRUTH 3 Pocket money in a coin purse

When Ruka-sama came to buy Kaname-sama's posters. A coin purse is easy to use...

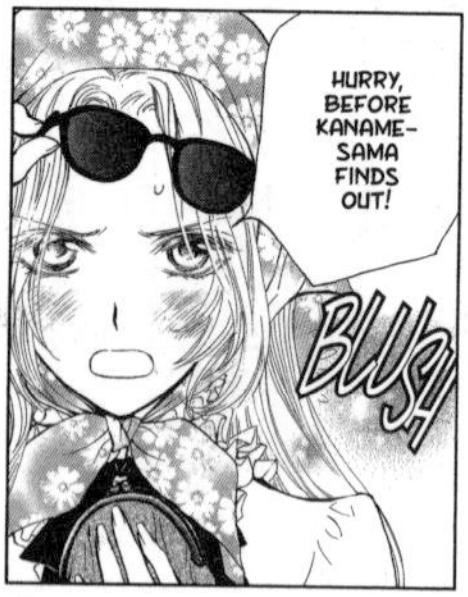
HURRY, BEFORE KANAME-SAMA FINDS OUT!
BLUSH

The way she wears her scarf is Showa era-like. How lovely! ➡

TRUTH 4 The detectives of justice?

These people want to form a group whenever several of them gather...

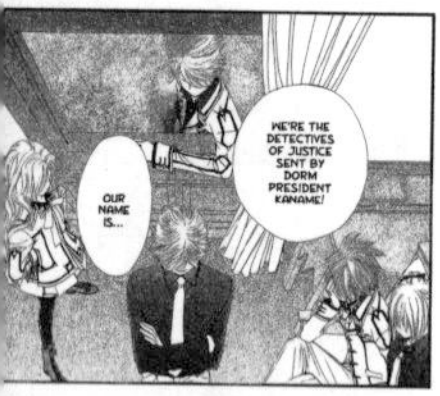
WE'RE THE DETECTIVES OF JUSTICE SENT BY DORM PRESIDENT KANAME!
OUR NAME IS...

⬅ They're investigating the incident in which a Day Class student was attacked by a vampire. Everyone's saying this and that, but they're all posing grandly. Do they like pretending...?

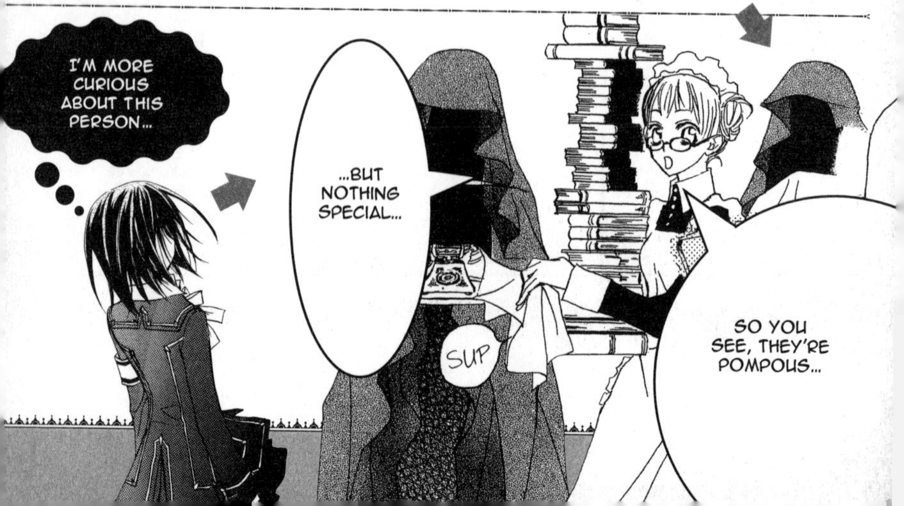
SO YOU SEE, THEY'RE POMPOUS...
...BUT NOTHING SPECIAL...
SUP
I'M MORE CURIOUS ABOUT THIS PERSON...

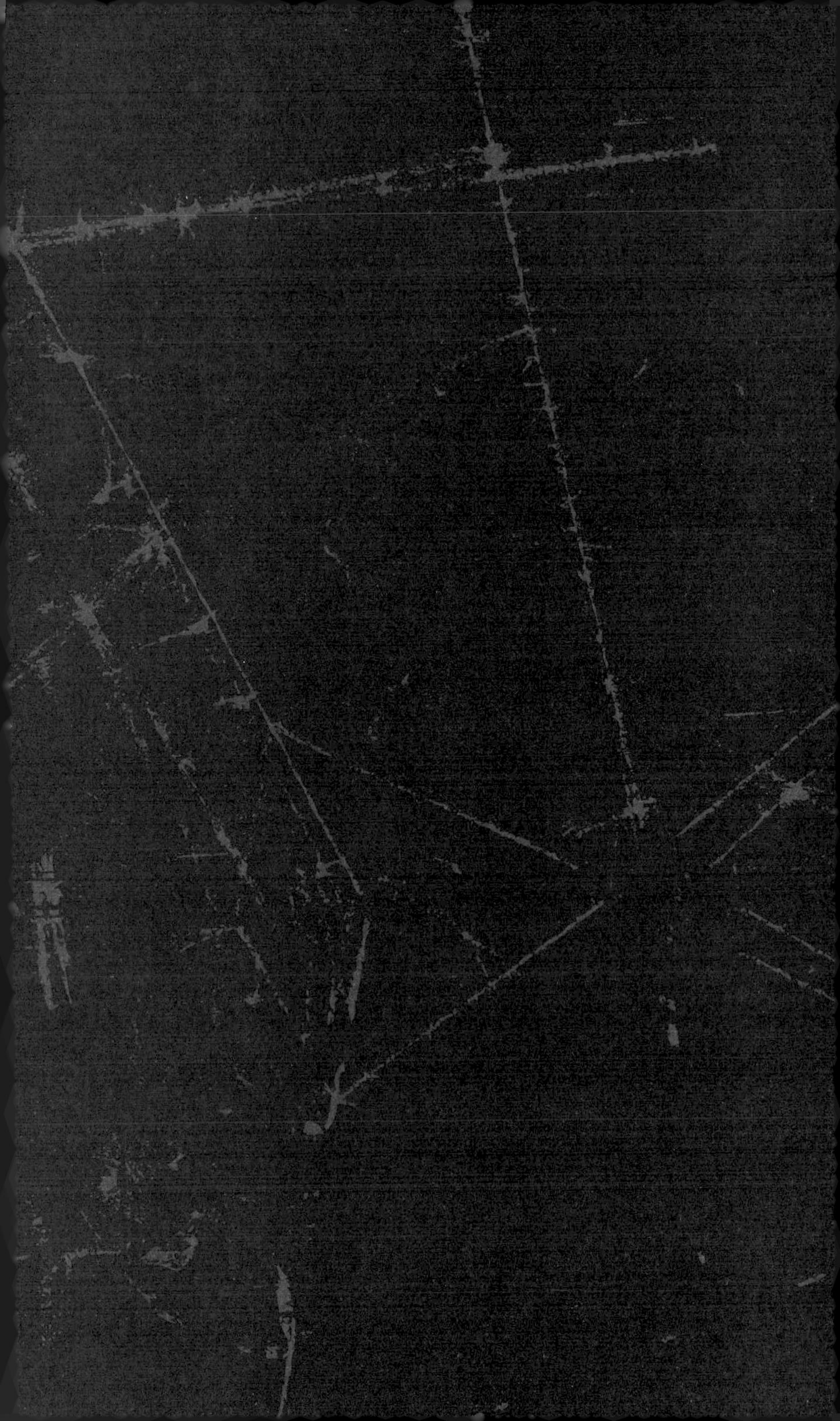

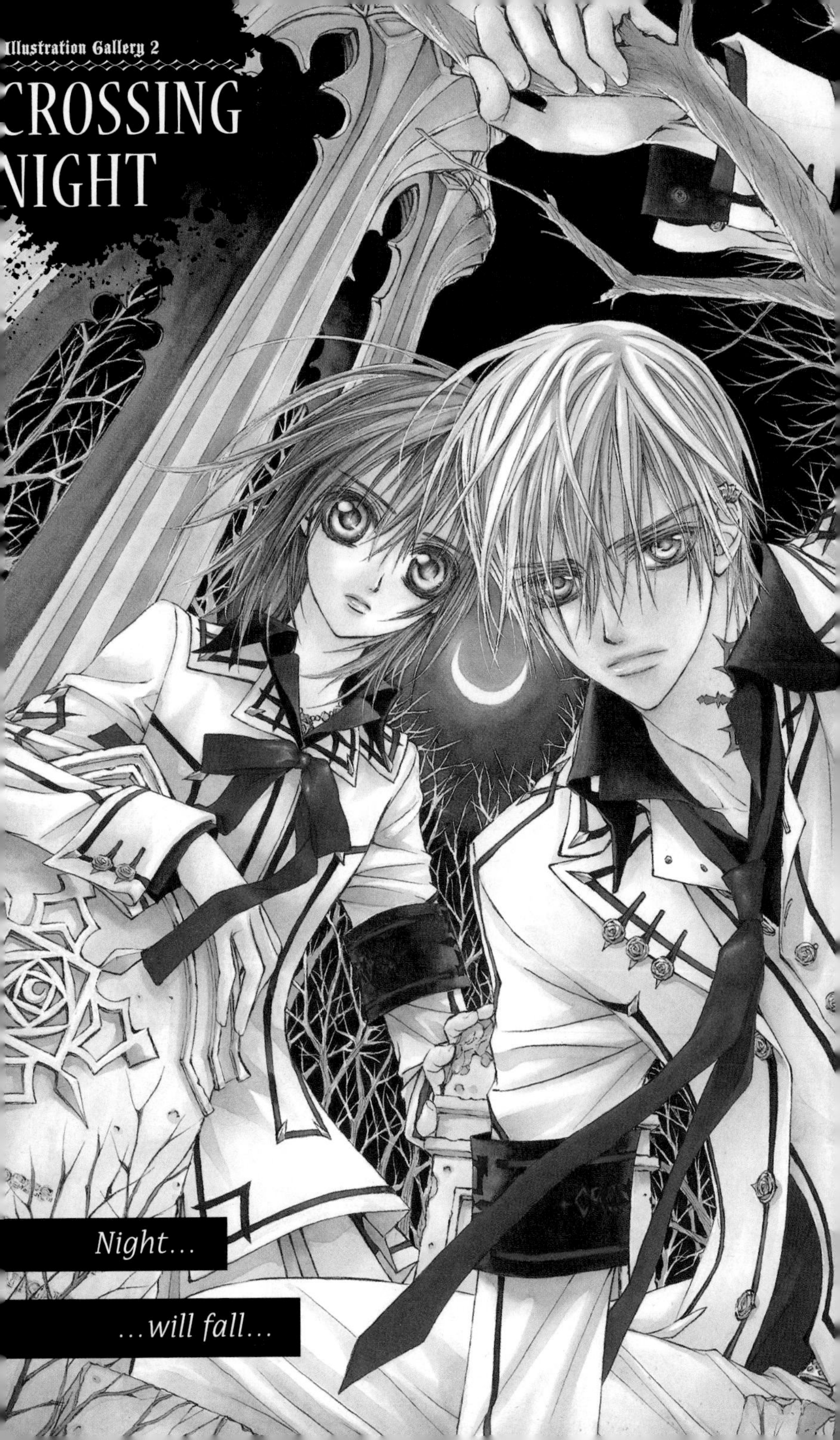
Illustration Gallery 2
CROSSING NIGHT
Night...
...will fall...

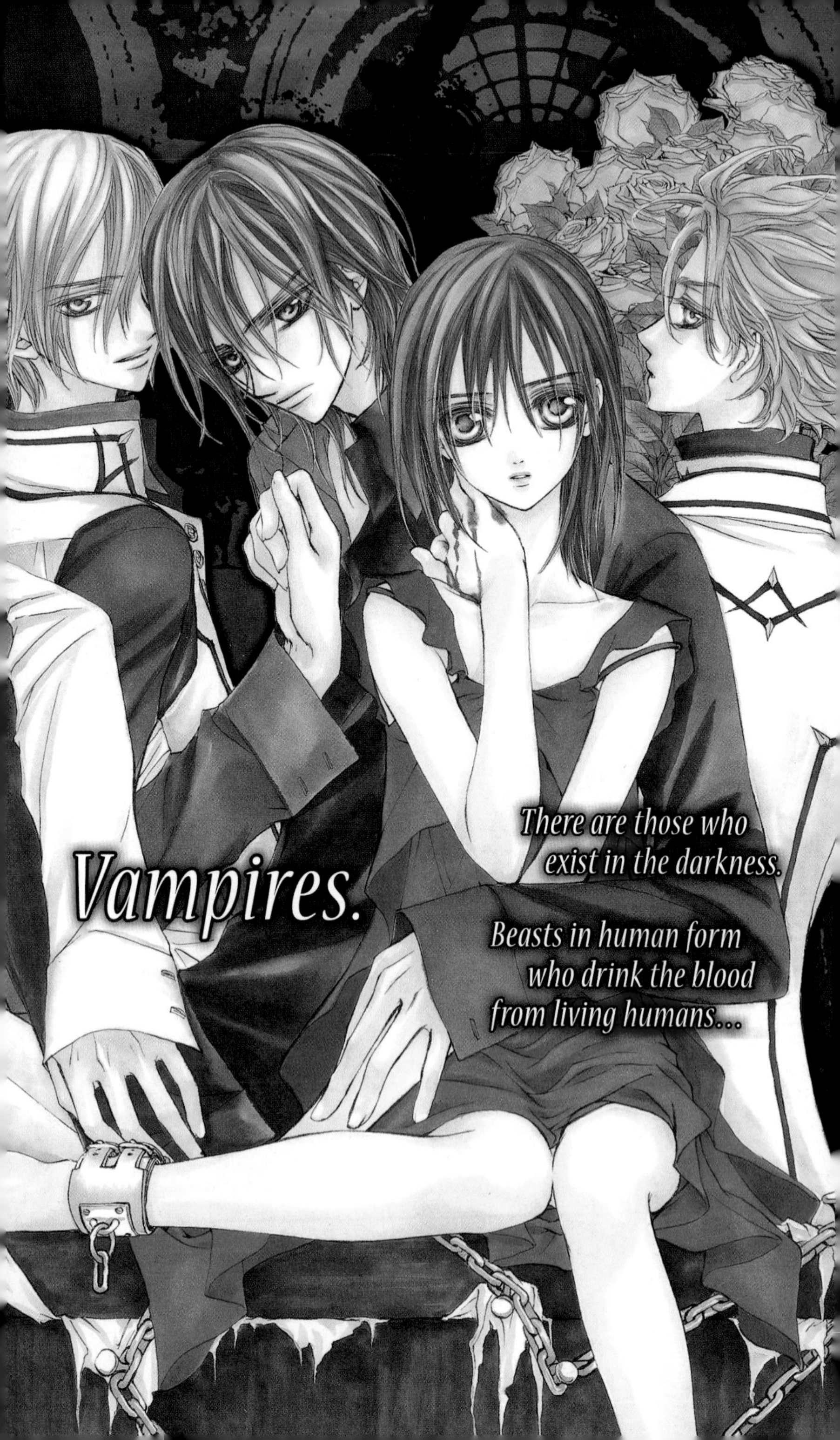
Vampires.
There are those who exist in the darkness.
Beasts in human form who drink the blood from living humans...

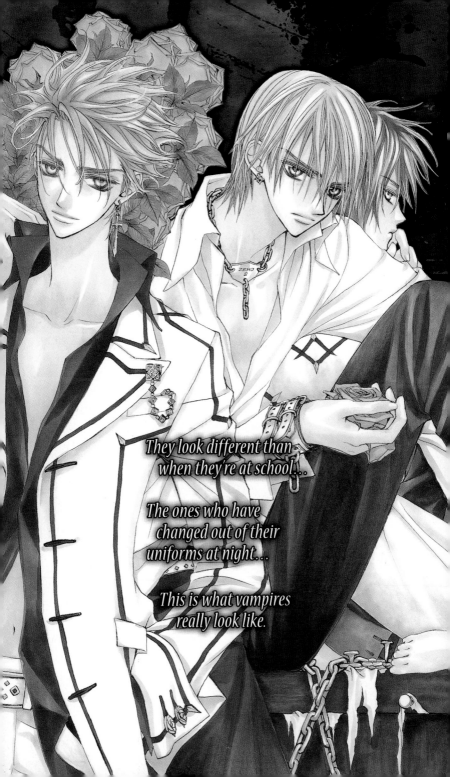

They look different than
when they're at school...

The ones who have
changed out of their
uniforms at night...

This is what vampires
really look like.

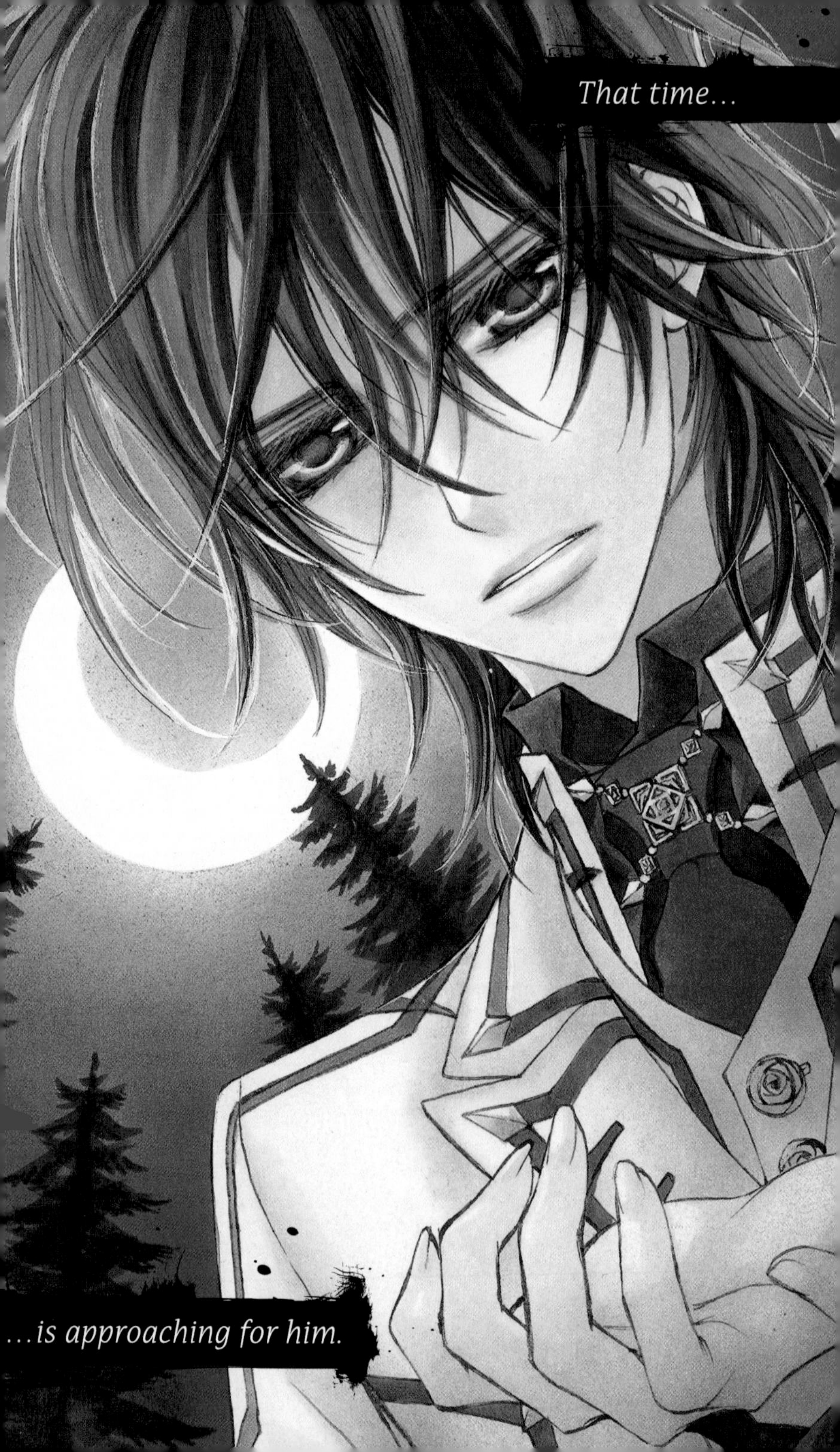
That time...
...is approaching for him.

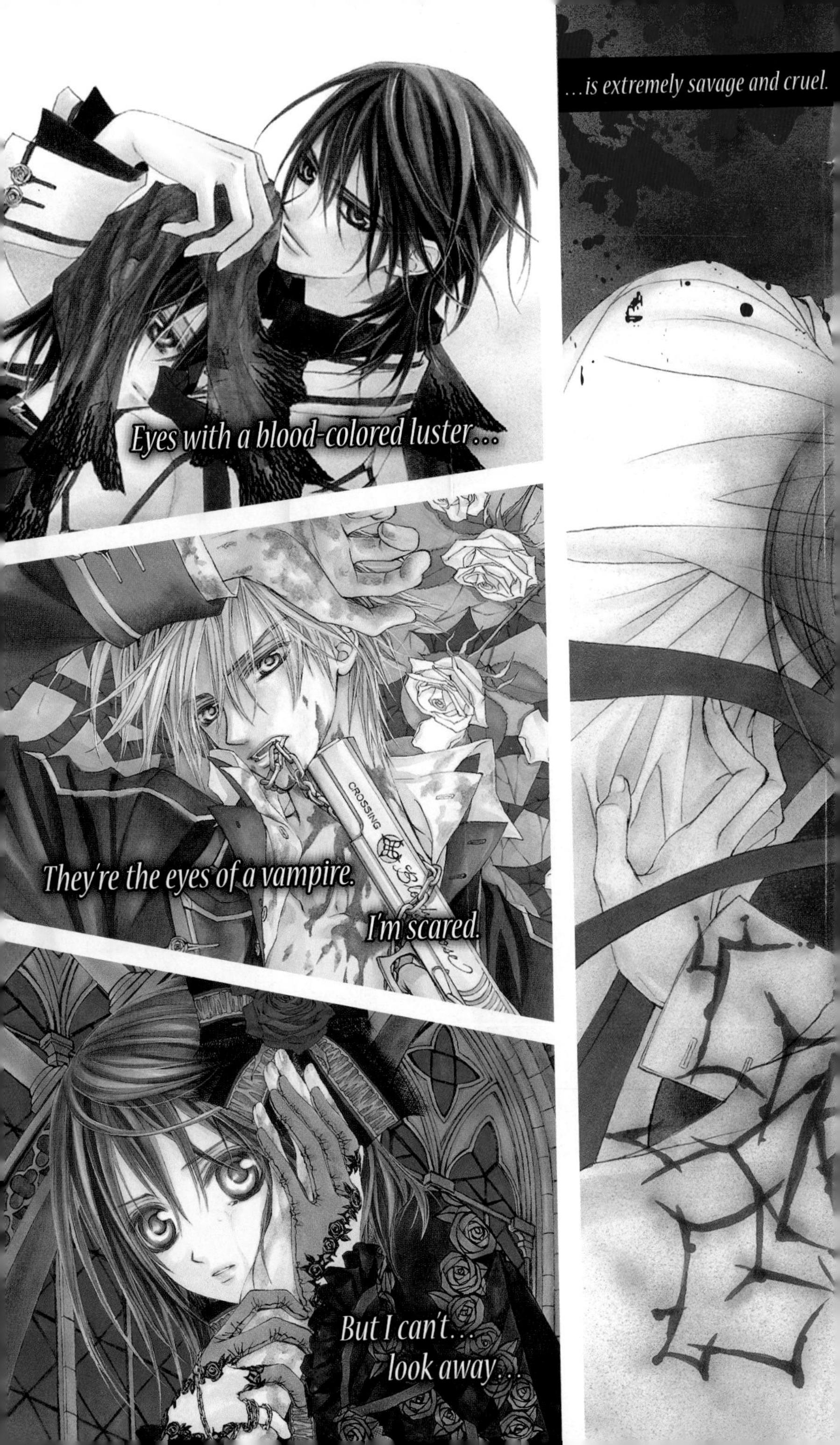
...is extremely savage and cruel.
Eyes with a blood-colored luster...
They're the eyes of a vampire.
CROSSING
I'm scared.
But I can't...
look away...

Has the girl...

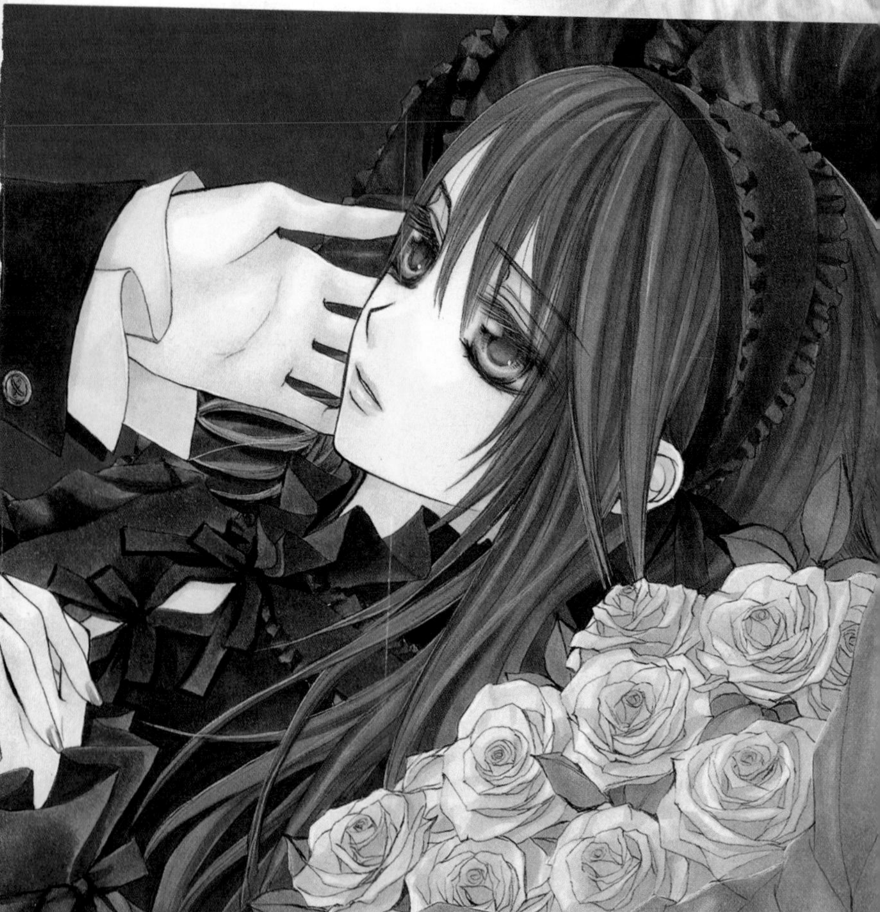

...woken from her nap?

VAMPIRE KNIGHT

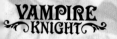

Intermission
Vampire Society

The World of Vampires That Humans Don't Know About

Vampires are residents of the world of darkness. We get close to their unknown biology, their mysterious society and secrets of hidden incidents!!

There are very few civilians who know the truth about the vampire world...

Vampire Report 1

The Biology of Vampires

We examine the characteristics of the beings called vampires.
What are the similarities and differences between vampires and humans?

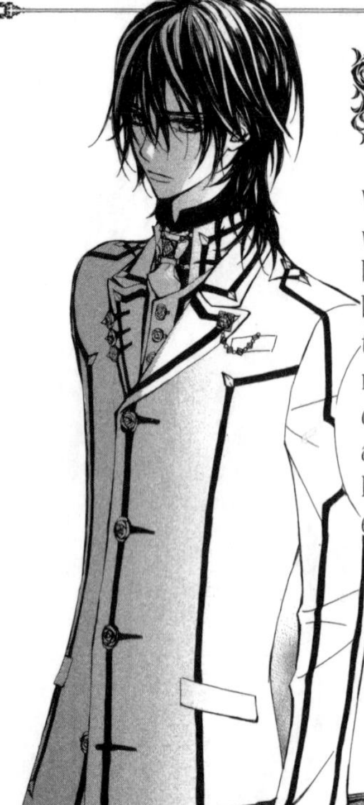

What are vampires?

Vampires were born in ancient times, and they are beings who are different from humans. They look like humans, but their canine teeth have developed into fangs to drink blood. Their vitality is amazingly strong. They live long, and there are those who have been living for over 3,000 years. In recent years, there are vampires who have taken advantage of their attractive looks, physical abilities and brains to work among humans in fields like sports, politics and business. Because vampires are superior in all areas, they can hide their existence from humans.

Looks — Generally beautiful

A vampire's attractive looks are one of its traits. Their beauty attracts humans, which allows them to drink blood from humans as they please.

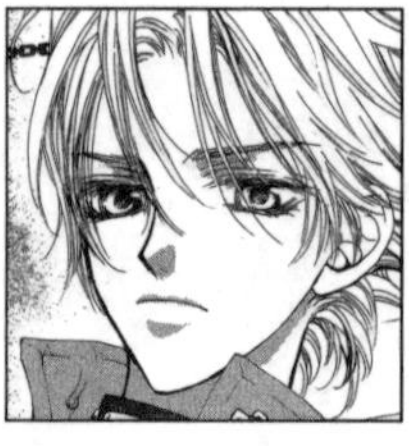

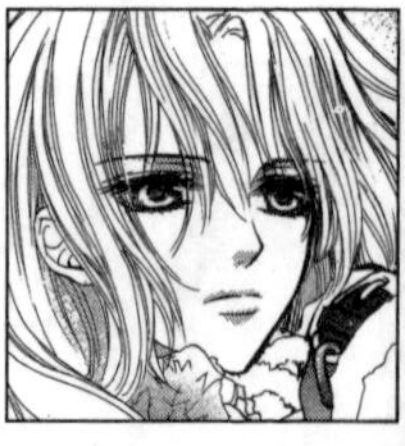

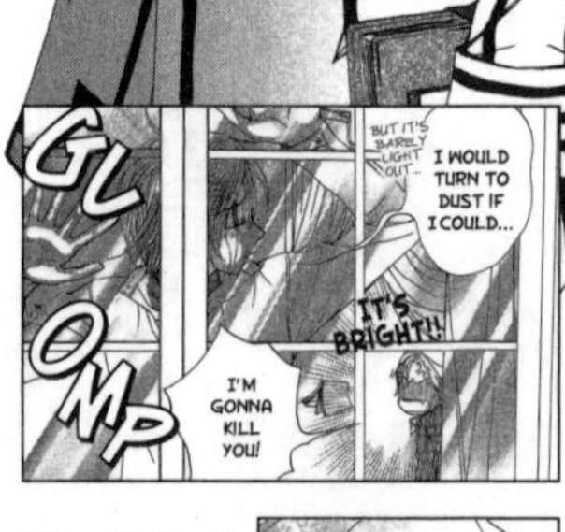
BUT IT'S BARELY LIGHT OUT...
I WOULD TURN TO DUST IF I COULD...
IT'S BRIGHT!!
GLOMP
I'M GONNA KILL YOU!

⬆ Even Aido doesn't like sunlight...

Nature — Don't like sunlight and are nocturnal

Vampires don't like strong sunlight since they have very sharp senses. This is why folklore such as "sunlight turns vampires to ashes" was born. But sunlight does not kill them. Vampires usually spend the day inside, and when they go out, they hide their skin from the sun.

Rima is a model, so she protects herself from the sun. ➡

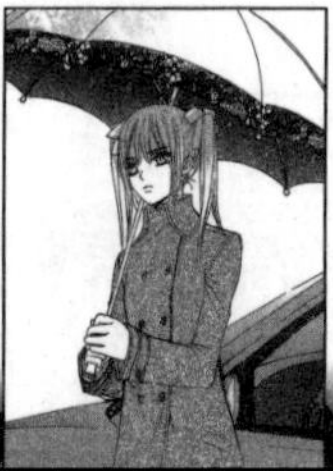

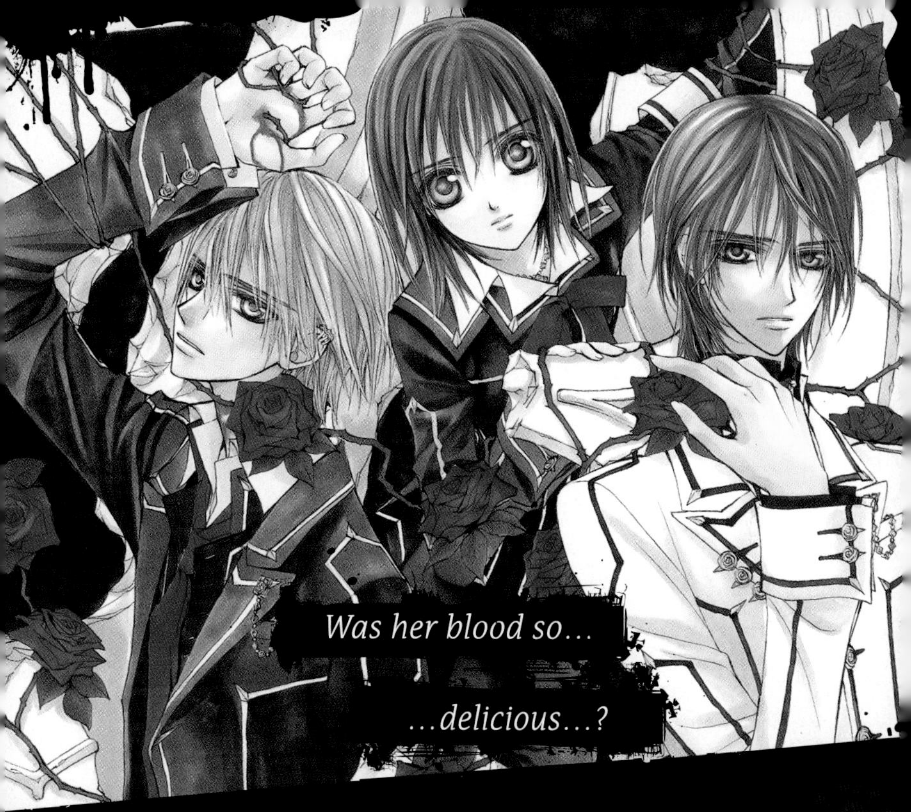
Was her blood so…
…delicious…?
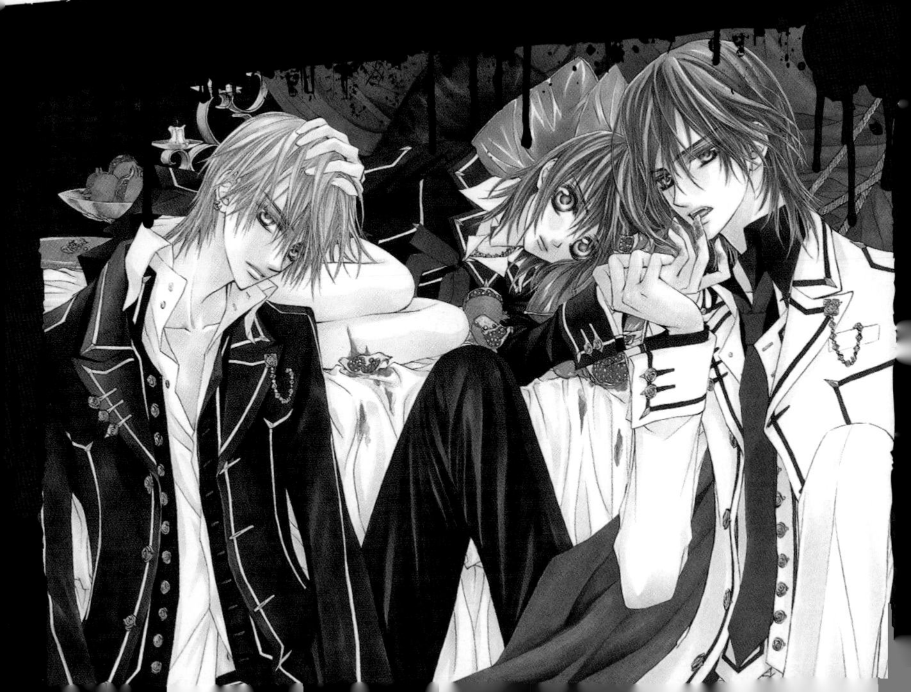

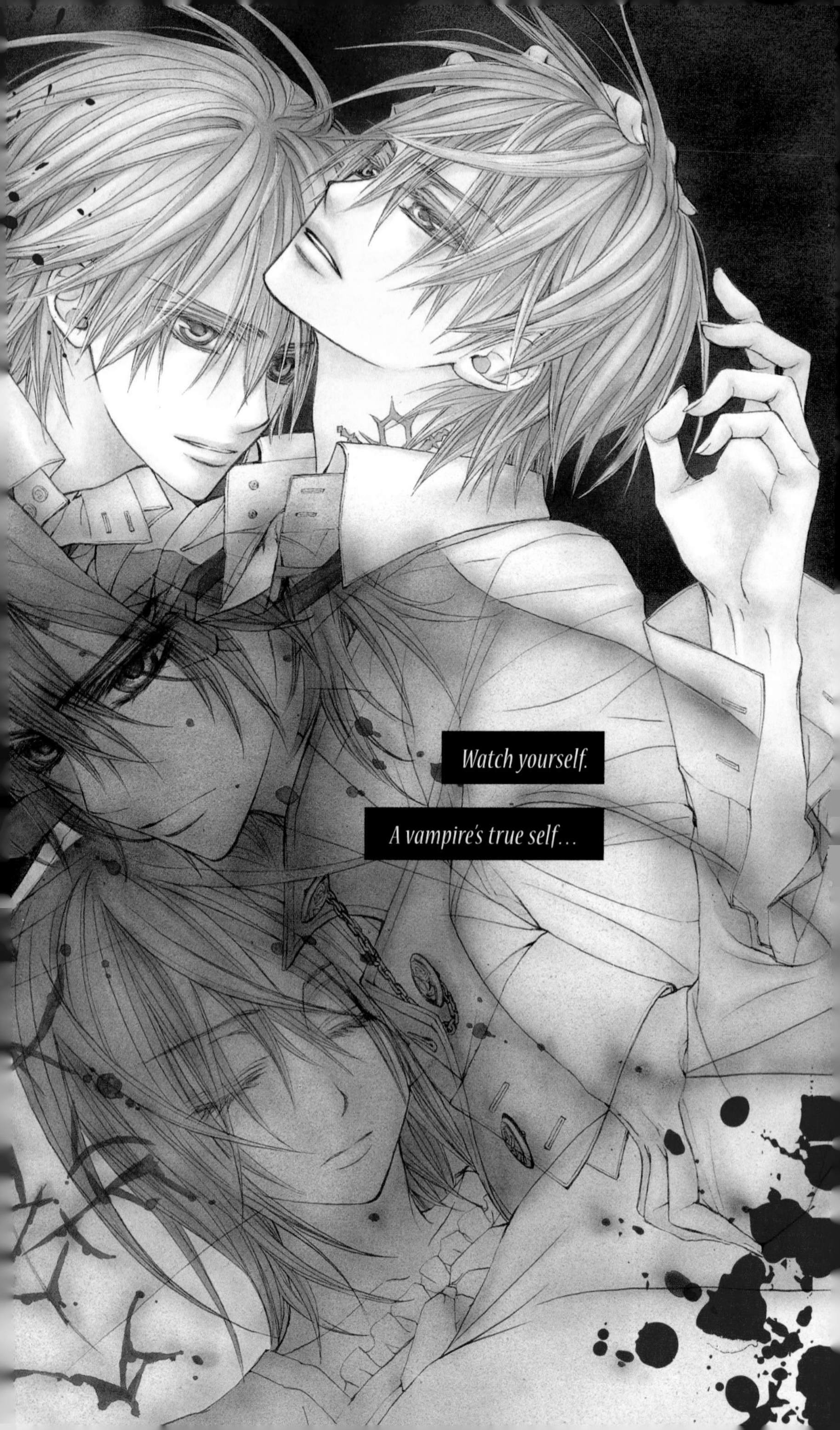
Watch yourself.
A vampire's true self...

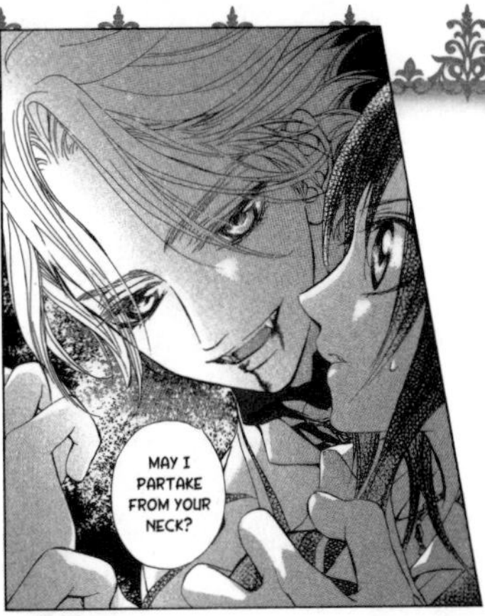
MAY I PARTAKE FROM YOUR NECK?

Taste — They love human blood

Vampires desire blood by instinct. Those who lose their reason will drink so much blood from a human that the human dies. Vampires do not drink blood for sustenance. They drink blood because they want to. Therefore, vampires do not die even if they do not drink blood. Blood tablets are available nowadays, so these can be used instead of drinking human blood. But human blood is special for a vampire, and they react quickly to its smell.

Special Note: Blood tablets

Tablets that restrain the urge to drink blood. The most popular tablet is BL-XXXV 06Σ. Kaname takes 06Ω.

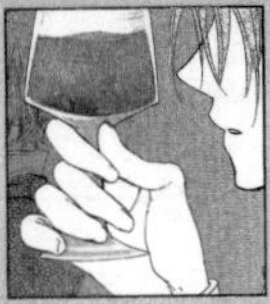

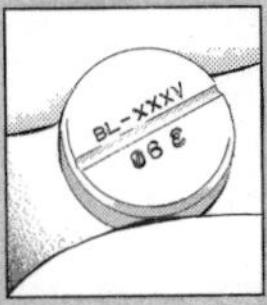
BL-XXXV

Special Note: The urge to drink blood

A strong desire to drink blood arises regularly. When vampires smell blood, they suddenly desire it.

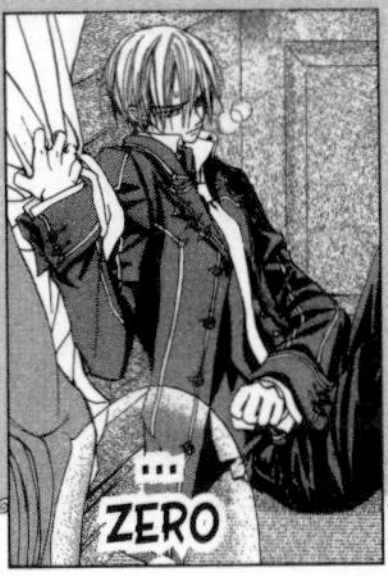
...
ZERO

Abilities — Intelligence and power that surpass human understanding

Vampires have physical abilities and intelligence that are far superior to those of humans. Those with strong vampire blood have special powers that are beyond human understanding, and they can manipulate forces of nature like ice, fire and electricity or even modify human memories.

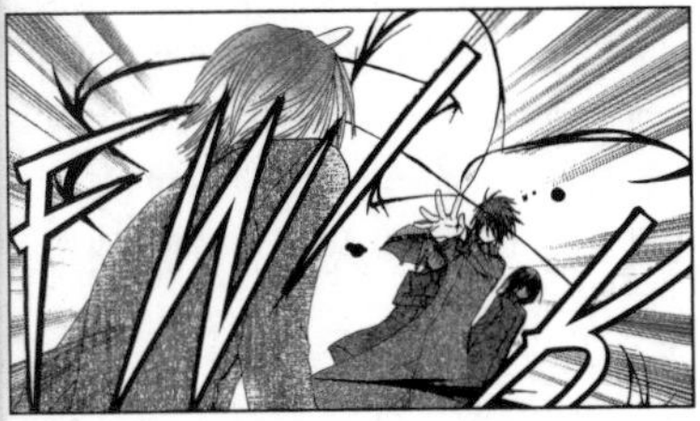
FWK

⬆ The ability to manipulate his blood at will. The strength of its power can pulverize rocks.

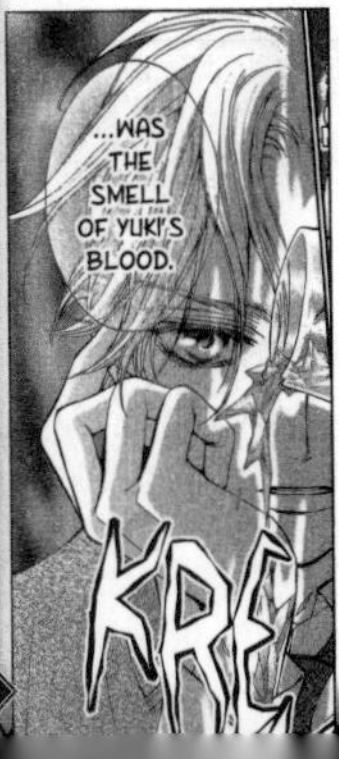
...WAS THE SMELL OF YUKI'S BLOOD.
KRE

⬅ The ability to turn water into ice instantly. Aido can also freeze molecules floating in the air.

They excel in sciences, and it was easy for them to create blood tablets while they were still students. ➡

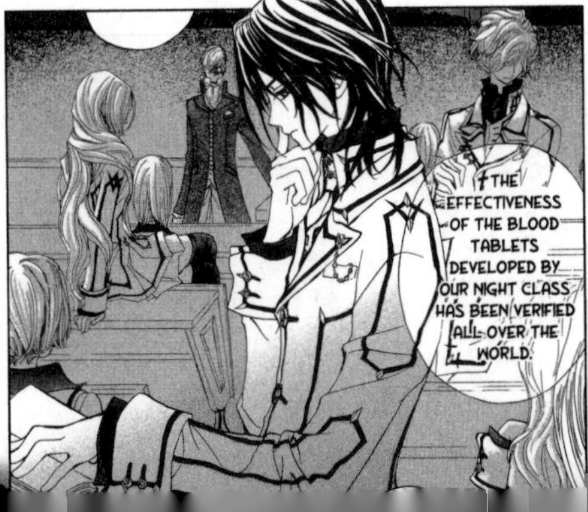
THE EFFECTIVENESS OF THE BLOOD TABLETS DEVELOPED BY OUR NIGHT CLASS HAS BEEN VERIFIED ALL OVER THE WORLD.

Vampire Report 2

The Life and Death of Vampires

How are vampires born, and how do they die?
What sort of powers do they possess? We unravel those mysteries.

The origin of vampires

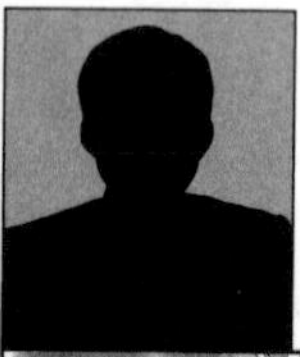

← The progenitor is supposed to have had powers much greater than those of vampires living today.

The battle between humans and vampires has continued since ancient times… ↓

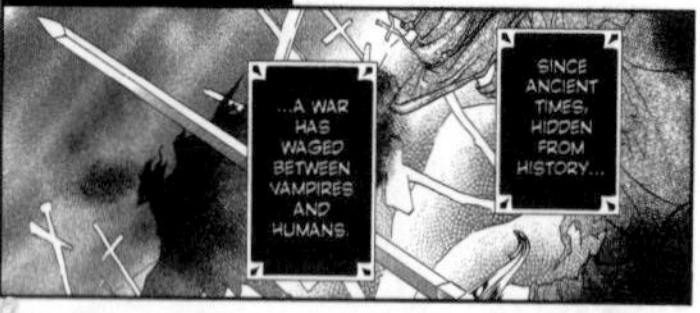
SINCE ANCIENT TIMES, HIDDEN FROM HISTORY...
...A WAR HAS WAGED BETWEEN VAMPIRES AND HUMANS.

In ancient times, human civilization almost perished. The progenitor of vampires was born around that time. Since then, vampires and humans have fought each other, but the number of vampires increased through marriage.

How vampires are born

They can have a family and bear children just like humans. →

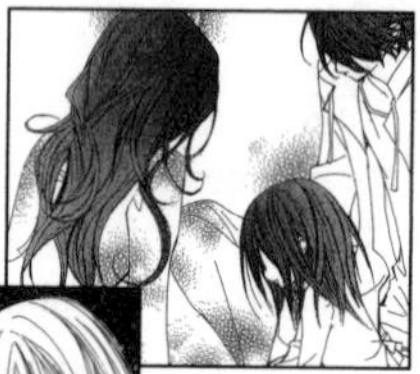

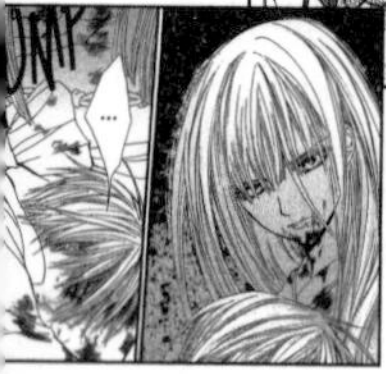

← There are those who increase their brethren by biting humans and transforming them into vampires…

Vampires bear children just like humans. A vampire's spouse can either be a vampire or a human. Children born between a vampire and a human are vampires, but their vampire abilities lessen. A human can be transformed into a vampire by being bitten by a pureblood—vampires with no human blood in their lineage.

How vampires die

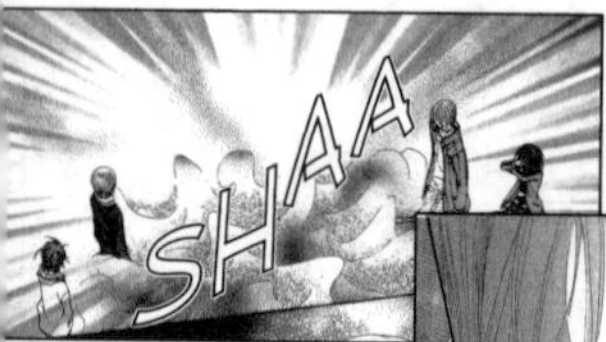
SHAA

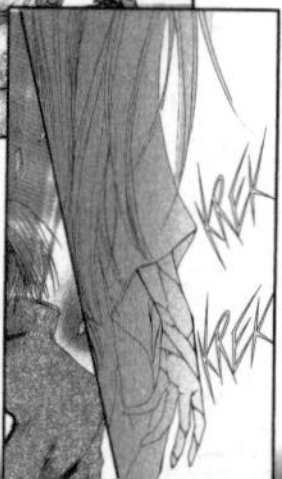
KREK
KREK

↑→ A dying vampire. The way they die differs depending on the type of vampire they are, and all the details are still not known…

Vampires have extremely high-level abilities to regenerate themselves. They can resurrect even under circumstances where other organisms would be dead. But if their head is severed or if they're attacked with certain weapons, they can die. In that case, their bodies disintegrate.

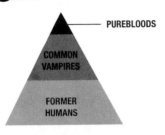

PUREBLOODS
COMMON VAMPIRES
FORMER HUMANS

Ways vampires are born and the differences in their abilities

Vampires are categorized into three classes—purebloods, common vampires, and former humans. Their abilities differ greatly depending on how they were born.

Abilities — Absolute power that allows them to rule

A pureblood can turn humans into vampires by drinking their blood. They can also manipulate humans like puppets. Common vampires cannot disobey a pureblood's will.

YOUR OVER-WHELMING YOUTH, POWER, BEAUTY...
HEY!
YOU WENT THROUGH THE WALL!

⬆ To a vampire, a pureblood is someone to admire and respect.

⬅ One can gain tremendous powers by drinking the blood of a pureblood.

PUREBLOODS

Vampires who do not have a single drop of human blood in their lineage since ancient times. They have special abilities far superior to other vampires. Their vitality is strong, and they live for a very long time.

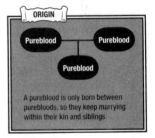

ORIGIN
Pureblood
Pureblood
Pureblood
A pureblood is only born between purebloods, so they keep marrying within their kin and siblings.

FORMER HUMANS

Humans who transform into vampires after a pureblood drinks their blood. They're different from common vampires in that they gradually lose their reason and lose control over their urge to drink blood. Those who attack humans indiscriminately are called "Level E."

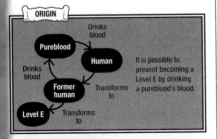

ORIGIN
Drinks blood
Pureblood
Human
Drinks blood
Former human
Transforms to
Level E
Transforms to
It is possible to prevent becoming a Level E by drinking a pureblood's blood.

VAMPIRE HUNTERS

The ancestor of vampire hunters supposedly devoured the progenitor of vampires, so they have some vampire genes in them.

COMMON VAMPIRES

Vampires born from a marriage between a vampire and a human. Their levels differ depending on the thickness of their vampire blood, and those who are close to purebloods are called aristocrats. They inherit a portion of the abilities that purebloods possess. The types of abilities differ by lineage, and their powers differ depending on the thickness of their vampire blood.

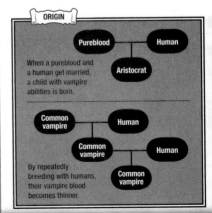

ORIGIN
Pureblood
Human
Aristocrat
When a pureblood and a human get married, a child with vampire abilities is born.
Common vampire
Human
Common vampire
Human
Common vampire
By repeatedly breeding with humans, their vampire blood becomes thinner.

Vampire Report 3

Vampire Society

What is the origin of vampires, and what sort of social system did they set up?
We unravel their history and analyze their social system.

How vampires organized themselves

1. When human civilization almost perished in ancient times, the progenitor of vampires appeared.
2. The number of vampires began to increase exponentially.
3. The Kurans became the royal family.
4. The king two generations ago abolished the monarchy.

The Senate was established.

Special Note: The beginning of the monarchy and the Senate

The Kurans became the royal family, and they had full authority over everything. But the head of the Kuran family two generations ago (Haruka Kuran's father) did not want this and decided to abolish the monarchy. He summoned the Senate to make them govern vampire society instead. Thus, vampires are now ruled by classes in the way we know today.

I'M SURPRISED YOU WERE ABLE TO MAKE IT HERE UNDER THE WATCH OF THE SENATE...
...BIG BROTHER.

Special Note: The birth of the progenitor and the vampires

Vampires and humans kept fighting each other. The power of a single vampire is strong, but humans had a numerical advantage and they fought back as a group. Vampires increased their brethren by turning humans into vampires. When the number of vampires increased exponentially, it was necessary to manage them by categorizing them into classes.

IN ANCIENT TIMES, HUMAN CIVILIZATION ALMOST PERISHED.
THE PROGENITOR OF VAMPIRES APPEARED AROUND THAT TIME.
THE PUREBLOOD LINEAGE HASN'T MIXED WITH THE HUMAN RACE AT ALL SINCE THEN.

The modern vampire society

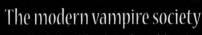
Pureblood rule and the relationship with humans

The vampire society is a class-based society under the control of the Senate. It is a complete pyramid structure from Level A down to Level E. Those who are aristocrats and above manage vampires who used to be human as well as hunt those who fall to Level E (End) status. Vampire hunters also hunt Level E vampires because they harm humans. However, because vampires and vampire hunters are at odds with each other, they do not cooperate. There are a number of rules to avoid clashes with human society. One of them is that vampire hunters monitor soirées. The crime of killing purebloods, which is the vampire society's gravest offense, applies to humans as well. If such an incident occurs, the Senate sends pursuers after the suspect and convicts him or her. The Hunter Society condones this to keep the peace.

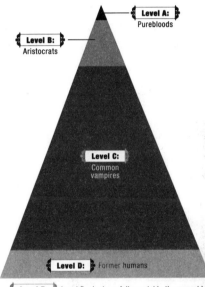

Level A: Purebloods

Level B: Aristocrats

Level C: Common vampires

Level D: Former humans

Level E: Level D who have fallen outside the pyramid

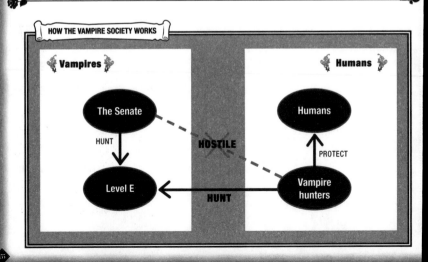

HOW THE VAMPIRE SOCIETY WORKS

Vampires

Humans

The Senate

Humans

HUNT

HOSTILE

PROTECT

Level E

Vampire hunters

HUNT

Vampire Report 4

Organizations Surrounding Vampires

Vampires and human organizations related to vampires are supposed to keep peace between the two societies, but the truth is each side has its own motives. What is their background…?

The Senate

The highest governing body that takes command of everything

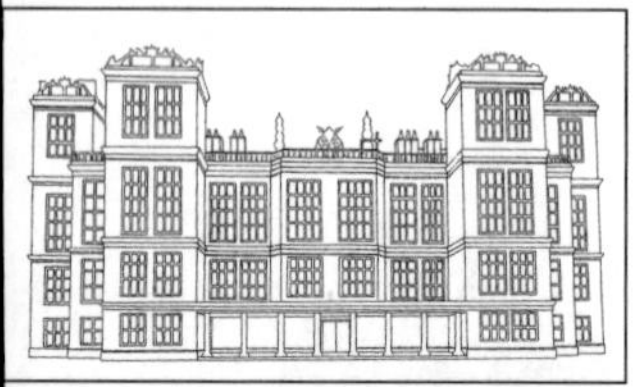

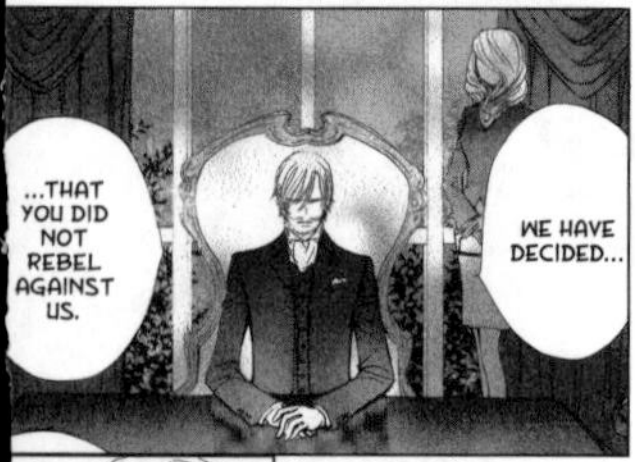
WE HAVE DECIDED...
...THAT YOU DID NOT REBEL AGAINST US.

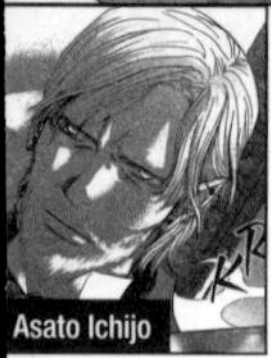
Asato Ichijo

⬆ He seems to be at odds with Kaname Kuran often.

⬅ Asato Ichijo is the head of the first family of aristocrats and has been a powerful Senate figure for a long time.

The Senate is an organization that was established two generations ago by the king related to Kaname Kuran. It is a council system, and its objective is vampire coexistence with humans. Senior aristocrats manage the Senate and act to smooth things out between humans and vampires by managing and executing vampires who harm humans. The Senate is the vampires' governing body, but the vampires do not revere it because it is not royal sovereignty. Therefore, the Senate is not monolithic—a factor that leads to the warped social structure. Ichio (Asato Ichijo), who was Kaname Kuran's legal guardian, holds the top position in the Senate.

Cross Academy

The bridge that aims for peaceful coexistence between humans and vampires

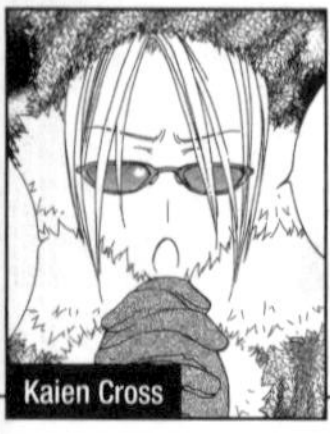
Kaien Cross

⬅⬇ Under Headmaster Cross's pacifism, vampires and humans study in the same buildings.

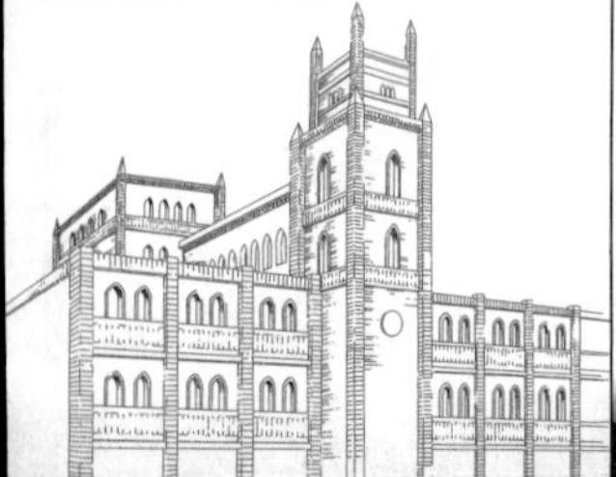

A private academy that espouses pacifism, Cross Academy was founded to function as a bridge between humans and vampires. With the pureblood Kaname Kuran as a key member, many young vampire aristocrats attend the academy alongside human students.

Political beliefs and factions

The Senate was supposed to be a governing body where many vampires would discuss and decide matters peacefully rather than have the purebloods with absolute power rule by force. However, the organization became a cruel institution that uses any method necessary to rule vampire society. Therefore, the Senate is now divided into two factions—one that supports the Senate and one that wants a return to the monarchy. The Ichijo family, the longest-serving members of the Senate, and the Shiki family are representatives of the pro-Senate faction. The Aido family is anti-Senate.

There are two notions regarding relationships with humans. One only sees humans as food, and the other wants coexistence with humans. Most vampires feel superior to humans because of their abilities, but lots of young vampires support the previous head of the Kuran family, who was a pacifist, and Kaname Kuran, who is spending time with humans at Cross Academy. They are aiming for coexistence with humans regardless of what their parents' beliefs are.

The pro-Senate faction consider Kaname Kuran to be trouble because he is at the core of this pacifism. The Kuran family name and their pureblood power are extremely important in controlling vampire society. This is why Asato Ichijo, the core member of the pro-Senate faction, tried to take advantage of Rido Kuran (who was expelled as head of the Kuran family) and Kaname Kuran. There are also humans who are trying to join forces with the Senate to take advantage of the powers of vampires. The vampires' various motives are tangled together and have become cause for strife.

YOUNG VAMPIRES
Hanabusa Aido
Akatsuki Kain
Ruka Souen
Rima Toya
LOYAL
THE KURAN FAMILY
Haruka
Juri
Kaname
HOSTILE
THE SENATE
Pro-Senate Faction
The Ichijo Family
Asato Ichijo
The Shiki Family
Anti-Senate Faction
The Aido Family
The Kain Family
and others
COMRADES
KAIEN CROSS
OBJECTIVES
To have humans and vampires interact and to create a peaceful world
OBJECTIVES
A portion of the pro-Senate faction: Institute absolute rule using Kaname as a puppet
Anti-Senate faction: A return to the monarchy

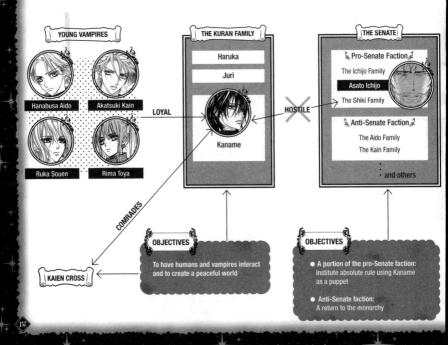

Vampire Report 5

Those Who Harm Vampires

In ancient times, humans and vampires were at war with each other.
In present times, vampire hunters only hunt the dangerous Level E vampires…

...ARE EITHER VAMPIRE HUNTERS OR THOSE WORKING FOR THE SOCIETY.

⬆ The Hunter Society is a place that many people like vampire hunters, intelligence-gathering staff and record keepers frequent. There are enough people related to the society to make up an entire town.

The Hunter Society president rules over all the vampire hunters. He issues hunting commands. He has great power in deciding whether a vampire lives or dies… ➡

The Hunter Society President

The Hunter Society

A secret society that has tacit government approval to protect humans

The Hunter Society was established to execute vampires who fell to Level E and were judged to be dangerous. In ancient times, individual hunters got rid of dangerous vampires themselves, but now the hunters are organized, and hunting is done accurately and efficiently. The society utilizes their own intelligence information to select targets to execute and to dispatch vampire hunters. The mission is accomplished under the obscure motto that killing vampires is not a crime. They also tame vampires who used to be human through spells and secretly use them for illegal missions.

⬆ Even now, there's a prison in Cross Academy from when it used to be the society's headquarters.

HERE WE ARE. THESE ARE OUR ARCHIVES.
THIS ROOM HOLDS EXTENSIVE RECORDS OF THE LONG WAR BETWEEN VAMPIRES AND VAMPIRE HUNTERS.

The Headquarters of the Hunter Society

The central anti-vampire office

The office that gives vampire hunters information about Level E vampires and issues commands to hunt them. Vampires cannot get close to this place because it is located in a town where many hunters reside and because it is protected by special spells. The headquarters was relocated to its current place recently, and Cross Academy was built on its former grounds.

⬅ The archives contain records of vampire-related incidents.

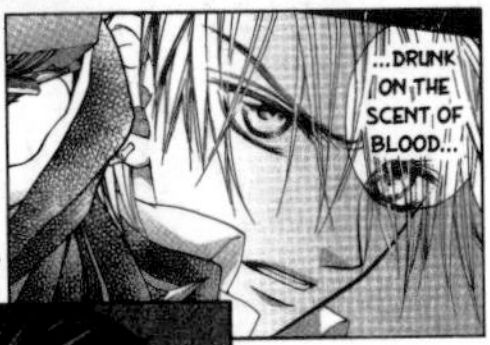
...DRUNK ON THE SCENT OF BLOOD...!

People have high expectations for Zero Kiryu as the son of gifted vampire hunters. ➡

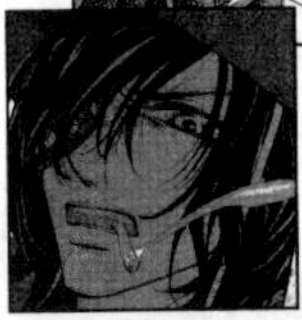

⬅ The No. 1 vampire hunter right now is Yagari.

Vampire Hunters

Those who hunt vampires

They are humans who make a living hunting vampires. They have high-level fighting abilities and execute their targets with anti-vampire weapons. Many of them hold public positions such as being students and teachers. The vampire hunters' ancestor is supposed to have gained the power to hunt vampires from devouring one of the progenitors of vampires.

How to Become a Vampire Hunter

Those who have talent begin training under a veteran vampire hunter while young and polish their skills. Once the Hunter Society recognizes them, they can become independent vampire hunters.

Special Note Aptitude

Even if you're born into a hunter family, you cannot become a hunter if you're judged to be unfit to become one. Ichiru Kiryu, Zero Kiryu's twin brother, could not become a vampire hunter.

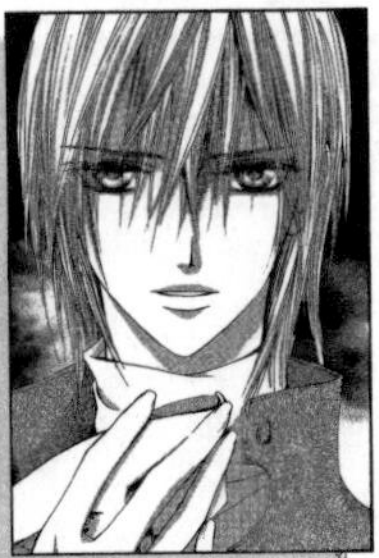

Special Note Hereditary system

Genetics often determine their powers, so hunters must be born into a family of hunters. The Kiryu family and the Cross family are distinguished hunter families.

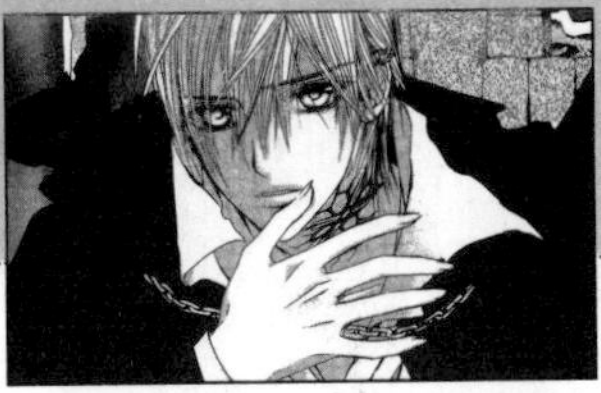

Vampire Hunters' Weapons

They have spells cast on them. The weapons can seriously wound vampires and slow their recovery. They're useless against humans.

Artemis

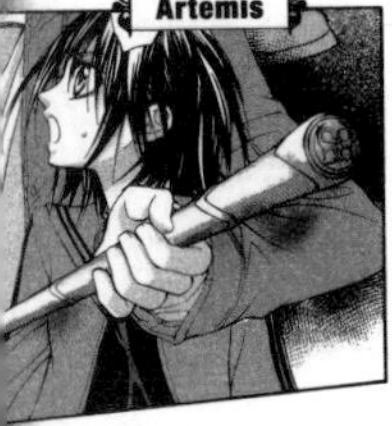

⬅ A sticklike weapon given to Yuki by her foster father, Kaien Cross. It is collapsible.

Bloody Rose Gun

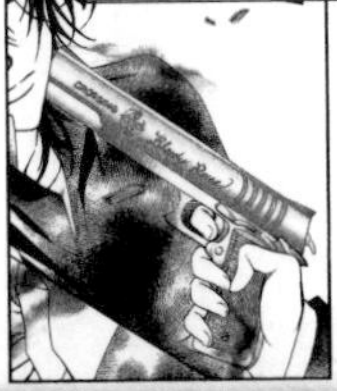

A gun that can shoot bullets that have been cast with spells. It can kill an ordinary vampire with one shot. ➡

How to Tame a Vampire

You can tame a vampire by inking a special tattoo on the vampire and soaking that vampire's blood onto a bracelet. This is a secret method that has been used by vampire hunters.

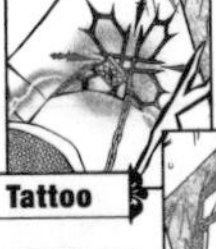

Tattoo

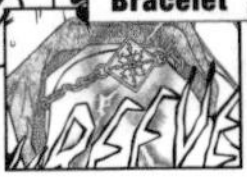

Bracelet

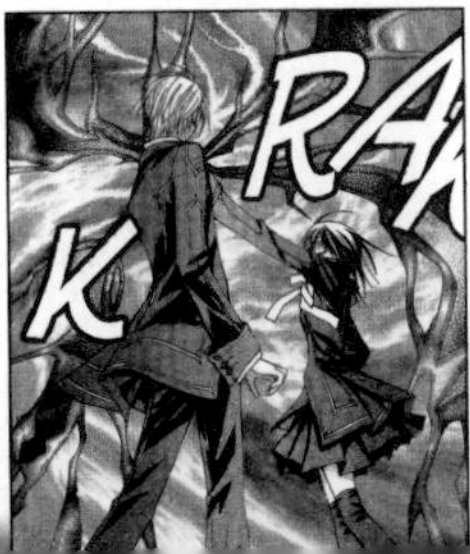

Vampire Report 6

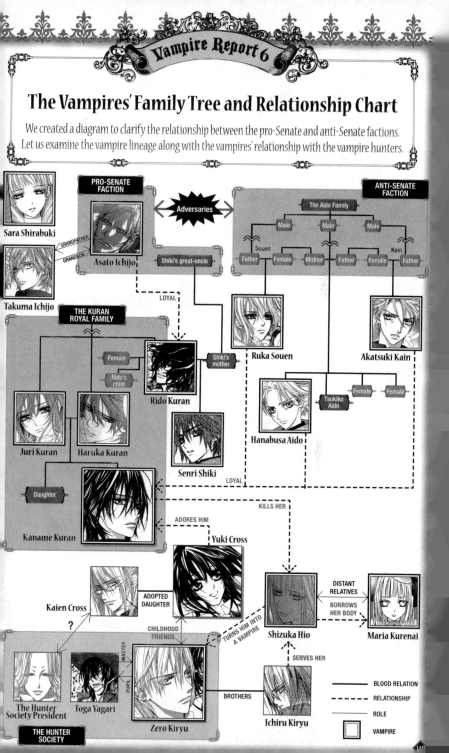

The Vampires' Family Tree and Relationship Chart

We created a diagram to clarify the relationship between the pro-Senate and anti-Senate factions. Let us examine the vampire lineage along with the vampires' relationship with the vampire hunters.

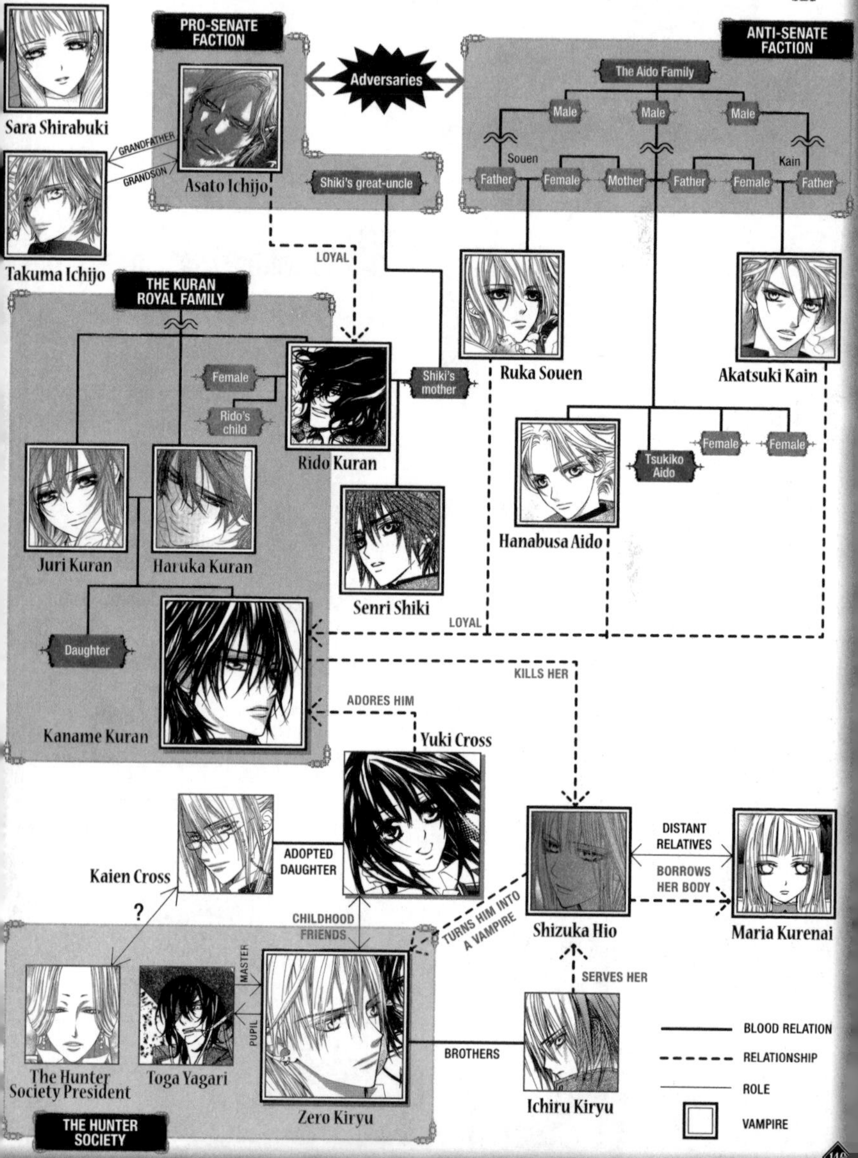

PRO-SENATE FACTION
Adversaries
ANTI-SENATE FACTION
Sara Shirabuki
GRANDFATHER
GRANDSON
Asato Ichijo
Takuma Ichijo
Shiki's great-uncle
The Aido Family
Male
Male
Male
Souen
Kain
Father
Female
Mother
Father
Female
Father
LOYAL
THE KURAN ROYAL FAMILY
Female
Rido's child
Rido Kuran
Shiki's mother
Ruka Souen
Akatsuki Kain
Tsukiko Aido
Female
Female
Hanabusa Aido
Juri Kuran
Haruka Kuran
Senri Shiki
LOYAL
Daughter
KILLS HER
ADORES HIM
Kaname Kuran
Yuki Cross
Kaien Cross
ADOPTED DAUGHTER
DISTANT RELATIVES
BORROWS HER BODY
?
CHILDHOOD FRIENDS
TURNS HIM INTO A VAMPIRE
Shizuka Hio
Maria Kurenai
MASTER
PUPIL
SERVES HER
BROTHERS
The Hunter Society President
Toga Yagari
Zero Kiryu
Ichiru Kiryu
THE HUNTER SOCIETY
BLOOD RELATION
RELATIONSHIP
ROLE
VAMPIRE

Chapter 3
Vampire & Hunter

An Unmentionable Existence and Those Who Hunt Them Down

The fierce war that has been perpetuated between humans and vampires secretly...

We comment on vampires, those who cooperate with them, and vampire hunters—all of them are participants in the war of the present age.

The fates of those who hunt and those who are hunted intersect...

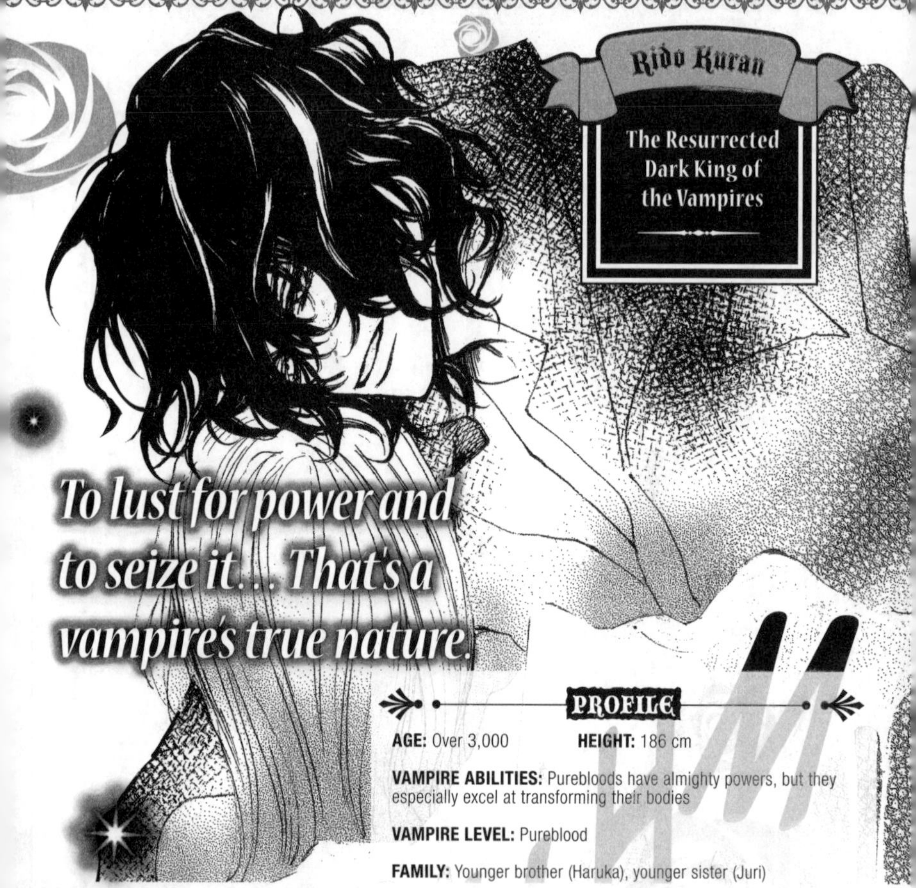

Rido Kuran

The Resurrected Dark King of the Vampires

To lust for power and to seize it... That's a vampire's true nature.

PROFILE

AGE: Over 3,000 **HEIGHT:** 186 cm

VAMPIRE ABILITIES: Purebloods have almighty powers, but they especially excel at transforming their bodies

VAMPIRE LEVEL: Pureblood

FAMILY: Younger brother (Haruka), younger sister (Juri)

RESPECTS: Juri

TASTE IN WOMEN: "A strong-minded woman like Juri."

HOBBIES: His Juri collection

FAVORITE FASHION: Clothes he looks good in

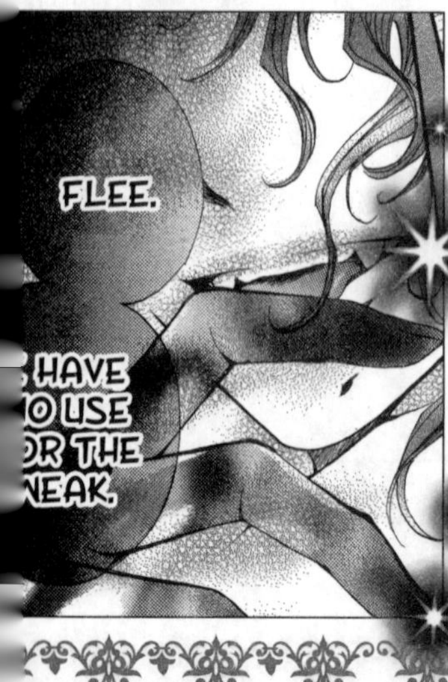
FLEE.

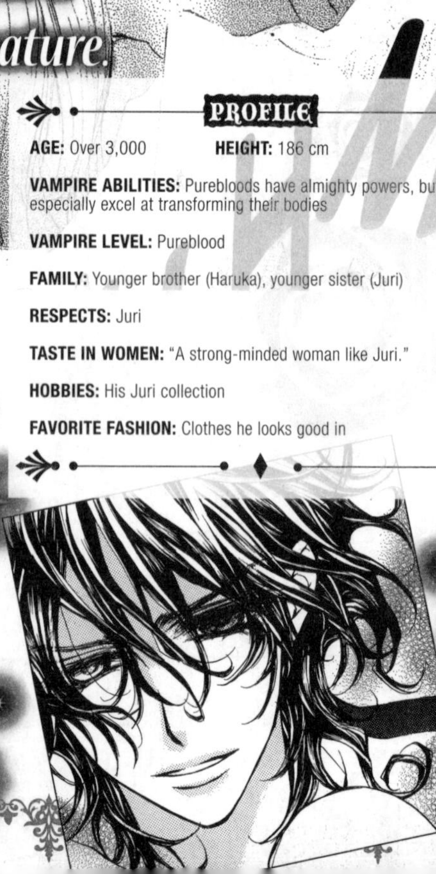

CHARACTER ANALYSIS

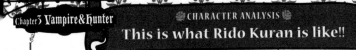

This is what Rido Kuran is like!!

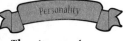

THEN THE WARM DAYS...
COME ...
...BE MY SACRIFICE.
...CAME TO AN ABRUPT END.

His younger sister Juri becomes his younger brother's wife… He attacks them with the intent to snatch their daughter!! ➡

Personality

The strongest vampire who acts ferociously by instinct

Rido's desire for power and love is strong, and he does not restrain himself. He loved his younger sister intensely, but his feelings were not returned. Because he feels that she was taken away by his younger brother, he decides to snatch away their dear daughter. Because of his self-centered personality and almighty power, no one can stop his evil actions!!

I'VE CHANGED MY MIND.
I'LL LOVE YOU...
...IN PLACE OF JURI...

⬅ Rido sees Juri in Yuki, so he tries to make Yuki his...

SLISH

Rido wielded the loathsome vampire hunter sword and slashed Haruka without hesitating. ➡

His Past

He destroyed Haruka in combat and was torn to pieces by Kaname

Ten years ago, Rido raided his brother Haruka's mansion. He destroyed Haruka using vampires under his command and vampire hunter weapons. Kaname tore Rido into pieces on the spot, but Rido was not completely destroyed. The Shiki family, who are part of the Senate, placed Rido under their protection. For ten years, Rido slowly regenerated his body and waited for the moment when he could be resurrected.

⬅ Rido was able to regenerate his body while sheltered in the basement of the Shiki family residence for ten years.

Haruka Kuran

The Legitimate Pureblood King

We've lived a long time. It's been more than enough.

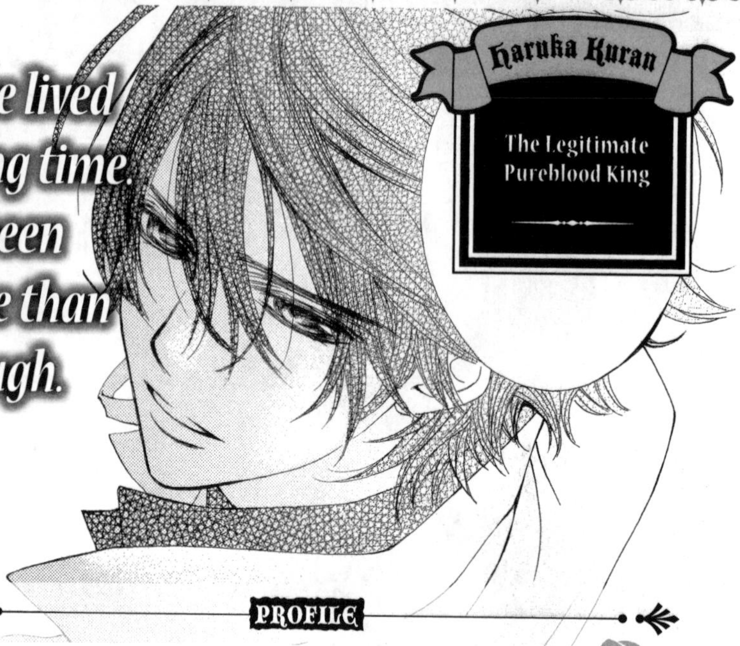

PROFILE

AGE: Over 3,000

HEIGHT: 185 cm

VAMPIRE ABILITIES: Excels in permeating others' bodies and transforming them

VAMPIRE LEVEL: Pureblood

FAMILY: Wife (Juri), son (Kaname), daughter

RESPECTS: His ancestors

TASTE IN WOMEN: "Juri."

HOBBIES: Playing chess with Kaname

FAVORITE FASHION: Comfortable clothes

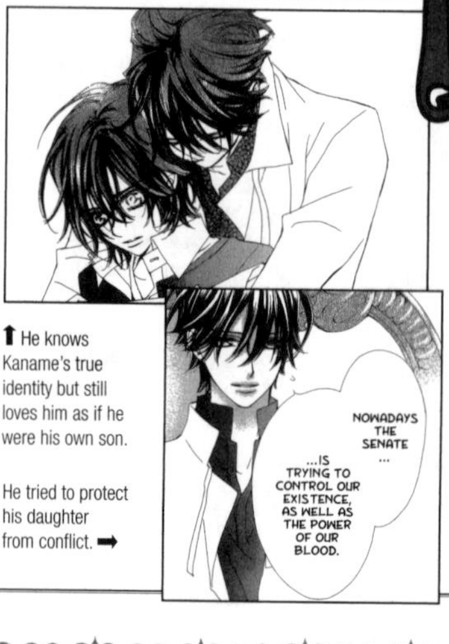
NOWADAYS THE SENATE ...
...IS TRYING TO CONTROL OUR EXISTENCE, AS WELL AS THE POWER OF OUR BLOOD.

⬆ He knows Kaname's true identity but still loves him as if he were his own son.

He tried to protect his daughter from conflict. ➡

CHARACTER ANALYSIS

This is what Haruka Kuran is like!!

Personality

A pacifist who believes in the future

He inherited the most rarified blood from the progenitor of vampires, but his personality is mild, and he prefers to live quietly. He was fearful about his family being taken advantage of and hoped for a peaceful future for his children. He lived for over 3,000 years, and Juri is the only woman he ever loved.

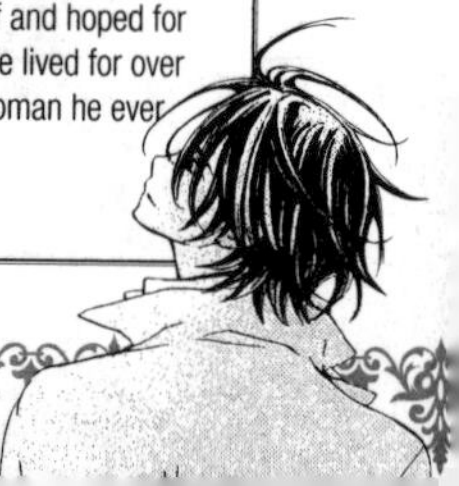

Juri Kuran

The Beautiful Mother Who Protected Her Daughter with Her Life

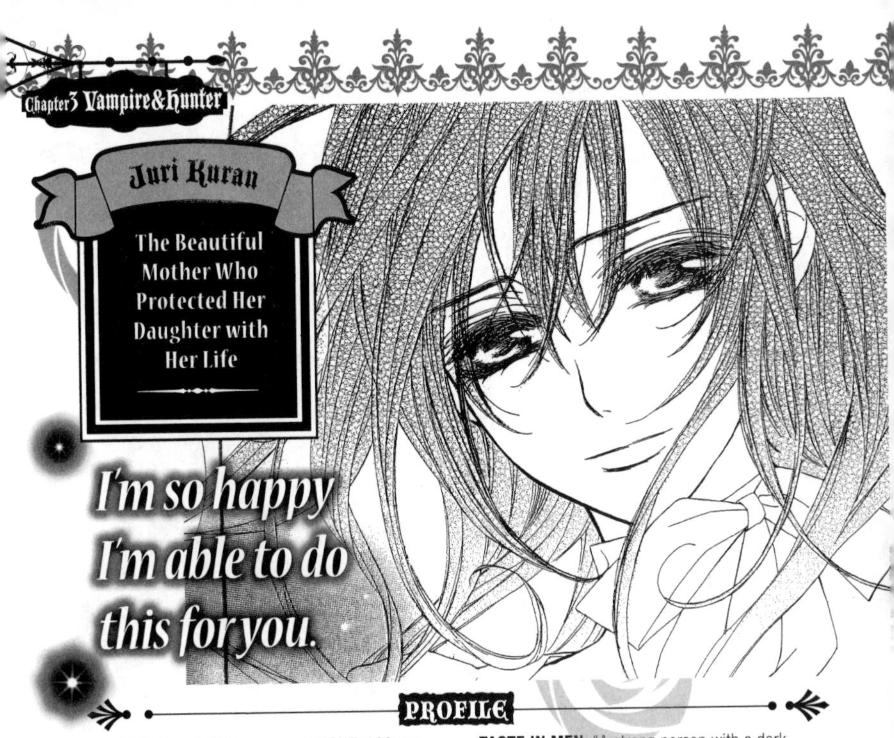

I'm so happy I'm able to do this for you.

PROFILE

AGE: Over 3,000

HEIGHT: 168 cm

VAMPIRE ABILITIES: Excels in using spells

VAMPIRE LEVEL: Pureblood

FAMILY: Husband (Haruka), son (Kaname), daughter

RESPECTS: Her parents

TASTE IN MEN: "A strong person with a dark side. Someone who has two faces."

HOBBIES:
When she was single → Buying snacks
After she had children → Playing piano and board games with her daughter and teasing Kaname

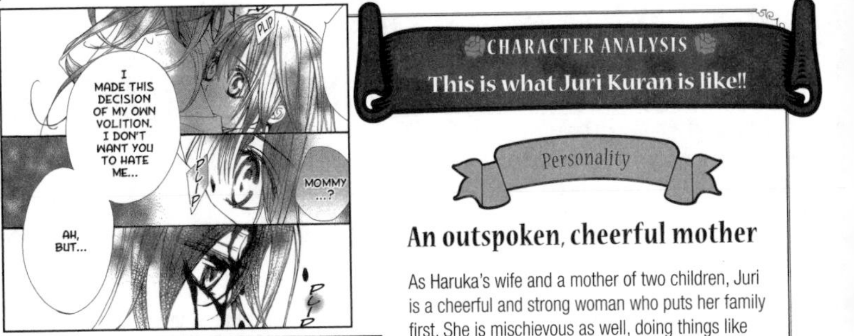
PLIP
I MADE THIS DECISION OF MY OWN VOLITION. I DON'T WANT YOU TO HATE ME...
PLIP
MOMMY ...?
AH, BUT...
PLIP

⬆ Juri casts a spell to seal her daughter's vampire genes.

She loves to toy with the serious Kaname. Her daughter calls it "being mean" though... ➡

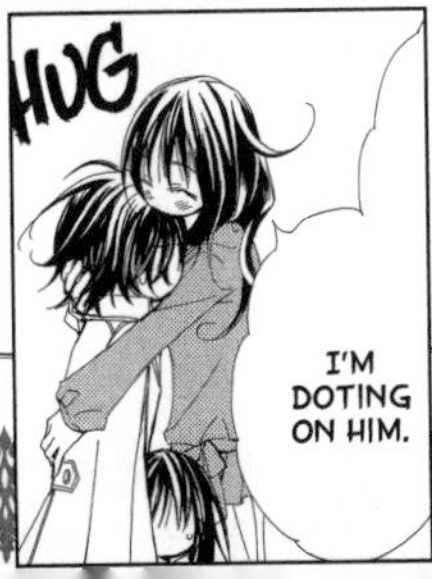
HUG
I'M DOTING ON HIM.

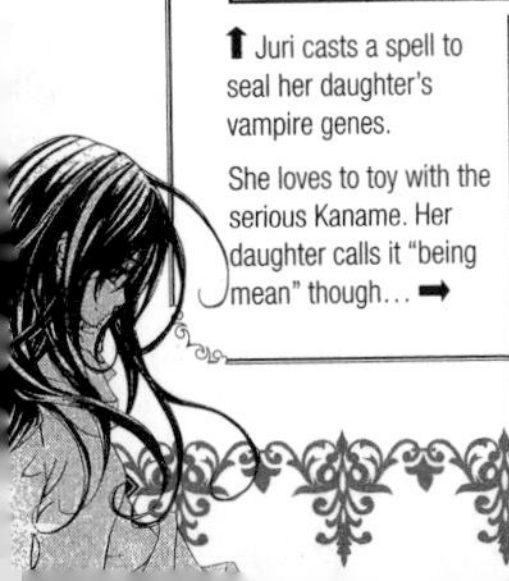

CHARACTER ANALYSIS

This is what Juri Kuran is like!!

Personality

An outspoken, cheerful mother

As Haruka's wife and a mother of two children, Juri is a cheerful and strong woman who puts her family first. She is mischievous as well, doing things like teasing Kaname about his straight-laced personality. She did not want her daughter to shoulder the harsh fate of being a pureblood, and she sacrificed her life to seal her daughter's vampire genes...

Shizuka Hio

The "Kuruizaki-hime" Who Met a Tragic Fate

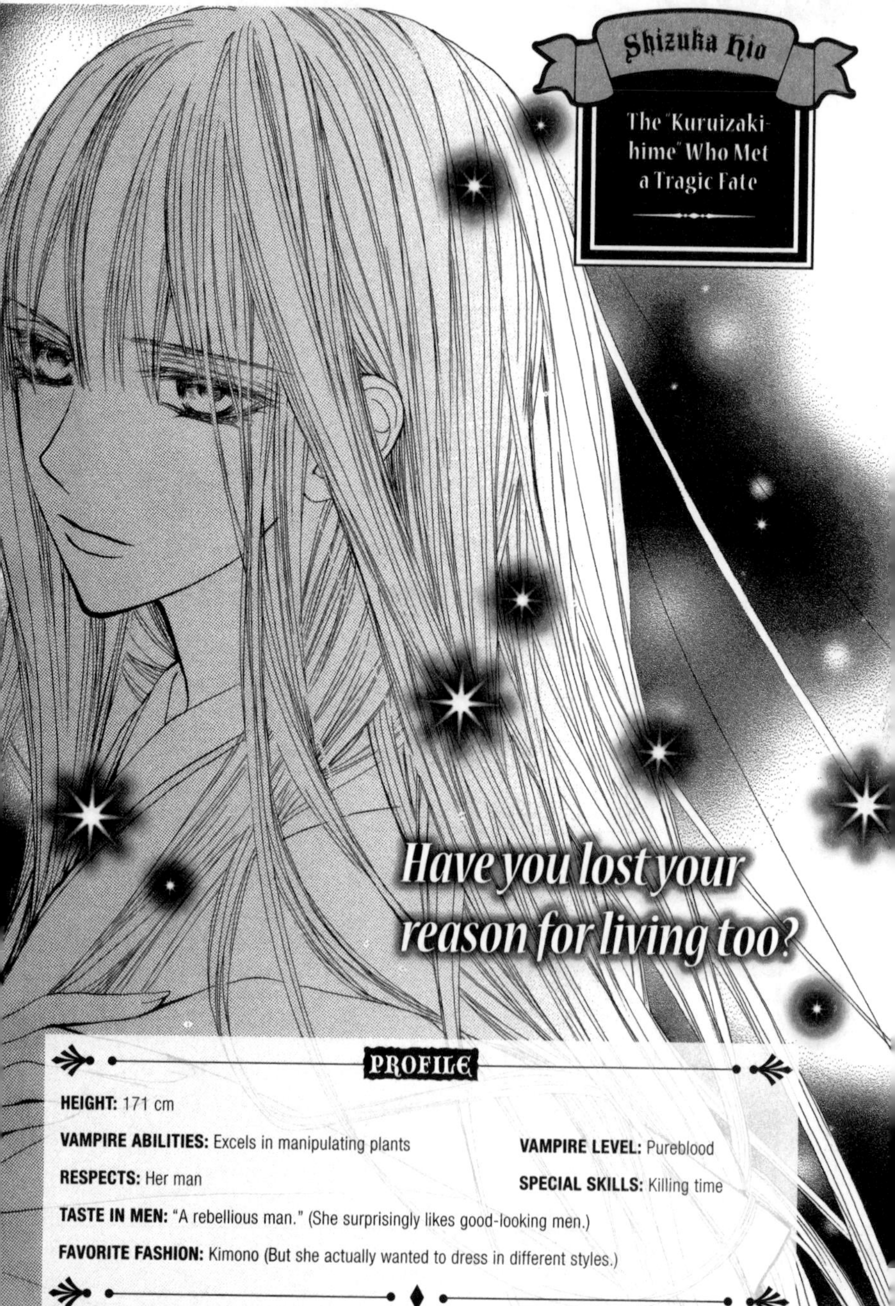
Have you lost your reason for living too?

PROFILE

HEIGHT: 171 cm

VAMPIRE ABILITIES: Excels in manipulating plants

VAMPIRE LEVEL: Pureblood

RESPECTS: Her man

SPECIAL SKILLS: Killing time

TASTE IN MEN: "A rebellious man." (She surprisingly likes good-looking men.)

FAVORITE FASHION: Kimono (But she actually wanted to dress in different styles.)

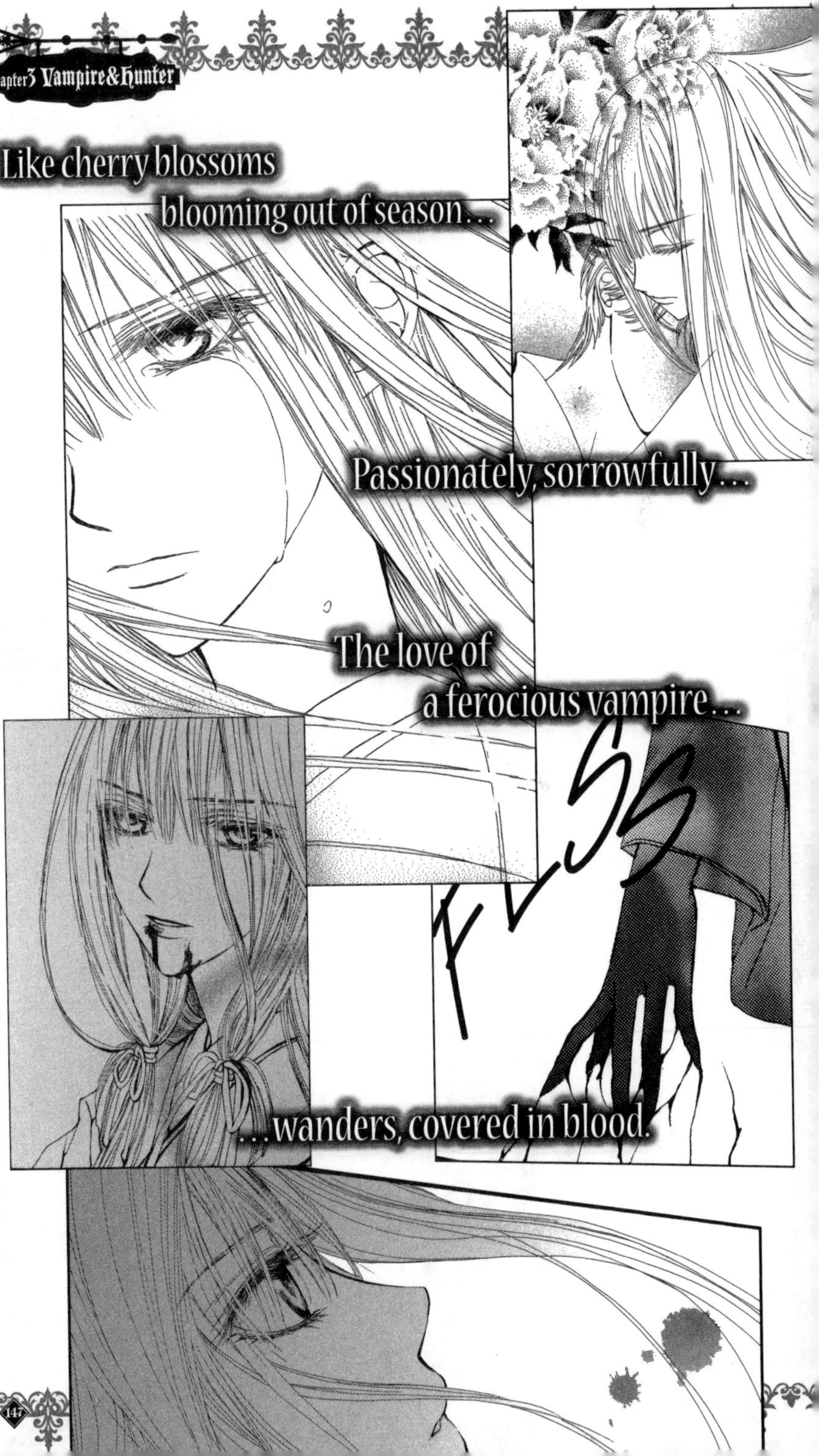
Like cherry blossoms
blooming out of season...
Passionately, sorrowfully...
The love of
a ferocious vampire...
FLSS
...wanders, covered in blood.

CHARACTER ANALYSIS
This is what Shizuka Hio is like!

Her Past

Her fierce passion explodes when she loses her beloved servant

She was locked in confinement right after she was born and given humans as food. She began to love a man, but he was executed by vampire hunters. She goes berserk with rage and sorrow and attacks her enemy, the Kiryu family. After that, she was labeled as a dangerous pureblood and hunted.

She butchered Zero's parents in front of him. She also bit Zero and turned him into a vampire. ⬇

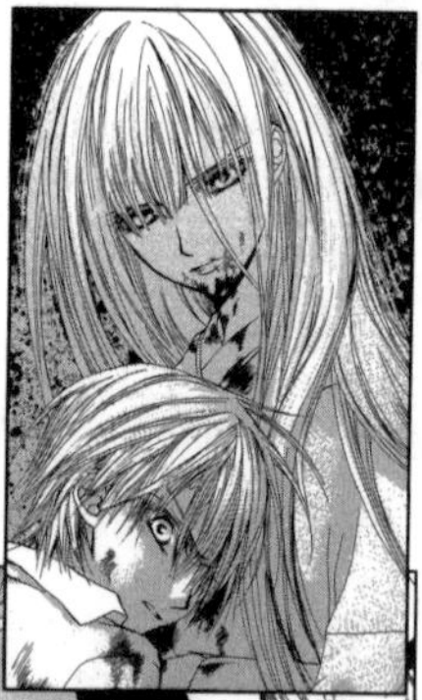

She killed Zero's parents, who were superior hunters, in an instant. She managed to do this while she was holding Zero. ⬇

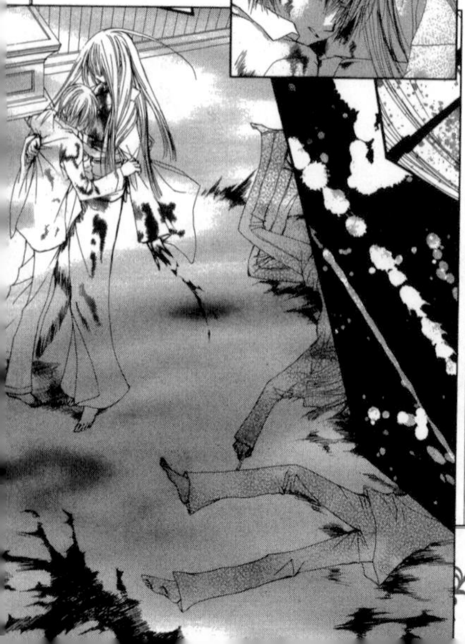

Personality

The aura and pride of a strong one

For Shizuka, who has the strongest power as a pureblood, ordinary vampires and human beings are nothing. Therefore, she is always relaxed in her words and actions. However, the Hio family has a history of members going berserk, so she was brought up in a cage. She also lost the one she loved, so she grew to have a peculiar sense of life and death.

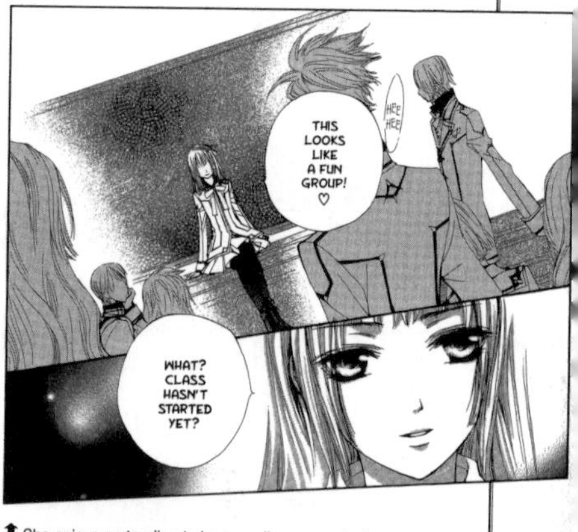
HEE HEE
THIS LOOKS LIKE A FUN GROUP! ♡
WHAT? CLASS HASN'T STARTED YET?

⬆ She enjoys pretending to be an ordinary vampire in Maria's body. She's very curious about what class is like since she's never experienced it before.

A merciless blow to Zero, who looked away while they were fighting. She does not condone servants who do not pay attention to her. ⬇

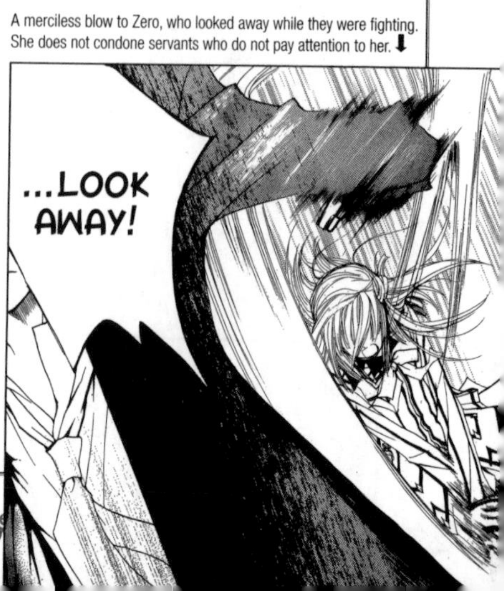
...LOOK AWAY!

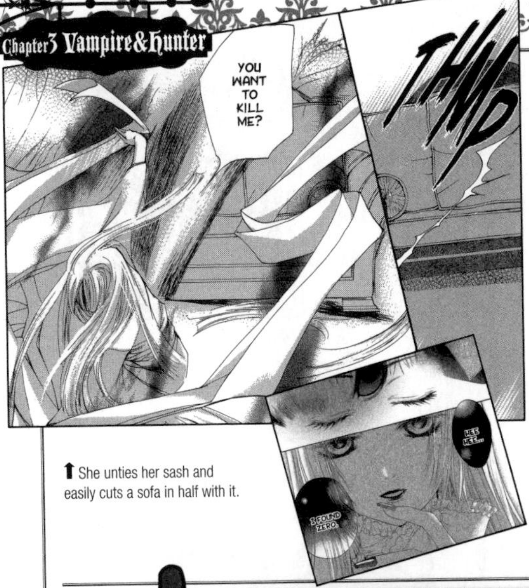
THMP
YOU WANT TO KILL ME?
HEE HEE...
I FOUND ZERO.

⬆ She unties her sash and easily cuts a sofa in half with it.

Fighting Ability

An almighty fighting power that can turn even a kimono into a weapon

She uses a Japanese sword, but she can fight with her bare hands too. She can use her powers to turn a kimono into a sharp blade or a shield to deflect bullets. She can also manipulate plants in such ways as making flowers bloom out of season.

⬅ She's good at transferring her senses to another being. She obtained Zero's information through a bird's eyes.

HER PRIVATE LIFE

Let's check out her actions!

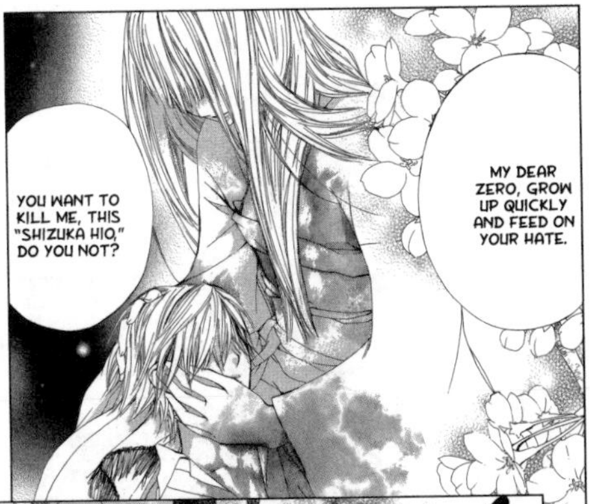
MY DEAR ZERO, GROW UP QUICKLY AND FEED ON YOUR HATE.
YOU WANT TO KILL ME, THIS "SHIZUKA HIO," DO YOU NOT?

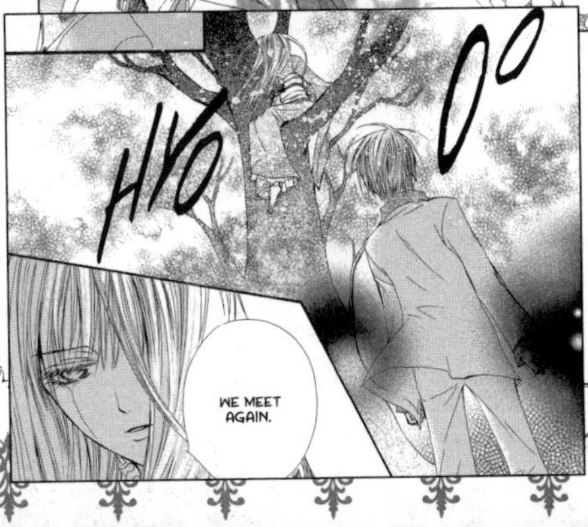
OO
HYO
WE MEET AGAIN.

The two bonds she created with her own blood

Shizuka grew up without love. After she lost the only man she loved, she began to desire peculiar bonds. She turned Zero into a vampire and forced him to chase her. She gave Ichiru her own blood and kept him by her side. These actions seem whimsical and sinful and were based on tragedy, but they still created inseparable bonds for Shizuka.

⬅ Shizuka sees in Zero the same thing that she saw in her lover and turns him into a vampire.

⬅ She felt something in Ichiru that's similar to herself, so she decides to keep him by her side.

Sara Shirabuki

A Rare Pureblood Princess

Please don't make a fuss.

PROFILE

AGE: (A little older than Kaname)

HEIGHT: 170 cm

VAMPIRE LEVEL: Pureblood

RESPECTS: The progenitor

TASTE IN MEN: "Kaname."

HOBBIES: Shopping, attending parties

THERE ARE FEW PUREBLOODS LEFT IN THIS WORLD...
...SO WE MUST SUPPORT EACH OTHER.

⬆ She tries to deal with Kaname through her role as a pureblood.

KANAME...

⬆ She attended the soirée sponsored by the Aido family because she heard that Kaname would attend. They hadn't seen each other in several years.

CHARACTER ANALYSIS

This is what Sara Shirabuki is like!!

Personality

Deep feelings hidden behind calm eyes...

She is prized as one of the few pureblood females, and due to her upbringing she appears to be gentle. However, she fully understands her position and acts cautiously. She seems to want a relationship with Kaname for the sake of their pureblood lineages...

Asato Ichijo

The Head of the Senate Who Has Lived a Long Time

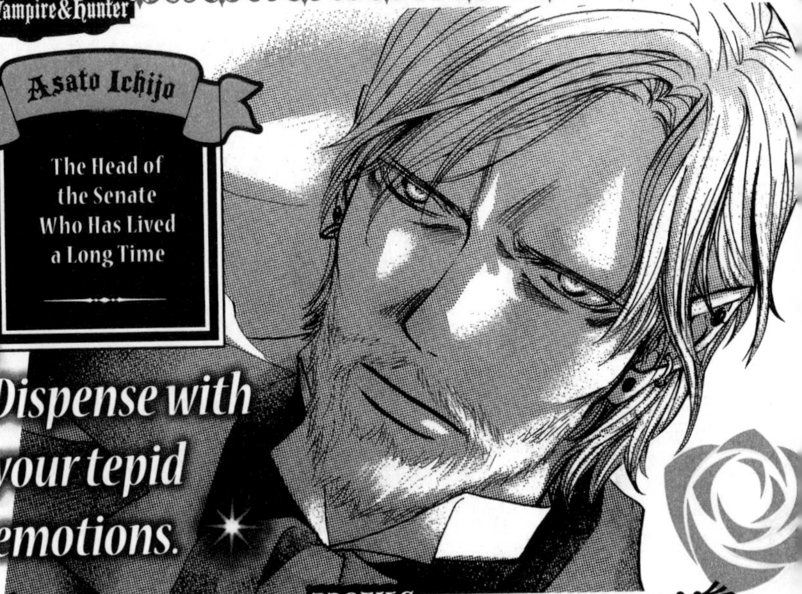

Dispense with your tepid emotions.

PROFILE

AFFILIATION: The Senate **HEIGHT:** 182 cm

VAMPIRE ABILITIES: Has a black aura

VAMPIRE LEVEL: Aristocrat

FAMILY: Son (living separately), grandson (Takuma)

RESPECTS: The head of the Kuran family two generations ago

TASTE IN WOMEN: A graceful, classy, modest and mischievous lady (like the actresses Sayuri Yoshinaga or Hitomi Kuroki)

GOOD AT: Iaido (traditional Japanese sword martial art), polo

FAVORITE FASHION: Formal clothes

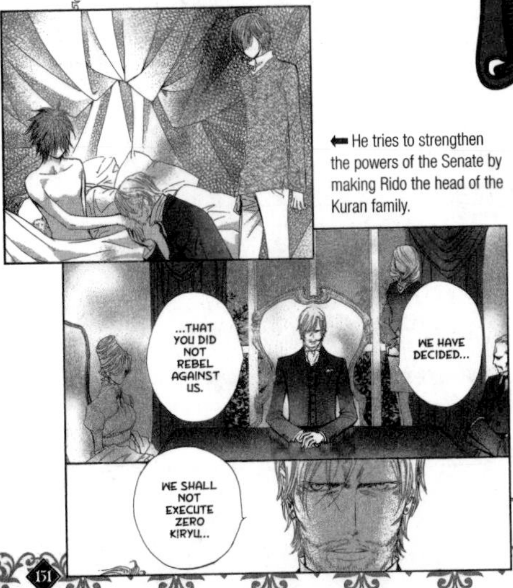
WE HAVE DECIDED...
...THAT YOU DID NOT REBEL AGAINST US.
WE SHALL NOT EXECUTE ZERO KIRYU..

⬅ He tries to strengthen the powers of the Senate by making Rido the head of the Kuran family.

CHARACTER ANALYSIS
This is what Asato Ichijo is like!!

Personality

A schemer who controls the vampire society

He uses every method possible to ensure that the Senate governs the vampire world. He sometimes makes cruel decisions. He is wary of those who want a return to the monarchy and has been keeping watch over Kaname because he is a symbol of the monarchy.

⬅ He tried to control Kaname by being his legal guardian.

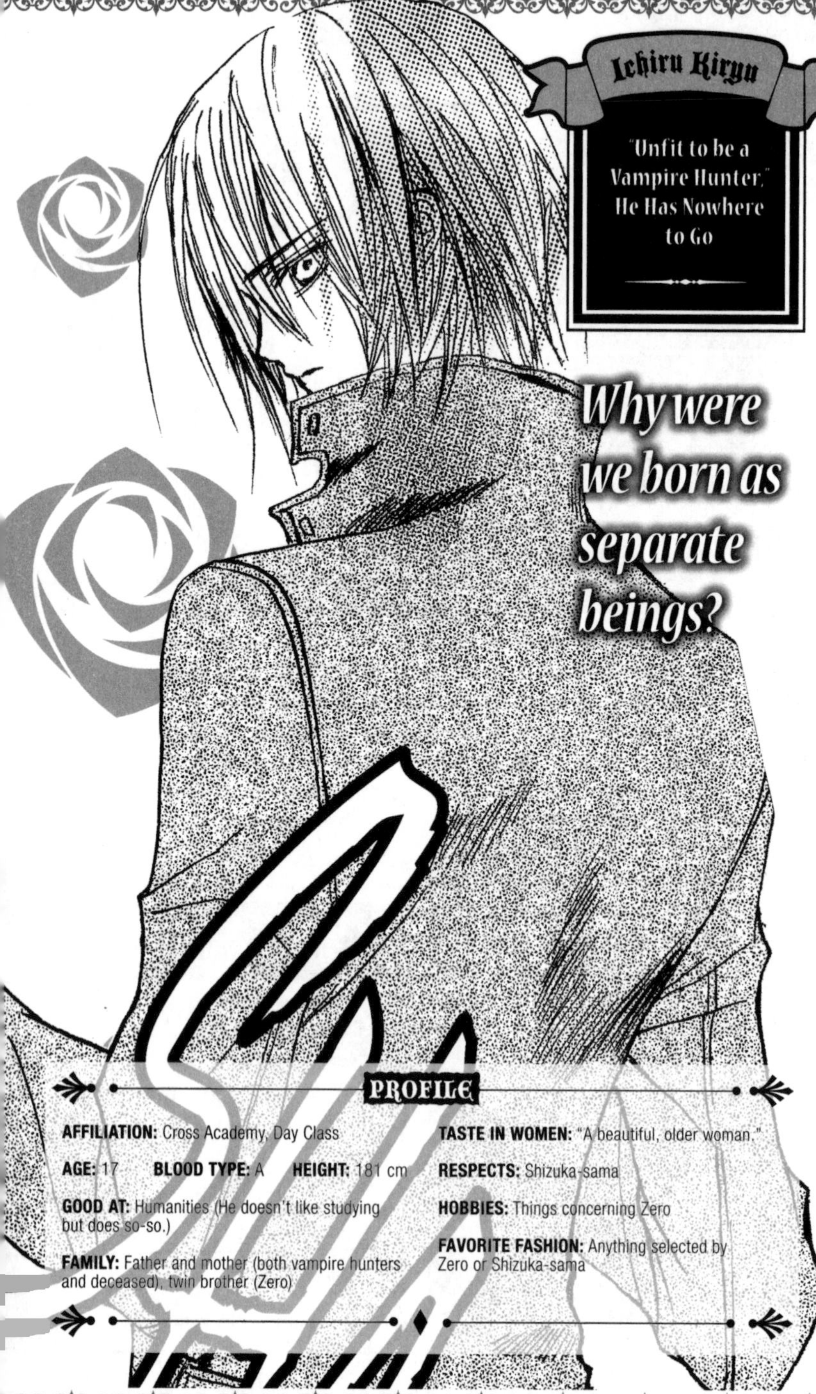

Ichiru Kiryu

"Unfit to be a Vampire Hunter," He Has Nowhere to Go

Why were we born as separate beings?

PROFILE

AFFILIATION: Cross Academy, Day Class

AGE: 17 **BLOOD TYPE:** A **HEIGHT:** 181 cm

GOOD AT: Humanities (He doesn't like studying but does so-so.)

FAMILY: Father and mother (both vampire hunters and deceased), twin brother (Zero)

TASTE IN WOMEN: "A beautiful, older woman."

RESPECTS: Shizuka-sama

HOBBIES: Things concerning Zero

FAVORITE FASHION: Anything selected by Zero or Shizuka-sama

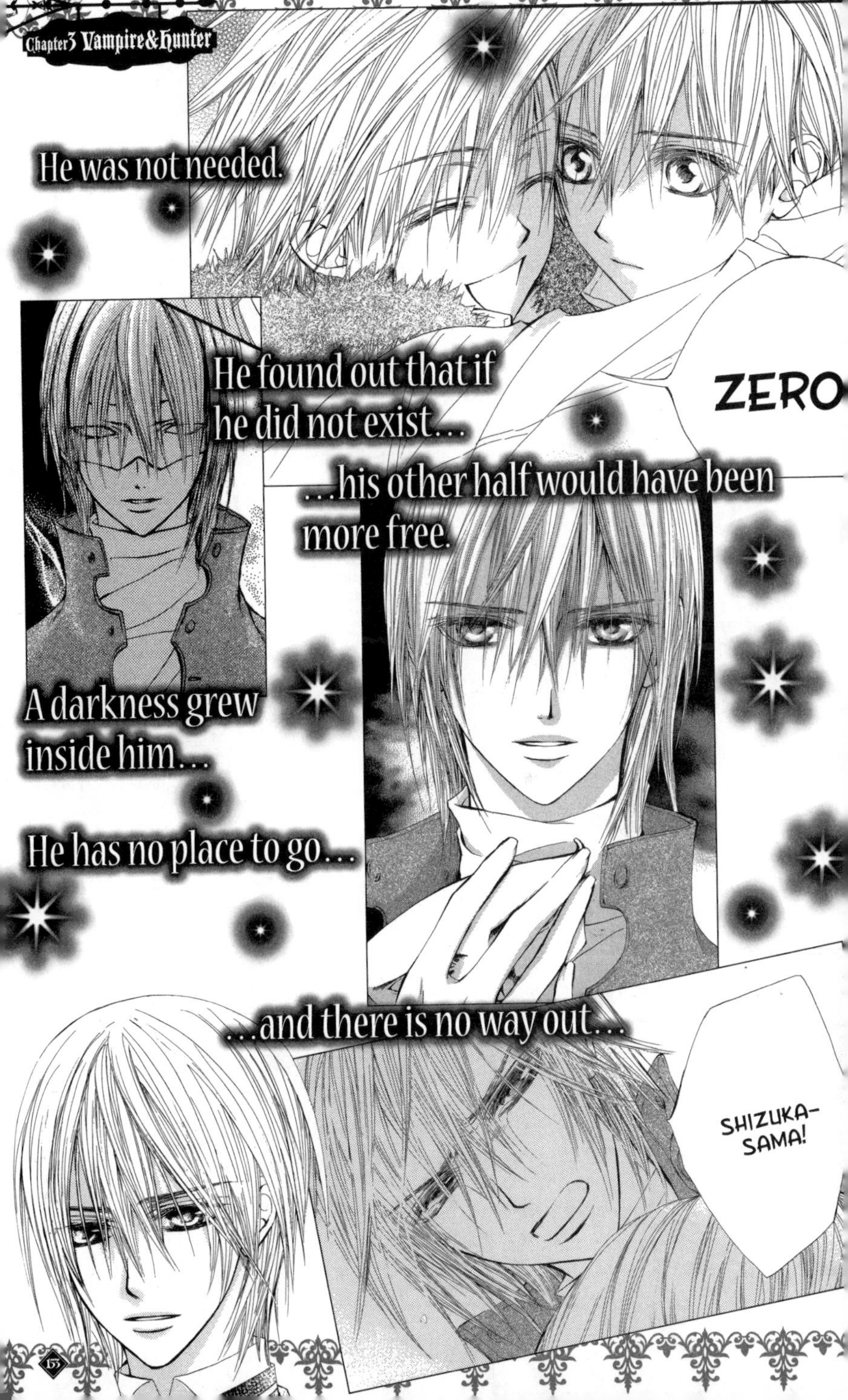
He was not needed.
He found out that if he did not exist...
ZERO
...his other half would have been more free.
A darkness grew inside him...
He has no place to go...
...and there is no way out...
SHIZUKA-SAMA!

CHARACTER ANALYSIS

This is what Ichiru Kiryu is like!

His Past

Looking for somewhere to go, he took the hand of Kuruizaki-hime

His parents deemed him unfit, and he felt that eventually there would come a day when he could not be with Zero anymore. When he met the crying Shizuka Hio, he was feeling as if he had no reason to live. Ichiru saw something in Shizuka that was similar to him, and he began meeting with her secretly. Then the tragedy occurred.

One night, he overheard his parents speaking and felt that he didn't belong anywhere. ➡

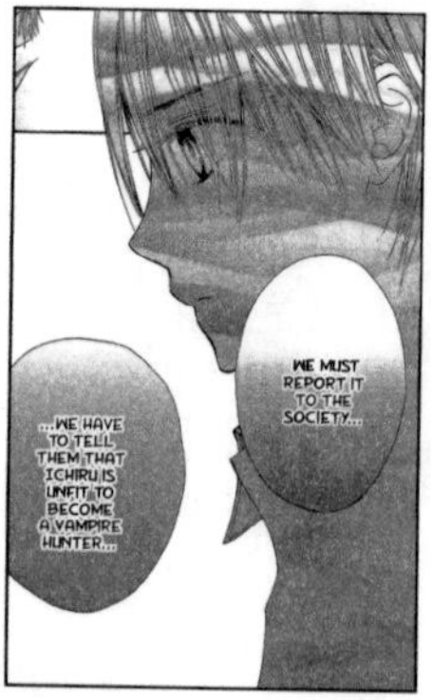
WE MUST REPORT IT TO THE SOCIETY...
...WE HAVE TO TELL THEM THAT ICHIRU IS UNFIT TO BECOME A VAMPIRE HUNTER...

He talks to the crying Shizuka, who is sitting on a branch of a cherry blossom tree that's not supposed to be in bloom. They slowly become close. ⬇

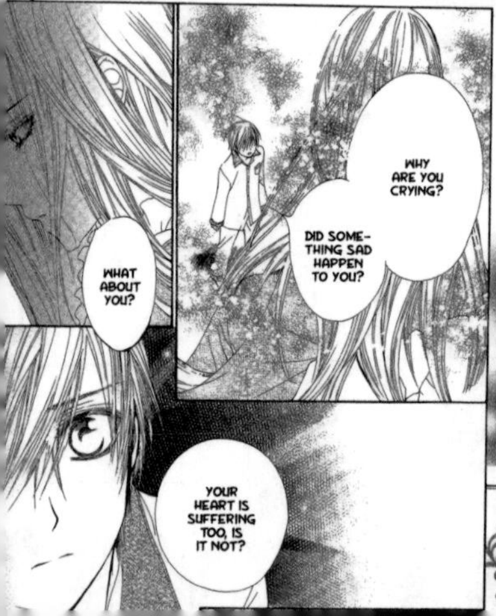
WHY ARE YOU CRYING?
DID SOME-THING SAD HAPPEN TO YOU?
WHAT ABOUT YOU?
YOUR HEART IS SUFFERING TOO, IS IT NOT?

Personality

He hid his true feelings under a mask...

He was born into a vampire hunter family, but he was frail and deemed unfit to become a hunter. Because he loved his gifted twin brother Zero, he stopped being able to reveal his true feelings. He used to be innocent and honest, but he began to conceal his heart, and dark feelings toward Zero began to grow inside him.

Days he spent with Zero... but complicated feelings festered inside him as well. ⬇

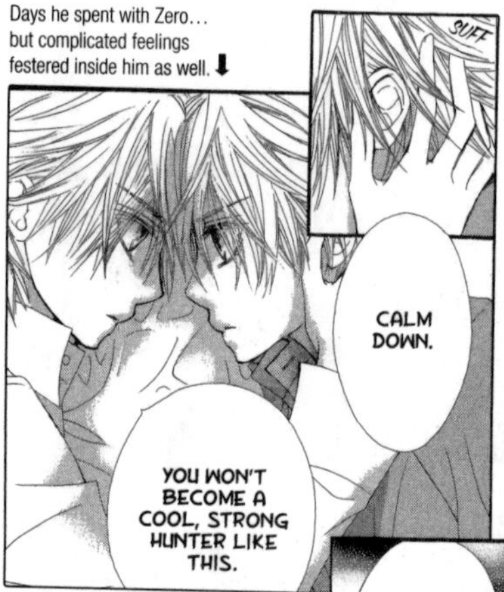
SUFF
CALM DOWN.
YOU WON'T BECOME A COOL, STRONG HUNTER LIKE THIS.

He meets Zero for the first time after four years as Shizuka's valet. He reveals his hatred of Zero. ➡

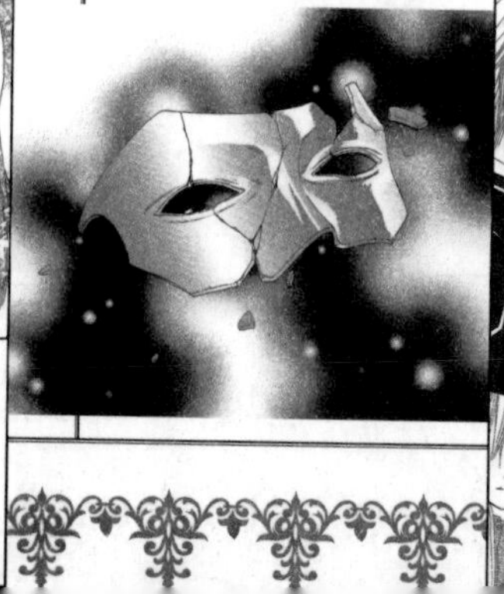

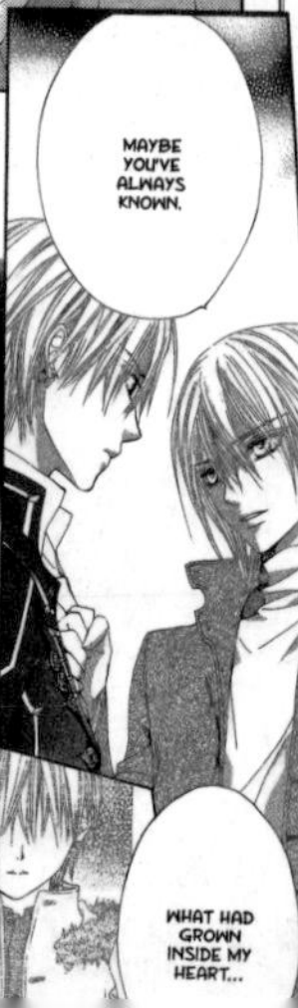
MAYBE YOU'VE ALWAYS KNOWN.
WHAT HAD GROWN INSIDE MY HEART...

Fighting Zero at Cross Academy. He can use a sword with either hand!! ⬇

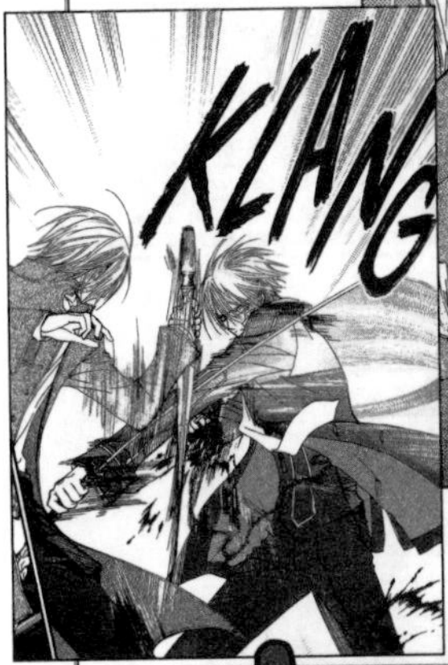
KLANG

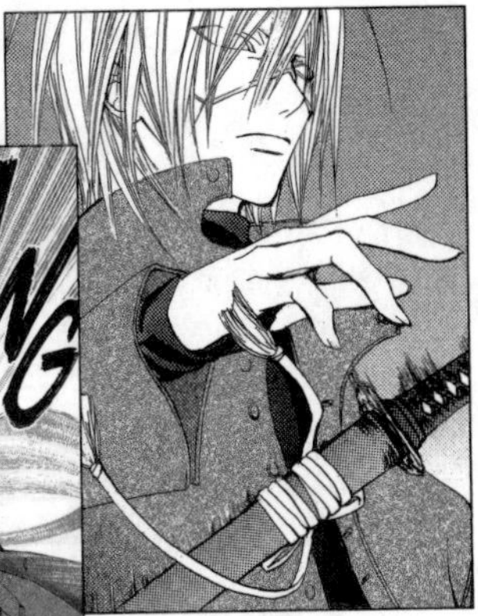

⬆ As Shizuka's valet, he carries her favorite Japanese sword. He uses it in fighting as well.

Fighting Ability

He handles short swords and Japanese swords

Because he drank blood from pureblood Shizuka, he is healthy now and can fight better than ordinary humans. When he fights, he instantly draws his collapsible short sword from his sleeve and pierces the enemy!! He often uses Shizuka's Japanese sword as well.

HIS PRIVATE LIFE

Let's check out his actions!

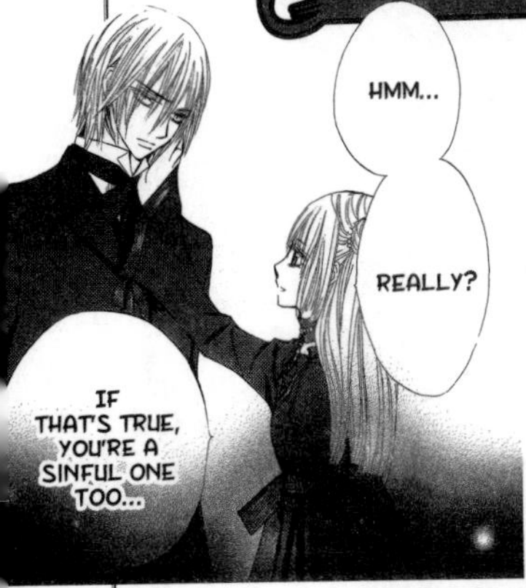
HMM...
REALLY?
IF THAT'S TRUE, YOU'RE A SINFUL ONE TOO...

Shizuka wanted Ichiru to live as a human until the very end. ⬇

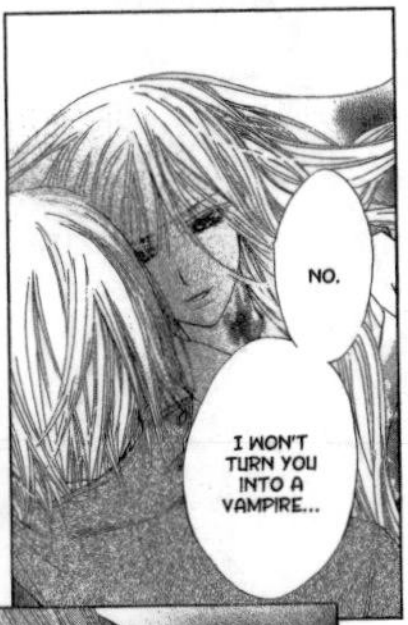
NO.
I WON'T TURN YOU INTO A VAMPIRE...

His four short years spent serving his master

He stood beside Shizuka as her bodyguard, but it was obvious that she did not need one. Yet Shizuka kept Ichiru by her side, and Ichiru demonstrated his loyalty to her. Ichiru hoped to become a vampire to be with Shizuka, but she did not want that. Ichiru's wish did not come true, and the relationship between the two who walked together for a fleeting moment came to an end…

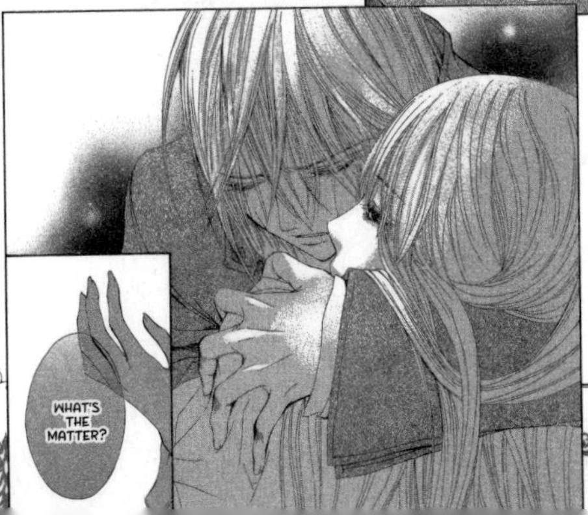
WHAT'S THE MATTER?

⬅ He cries while holding the dying Shizuka. She saved his lonely soul.

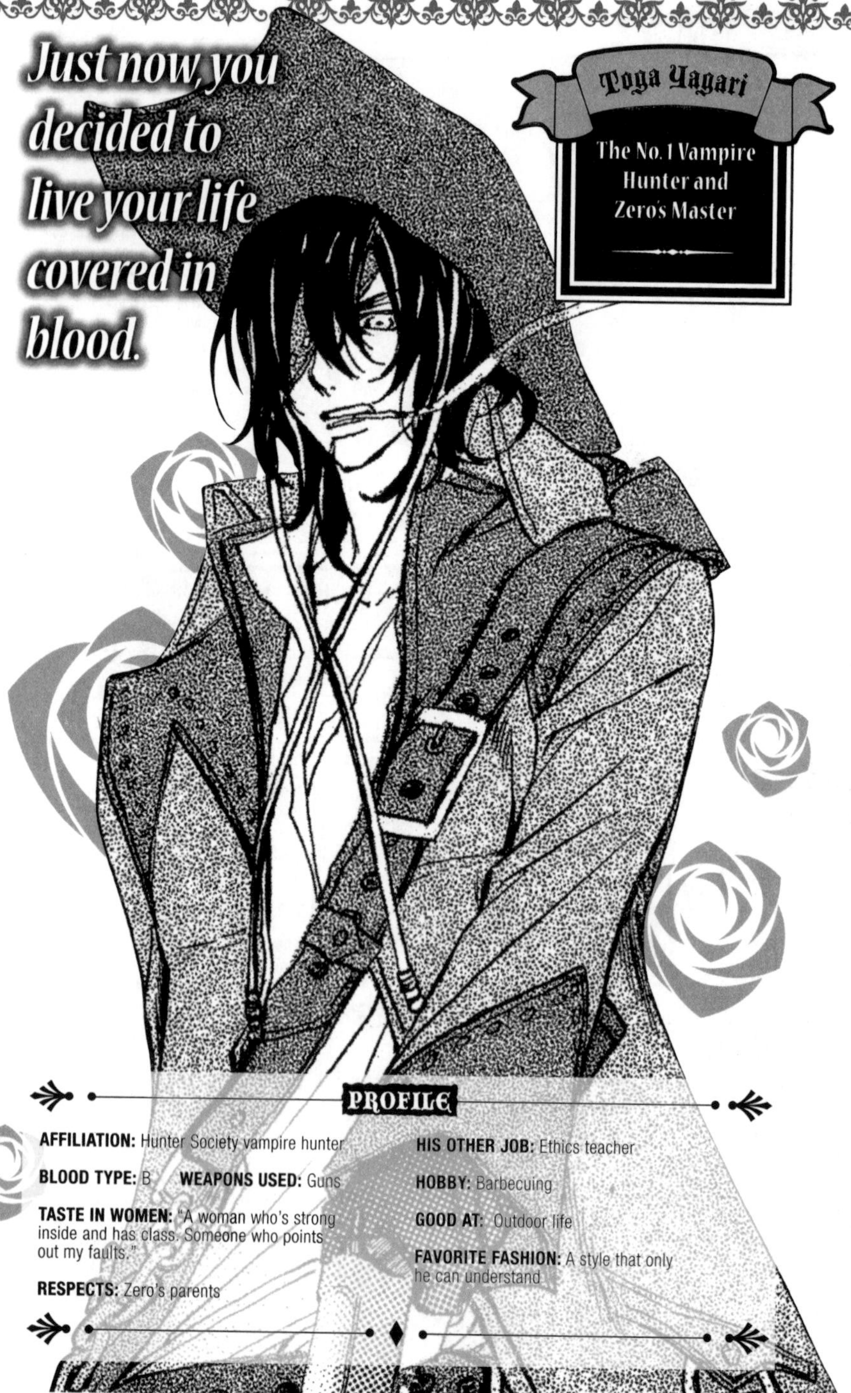
Just now, you decided to live your life covered in blood.
Toga Yagari
The No. 1 Vampire Hunter and Zero's Master

PROFILE

AFFILIATION: Hunter Society vampire hunter

BLOOD TYPE: B **WEAPONS USED:** Guns

TASTE IN WOMEN: "A woman who's strong inside and has class. Someone who points out my faults."

RESPECTS: Zero's parents

HIS OTHER JOB: Ethics teacher

HOBBY: Barbecuing

GOOD AT: Outdoor life

FAVORITE FASHION: A style that only he can understand

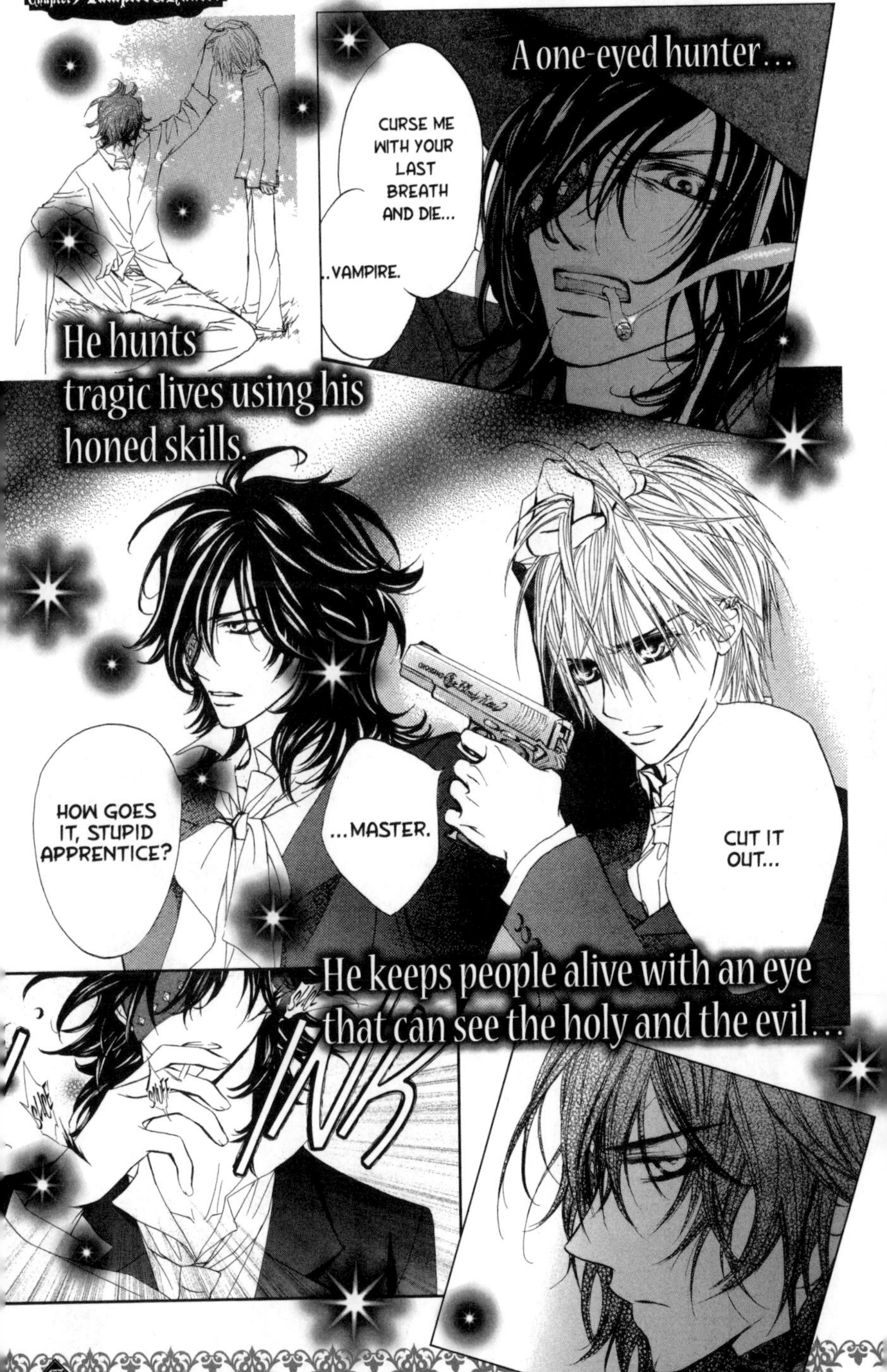
A one-eyed hunter…
CURSE ME WITH YOUR LAST BREATH AND DIE...
..VAMPIRE.
He hunts tragic lives using his honed skills.
HOW GOES IT, STUPID APPRENTICE?
...MASTER.
CUT IT OUT...
He keeps people alive with an eye that can see the holy and the evil…

CHARACTER ANALYSIS

This is what Toga Yagari is like!

His Past

A young life he protected in exchange for an eye

When Zero was still in elementary school, the doctor of his school turned into a Level E. Zero didn't know how terrifying a Level E could be, and Yagari lost an eye while protecting Zero. Yagari taught Zero about a vampire hunter's duties and a need for readiness in his actions.

A Level E gouged out Yagari's eye with its claws while he was protecting Zero. ⬇

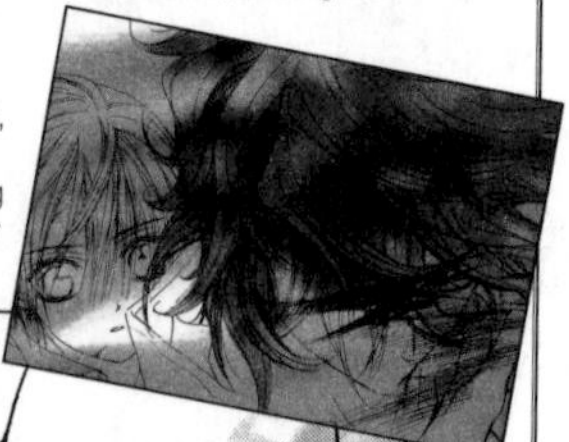

He reprimands Zero, who is losing his nerve about drinking Yuki's blood in order to survive. ⬇

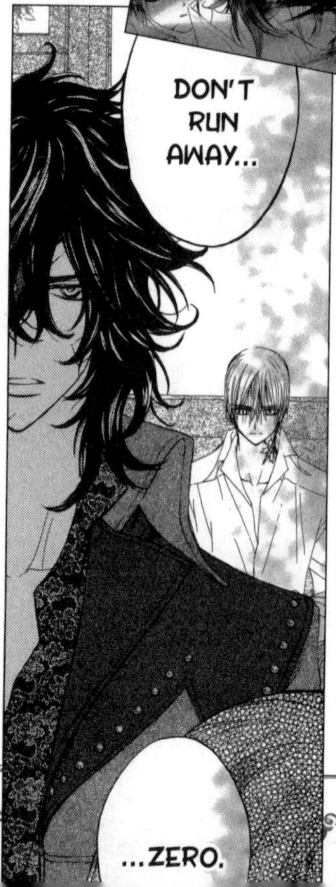
DON'T RUN AWAY...
...ZERO.

Personality

Harsh actions for the sake of being a hunter

He is very professional as a vampire hunter and methodically destroys vampires on his list. He is brutally merciless because he understands the harm that Level E vampires can do, and he knows that hesitating can cost him his life. There are no exceptions, even when he's facing his beloved former pupil!!

He's angry because he feels that vampire aristocrats are destroying vampires who used to be human as if they're enjoying hunting them down. ⬇

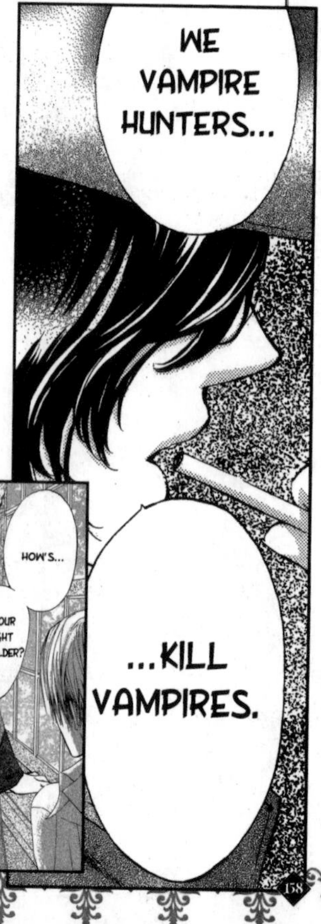
WE VAMPIRE HUNTERS...
...KILL VAMPIRES.

He tests Zero to see how close he is to Level E. He's prepared to execute him if necessary!! ⬇

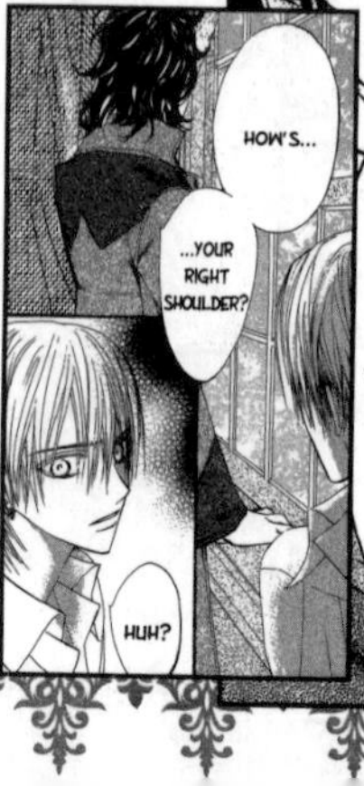
HOW'S...
...YOUR RIGHT SHOULDER?
HUH?

Fighting Ability

Well-sharpened skills used to chase and destroy the enemy

Yagari is number one in shooting accuracy, making appropriate judgments on the spot and other various skills. He is excellent at tracking down his target, and he never lets them get away. His skills are famous in the vampire world too.

VAMPIRES WHO'VE BEEN TAMED BY VAMPIRE HUNTER SPELLS ARE HERE.

He can figure out information about a vampire through its ashes. ➡

P-
TOOM

He can shoot the vitals of a vampire with one shot and destroy it. ⬇

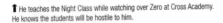

SCHOOLTIME

His activities at school!

Teaching

He's a teacher in ethics

He has a teaching certificate in ethics. He knows a lot about vampires, so he taught the Night Class of Cross Academy once.

I'M TOGA YAGARI. I'LL BE YOUR TEMPORARY LECTURER FOR THIS ETHICS CLASS.
NICE TO MEET YOU, VAMPIRES...

⬆ He teaches the Night Class while watching over Zero at Cross Academy. He knows the students will be hostile to him.

⬆ He calmly deals with a flying knife. There was no trouble in particular, and the class ended safely!!

Kaien Cross

The Founder of the Academy Who Aimed to Create Paradise

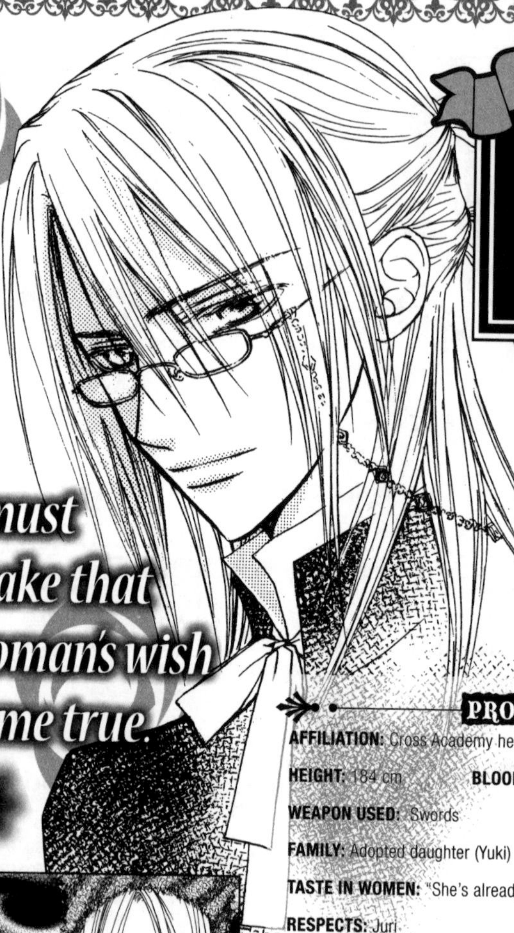

I must make that woman's wish come true.

PROFILE

AFFILIATION: Cross Academy headmaster

HEIGHT: 184 cm **BLOOD TYPE:** AB

WEAPON USED: Swords

FAMILY: Adopted daughter (Yuki)

TASTE IN WOMEN: "She's already married, so..."

RESPECTS: Juri

HOBBIES: Cooking. Always makes elaborate dishes in his own "style."

FAVORITE FASHION: Lots of layers

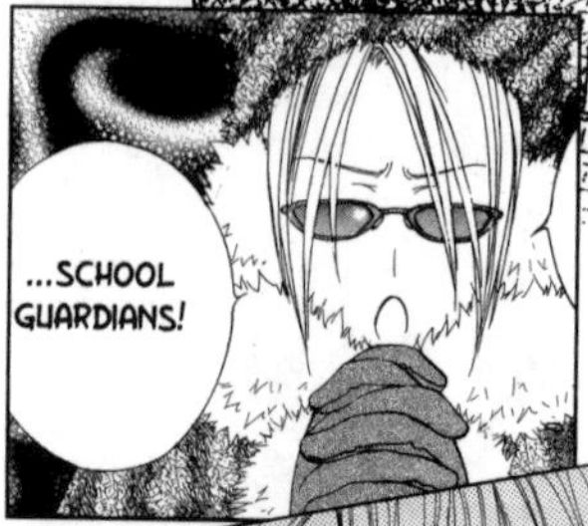
...SCHOOL GUARDIANS!

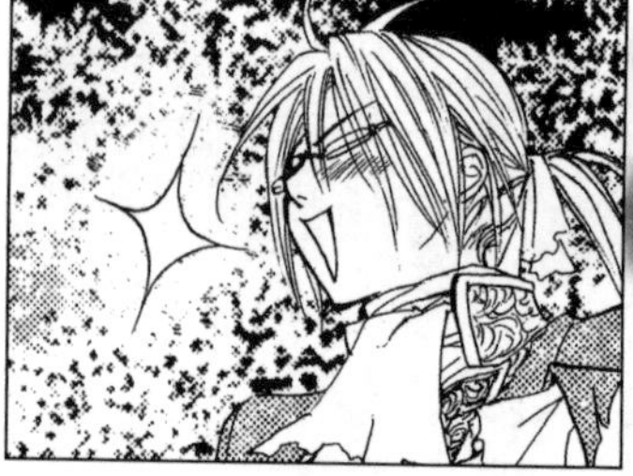

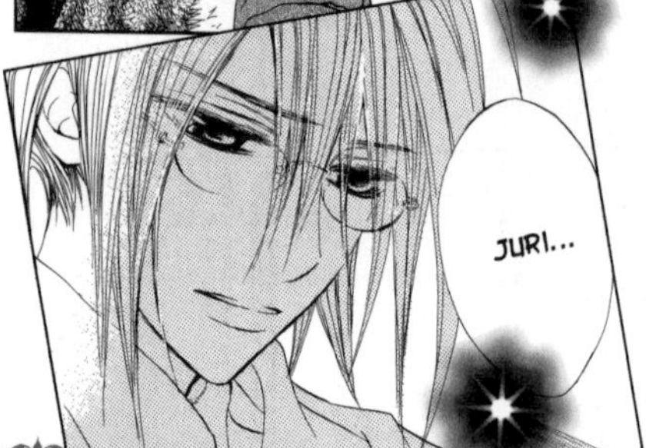
JURI...

CHARACTER ANALYSIS

This is what Kaien Cross is like!!

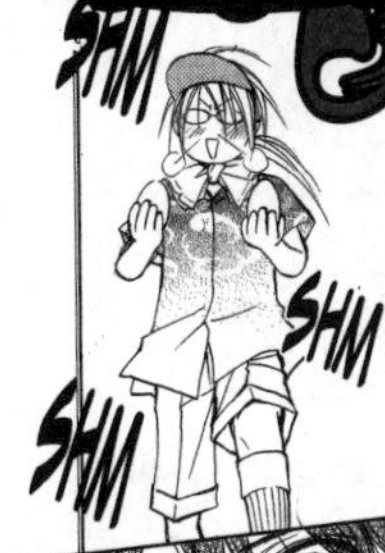
SHM
SHM
SHM

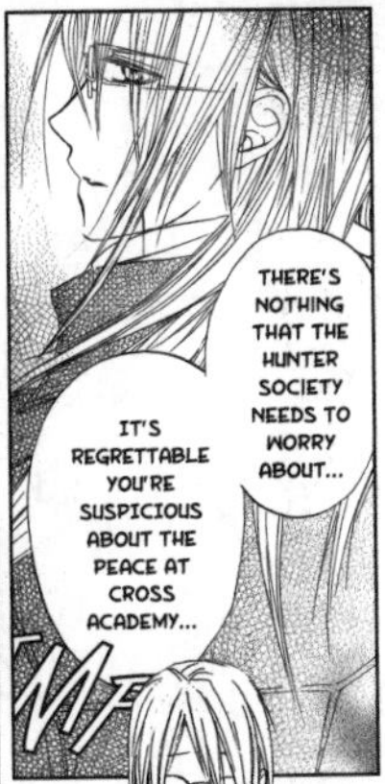
THERE'S NOTHING THAT THE HUNTER SOCIETY NEEDS TO WORRY ABOUT...
IT'S REGRETTABLE YOU'RE SUSPICIOUS ABOUT THE PEACE AT CROSS ACADEMY...

He restrains the Hunter Society, which tried to meddle with the academy when Zero turned into a vampire.➡

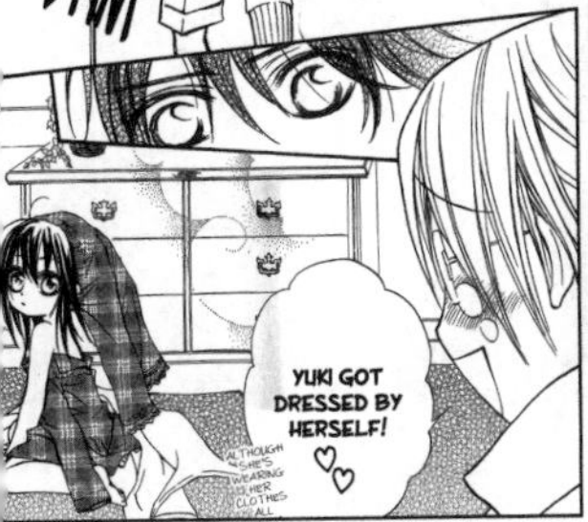
YUKI GOT DRESSED BY HERSELF! ♡ ♡
ALTHOUGH SHE'S WEARING HER CLOTHES ALL

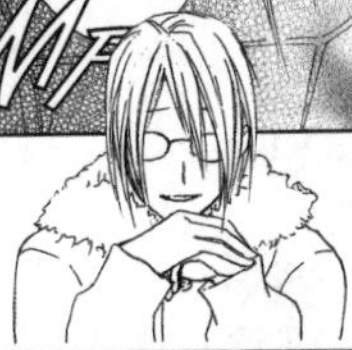

⬆ He cried for joy when Yuki put on clothes by herself.

Personality

A man who looks to the future and protects the academy he founded in addition to being a doting parent

He may seem unworldly, but he's a schemer who engages in a battle of wits with the Hunter Society to maintain the academy. He's basically a pacifist and hates conflicts. He loves his adopted daughter Yuki so much it's ridiculous.

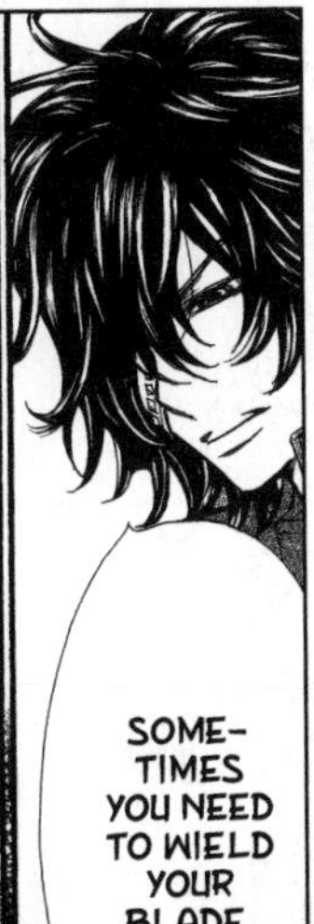
SOME-TIMES YOU NEED TO WIELD YOUR BLADE.

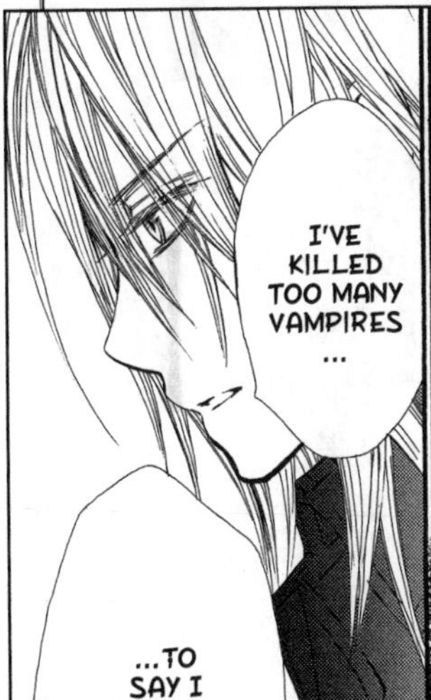
I'VE KILLED TOO MANY VAMPIRES ...
...TO SAY I UNDER-STAND THEM.

⬆ He regrets the time he thought of vampires as beings without emotions and hunted them.

His Past

He was a master vampire hunter affiliated with the Hunter Society until 16 years ago

He used to be a strong hunter who destroyed countless vampires by himself. After he met Juri Kuran and heard her wish, however, Kaien changed. He then founded Cross Academy with the aim of having a peaceful coexistence between vampires and humans.

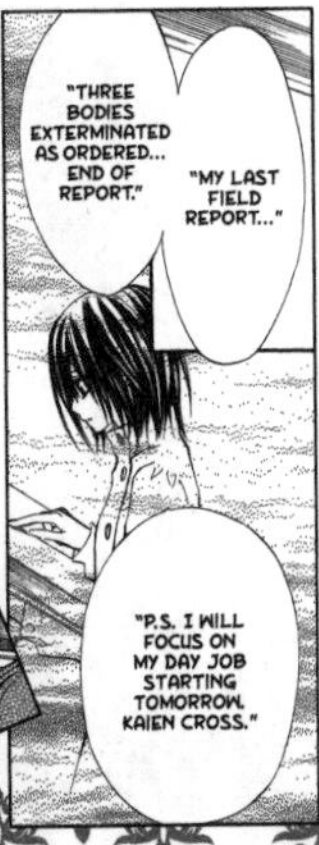
"THREE BODIES EXTERMINATED AS ORDERED... END OF REPORT."
"MY LAST FIELD REPORT..."
"P.S. I WILL FOCUS ON MY DAY JOB STARTING TOMORROW. KAIEN CROSS."

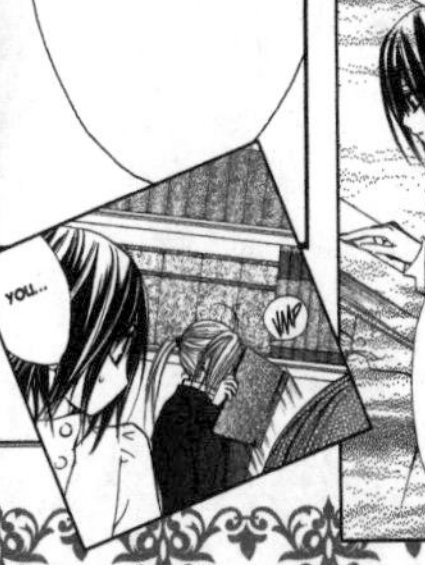
YOU...

⬅ The archives of the Hunter Society contain records of when Kaien was active as a vampire hunter.

Read these pages at your own risk!
Only for those who really want to know the truth!!

Yuki, Kaname, Zero—*The Truth About the Three!!*

Yuki, Kaname, and Zero are supposed to be students at a peaceful academy. In actuality, each of them is a key player in the coexistence between vampires and humans…

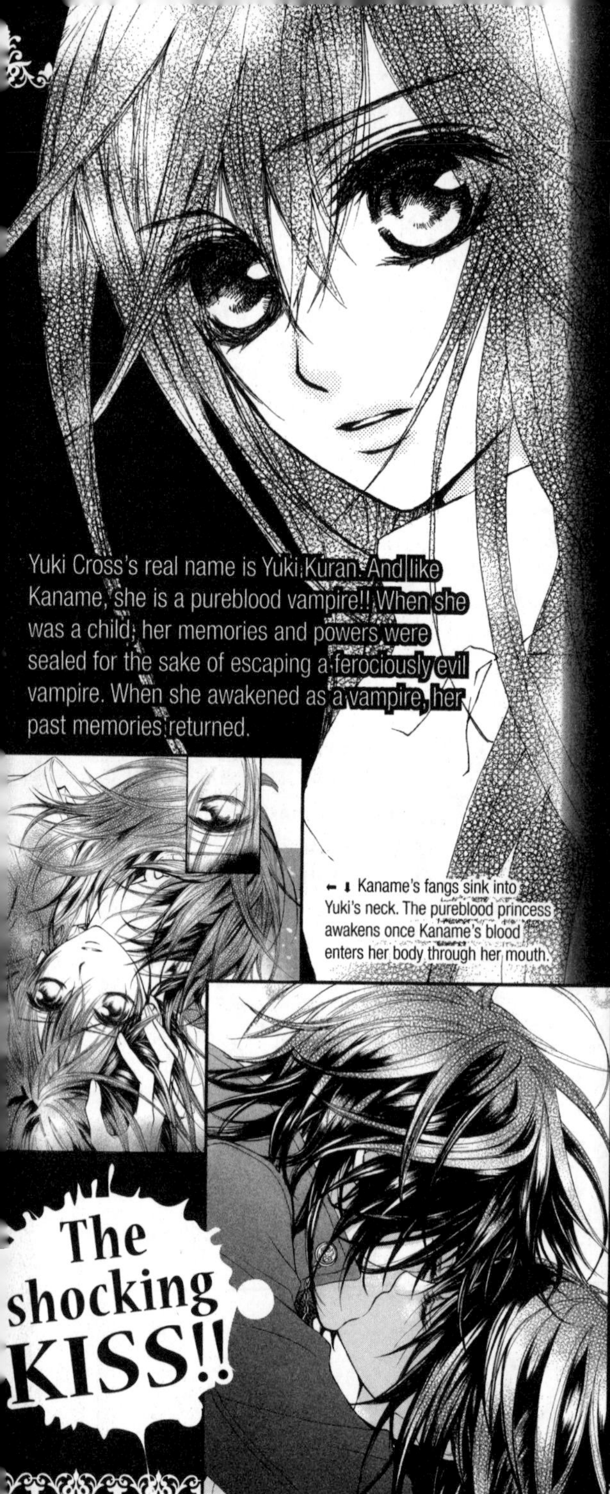

Yuki Cross's real name is Yuki Kuran. And like Kaname, she is a pureblood vampire!! When she was a child, her memories and powers were sealed for the sake of escaping a ferociously evil vampire. When she awakened as a vampire, her past memories returned.

← ↓ Kaname's fangs sink into Yuki's neck. The pureblood princess awakens once Kaname's blood enters her body through her mouth.

The shocking KISS!!

Yuki Kuran

Her sealed memories return!!

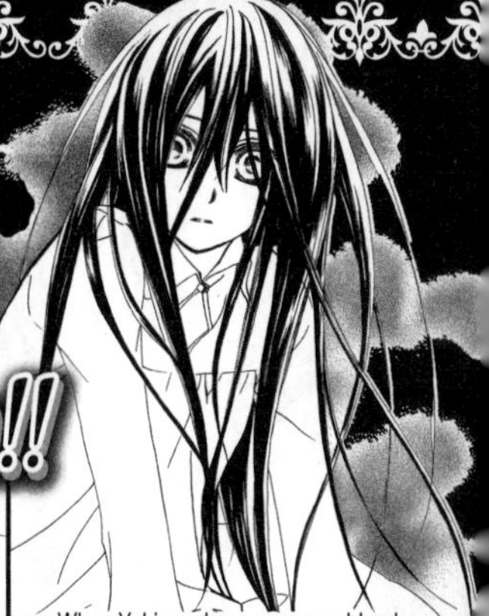

↑ When Yuki awakens as a pureblood, her looks change too. Her hair grows long to her waist. Her expression is different as well…

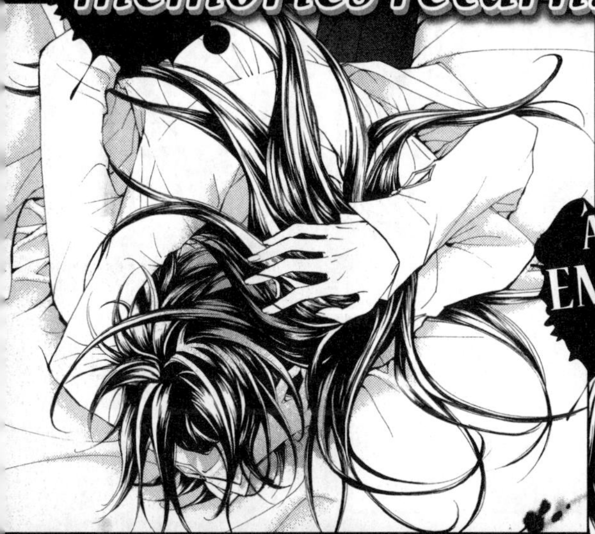

A passionate EMBRACE with KANAME!!

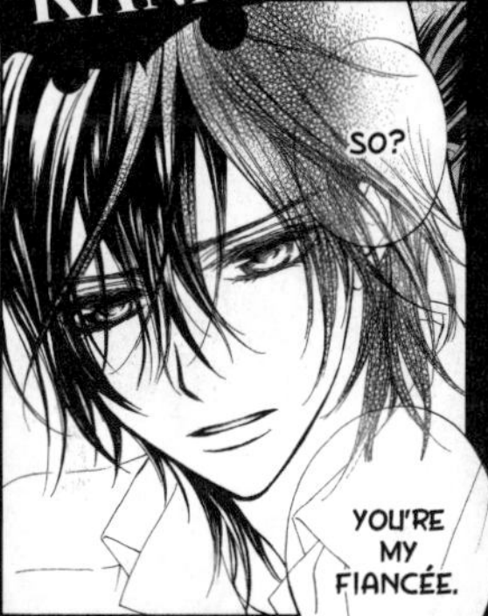
SO?
YOU'RE MY FIANCÉE.

↑ Kaname tells Yuki that they're lovers!!

When Yuki awakens as a pureblood, she realizes that Kaname is the big brother she adored and her fiancé. Just as her parents Haruka and Juri Kuran were siblings, Yuki and Kaname were born to marry each other.

Ten Years Ago — Her memory is robbed due to her parents' deep love!!

Yuki is the daughter of Haruka and Juri Kuran. Her mother Juri sacrificed her life in order to hide and protect Yuki from her uncle Rido Kuran. Yuki's father Haruka also lost his life protecting his family. When Kaname awakens Yuki as a pureblood, she remembers this bloody incident.

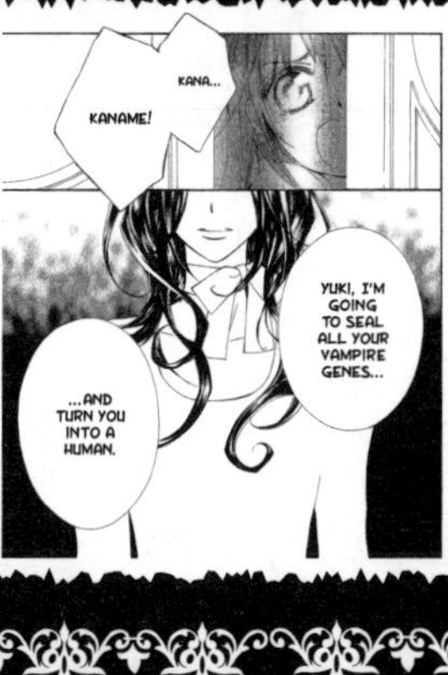
KANA...
KANAME!
YUKI, I'M GOING TO SEAL ALL YOUR VAMPIRE GENES...
...AND TURN YOU INTO A HUMAN.

← Yuki's mother Juri puts a special spell on her and seals her vampire genes. This is why Yuki's memories were lost.

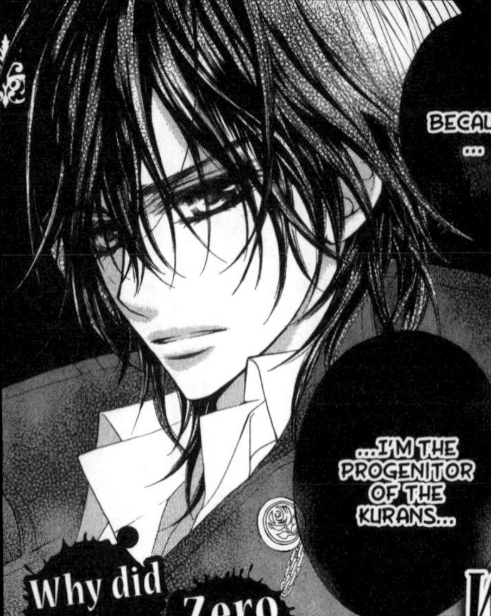
BECAUSE ...
...I'M THE PROGENITOR OF THE KURANS...

Kaname Kuran

The man who rules the Night Class! Who is he really?!

Why did he keep Zero alive?!

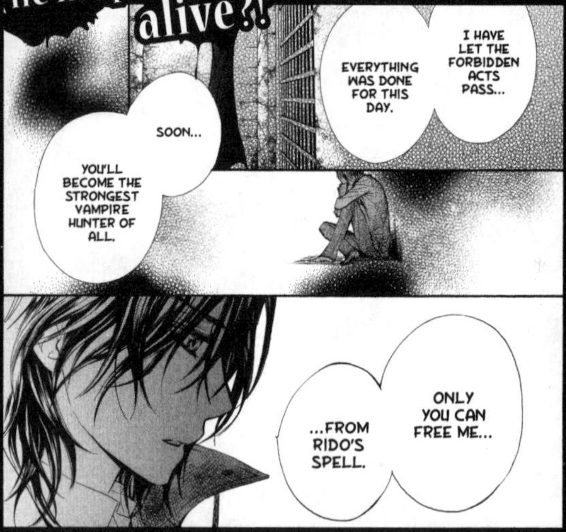
I HAVE LET THE FORBIDDEN ACTS PASS...
EVERYTHING WAS DONE FOR THIS DAY.
SOON...
YOU'LL BECOME THE STRONGEST VAMPIRE HUNTER OF ALL.
ONLY YOU CAN FREE ME...
...FROM RIDO'S SPELL.

When Rido is resurrected, Kaname reveals a shocking truth—that he is the progenitor of the vampires and that he cannot escape the curse of Rido, the master who resurrected him. He also tells Zero that only he can free him.

← Kaname kept Zero alive and kept making him stronger!! It was all done to free himself from Rido's curse...

Ten Years Ago — Kaname's "master" is his nemesis—Rido Kuran!!

Kaname loathes Rido the most because Rido destroyed Kaname's foster father Haruka and continues to target Yuki. He almost killed Rido once but could not deal the final blow. The reason is that Rido became Kaname's master when he awakened Kaname from his coffin. That's why Kaname charges Zero with protecting Yuki and destroying Rido...!!

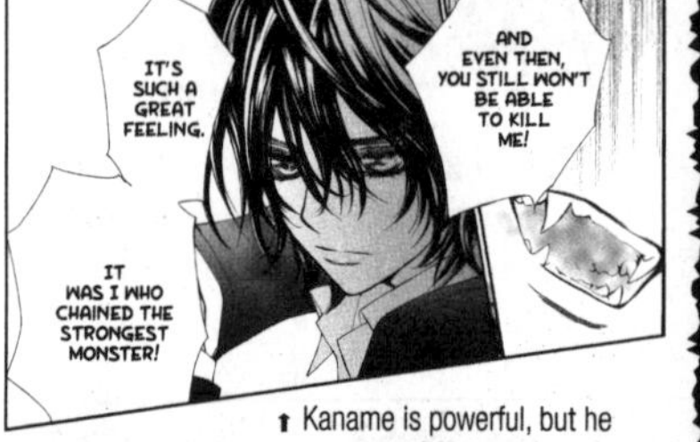
AND EVEN THEN, YOU STILL WON'T BE ABLE TO KILL ME!
IT'S SUCH A GREAT FEELING.
IT WAS I WHO CHAINED THE STRONGEST MONSTER!

↑ Kaname is powerful, but he cannot completely destroy Rido...

Zero Kiryu

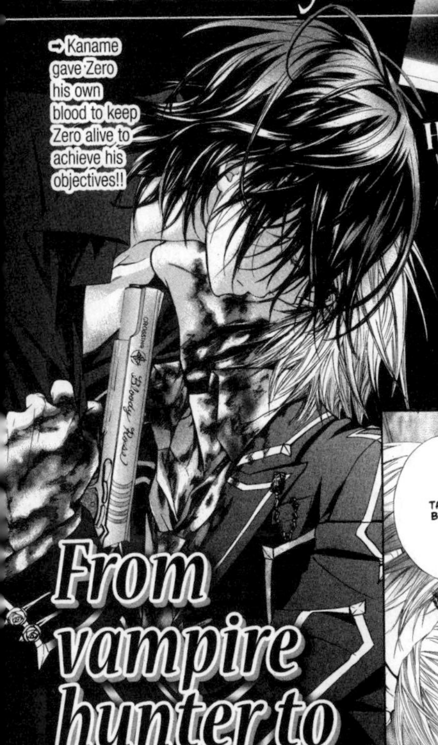

➡ Kaname gave Zero his own blood to keep Zero alive to achieve his objectives!!

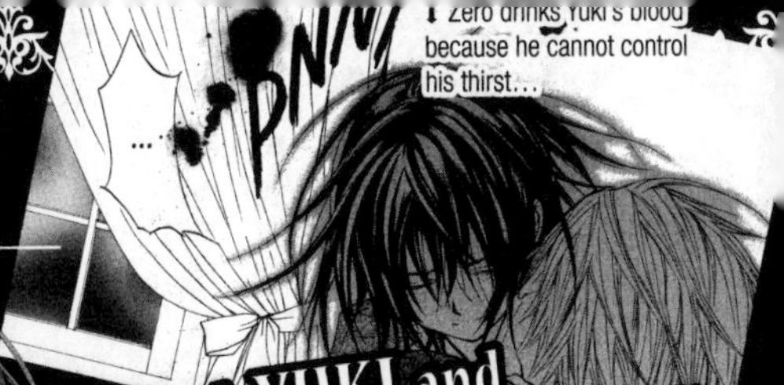
...

⬇ Zero drinks Yuki's blood because he cannot control his thirst…

He drank YUKI and KANAME'S blood…!!

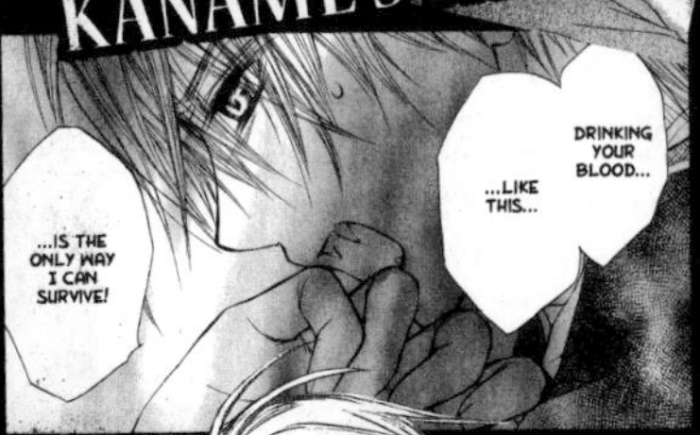
DRINKING YOUR BLOOD...
...LIKE THIS...
...IS THE ONLY WAY I CAN SURVIVE!

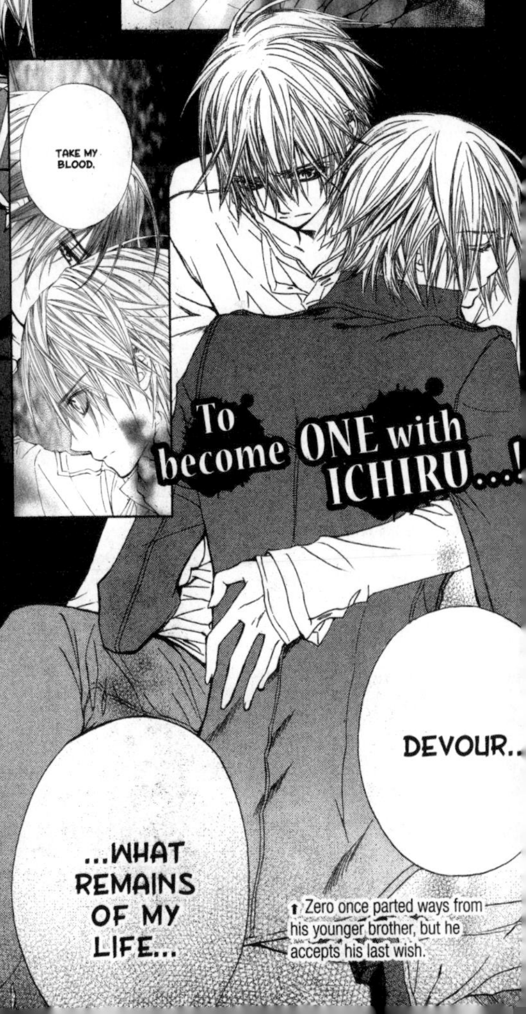
TAKE MY BLOOD.
DEVOUR...
...WHAT REMAINS OF MY LIFE...

To become ONE with ICHIRU…!

⬆ Zero once parted ways from his younger brother, but he accepts his last wish.

From vampire hunter to vampire… Where is he headed?!

Kaname devoured Shizuka, and Yuki gained power once she awakened as a pureblood… Zero has both of their blood stirring inside him. Zero also devours his twin Ichiru and becomes the strongest vampire hunter of all!!

The Hidden Case Files

Regarding Yuki and those related to her

Sixteen years ago

- Kaien Cross quits being a vampire hunter.

Ten years ago

- The Kurans die. Kaname defeats Rido.
- Kaname rescues Yuki when she's being attacked by a vampire. Headmaster Cross adopts her.

A little over four years ago

- Rido orders the Senate to get rid of Shizuka's servant.
- The Hunter Society sends the Kiryu family (Zero's parents) to carry out the Senate's orders. Shizuka's servant is executed by the Kiryu family.

Four years ago

- Shizuka attacks the Kiryu family. Shizuka kills Zero's parents and bites Zero. Kaien Cross starts taking care of Zero.
- It turns out Ichiru led Shizuka to his parents.

Present Day

- Shizuka borrows Maria's body to transfer to the Night Class. She attacks Zero but is destroyed by Kaname.
- The Hunter Society issues a restraining order for Zero, but Yagari and the Headmaster block it.
- The Hunter Society enters Cross Academy and decides to purge the Night Class.
- Rido is resurrected.

WHAT will happen at these TWO BATTLES?!

The final battle to defeat their nemeses!!

To protect Cross Academy, Yuki goes into battle holding her Artemis rod!! Zero is shocked to discove that Yuki is one of the purebloods that he loathes, but he fights beside her against Rido. Meanwhile, Kaname heads off to a final battle with the Senate—a powerful, Machiavellian organization.

YUKI and ZERO vs. RIDO!!
KANAME vs. the SENATE!!
HAVE YOU COME TO DESTROY ME?
THAT ONE OF OUR HOLY PROGENITORS WHO WAS RESURRECTED HAS TAKEN THE TROUBLE TO COME HERE...
YOU TOOK CARE OF ME, ASATO ICHIJO...
AND I'VE REGAINED THE CONDITION I WAS IN BEFORE I WENT TO "SLEEP"...

→ As a pureblood, Yuki is his enemy. But Zero chooses to fight Rido!!

← Kaname goes to see Ichio. After ten years of using each other, the time has come to declare war!!

Vam☆Fan Hall

Announcement ①

Acting President Ichijo's Special Power Research Lab

The elite vampire abilities that people came up with are all amazing!!

ABILITY 1 Kamaitachi (Sharp Slashes)

Use fans to create wind and slash the enemy. Can make slashes with one hand only, but slashes created with both hands crossed are very effective. This move is effective against objects as well as people. Can also just blow the enemy away instead of slashing them.

-Kii Kurohina, Aichi Prefecture

With a vampire's physical strength and taijutsu training, this ability becomes as fast as drawing a sword at lightning speed!

ABILITY 2 Sharing Abilities

By drinking another vampire's blood, you can temporarily use that vampire's voice and part of his or her special abilities.

-Mittan 6-go, Tokyo

Everyone would want to copy the powers of the almighty Kaname...

ABILITY 3 The Power of Tears

A vampire's tears can make a human three times more beautiful.

-Hitomi Watanabe, Niigata Prefecture

If we turn this into a product, it might be popular among women who want to become beautiful...

ABILITY 4 Blood Testing

When you drink someone's blood, you can instantly know things about that person's health like blood pressure, the total amount of blood that person has, illnesses and the like.

-Fumika Honda, Gunma Prefecture

If you're drinking human blood, it's good manners to comprehend the health of that person.

ABILITY 5 Duplication

By putting your blood on a mirror when you're looking at it, you can create a clone of yourself.

-Tochi no mi, Tokyo

If I had a clone of myself, I'd have it run my grandfather's errands and go to my classes for me.

ABILITY 6 Charming Melody

Words and songs in high tones are for capturing. Words and songs in low tones can kill. Ordinary conversations do not have these effects because your eyes would be open (i.e., the abilities are effective only when you have your eyes closed).

-Mamepon, Hokkaido

This is a convenient skill where you can capture your enemy while they're listening to you sing. ☆

Vice president Shiki's recommended abilities

Here are the abilities I took notice of...

ABILITY 7 Aftereffect

If a pureblood drinks your blood, you turn into a vampire. A few days later, the bitten area starts itching as if a mosquito bit you.

-Voice Actor Hopeful, Tokyo

Is it a million times more itchy than if a mosquito were to bite you?

ABILITY 8 Even Insects Avoid You

Mosquitoes and vampires both suck blood, but mosquitoes hate vampire blood, so vampires don't actually know how itchy mosquito bites are.

-Sakuran, Tokyo

So how itchy are mosquito bites?

ABILITY 9 Can Manipulate Mosquitoes

Limited to summertime only. Use the mosquito to gather fresh blood in the academy even though drinking blood is prohibited. If the mosquito is squashed, the one manipulating it feels pain like a slap.

-Rei, Aichi Prefecture

It would be convenient if mosquitoes gathered blood instead.

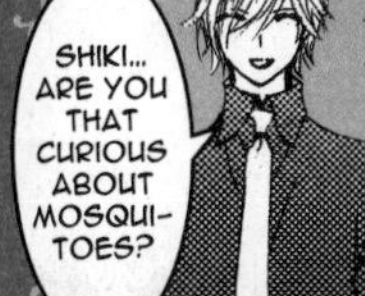
SHIKI... ARE YOU THAT CURIOUS ABOUT MOSQUITOES?

Vam☆Fan Hall
Announcement ②

Created by I&W of the Night Class

SECRET

INVESTIGATION REPORT

On Those Who Want to Give Blood

"Who do you want to drink your blood?" The I-W pair hid their identity and asked around. Here are the results!!

#1 Kaname Kuran

It is ultimate bliss to have him drink my blood.

Previously No.1

I think my stiff shoulders would heal. (Smile)
-Chakura, Hyogo Prefecture

I want him to coldly say, "Your blood doesn't taste good" after he finishes. ♥
-Ichigo, Hokkaido

If Kaname-sama drank my blood, I wouldn't mind becoming a vampire.
-Syuri Shinbo, Tokyo

I want to see Kaname-sama with blood around his mouth.
-Sumire Ameya, Tokyo

I want to look at Kaname-sama's face at close range.
-Jun x 2, Okayama

I want Kaname Kuran to drink my blood and fall asleep with sweet dreams.
-Satomi Sato, Aichi Prefecture

I'm sure he'll drink my blood politely, beautifully and lovingly!
-Miyuki Kondo, Kanagawa Prefecture

#4 Akatsuki Kain

I want him to drink my blood wildly.

Previously No.6

I'd melt in an instant if that muscular body that I can see from beneath his shirt touched me. ♥ I'm lured by his sexy body. (Smile)
-Aoi, Ehime Prefecture

If something happened, I think he'd be strong. He's like a big brother, so I always want him by my side.
-Miyucchi, Saitama Prefecture

When I imagine him holding me tenderly but firmly... ♥
-Nayuta, Gunma Prefecture

I love cool Akatsuki!! I wish he'd marry me...
-Yura, Ibaragi Prefecture

#3 Senri Shiki

I want him to beg when he feels like it.

Previously No.4

I want him to look at me with those eyes that don't tell you what he's thinking. ♥ And if he mumbled, "That was good" in the end...!!
-Jehann Darc, Chiba Prefecture

If he casually asked me to let him drink my blood or if he came at me with an unemotional expression, I would...
-Miki, Gifu Prefecture

I want him to drink my blood in the classroom at night, saying, "Your blood...exists just for me."
-Miwa, Tokyo

The way he's naturally himself is cute, and the way he's cool is awesome!!
-Shi-chan ☆, Hokkaido

INSIDE STORY

I&W's heart-pounding inside story on how they created this report?!

Getting All the Data Together

*We altered their voices in the following exchange.

Hey Ak— (whap)

Be quiet. If the president finds out we've been doing something like this…

I: What do you mean, something like this!! I just thought it would be useful to find girls who'd give us blood in case of emergencies… In case something happened to Kaname-sama!!

W: Oh, really.

I: What? The girls are volunteering themselves!! Take a good look at the report!!

W: All right, all right. Don't get so worked up. I just hope the president, Ruka, and the others don't find out about this… Let's finish up quickly.

Such an exchange took place… Or maybe not…

#2 Zero Kiryu

Lots of volunteers because he's suffering so?!

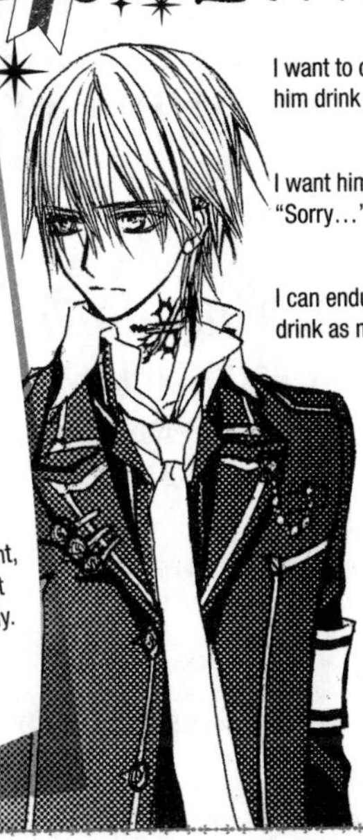

I want to console his body and heart by having him drink my blood. I also want to be soothed. ♥

-Naoko Toida, Tokyo

I want him to push himself onto me, saying, "Sorry…" ♥

-Yuriko Kamijo, Nagano Prefecture

I can endure the pain for Zero's sake. He can drink as much as he wants.

-Kasumi Koga, Miyazaki Prefecture

I don't want him to hesitate. I want him to gulp my blood. ★

-Haruchi, Saitama Prefecture

He hates drinking blood but he can't control his urges… If Zero looked as if he was suffering, I'd want him to drink my blood.

-Sayaka Ota, Kanagawa Prefecture

Previously No. 2

#6 Hanabusa Aido

I want to offer my blood to the school idol!

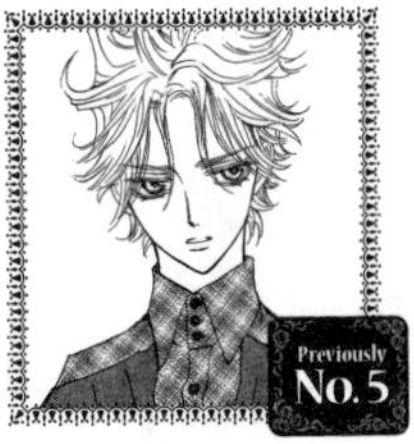

Aido is the most dazzling one, so I'd like to give all my blood to the Aido I love.

-Akira Shigure, Fukuoka Prefecture

Previously No. 5

I think he'll really gulp it down, but I don't want to become anemic, so please don't drink too much. (Smile)

-Megumi Ishizuka, Hyogo Prefecture

The way he's not honest with himself is very cute.

-Hotaru, Akita Prefecture

I'd pester him until the very end. I'd drive Wild out and become his roommate!!

-Kureha, Shiga Prefecture

#5 Takuma Ichijo

The number 1 nice guy

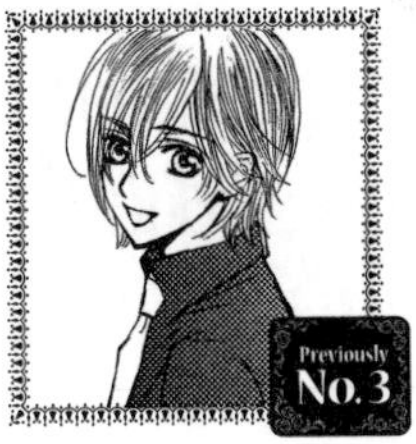

I've never seen Takuma-sama drink blood, so I want him to drink my blood tenderly.

-∞ Kako ∞, Ibaragi Prefecture

Previously No. 3

If the last thing I see before I die is Takuma-sama, I'll have no regrets.

-Raimu, Toyama Prefecture

I think he'll do it well, like a nurse who's used to drawing blood.

-Yusei, Kochi Prefecture

I want him to be cool and sexy when drinking blood.

-Mikan ☆, Gunma Prefecture

I want to see Ichijo drinking blood. ♥ And I want him to drink my blood!!

-Mayu Aiba, Hyogo Prefecture

Vam☆Fan Hall

They **struck** the hearts of girls across the country!

Great Lines

That IMPRESSED and EXCITED You

Even Ruka agrees? We publish everyone's passionate opinions!!

BEST 5

Announcement 3

1 — Thirtieth Night

I love you. More than anyone else in the entire world.

— Kaname Kuran

I LOVE YOU.

MORE THAN ANYONE ELSE IN THE ENTIRE WORLD.

He declared his true feelings to Yuki, who was at a loss…

• Even as a reader, my heart went "ba bump." I love this scene!!

-Kokoro, Chiba Prefecture

• I cried, because the line encompasses the suffering and love that Kaname had been holding inside for so long!

-Suiryori, Kanagawa Prefecture

• I'd die if someone said this to me. ♥

-Yubo Tachikawa, Aichi Prefecture

• I understood his deep love for Yuki.

-Kyanametti, Saitama Prefecture

• I feel like it's being said to me. If Kaname-sama said this to me, I'd die. (Smile)

-Haruka, Shiga Prefecture

• I understood that he really cared about Yuki, and I felt like my heart was being squeezed.

-Sakuraka, Nagano Prefecture

• It's not an ordinary love confession. It has class… It's a beautiful way to put it, which is very much like Kaname-sama.

-♡ Sato ♡, Osaka

2 — Twenty sixth Night

Will you become a monster that devours blood… and live the long flow of time with me?

— Kaname Kuran

He said this to Yuki, who was trying to keep her distance from him…

…AND LIVE THE LONG FLOW OF TIME…

…WITH ME?

• I thought something was gonna happen to me, I was so excited!

-Seika, Oita Prefecture

• I thought it was cool that he wanted to drink Yuki's blood but didn't because he didn't want to turn her into a vampire.

-Miho Shimizu, Yamanashi Prefecture

• If someone declared his love to me like this, I'd be SO happy, I'd vow to be with him forever.

-Reika Kurenai, Okayama

• If the Kaname-sama I adore said this to me, I'd answer, "Yes!!" without hesitation.

-Iku, Ibaragi Prefecture

• If Kaname-sama said this to me, I'd be with him forever, even if he refused!

-Chinatsu, Hokkaido

3
Fifteenth Night

I think I was able to live on because you were beside me, Yuki.

-Zero Kiryu

I THINK I WAS ABLE TO LIVE ON...
...BECAUSE YOU WERE BESIDE ME, YUKI.

The night Zero made up his mind as Shizuka's shadow approached him...

• This was the first time Zero expressed his feelings for Yuki, and this says it all.

-Emiko, Kanagawa Prefecture

• I think there's the feeling that he likes Yuki, and he's also expressing his gratitude and saying thanks.

-Kuma, Hokkaido

4
Twenty-fourth Night

I want her gentle hands... Her smile...

-Zero Kiryu

The regret Zero feels for wanting blood and the warmth of Yuki...

• He knows his feelings are forbidden, but he can't keep his feelings for Yuki contained inside.

-Raspberry, Hokkaido

• I can see that Zero really, really likes Yuki.

-Hiromi Nagato, Nagasaki Prefecture

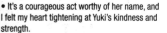

I WANT...
HER GENTLE HANDS...
HER SMILE...

5
Eighth Night

We'll do... the most forbidden act of all...

-Yuki Cross

...THE MOST FORBIDDEN ACT OF ALL...

The answer Yuki came up with to rescue the suffering Zero...

• It's a courageous act worthy of her name, and I felt my heart tightening at Yuki's kindness and strength.

-Rumitan ♥, Miyagi Prefecture

• Y-Y-You can't do this!

-Kuma, Hokkaido

• Because their relationship began with this line.

-Mana, Osaka

• This line stabbed my heart.

-Marii Suwicchi, Chiba

I'll also announce No. 6-10

6 *That's why I don't mind using what's left of my life for you.*

-Zero Kiryu
Twenty-ninth Night

It left an impression in my heart, because it seemed as if he was saying, "I'd risk my life to protect Yuki."

-Miwa Ueto, Miyagi Prefecture

7 *I don't think of you as a child. I only wanted to protect you.*

-Kaname Kuran
Seventeenth Night

Kaname is trying to protect Yuki in his own way.

-Natsumi Yoshida, Ibaragi Prefecture

8 *...I trust him. But even if he were to double-cross me, I'd be fine with it.*

-Yuki Cross
Twenty-third Night

I felt Yuki's firm determination and her absolute trust and love for Kaname-sama.

-Tomoe Shimotsuki, Saitama Prefecture

9 *You don't need to care for me so much!*

-Zero Kiryu
Twentieth Night

They're Zero's tender words toward Yuki, who risked her life to save him. And he's relieved that he's safe.

-Aki, Yamaguchi Prefecture

10 *I will not do anything that goes against my friend's best interests.*

-Takuma Ichijo
Tenth Night

I can feel that Kaname is a really good friend to him.

-Shion, Hyogo Prefecture

KANAME-SAMA'S WORDS ARE THE BEST.

Chapter 4
The Making of Vampire Knight

From Matsuri Hino's Workplace

You can see sketches that have never been made public before as well as read comments from Matsuri Hino and the cast of the Japanese anime!!

When the various essences of the *Vampire Knight* world cross over each other, the work becomes richer.

Manga pages are created this way!

It takes about three steps for manga pages to be completed after the story is ready.

Storyboards	The page composition (panel layouts and character dialogue) is determined here.
Rough Sketches	Carefully draw the characters on manga manuscript paper.
Inking & Finishing Touches	Ink over your rough sketch lines. Finish by inking large areas and applying screen tones.

This is how the detailed story is created!!

Check out these story-boards—the blueprints for the manga!!

These storyboards were done six months before the series started and were finished in great detail.

Storyboards that are almost like rough sketches!!

First Night

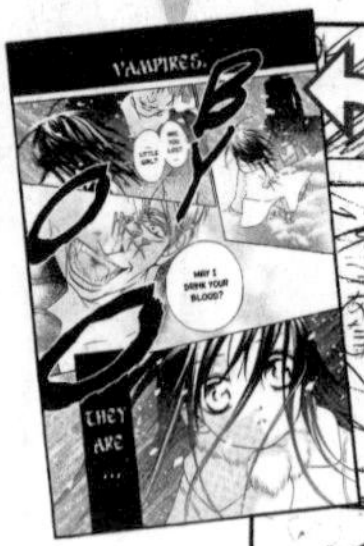
VAMPIRES.
MAY I DRINK YOUR BLOOD?
THEY ARE ...

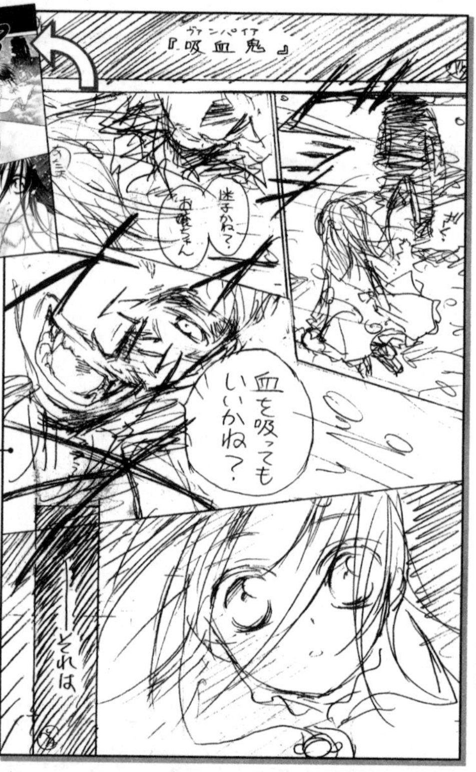
ヴァンパイア
『吸血鬼』
迷子かね？ お嬢ちゃん
血を吸ってもいいかね？
ーそれは

This is the storyboard for the first page of "First Night" that was published in *LaLa* magazine. The ferociousness of the vampire and Yuki's expression of terror are emphasized.

Readers don't usually get to see the artist's storyboards. But here, we can examine the roots of the story by looking at the blueprints for the manga.

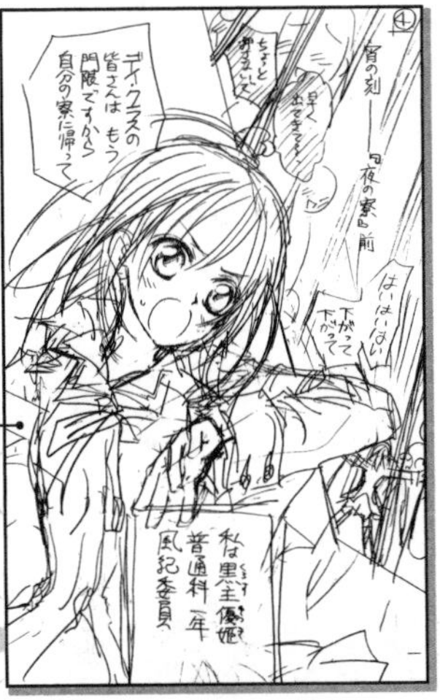
デイ・クラスの皆さんは もう門限ですから自分の家に帰って
はいはいはい 下がって下がって
私は黒主優姫 普通科一年 風紀委員

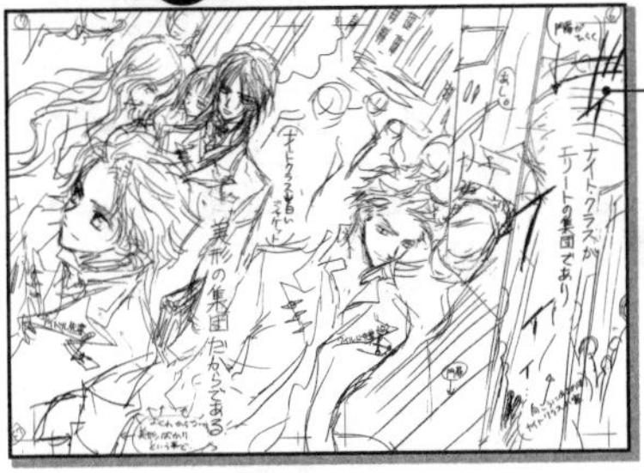
ナイトクラスがエリートの集団であり

You get to see the group of Night Class students. Their individuality stood out thanks to the detailed drawing.

The scene where Yuki first appears as a student. Her lively expression and pose show her energetic personality.

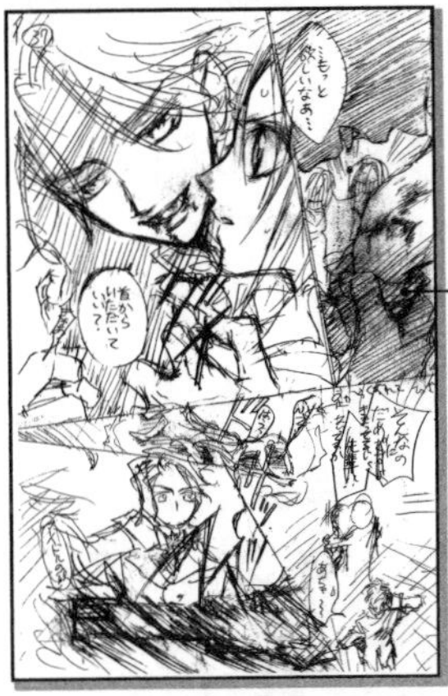

Aido's erotic expression sets up the atmosphere for the first blood-drinking scene. Yuki is surprised when he gazes at her face!

In order to give impact to Zero holding his gun ready, the drawing technique of perspective was used here.

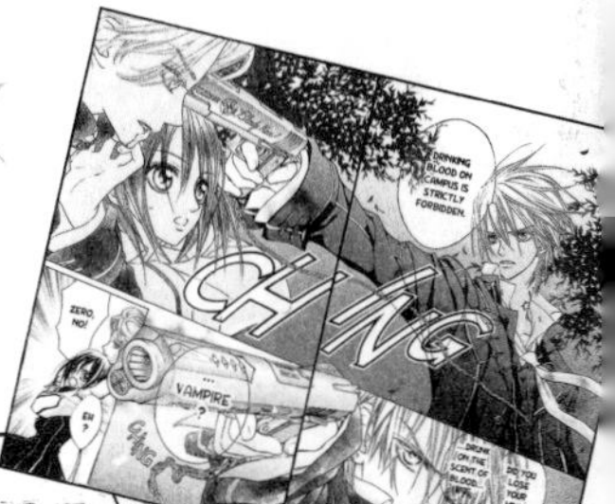
DRINKING BLOOD ON CAMPUS IS STRICTLY FORBIDDEN.
CHING
ZERO, NO!
VAMPIRE...?
EH?
DRUNK ON THE SCENT OF BLOOD...?
DID YOU LOSE YOUR MIND?

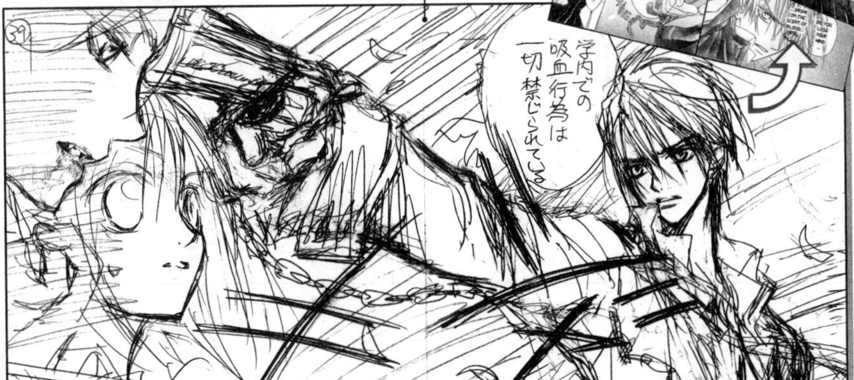
学内での吸血行為は一切禁じられている
血の香りに酔って正気を失ったか
へぇ…?

Putting all her energy into the highlight panels!!

Third Night

Matsuri Hino challenged herself to draw a vampire story for the first time with this series!! She'd been wanting to draw a vampire-themed story for a while. In contrast to her previous romantic comedies, there are more shocking scenes in this series, and a lot of large panels that spread across two pages are used.

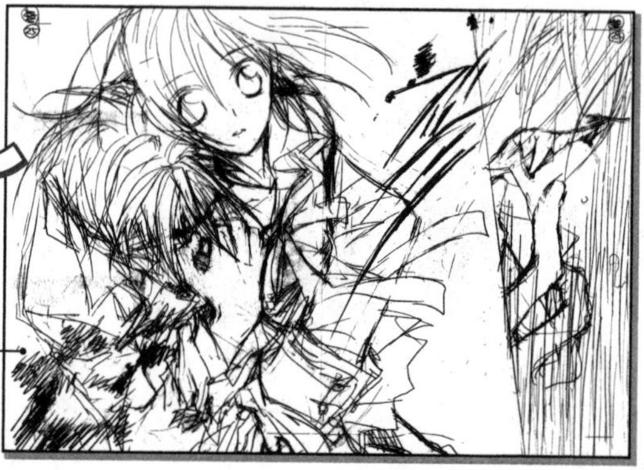

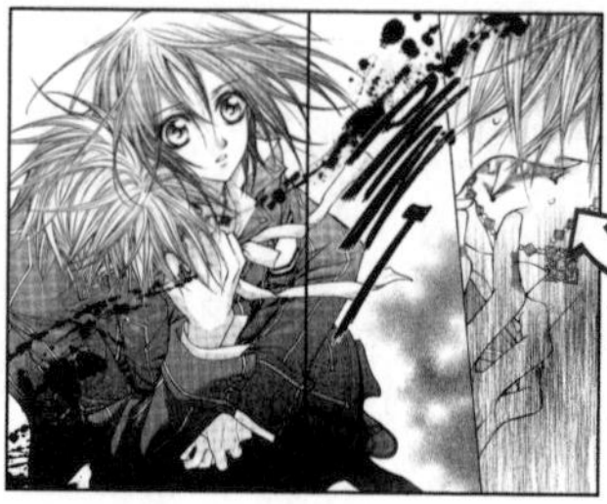

The shocking scene where Zero devours Yuki's blood for the first time was boldly drawn using a two-page spread.

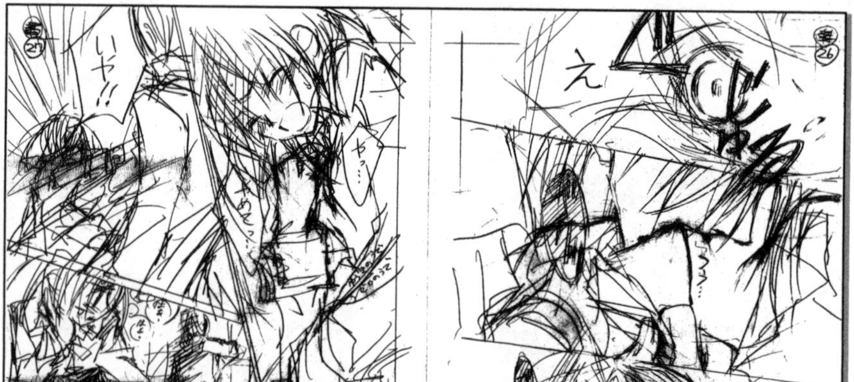
え
なに
なんなの これは…!!
いや!!
血色に底光りする瞳ー

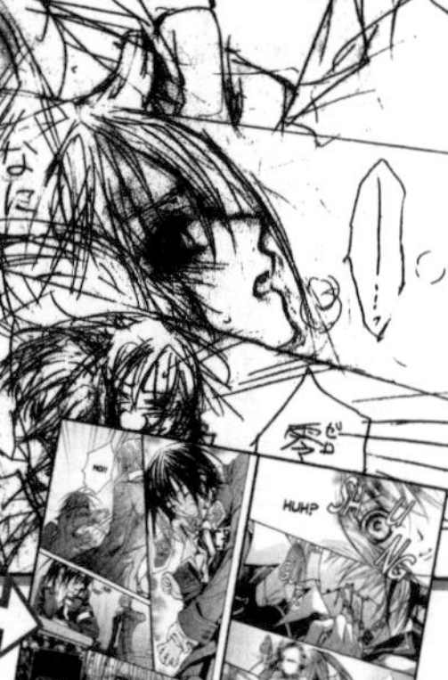

Yuki panics because Zero suddenly bites her. Her feelings are conveyed through the random-shaped panels that are separated by slanted lines.

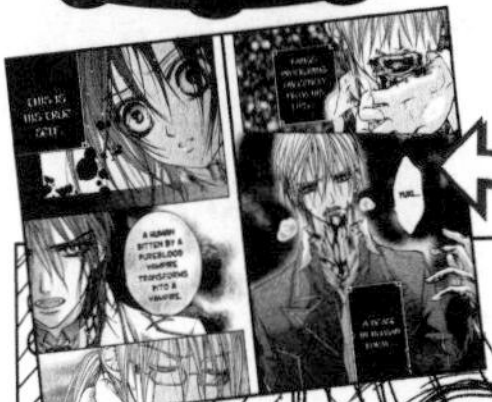

Zero's vacant eyes make him look inhuman. On the other hand, the vampire Kaname has power in his eyes.

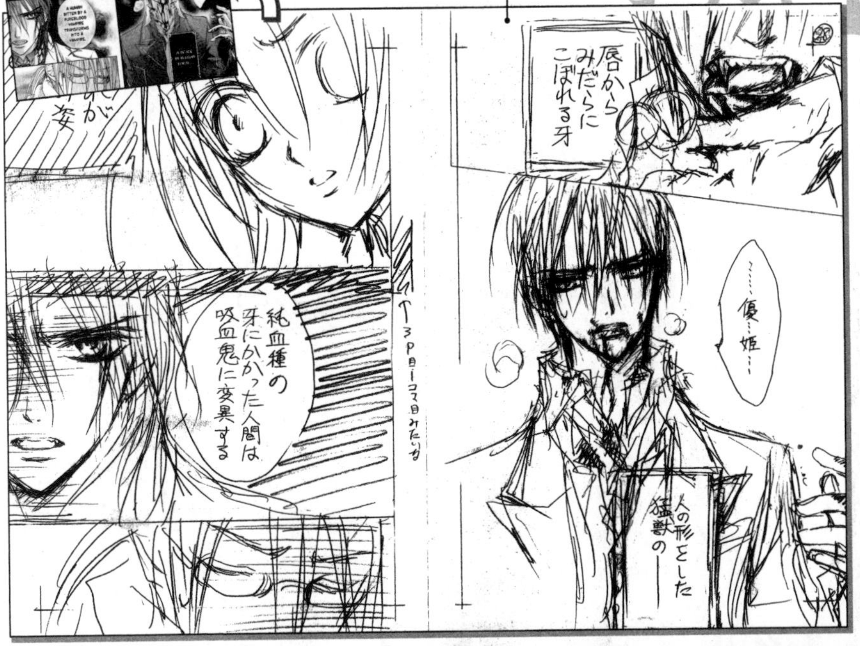
唇から
みだらに
こぼれる牙
……優…姫……
人の形をした
猛獣の——
↑3P目1コマ目みたいな
純血種の
牙にかかった人間は
吸血鬼に変異する
が
姿

Inside Story

Now that the story is heating up, the storyboards are becoming more white...?!

The old storyboards were drawn in great detail... The story is moving really fast now, so the emphasis seems to be on speed. -Editor

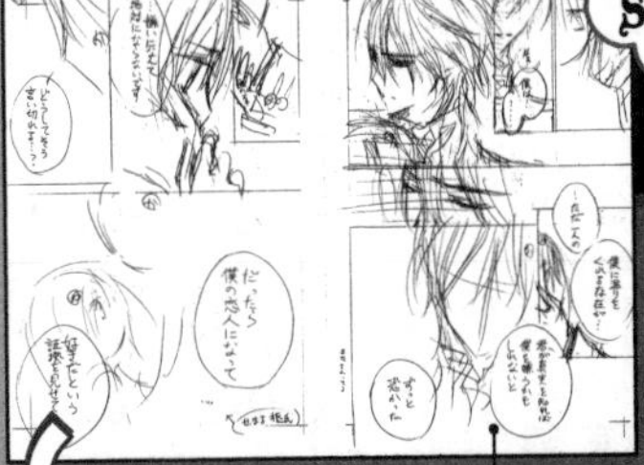

The love scenes move slowly.

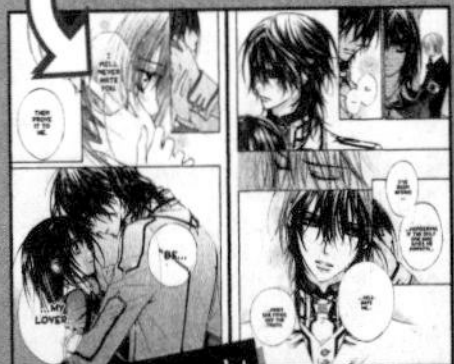

Thirty second Night

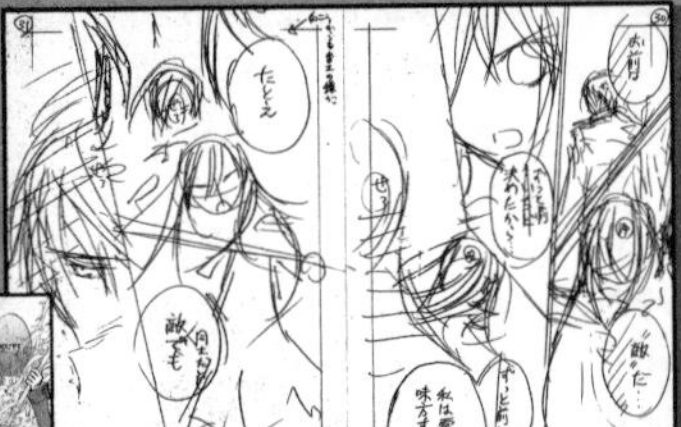

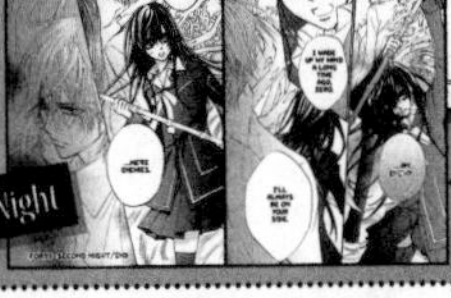

Forty second Night

There's more variation in the panel layouts to synchronize with a climax in the story.

Female Uniforms

The standard style is a combination of a jacket, shirt, and skirt. It's designed well and is also easy to move around in.

(Darts)

Girls

The shirt can be tucked inside or outside the skirt.

A Cross Academy rule dictates that the skirt must extend at least ten centimeters below the bottom of the jacket.

Petticoats can show when skirts flutter.

And Yuki wears short leggings. ☆ (So she can move about.)

Excavated from Matsuri Hino's atelier!!

Concept Illustrations for Cross Academy Uniforms

You can see plenty of concept illustrations for the uniforms, which are full of Matsuri Hino's details. Readers keep saying, "I want to wear the uniform"!!

The uniform design is both elegant and cute

Full-length diagram

The uniform is designed in a sophisticated style, but it's easy to move around in. The color of the shirt is pure white, and the knee socks are black.

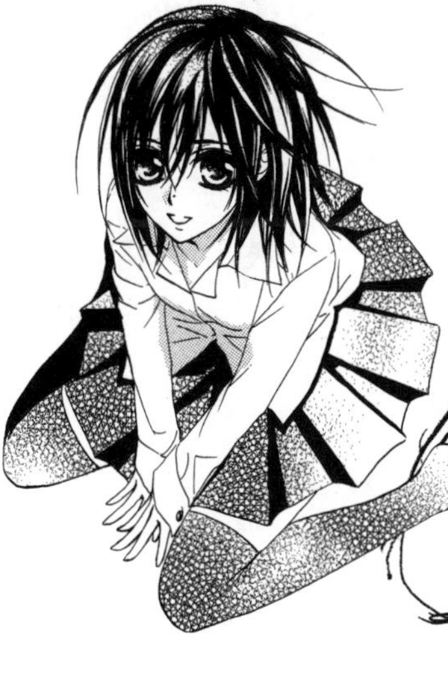

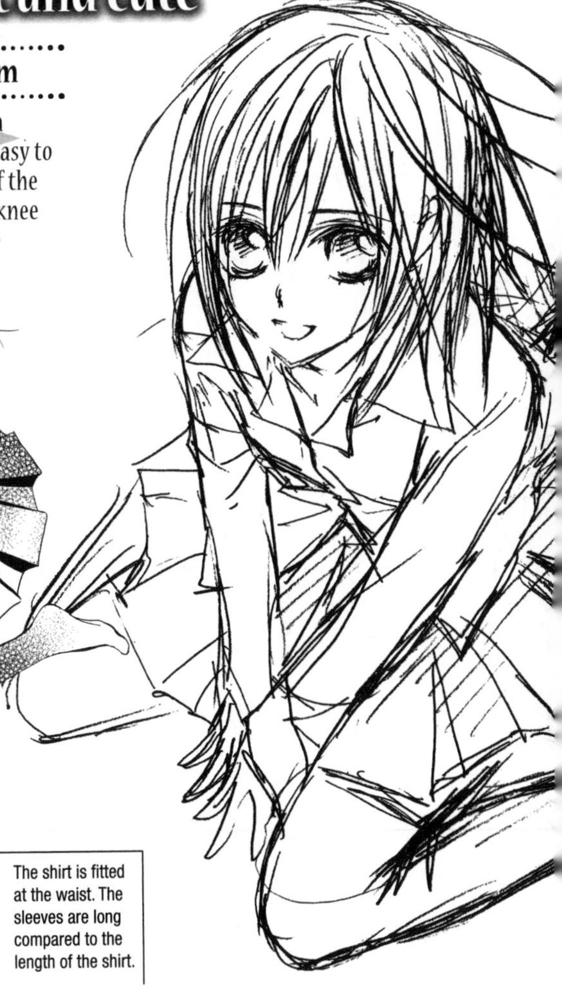

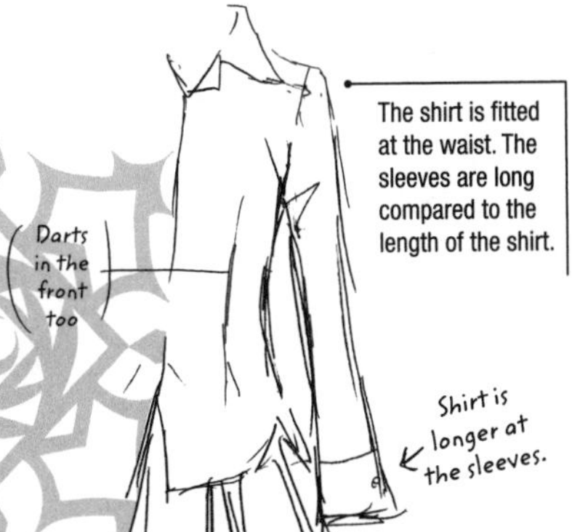
Darts in the front too
Shirt is longer at the sleeves.

The shirt is fitted at the waist. The sleeves are long compared to the length of the shirt.

The jacket length is slightly longer. The exact sleeve length is specified as well.

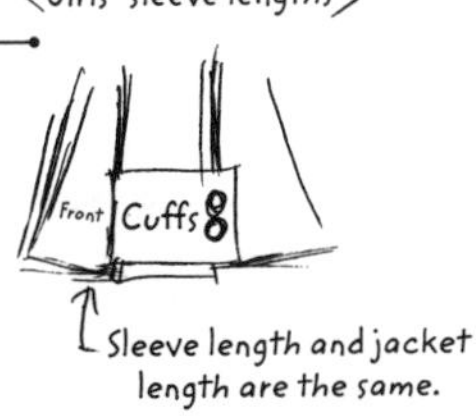
<Girls' sleeve lengths>
Front
Cuffs
Sleeve length and jacket length are the same.

The Day Class and the Night Class—Both uniforms stand out

Jackets

The Day Class jacket is in traditional black. The Night Class jacket is in noble white. The design of the trim on the lapels and hems of the Day Class and Night Class uniforms is slightly different.

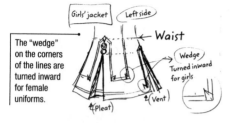

Girls' jacket
Left side
Waist
Wedge
Turned inward for girls
Pleat
Vent

The "wedge" on the corners of the lines are turned inward for female uniforms.

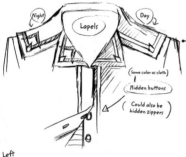

Night
Day
Lapels
Same color as cloth
Hidden buttons
Could also be hidden zippers

You fasten the jacket buttons from the inside. Placing the buttons where you can't see them makes for a cleaner look.

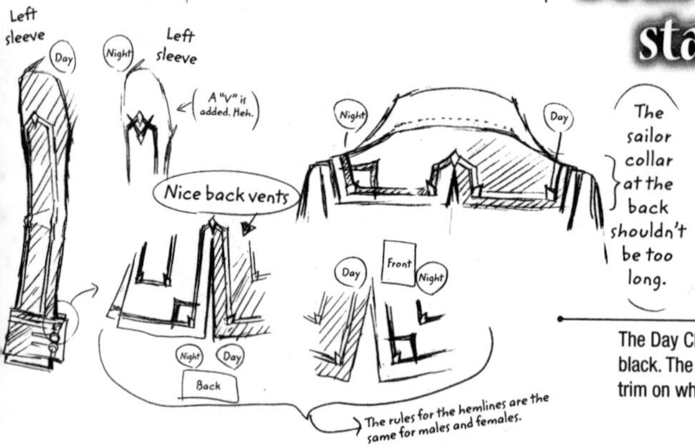

Left sleeve
Day
Night
Left sleeve
A "V" is added. Heh.
Nice back vents
Night
Day
The sailor collar at the back shouldn't be too long.
Day
Front
Night
Night
Day
Back
The rules for the hemlines are the same for males and females.

The Day Class jacket has white trim on black. The Night Class jacket has black trim on white.

Jacket lapels
The edges
Are about 1 cm away from the tip of the shoulder.
Girls' shirts are open-collar.
But they shouldn't be too open.
Lapels
Can be flat
Can be a bit upright
Both are OK
Buttons are hidden for both male and female shirts.

The layering of the shirt and jacket lapels looks cool. The ribbon color is "cardinal red," which is red with vermilion in it.

Shirts are made so that you can't see the buttons. They're high-quality shirts that give a beautiful silhouette naturally.

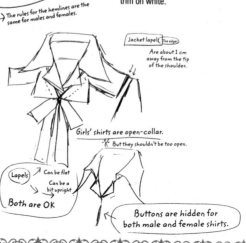

Skirts

The jacket and skirt are closely fitted, but the skirt has large pleats that enable movement.

Side pocket
Back zipper
Left side

There's a large pocket on the left side of the skirt. The skirt has a zipper so you can put it on easily.

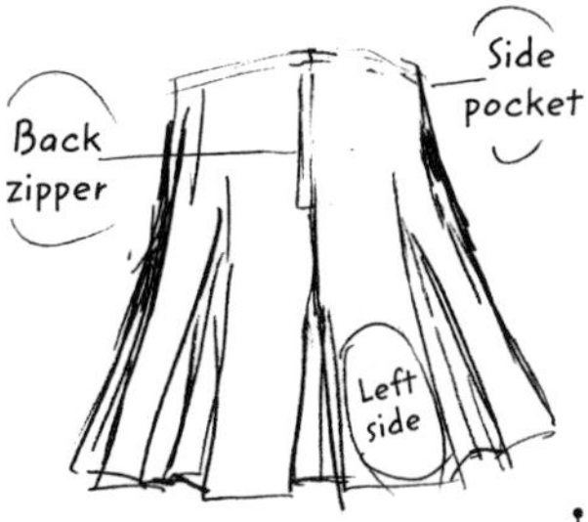

The Artemis rod is hidden under Yuki's skirt

It's just hidden under the skirt somehow...
Skirt
Leggings
Holder for Artemis.
Seen from the front.
The holder has snaps.
Seen from the back.

Yuki's weapon "Artemis" is kept in a holder on her left thigh. She can draw it in an instant when necessary.

Both casual and proper

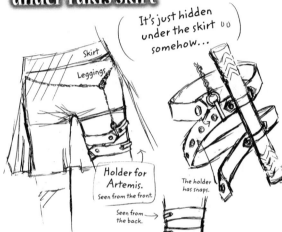

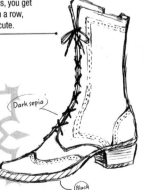

Short boots

The elegant boots go very well with the above-knee-length skirt and knee socks.

The boots are short, but there are lots of shoelace holes—13 in all. When you lace a boot up with thin shoelaces, you get six crosses in a row, which looks cute.

Dark sepia
Black

The toe doesn't have to be as pointed as the male shoes.
Top view

The slightly narrow, rounded toe isn't too pointed or too round, giving an elegant feeling.

Back view

The sole is thick and sturdy. They're easy to walk in, and it's okay to run in them every now and then as well.

Vests

The vest is an item that the female uniform does not have. Boys must wear one over the long-sleeve shirt and underneath the jacket.

Male Uniforms

Guys wear a jacket, a vest and a long-sleeve shirt. A narrow, long silhouette like the female uniform is a distinguishing feature.

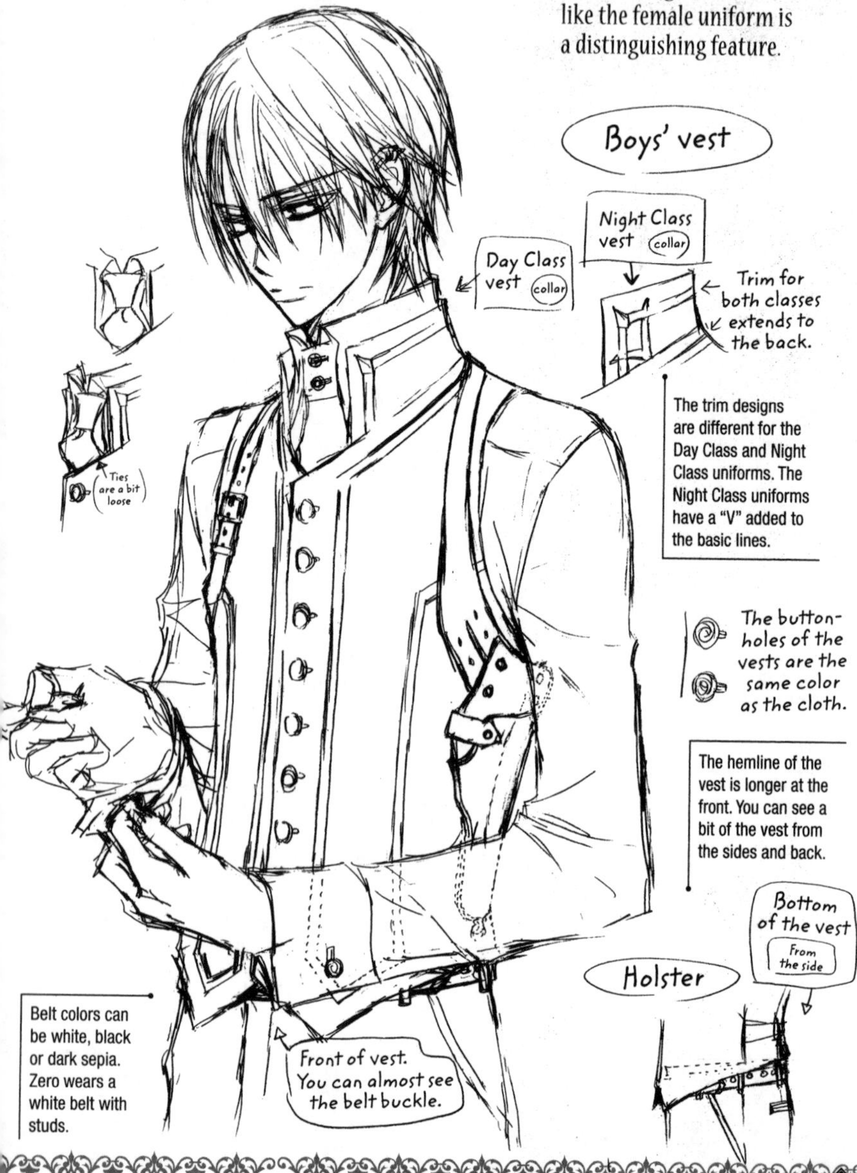

Boys' vest
Night Class vest (collar)
Day Class vest (collar)
Trim for both classes extends to the back.
The trim designs are different for the Day Class and Night Class uniforms. The Night Class uniforms have a "V" added to the basic lines.
Ties are a bit loose
The button-holes of the vests are the same color as the cloth.
The hemline of the vest is longer at the front. You can see a bit of the vest from the sides and back.
Bottom of the vest
From the side
Holster
Belt colors can be white, black or dark sepia. Zero wears a white belt with studs.
Front of vest. You can almost see the belt buckle.

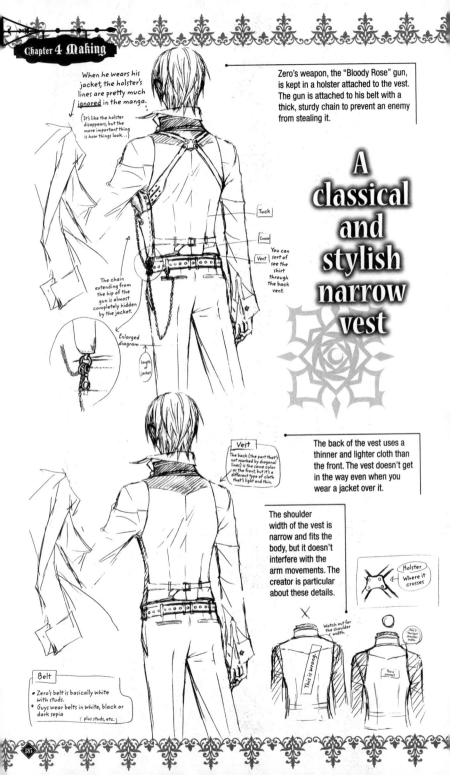

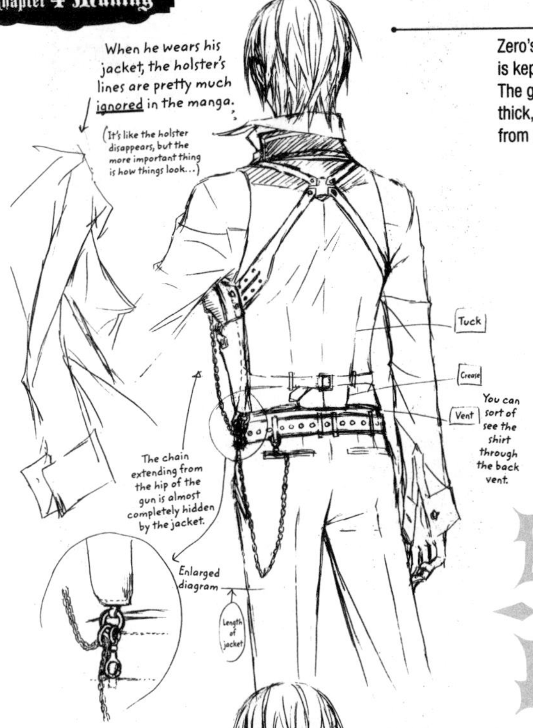
When he wears his jacket, the holster's lines are pretty much ignored in the manga.
(It's like the holster disappears, but the more important thing is how things look…)
Tuck
Crease
Vent
You can sort of see the shirt through the back vent.
The chain extending from the hip of the gun is almost completely hidden by the jacket.
Enlarged diagram
Length of jacket

Zero's weapon, the "Bloody Rose" gun, is kept in a holster attached to the vest. The gun is attached to his belt with a thick, sturdy chain to prevent an enemy from stealing it.

A classical and stylish narrow vest

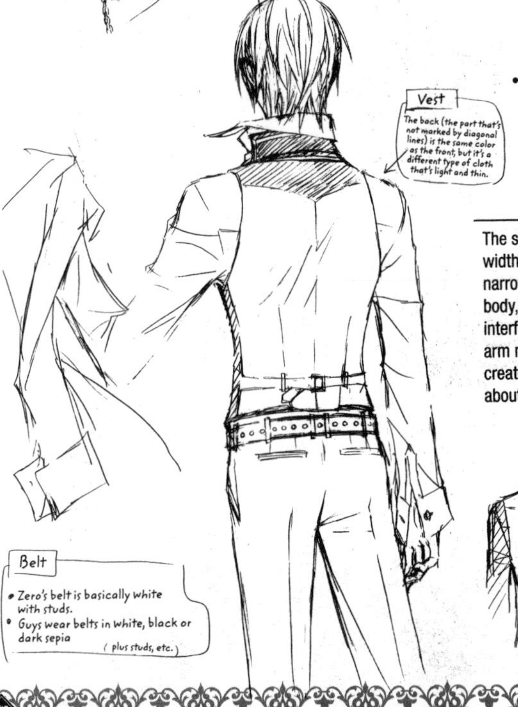
Vest
The back (the part that's not marked by diagonal lines) is the same color as the front, but it's a different type of cloth that's light and thin.
Belt
• Zero's belt is basically white with studs.
• Guys wear belts in white, black or dark sepia (plus studs, etc.)

The back of the vest uses a thinner and lighter cloth than the front. The vest doesn't get in the way even when you wear a jacket over it.

The shoulder width of the vest is narrow and fits the body, but it doesn't interfere with the arm movements. The creator is particular about these details.

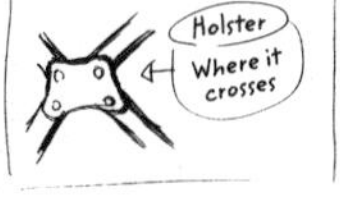
Holster
Where it crosses

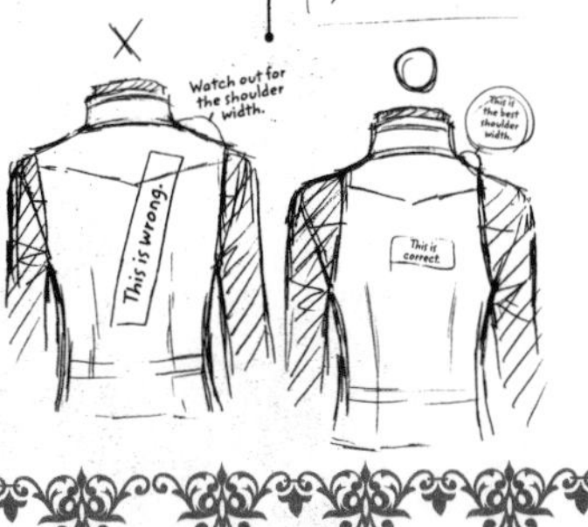
Watch out for the shoulder width.
This is wrong.
This is the best shoulder width.
This is correct.

Jackets

Male jackets are slightly longer in length. They have pockets that the female jackets don't have, which is another difference in details.

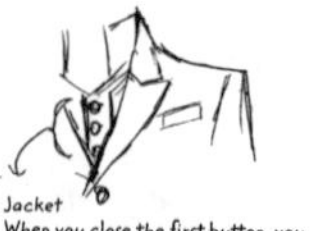
Jacket
When you close the first button, you can see about three vest buttons.
Everyone has the fourth button of their jackets unbuttoned. (Even Kaname.)

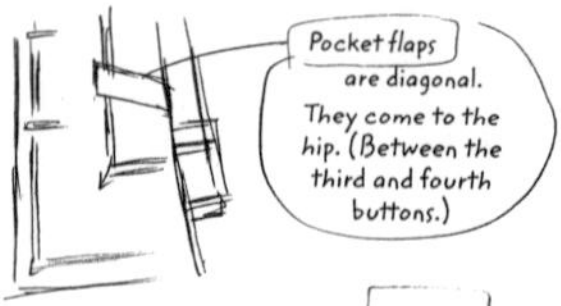
Pocket flaps are diagonal.
They come to the hip. (Between the third and fourth buttons.)
Male jacket

The standard way to wear the jacket is to unbutton the fourth button.

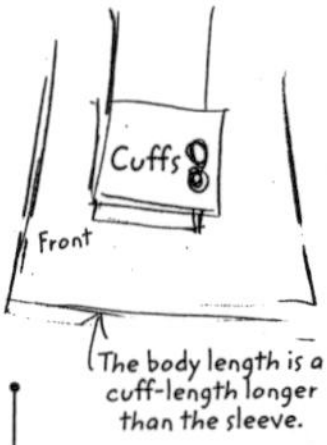
< Male sleeve length >
Cuffs
Front
The body length is a cuff-length longer than the sleeve.

A distinguishing feature of the male uniforms is that the body length is a cuff-length longer than the sleeve length.

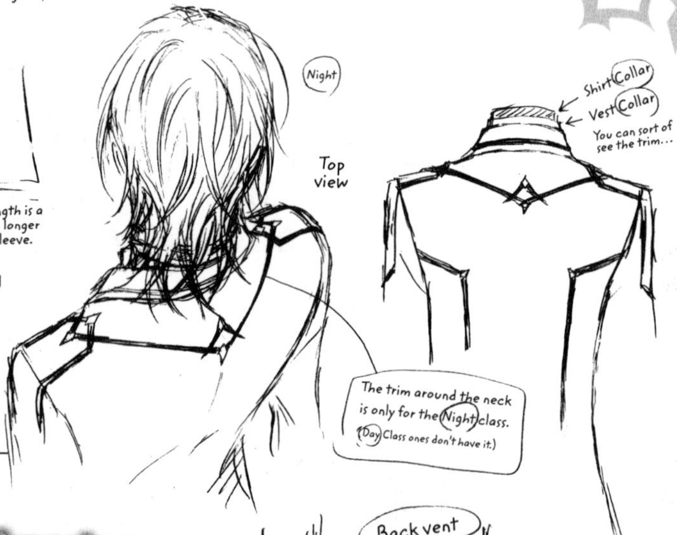
Night
Top view
Shirt Collar
Vest Collar
You can sort of see the trim...
The trim around the neck is only for the Night class.
(Day Class ones don't have it.)

The layering of the collars has an urban essence

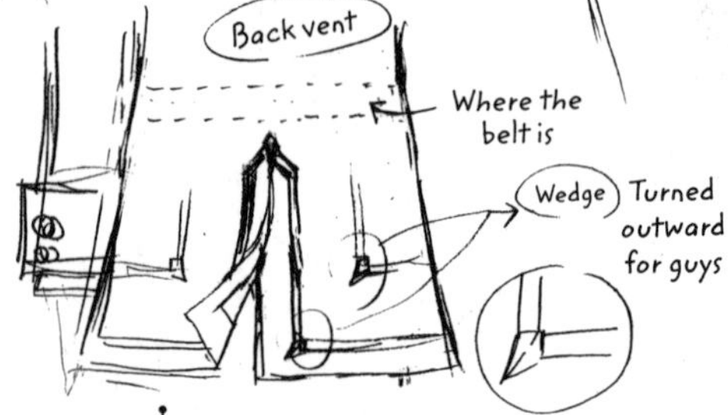
Back vent
Where the belt is
Wedge
Turned outward for guys

The trim on the hem of the jacket stands out. With male uniforms, wedges are turned outward.

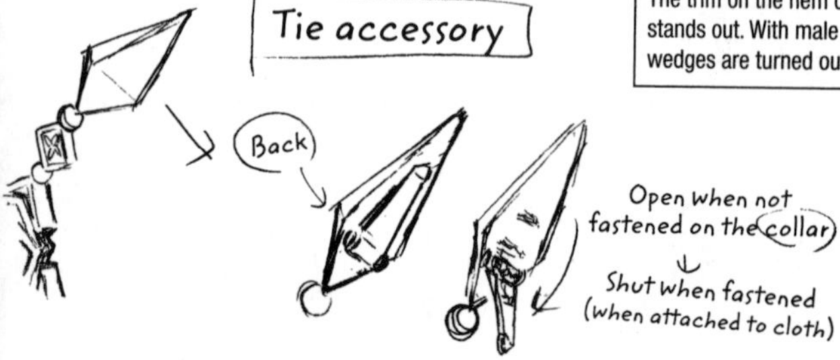
Tie accessory
Back
Open when not fastened on the collar
Shut when fastened (when attached to cloth)

The cardinal red tie is fastened by a silver tie clasp.

A sharp-looking shirt with a decorous look

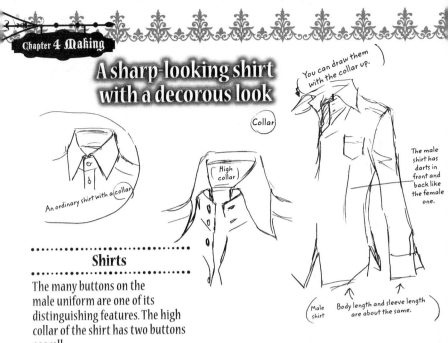

An ordinary shirt with a collar

Collar
High collar

You can draw them with the collar up.
The male shirt has darts in front and back like the female one.
Male shirt
Body length and sleeve length are about the same.

Shirts

The many buttons on the male uniform are one of its distinguishing features. The high collar of the shirt has two buttons as well.

Shoes

The formal shoes make the jacket style even more elegant.

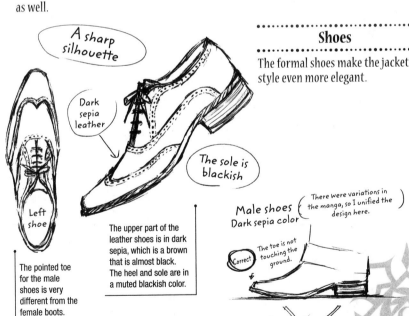

A sharp silhouette
Dark sepia leather
The sole is blackish
Left shoe

The pointed toe for the male shoes is very different from the female boots.

The upper part of the leather shoes is in dark sepia, which is a brown that is almost black. The heel and sole are in a muted blackish color.

Male shoes
Dark sepia color
There were variations in the manga, so I unified the design here.
Correct
The toe is not touching the ground.
This is wrong.

There is even a correct shape for the sole. The curve of the toe part helps one walk naturally.

Sophisticated items that make guys look cool

Common details in both male and female uniforms

Cuffs that are specified to the centimeter and detailed buttons—surprising details you don't see in other manga.

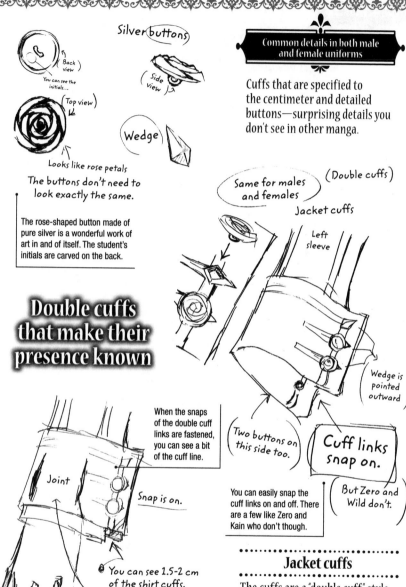

Silver buttons
Back view
You can see the initials...
Side view
Top view
Wedge
Looks like rose petals
The buttons don't need to look exactly the same.

The rose-shaped button made of pure silver is a wonderful work of art in and of itself. The student's initials are carved on the back.

Double cuffs that make their presence known

Same for males and females
(Double cuffs)
Jacket cuffs
Left sleeve
Wedge is pointed outward
Two buttons on this side too.
Cuff links snap on.
But Zero and Wild don't.

You can easily snap the cuff links on and off. There are a few like Zero and Kain who don't though.

Joint
Snap is on.
You can see 1.5-2 cm of the shirt cuffs.
The narrowest part of the wrist is hidden.
The sleeves seem difficult to study in...

When the snaps of the double cuff links are fastened, you can see a bit of the cuff line.

Jacket cuffs

The cuffs are a "double cuff" style where the sleeves are turned up and fastened. With vertical twin buttons on the side, these cuffs create a distinguished nuance.

There are two options for sleeve cuffs—"single button" or "twin button." Students can choose between these two styles.

Single cuff links are special

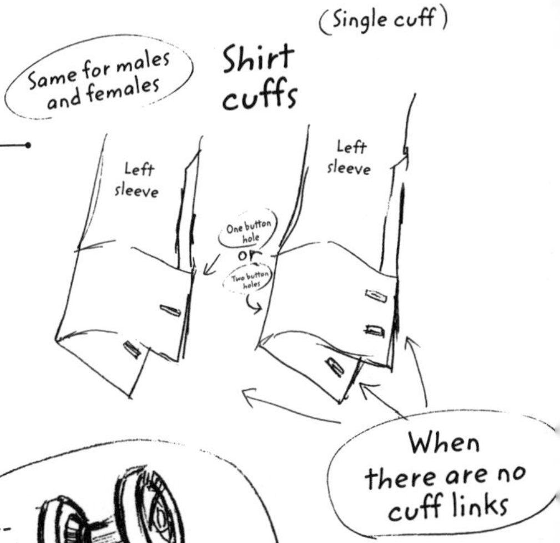
(Single cuff)
Shirt cuffs
Same for males and females
Left sleeve
Left sleeve
One button hole
or
Two button holes
When there are no cuff links

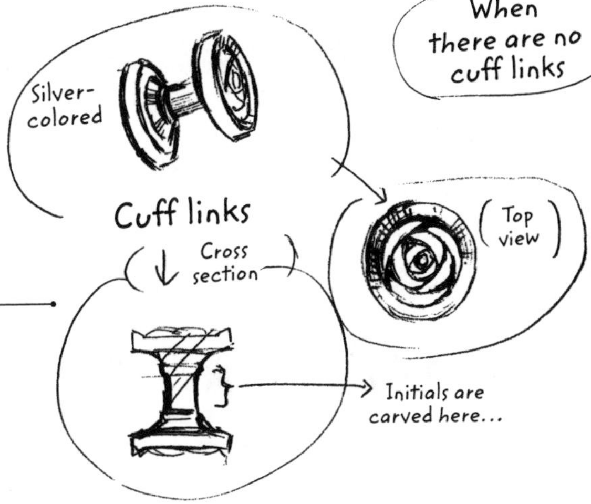
Silver-colored
Cuff links
Cross section
Top view
Initials are carved here...

A student's initials are carved on the part that you can't see when the cuff links are on. So this is being really stylish?!

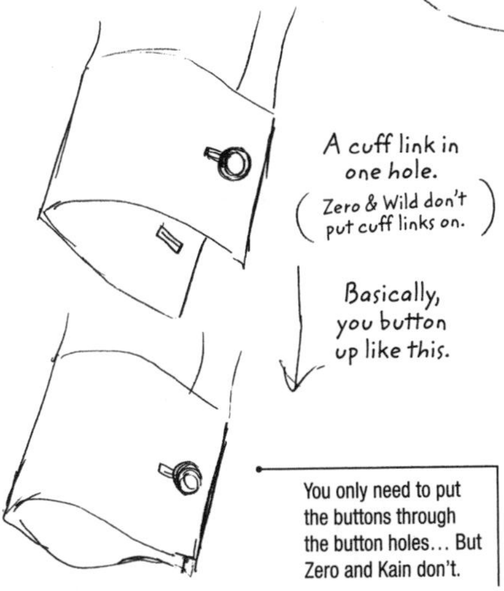
A cuff link in one hole.
(Zero & Wild don't put cuff links on.
Basically, you button up like this.

You only need to put the buttons through the button holes… But Zero and Kain don't.

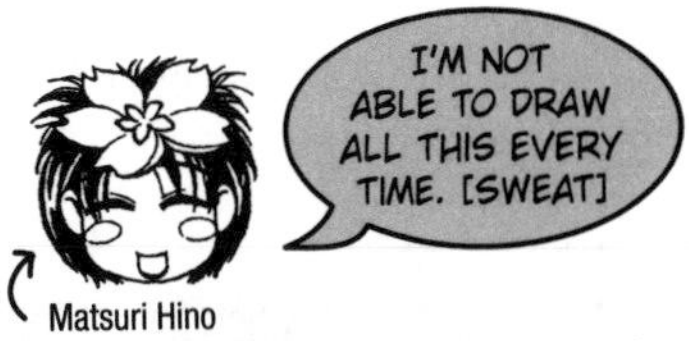
I'M NOT ABLE TO DRAW ALL THIS EVERY TIME. [SWEAT]
Matsuri Hino

Shirt cuffs

A "single cuff" style where the sleeves aren't folded up. The 3-D shape of the cuff links give the simple shirt character.

♣ Yuki Cross ♣

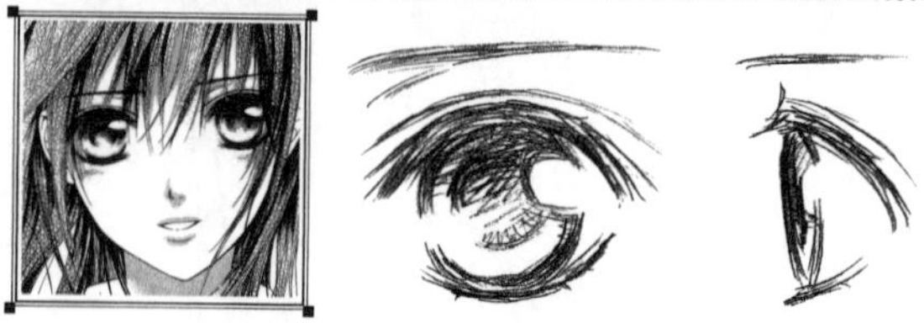

Round pupils give an impression of honesty

Her eyes aren't that wide, but they have height. The distinguishing feature of Yuki's eyes is the big and round irises. Straight eyebrows and moderate eyelashes give her a tomboy feel.

♣ Ruka Souen ♣

Her long eyelashes are sexy

She has gorgeous, lush eyelashes, but she looks elegant because the outer ends of her eyebrows are thin.

♣ Sayori Wakaba ♣

Soft eyes that make her look kind

She has thick eyelashes. Her soft eyes with their large irises make her look easygoing and cute.

♣ Seiren ♣

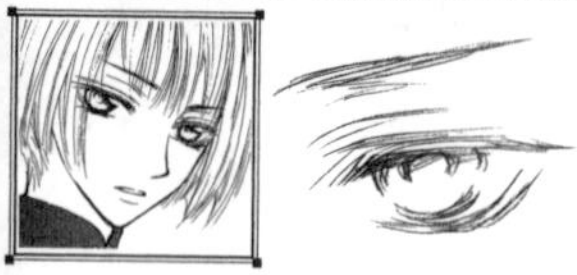

Eyes that show her strong will

Her eyes turn up at the corners, and her eyebrows are slightly short and sharp. They give her a restrained expression.

♣ Rima Toya ♣

Fascinating eyes that look like a doll's

Eyes that turn up slightly at the corners. Straight eyebrows that turn up a little!! Her demeanor is self-assured and cool.

♣ Shizuka Hio ♣

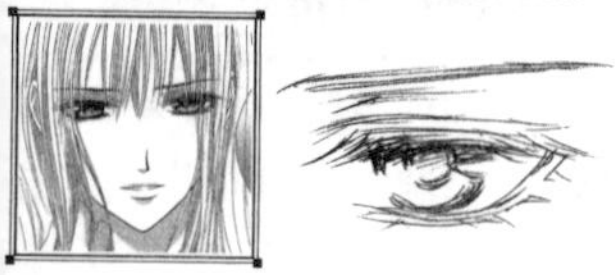

An erotic look

Her eyes look like Zero's, but her eyelashes show off her femininity. The expression of her eyes is sexy.

♣ Maria Kurenai ♣

Her straight eyebrows emphasize her sincerity

Her eyebrows and eyelashes are like Yuki's. Her eyes aren't as dewy, and they turn up slightly at the corners.

Who do you want to look in the eye?

Concept Illustrations for the Eyes

The length of the eyebrows, the thickness of the eyelashes, the shapes of the pupils… The eyes, which determine a character's personality, are drawn differently for each character.

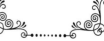

Zero Kiryu

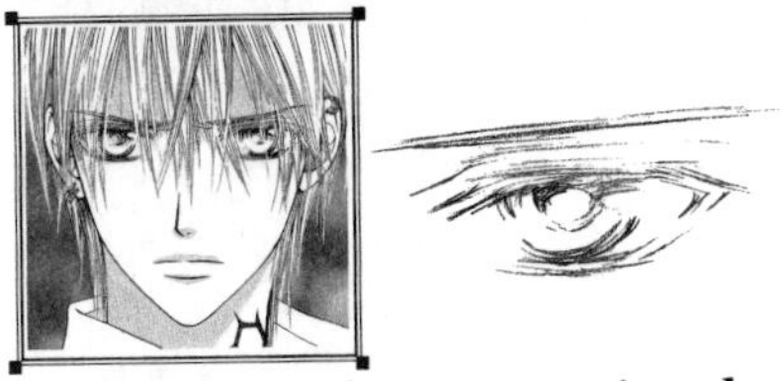

The secret to his unemotional expressions is his eyes

His eyes don't look dewy at all. His gaze looks as if he has his eyes fixed on something—it appears unemotional. His upper and lower eyelashes are parallel to each other.

Akatsuki Kain

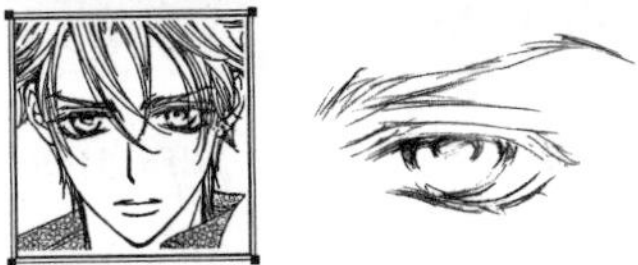

His grown-up-looking, drooping eyes are wild

His thick, arched eyebrows are very masculine. His gentle-looking, drooping eyes make him look sexy.

Senri Shiki

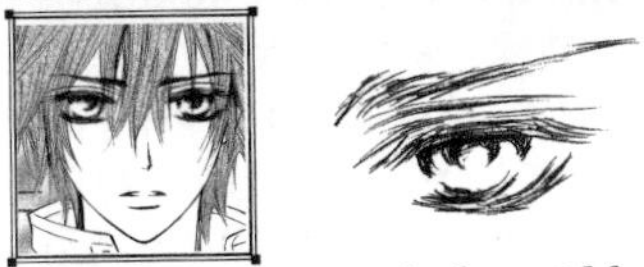

His eyes have a particular languid feeling

The inner ends of his eyebrows are thick, and the outer ends are thin. His eyes turn up at the corners and look sharp, but his eyelashes give a languid feeling.

Kaien Cross

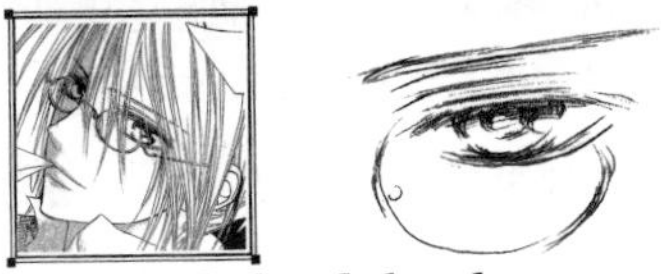

The eyes behind the glasses are super-cool

His eyebrows are thin like a woman's. The expression of his eyes is cool. You can catch a glimpse of what the Headmaster is really like through his eyes.

Kaname Kuran

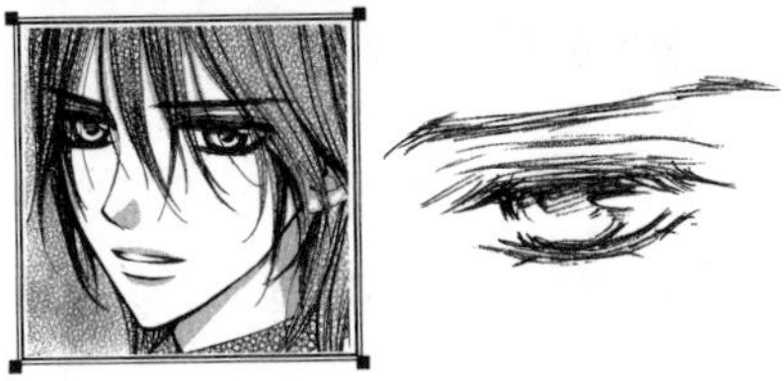

Languorous but graceful eyes

He has longer and thicker eyelashes than the average male. Therefore, when Kaname looks down, he often has an aloof attitude about him.

Hanabusa Aido

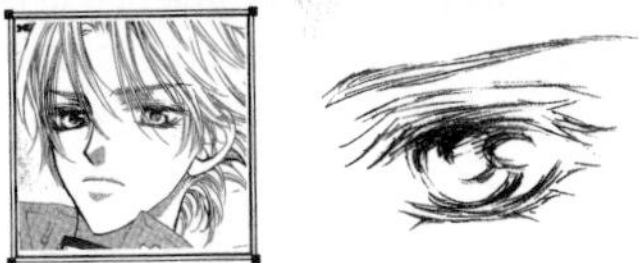

Sparkling eyes like an idol's

The thick inner ends of his eyebrows express Aido's strength of will. His lush eyelashes are like a girl's.

Takuma Ichijo

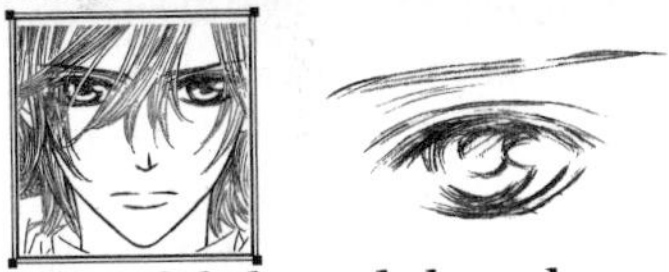

Beautiful almond-shaped eyes

His almond-shaped eyes have height and give color to his abundant expressions.

Toga Yagari

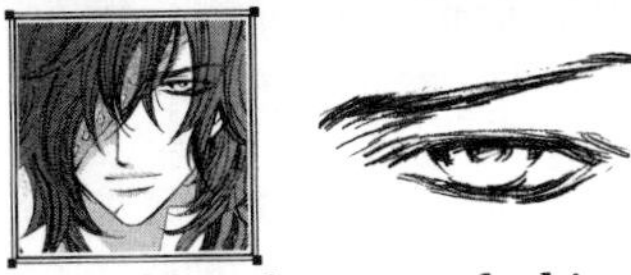

His wild eyebrows make him a man among men

He doesn't take care of his eyebrows. He doesn't have many eyelashes, and he has single eyelids with drooping eyes. Thus, his stark expressions stand out.

me working, he or she would probably notice them though.

❹ How would you describe your personality?

A bother to deal with. (Oh dear… ☹)

❺ What would you want to be reincarnated as?

A human or a space alien? A life-form that can experience the joy of creating.

❻ What do you recommend about Hokkaido?

It's large and there's a sense of space. Seasonal food, dairy products, and rice called *oborozuki* are delicious here. That's why I enjoy spending my days driving, looking for good food and great scenery.

❼ What are some places that you've traveled to that you remember?

Takayama City, Mount Norikura where I stayed at a mountain hut the day before the first day of snow, Garo Falls, Shiretoko, Akan, Kushiro Wetlands, the stage of Kiyomizu-dera temple that was under construction, the Merlion that was under construction and therefore not spouting out water, the old part of Lijiang, my first overseas autograph session in the U.S., and gathering material in central Europe when the weather was sunny the whole time (despite the fact that I tend to cause rain wherever I go, it was the neighboring countries that had terrible weather then—to the point that the Danube River flooded).

❽ What brings you peace of mind?

Cats. Letters from all my readers. Delicious sweets I buy at the airport when I go to Tokyo.

Interview with MATSURI HINO

She gives frank answers about her private life, life as a manga artist, and *Vampire Knight*!!

⭐ Private Life

❶ Are you a morning person or a night person?

I can be in a good mood and work in the morning. But if I get stuck on something, I end up waking up at night… Then I get sleepy before dawn…

❷ What are your favorite foods?

Seasonal fruits, seasonal seafood, mushrooms, plums, tomatoes, Italian dishes, Japanese dishes, dishes with lots of ginger in them, hot and sour dishes, tachi soup with lots of root vegetables and mushrooms, Ishikari-nabe, blowfish soup, pork miso soup, lamb shabu-shabu, sarashina soba, my mother's beef stew, my home-baked bread, rice cooked in an earthen pot, delicious sweets… I can't make the list shorter. Basically, I like anything that tastes good.

❸ What are some strange habits you can't help doing?

I'm probably full of all sorts of strange and weird habits, but I'm scared that I don't know about them. If some levelheaded person saw

❸ What's your favorite stage in the manga-creating process?

I like making the storyboards because I really feel like I'm creating something. Only if I have the time to do them though.

❹ What's your least favorite stage?

Drawing the rough sketches. When I don't have time, sketching is difficult.

❺ How do you come up with your storyboards?

This past year, I've been working at various jobs for ten to fourteen days after completing my manga deadlines. (It's not enough, and I'm barely managing things by borrowing money.) After those jobs, I start working on my storyboards. I simply think at my desk. Even when I'm brushing my teeth, I'm thinking. I'm tempted to think while driving, so I try not to drive while thinking about my storyboards.

❻ When you draw your characters, where do you start?

I decide where the head will be and start from the silhouette of the face.

❼ How long does it take you to draw your color pages?

From deciding the composition to doing the finishing touches, it takes about three days.

❽ How do you give yourself breaks?

Nowadays, I have no time for breathers even if I get stuck, so I have to force myself to continue thinking. I want to use my time more wisely… Agh…

❾ When you're working, do you listen to music or watch TV?

When I'm working on my storyboards, I pick

❾ I've heard that you like making dolls?

I like making things in general, not just dolls. At home, I have Super Dollfie dolls that are in the process of being transformed to Airi, Aram, Jeile, and Arto. I have eight Super Dollfie dolls in all, but I have no time to work on them. I'm thinking about asking a professional to do it… [*Tearful*]

★ Life as a Manga Artist

❶ When did you start drawing manga?

The first time I drew something manga-like was with a pencil in a notebook around sixth grade. But the first time I drew manga properly was during freshman year of college, I think. That was the first piece I submitted to a magazine… I drew three stories that I sent to three magazines, but I was a ways from receiving the top prize. One of those magazines, *LaLa*, told me I had no talent for drawing manga, so I gave up on becoming a manga artist. Then the bubble economy burst during my senior year, and my job hunting didn't go too well. (Granted, I wasn't too serious about finding a job.) At that time, the only thing I could really concentrate on was the manga I loved, so I convinced my parents to let me draw and submit a story instead of looking for a job. I was determined to make a living through drawing manga. I didn't realize then that things remain difficult even after you make your debut.

❷ What would you be if you hadn't become a manga artist?

I think I would've ended up with a job in architecture or in a field where I get to create things.

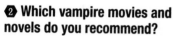

continued from question 9

a song that makes me hyper and listen to it on repeat. At other times, I listen to a minidisc endlessly. I feel I often choose music that matches *Vampire Knight*, but if it makes me happy, anything will do. I also watch TV as long as it doesn't interfere with my work. I watch programs I can just listen to and understand easily.

2 Which vampire movies and novels do you recommend?

If you share my taste, then I think you've found them already, but I'll list them here just in case. The movie *Blade* and the novel *Vampire Hunter D* fulfill my number one desire of wanting vampires to be cool and strong. The movie *Interview with a Vampire* fulfills my number two desire of wanting vampires to look handsome and alluring. However, my number one desire is much higher on the priority list… There are plenty of works that fulfill my number three desire of creepiness too…

3 Which character would you like to give blood to?

I'll say no one. [*Smile*] If I become more anemic, I won't be able to draw *Vampire Knight*! Oh, I'd like Kaname's blood, because I think it'll give me more physical strength. I wouldn't mind having Yuki's blood either, but I don't want to make her suffer.

4 Which character is very similar to you?

Take Yuki, Zero and Kaname, and mix in Ichiru, Juri, Ichio and the Headmaster. You'll get a chemical reaction, and when the mixture explodes, the leftover cinders are me…

5 Which character would you want as your lover and which would you want as your brother?

I'd like His Highness Jeile as my lover. No, I want Ichijo to be my lover. (I may want to marry Kain?) Zero would be my little brother, Yuki would be my little sister, and Kaname would be the young man next door who's a shut-in… I'm sorry. I may not be quite myself because I've been forced into a corner…

10 What's the atmosphere of your workplace like?

I try to make sure the atmosphere doesn't get tense, but my hands are moving in rapid motion… Getting tense just makes me feel worse though, and I become less efficient as a result.

11 What are your must-haves while working?

Ingredients for making café au lait, [caffeine drink] Minmin-daha, sweets, Milo, jelly drinks, SOYJOY bars.

12 Which manga artists do you respect?

My predecessors. People whose single-mindedness show in their work.

About *Vampire Knight*

1 How did you gather reference material for creating this manga?

I started watching various vampire movies in junior high, and when I was in college, I researched folklore as a hobby. These were in my head as reference material, so I didn't go out and gather new material regarding vampires… Sorry. I dug up this material that was stored in my brain and added my own interpretation, so I kind of felt that true vampire buffs would hate the series… Regardless, I forged ahead anyway.

I want to be Ichijo, mess with Kaname and make him explode. I want to become Yuki, mess with Zero and make him explode. I'm a masochist though.

⑪ Do vampires have blood types?

I think they do. Let's just say that they won't make it public.

⑫ How was this manga conceived?

Before *MeruPuri* ended, I started talking with my editor about my next series. Uh, this is gonna be long. [*Smile*] My editor insisted that we have lots of guys appear in it. To tell you the truth, I didn't want to do that, so I resisted until the very end. I was thinking I'd like to draw lots of girls. We tried to compromise and settled on the idea that if the story took place at a school, lots of guys would be forced to appear. I managed to have two heroes rather than have things turn into a male harem manga. We then argued over the fantasy elements. I'd been drawing fantasy stories, so I was eager to challenge myself by drawing a non-fantasy manga. However, my editor insisted on fantasy, saying, "Do you think readers expect you to provide an ordinary worldview?" Well, here things came to a standstill while we decided on what the theme would be. I really didn't have much time then, so now that I think about it, I'm impressed with how things took shape. My editor and I were chatting when I happened to say, "I'd like to draw a vampire one-shot story someday." My editor exclaimed, "That's it!" but I responded with, "Even as a one-shot, it'll be dark. If I make it into a series, I'll do everything I can to make the story really dark and bleak." My editor countered, "Let's make it a comedy." "But I want to draw a serious vampire story," I said. There was endless back-and-forth before we came to an agreement. At the same time, I decided that

⑥ Do you still have nicknames for the characters?

My editor sometimes calls Zero "Ero... I mean, Zero." Once when I met with my editor, Kaname was called Deep Impact* at the soirée being held at the Aido residence. (I'm sorry for being vulgar. Agh...) Due to the influence of the anime version of the class rep Kageyama, we call Ruka "Ruka-shan." In addition to the nicknames that I mentioned in volume 1, recently there have been nicknames like "the one whose gaze looks evil," "the one who's smiling in an erotic way," "the one whose gaze is lecherous," "the one whose lower eyelashes are drooping," "the one who's really grouchy," and so on... The nicknames change depending on the scene and the mood. It's a twisted game that people play when they're feeling cornered right before a deadline... Please overlook it. [*Sweat*] We do it because we love the characters.

*Deep Impact is a retired champion racehorse that's a stud now.

⑦ What size are Yuki's boobs?

Not big enough to fill soup bowls... Now they're about the size of those red lamps on alarms?

⑧ What are you careful about when drawing Kaname?

I'm so tense when I draw him I can't even explain it. It's because all the details related to him are core elements to the series.

⑨ What about summer uniforms? Is the school in a cold place?

It's cold, but I think there's a short summer there. It's cool enough that you only need to dress lightly, so you don't really need summer clothes.

⑩ Who would you like to be, and what would you like to do as that character?

continued from question 12

13 What's going to happen to the story now?

I have the rough plot ready. That came first, and the school setting was tacked on. If you look at my answer for question 12, you might be able to guess.

14 What is *Vampire Knight* to you?

A troublesome homework assignment that's worth doing. A challenge to myself. A vampire manga that's done my way. I'll keep forging ahead, believing that there are people out there who like this sort of manga.

the vampires would all attend school. (Since I'd first decided that the story would take place at a school…) And thus, *Vampire Knight* was born. If this had been a comedy, the title might have had the temporary title *Welcome to 9-bankan*!* [*Smile*] My editor and I always clash with each other passionately, but we work toward a common goal of creating as interesting a manga as possible. We're like comrades-in-arms. My feelings of gratitude are always whirling in my head.

* There's a shojo manga called *Welcome to 5-bankan*.

Matsuri Hino's profile

Born in Sapporo, Hokkaido, on January 24. Debuted with *Kono Yume ga Sametara* (When This Dream Is Over) in 1995.

List of Past Works

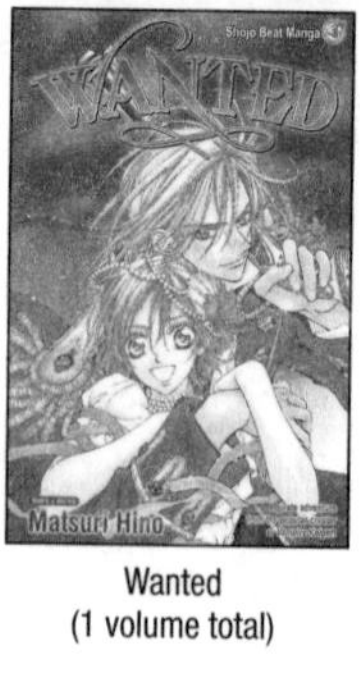
Shojo Beat Manga
WANTED
Matsuri Hino

Wanted
(1 volume total)

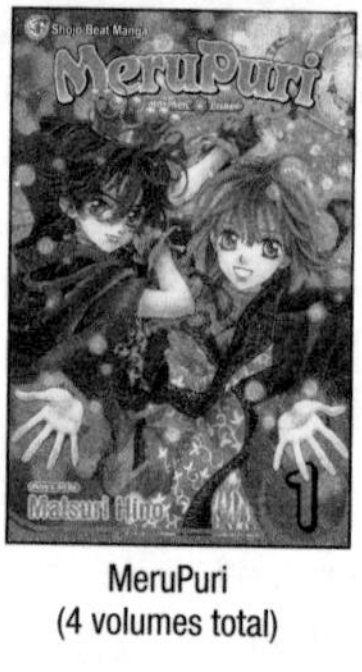
Shojo Beat Manga
MeruPuri
Matsuri Hino
1

MeruPuri
(4 volumes total)

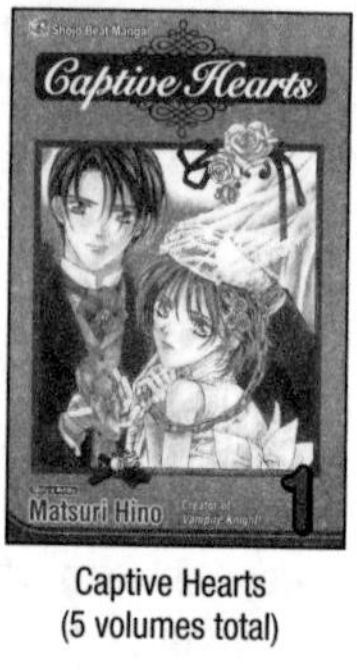
Shojo Beat Manga
Captive Hearts
Matsuri Hino
1

Captive Hearts
(5 volumes total)

PEOPLE WHO SENT IN QUESTIONS

Saori Yamagata, Hokkaido
Konoha, Ibaragi Prefecture
Misaki Inoue, Saitama Prefecture
Abe Maria, Tokyo
Tokimori Yue, Tokyo
Yuzuha Takashina, Fukui Prefecture
Rin, Gifu Prefecture
Genevieve, Kyoto
Yoi no Tsukihime, Ehime Prefecture
Toranpetto, Saga Prefecture

Special thanks to you!♥

Special Messages

with autographs and comments

From the Japanese anime cast

Here are some enthusiastic comments from the voice actors who played the main characters in the Japanese anime!!

① About the character I played
② About *Vampire Knight*

優姫♥

Yuki Cross

Performed by

Yui Horie

① I always pray for Yuki's happiness. ♥♥ She's a dear character that I'm deeply attached to. ♥

② The atmosphere of the story is very beautiful and serious, but our workplace was completely the opposite. Things were always merry, and I had lots of fun. ♪

零

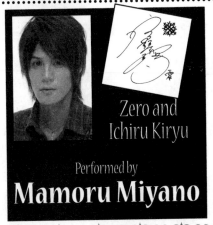

Zero and Ichiru Kiryu

Performed by

Mamoru Miyano

① Being Zero taught me about the strength of a heart that fights against fate, no matter how harsh it feels. I hope I can live that way too! Zero, thank you so much! I'm glad I was able to meet you!!

② From the drama CDs to the anime, I'm really happy that I've been involved with this work for so long!! I don't want it to end… I wonder if there will be a third season… [*Smile*] I want to keep being Zero!! So please consider it. [*Smile*]

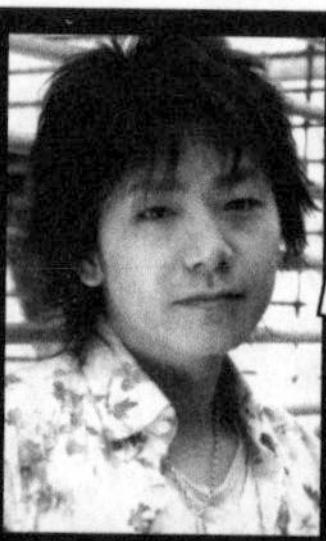

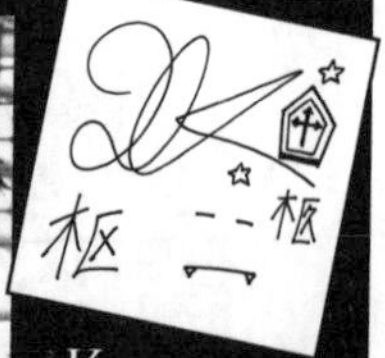

Kaname Kuran

Performed by

Daisuke Kishio

① I'll say it again and again. I love vampires, so I was really happy to play Kaname. Kaname is wonderful and a character that's easy to develop, so I love him!!

② I was happy I could work on both the drama CDs and the anime every week. The work itself is intense, but people were always laughing at the workplace. Everyone was hyper, and the studio was hot.

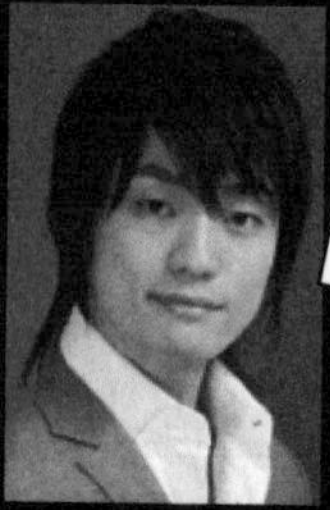

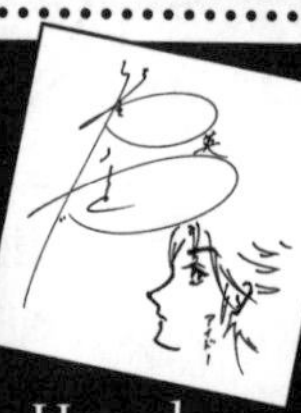

Hanabusa Aido

Performed by

Jun Fukuyama

① The anime featured Aido a lot more than I thought it would, so I was able to record both funny and serious scenes. I like his charm!

② The story brought together beautiful characters. Since Aido was in charge of keeping the rhythm, I was able to act fiercely and happily while being cool. I found it very interesting.

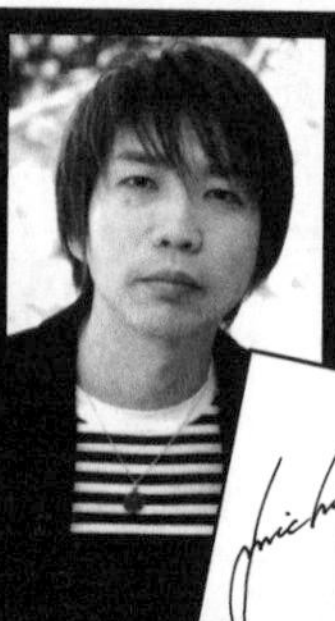

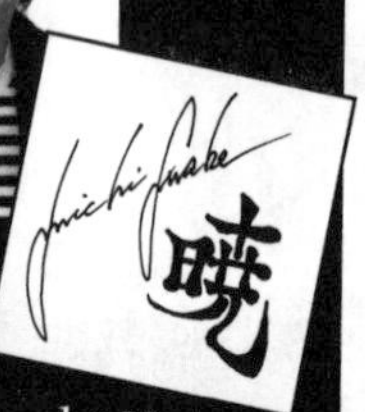

Akatsuki Kain

Performed by

Junichi Suwabe

① He speaks with his actions rather than with his words. That's Akatsuki Kain. He's a cool guy who watches over the situation calmly and objectively from a distance, but like the flames he manipulates, he has something passionate hidden inside himself... That was my impression of him. I did my best to act him out in a subdued way, but I also wanted to express his presence. I'm happy if I was able to etch him into your hearts a bit. While performing, I had this thought regarding his love situation: "Be more greedy and go for it!" [*Smile*]

② I was happy I could play the same character in both the drama CDs and the anime. I was immersed in this beautiful world with these wonderful characters for six months. I think it's rare that the main characters talk so little though. Recording didn't go smoothly because the microphones kept picking up noise. [*Smile*]

Takuma
Ichijo

Performed by

Susumu Chiba

① His kindness and flexibility. I was impressed by how much he cares for others, especially Shiki. I think if you asked him to plan a trip, it'd be fun traveling with him.

② The recording was really fun to do. Our team worked well together, and we loved our characters. I'm grateful I was able to come across such wonderful work.

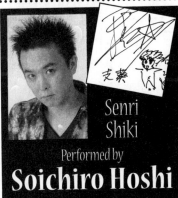

Senri
Shiki

Performed by

Soichiro Hoshi

① Amazing things happened in the middle, but Shiki stayed Shiki from the beginning to the end. [*Smile*]

② I'm glad I was able to take my time playing Shiki in the drama CDs as well as in the first and second seasons of the anime. I don't feel that the story is complete yet, so I'd like there to be a new series featuring Shiki.

Various official items full of the characters' charms!!

TREASURE COLLECTION

We show you things based on the series like novels and drama CDs as well as special goods. They're official *LaLa* items!!

Novels

Side stories where Aido and Kain are featured!!

The novels contain original stories about the main characters' pasts!!

樋野まつり
藤咲あゆな

LaLa Novels

Vampire Knight The Ice Blue Sin
By Matsuri Hino,
Written by Ayuna Fujisaki
(Published on April 5, 2008)

A sad but beautiful love story between Aido and a girl who adores him. Also contains a story about when Zero was younger.

LaLa Novels

Vampire Knight The Noir Trap
By Matsuri Hino,
Written by Ayuna Fujisaki
(Published on October 3, 2008)

A mysterious incident in showbiz that occurred when Yuki was in junior high…? Also contains short stories about love in the academy.

樋野まつり
藤咲あゆな

Drama CDs

Scripts are written by Matsuri Hino!!

Hino Matsuri

There are seven drama CDs that were either zenin service items or extras that came with *LaLa* magazine. The original scripts revealed surprising sides to Zero, Kaname, and the others.

LaLa
Midnight CD-PACK
Hino Matsuri

Vampire Knight Midnight CD-PACK
(2006 - February, March issues of *LaLa*, March issue of *LaLa DX*) [zenin service]

Contains two scripts: "Cross Academy Night Class" (which depicts the beginning of the manga) and "Night Class Personal Interview" (where funny dialogue makes you laugh)

Vampire Knight Moonlight CD-PACK
(2007 - July, August issues of *LaLa*, July issue of *LaLa DX*, August issue of *LaLa Special*) [zenin service]

Your heart flutters at the private life of the main characters depicted in "Visitor at Midnight" and "Moon Dormitory Spot Check."

Moonlight CD-PACK

LaLa magazine's super gorgeous extras

LaLa Kirameki ★ drama CD (September 2005 issue) [extra]
LaLa Gorgeous ♥ drama CD (November 2006 issue) [extra]
LaLa Treasure ★ drama CD (October 2007 issue) [extra]
LaLa Premium ♥ drama CD (May 2008 issue) [extra]
LaLa Excellent ★ drama CD (November 2008 issue) [extra]

Hino Matsuri

LaLa Original Goods

Not-for-sale goods that only LaLa readers were able to get!!

Various exciting goods and stationery that were put together by *LaLa*

* Reader giveaway [RG]
Zenin service [ZS]
Magazine extra [ME]
Thank-you giveaway [TG]

ZERO KIRYU

■ Cross Academy Alarm Clock
(2008 - June issue of *LaLa Special*, July and August issues of *LaLa*, May issue of *LaLa DX*) [ZS]

Even sleepyheads can wake up with the fascinating voices of seven characters! ♥

■ Good Night Set (Big bedsheet & good night CD)
(2008 - November and December issues of *LaLa*, November issue of *LaLa DX*) [ZS]

You can enjoy sleeping on a big bedsheet with Zero or Kaname on it. The CD contains voices of six male characters.

THERE WERE LOTS OF OTHER ITEMS TOO!

■ Night Class electric toothbrush and mini-towel set (2005 - January issue of *LaLa*) [RG]
■ Postcards (2005 - January issue of *LaLa*) [RG]
■ Eye shadow palette (2005 - February issue of *LaLa*) [RG]
■ Hot sandwich maker (2005 - March issue of *LaLa*) [RG]
■ Coaster (2005 - March issue of *LaLa*) [RG]
■ Guardian armband (2005 - April issue of *LaLa*) [RG]
■ Original telephone card (2005 - April issue of *LaLa*) [RG]
■ Night Class pocket notebook (2005 - April issue of *LaLa*) [RG]
■ Cross Academy pass case (2005 - April issue of *LaLa*) [RG]
■ Vampire Set <Cloak, fake blood, cross> (2005 - April issue of *LaLa*) [RG]
■ Yuki's first-aid set (2005 - April issue of *LaLa*) [RG]
■ Address memo sheets (2005 - April issue of *LaLa*) [RG]
■ QUO card (2005 - June issue of *LaLa*) [RG]
■ Kira ★ chara key ring (2005 - September and October issues of *LaLa*, September issue of *LaLa DX*) [ZS]
■ Secret ♥ memo pad (2005 - November issue of *LaLa*) [ME]
■ Zero vs. Kaname telephone card (2005 - November issue of *LaLa*) [RG]
■ Telephone card (December 2005 and January 2006 issues of *LaLa*, January 2006 issue of *LaLa DX*) [ZS]
■ Plastic file case and message card (2006 - January issue of *LaLa*) [RG]
■ Fleece blanket (2006 - February issue of *LaLa*) [RG]
■ Cross Academy school emblem necklace (2006 - March issue of *LaLa*) [ME]
■ Rose tin pencase (2006 - October issue of *LaLa*) [ME]
■ Original tosho card (2006 - October issue of *LaLa*) [TG]

■ 3 STARS CALENDAR (2007 - January issue of *LaLa*) [ME]
■ Original bag (2007 - January issue of *LaLa*) [RG]
■ Message card (2007 - January issue of *LaLa*) [RG]
■ Telephone card (2007 - January issue of *LaLa DX*) [RG]
■ Bath light (2007 - February issue of *LaLa*) [RG]
■ Cross tattoo bracelet (2007 - March issue of *LaLa*) [ME]
■ Lunch box (2007 - March issue of *LaLa*) [RG]
■ Plate (2007 - March issue of *LaLa*) [RG]
■ Transform ★ illusion mug (2007 - May and June issues of *LaLa*, May issue of *LaLa DX*) [ZS]
■ Gold & silver gel pen set (2007 - July issue of *LaLa*) [ME]
■ Parasol & cell phone cleaner (2007 - August issue of *LaLa*) [RG]
■ Very sweet ♥ voice card (2007 - September and October issues of *LaLa*, September issue of *LaLa DX*) [ZS]
■ Colorful ♥ greeting stamp set (2007 - October and November issues of *LaLa*) [RG]
■ Sparkling rose mirror (2007 - December issue of *LaLa*) [ME]
■ LaLa Memorial Calendar (2008 - January issue of *LaLa*) [ME]
■ Tosho card (2008 - January issue of *LaLa*) [TG]
■ Cross Academy-style tie (2008 - February issue of *LaLa*) [RG]
■ Cross Academy accessory set <Zero version/ Kaname version> (2008 - May and June issues of *LaLa*, May issue of *LaLa DX*) [ZS]
■ Book cover (2008 - June issue of *LaLa*) [RG]
■ Cross Academy pass case (2008 - June issue of *LaLa*) [ME]
■ Portable DVD player (2008 - June issue of *LaLa Special*) [RG]
■ Zero & Kaname plastic pouch (2008 - July issue of *LaLa*) [ME]
■ Memorial ♥ original stamp sheet set <stamp sheet, file, postcards> (2008 - September and October issues of *LaLa*) [ZS]
■ Silver stickers (2008 - October issue of *LaLa Special*)
■ Rose-thorned handkerchief (2008 - December issue of *LaLa*)

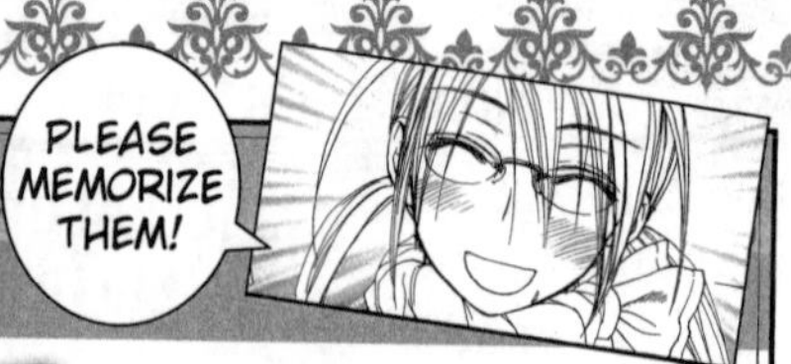
PLEASE MEMORIZE THEM!

Vampire Knight Glossary

Noteworthy Characters, Things, and Words

We feature various things from *Vampire Knight* that people want to know more about!!

This glossary is arranged alphabetically by category. Each source is listed in brackets with the volume number and chapter number separated by a dash. "S" means "side story," "N-S" means the novel *Setsuna no Toki*, and "N-I" means the novel *The Ice Blue Sin.*

building. Each gate has a Night Class student's name on it, and the Night Class students receive chocolates from girls lining up at these designated gates.

Experiment to test the strength of sand materials [6-28]
A test to see how big a circular cone tower you can build with sand from the sand pile in the garden. Also called playing with sand. Aido used to do this when he was a child.

Friendship Evening [2-S]
A party sponsored by Headmaster Cross. The purpose of it is so that the Day Class and Night Class students can get to know each other. It's usually held on the evening before the entrance ceremony.

The holidays [6-26]
When classes at Cross Academy are not held for a long time. Most students go back to their parents' place or travel. The Night Class students are no exception, and they all leave the academy.

Soirée [6-25]
A gathering of vampire aristocrats. There are various soirées held among the aristocrats like regular soirées. At large soirées, vampire hunters dispatched by the Hunter Society are on hand to supervise them.

ANIMAL

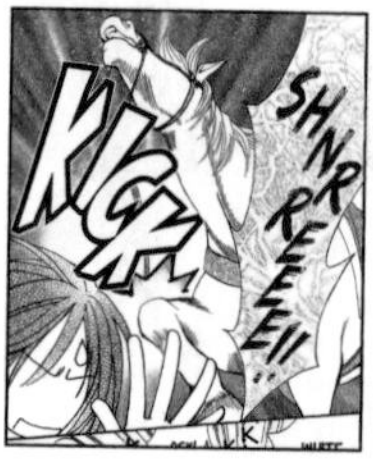
KICK
SHNRREEE!!

White Lily [2-6]
A white horse that's also called "the wild horse from hell." She will kick you if you look away. She is attached to Zero because he used to give her milk when she was a foal.

EVENT

The Ball [4-17]
One of the few official events that the Night Class and Day Class hold together. Girls dress up, guys wear their uniforms properly with a rose in their jacket breast pockets, and they dance together. The class that comes in last in the school exams held right before the ball has to work at the ball.

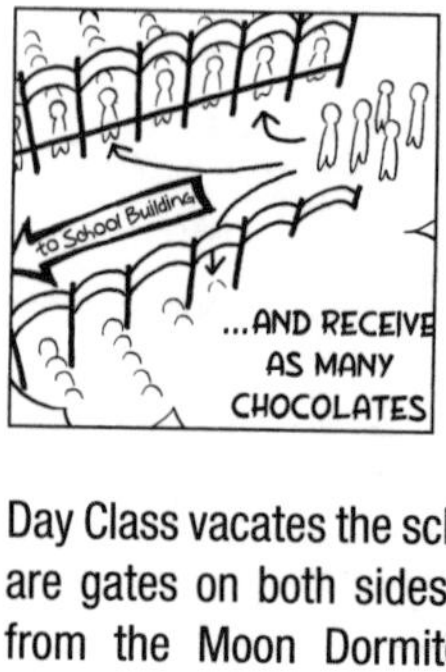
to School Building
...AND RECEIVE AS MANY CHOCOLATES

The "chocolate handoff" race [1-2]
An event that occurs on St. Xocolatl's day when the Night Class walks to class and the Day Class vacates the school building. There are gates on both sides of the road going from the Moon Dormitory to the school

Shio ramen [2-6]
One of the things you can eat in town. Zero wanted to eat this when he and Yuki went out shopping.

Stir-fried liver and leeks, my style [2-7]
Headmaster Cross's homemade cooking. It's not an ordinary stir-fry, but has been seasoned "my style." But that makes the food taste a little strange.

Related terms: A melt-in-your-mouth stew of bok choy and filet, my style

Sweets at the café [2-6]
Several menu items at the town café. Aido likes them and sometimes comes to the café to eat them.

GROUP

Detectives of Justice [5-24]
The Night Class students created this organization to investigate the blood-drinking incident that occurred at Cross Academy. It consists of members appointed by Kaname Kuran. Takuma Ichijo named the group, but there's no official name yet.

The Ichijo Group [3-10]
A company so huge that all human business transactions are involved with this company. Asato Ichijo grew it to this size.

The Kettle Club [2-S]
A Night Class club where you put kettles of different shapes on your head. Aido, Ichijo and Seiren are members…?

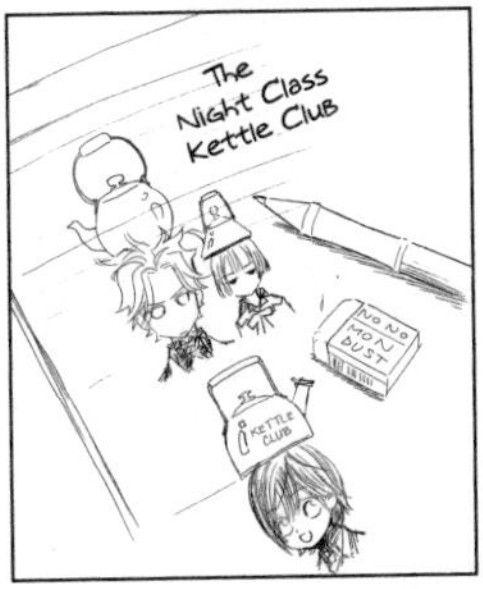
The Night Class Kettle Club
KETTLE CLUB

St. Xocolatl's Day [1-2]
A special day at Cross Academy where girls give chocolates to the guys they like and declare their love.

The thousand-questions survey [3-12]
When the Night Class was established at Cross Academy, vampires who wanted to enter the academy had to take time to fill this out. The survey became huge as Headmaster Cross worked on it eagerly…

FOOD

Ginger stir-fry set [2-S]
The morning "B set" menu. A fascinating dish that makes Yuki wake up at once.

Handmade chocolate [1-2]
The one chocolate Yuki successfully made on St. Xocolatl's day.

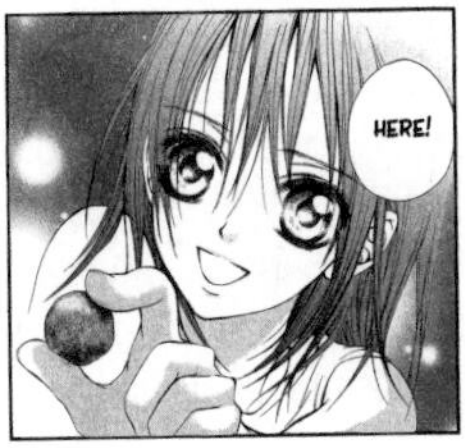
HERE!

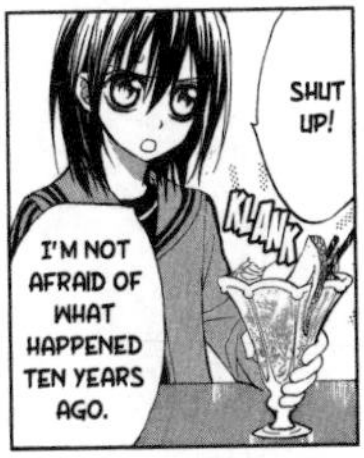
SHUT UP!
KLANK
I'M NOT AFRAID OF WHAT HAPPENED TEN YEARS AGO.

Parfait at the café [2-6]
Yuki's favorite parfait at the town café. Yuki can eat two in an instant.

Pokkin choco [3-14]
Sweets that Hanabusa Aido brought to school. These are biscuits in stick form that are coated with chocolate.

Rose tea [7-30]
Kaname got this for Headmaster Cross as a souvenir when he was away during the holidays.

Rose that blooms only once every ten years [7-30]

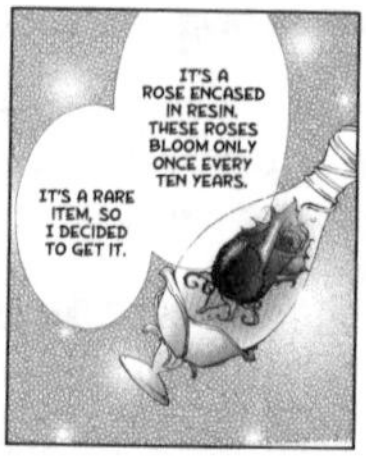
IT'S A ROSE ENCASED IN RESIN. THESE ROSES BLOOM ONLY ONCE EVERY TEN YEARS.
IT'S A RARE ITEM, SO I DECIDED TO GET IT.

The souvenir Kaname gave Yuki when he came back after the holidays. It's a rose that blooms only once every ten years, and it's encased in resin in a bottle. Kaname promised her ten years ago that the next time the rose bloomed, he would show it to her.

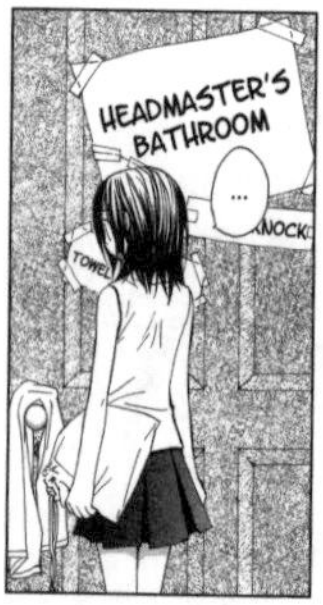
HEADMASTER'S BATHROOM
...

Towel [3-12]

You put this on the outside doorknob to show that you're using the bathroom at the Headmaster's living quarters. Yuki and Zero kept quarreling about using the bathroom, so this rule was decided between the two of them. But Yuki keeps opening the door without realizing he's using it.

Twenty tickets for Yuki's shoulder massage [1-2]

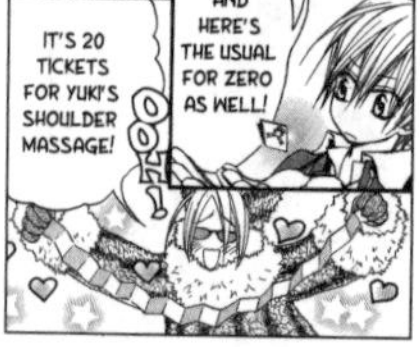
IT'S 20 TICKETS FOR YUKI'S SHOULDER MASSAGE!
AND HERE'S THE USUAL FOR ZERO AS WELL!

Yuki gave the Headmaster this as a St. Xocolatl's Day gift. She gives this to him every year.

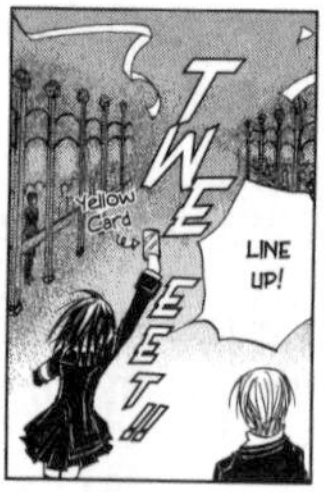
TWEEEET!!
LINE UP!
Yellow Card

Yellow card [1-2]

The card the Disciplinary Committee shows a student who resorts to dangerous acts on St. Xocolatl's Day.

Related term: Red card

"Kuran" and "Ichijo" [4-S]

Factions that existed for a very short time among a very small group of students in the Moon Dormitory. It started when Ichijo called Shiki—who's attached to him—an "Ichijo." Aido then tried to confirm whether Kaname or Ichijo is more popular by holding an election. Aido and Ruka declared themselves "Kurans." The election had no effect at all, however, because the Night Class students weren't interested. By the way, Kaname declared himself an "Ichijo."

ITEM

Bucket [1-S]

When Aido angers Kaname, punishment consists of a water-filled bucket being placed on his head. Aido has to hold water-filled buckets with his hands too.

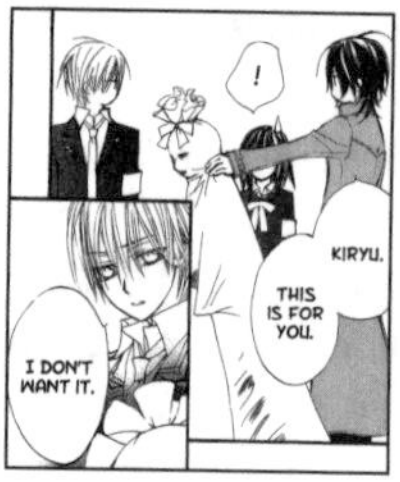
!
KIRYU.
THIS IS FOR YOU.
I DON'T WANT IT.

Cursed life-size doll [7-30]

A souvenir Kaname gave Zero when he came back to school after the holidays. The doll has supposedly been passed down since ancient times.

Errand ticket [1-2]

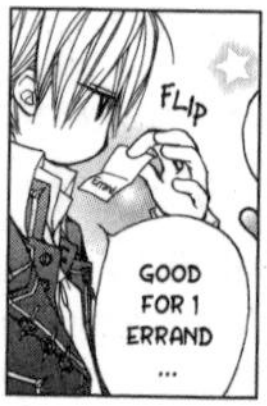
FLIP
GOOD FOR 1 ERRAND
...

Yuki gave this to Zero as a St. Xocolatl's Day gift. She apparently gives him the same thing every year.

Hidden camera [6-26]

A female Day Class student wanted to set up a hidden camera in the Moon Dormitory because the Night Class students would be gone during the holidays. The idea was rejected through Zero's silence.

Would you have preferred food instead? [7-30]

Yuki looked at the rose encased in resin that Kaname gave her as a souvenir in puzzlement, so he said this out of consideration. So he thinks she eats a lot…?

"Yuki…" series [3-11][3-S]

Lines related to Yuki that Headmaster Cross uses to have Kaname come over. They're 100% effective.

Example 1: "A vampire chased Yuki and attacked this place." The Headmaster used this line ten years ago. It was a lie, but Kaname believed it and rushed over.
Example 2: "Yuki has been kidnapped." The Headmaster used this line nine years ago. It was a lie, but Kaname believed it.
Example 3: "Yuki collapsed with a high fever." Kaname rushed over, but this time it was true.

NICKNAME/CHARACTER DESCRIPTION

Beasts in human form [1-1]

Zero referred to vampires this way with hate.

Gang leader [2-S]

Kain came up with this nickname for Kaname. It's just like Wild to say this.

Hana [6-28]

Hanabusa Aido's nickname when he was a child. His big sisters called him this.

He's beginning to get on my nerves [6-S]

Refers to Aido. When the young Aido appeared on TV and went on and on, Kaname bluntly said this about him.

He's just doing what he wants [5-23]

Refers to Aido, who ran away from the Moon

Yuki's whistle [1-2]

A whistle that says "Yuki's whistle!! Keep your mitts off, Zero!" Yuki uses it to quiet the students down.

LINE

Fighting is prohibited! [1-3]

The Cross Academy student handbook says so. If you still want to fight, Yuki insists that you first fight her since she is a member of the Disciplinary Committee.

In ten years, that's the only thing that has changed. [2-9]

What Kaname said to Yuki when he pointed out that she had stopped telling him everything like before. On the other hand, everything else has stayed the same for the past ten years. Like her having no boobs…

It's not food either… [7-30]

Kaname said this when Yuki stared at the souvenir he got for Zero. So he thinks she eats a lot…?

May I drink your blood? [1-1]

In Yuki's memories, the vampire who attacked her said this. There's probably no one who would actually answer yes.

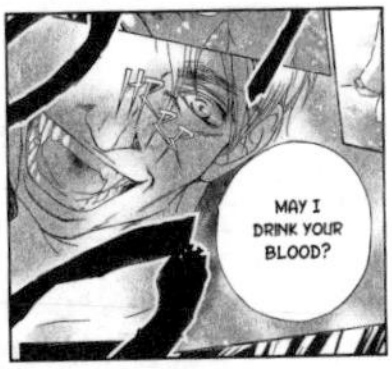
MAY I DRINK YOUR BLOOD?

Only I am witnessing this rare event with Kaname-sama! [2-S]

Only Aido was able to witness Kaname-sama smiling, holding a bucket, and filling up the bucket using a water hose. But if Aido showed that he was happy witnessing this rare event, he would have been punished even more.

Practically ran away from home [6-28]
Refers to Kaname. He doesn't want to go back to his own home, which Asato Ichijo manages, so Kaname usually stays at the Aido family vacation home when school is closed. Aido ended up blurting this out because he felt sympathy for Kaname.

Retired twit [2-8]
One of the several names Toga Yagari calls Headmaster Cross.

Rising star of the Day Class [2-6]
Refers to Zero. The male Day Class students have high hopes for him because he's the only one who can glare fearlessly at Kaname Kuran.

Savage brute [6-29]
Refers to Rido. Senri Shiki's mother accurately described Shiki's father, Rido, this way.

The Senate's henchmen [5-22]
Refers to the assassins who came to execute Zero on the charge of killing the pureblood Shizuka Hio. Kaname said this term with hate. Haruka also used this term a long time ago.

Silly twit [2-8]
One of the several names Toga Yagari calls Headmaster Cross.

Supreme gang leader [2-S]
Refers to Kaname. Aido blurted out this nickname.

This fool [1-1]
Refers to Aido, who had bitten Yuki. Kaname cut him down with these words.

Wild [2-S]
Akatsuki Kain's nickname. When Hanabusa Aido was nicknamed "Idol," Kain became Dormitory and started staying in Headmaster Cross's private quarters. Aido kept complaining, but he ate everything Zero cooked, so Yuki said this about Aido.

AS SOON AS IT WAS READY, HE ATE IT!
WELL ...
I WAS ABLE TO EAT IT...
IT WAS ALL RIGHT.
TINK

Homeless me [6-28]
Refers to Kaname. Aido mentioned how Kaname had practically run away from home, so Kaname countered with this description of himself. Maybe he's enjoying Aido feeling guilty…?

Idol [2-S]
Hanabusa Aido's nickname. During Friendship Evening, new student Yuki had mumbled, "Aido's like an idol…" and the female students around her took to her comment.

Related term: Wild

Kaname-sama [3-11]
Refers to Kaname. When Yuki was a child, she called Kaname this. She didn't seem to understand the meaning of "sama" then.

Kaname-sama's right-hand men [2-7]
The Night Class students call Aido and Kain this.

Miracle Genius [1-5]
Refers to Aido. The academic world calls him this.

Related term: Handsome boy genius

Moron [1-S]
Refers to Aido. Ruka said there's no one else who suits this word so well.

garden, and rare-colored roses bloom all year round. It is a comfortable place to stay, so Kaname and the other students often visit here.

Café [2-6]
Yuki and Aido frequent this place, which is in a town near Cross Academy.

Tropical island [7-S]
Headmaster Cross took Yuki and Zero here during vacation. The sunlight shines brightly, so it was a harsh environment for Zero.

SCHOOL LECTURE

Macroeconomics [2-8]
One of the lectures in the Night Class. In macroeconomics, you research economic activities on a national scale like the nation's income and the labor market. You usually study this in a college economics class. Kaname wasn't interested in "that old man's macroeconomics" lecture though.

SOUND EFFECT

Lunk… [2-6]
The sound that occurred when Zero put the huge sack of goods that he got at the Headmaster's request on his shoulders. The contents were never shown.

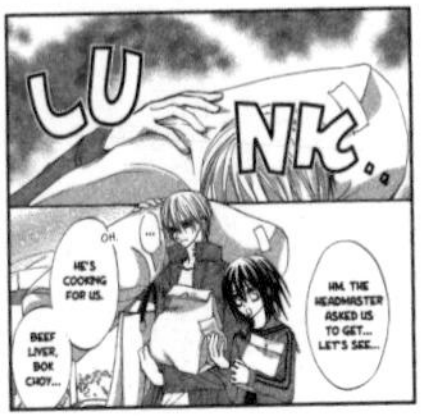
LUNK..
HM. THE HEADMASTER ASKED US TO GET... LET'S SEE...
...
OH.
HE'S COOKING FOR US.
BEEF LIVER, BOK CHOY...

Rsst rsst [6-25]
When Yagari grabs Zero's hair, this is the sound that it makes. He's been doing this as a way to greet Zero since Zero was a child.

a victim of circumstances and got this nickname because he looks wild.

Related term: Idol

PERSON

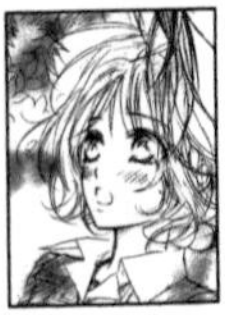

Fuka Kisaragi [N-I]
A female Day Class student. She has a secret.

Kaito [N-S]
A vampire hunter candidate who trained briefly with Zero under Yagari when Zero was a child. He later became an outstanding vampire hunter.

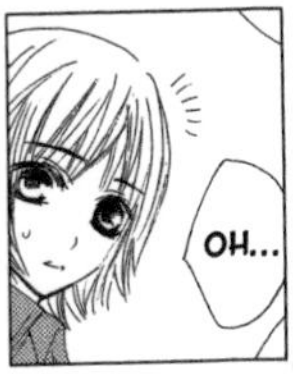
OH...

Maki [9-39]
A girl who keeps trying to sneak into the Moon Dormitory. She was almost attacked by one of Rido's servant vampires.

Waitress at the café [2-6]
Waitress at the café near Cross Academy. She's a sharp person who talked to Zero, sensing that he looked "a little different from ordinary people."

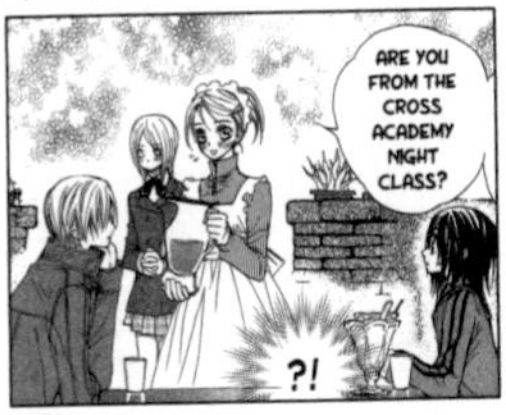
ARE YOU FROM THE CROSS ACADEMY NIGHT CLASS?
?!

PLACE

Aido family vacation home [6-28]
The place where Kaname Kuran and other Night Class students spend their holidays. It is one of the many vacation homes that the Aido family owns. This one is so far away from the academy that the weather is different here. The courtyard has a rose

VAMPIRE KNIGHT OFFICIAL FANBOOK
SB PROFILES

STORY AND ART BY
MATSURI HINO

Translation & Adaptation / Tomo Kimura
Lead Design / Frances O. Liddell, Fawn Lau
Graphic Design / Ronnie Casson
Editor / Amy Yu

VAMPIRE KNIGHT KOUSHIKI FANBOOK X by Matsuri Hino

First published in Japan in 2008 by HAKUSENSHA, Inc., Tokyo.
English language translation rights arranged with HAKUSENSHA, Inc., Tokyo.

The rights of the author(s) of the work(s) in this publication to be so identified have been asserted in accordance with Copyright, Designs and Patents Act 1988. A CIP catalogue record for this book is available from the British Library.

Printed in the U.S.A.

Published by VIZ Media, LLC
P.O. Box 77010
San Francisco, CA 94107

10 9 8 7 6 5 4 3 2 1
First printing, October 2010

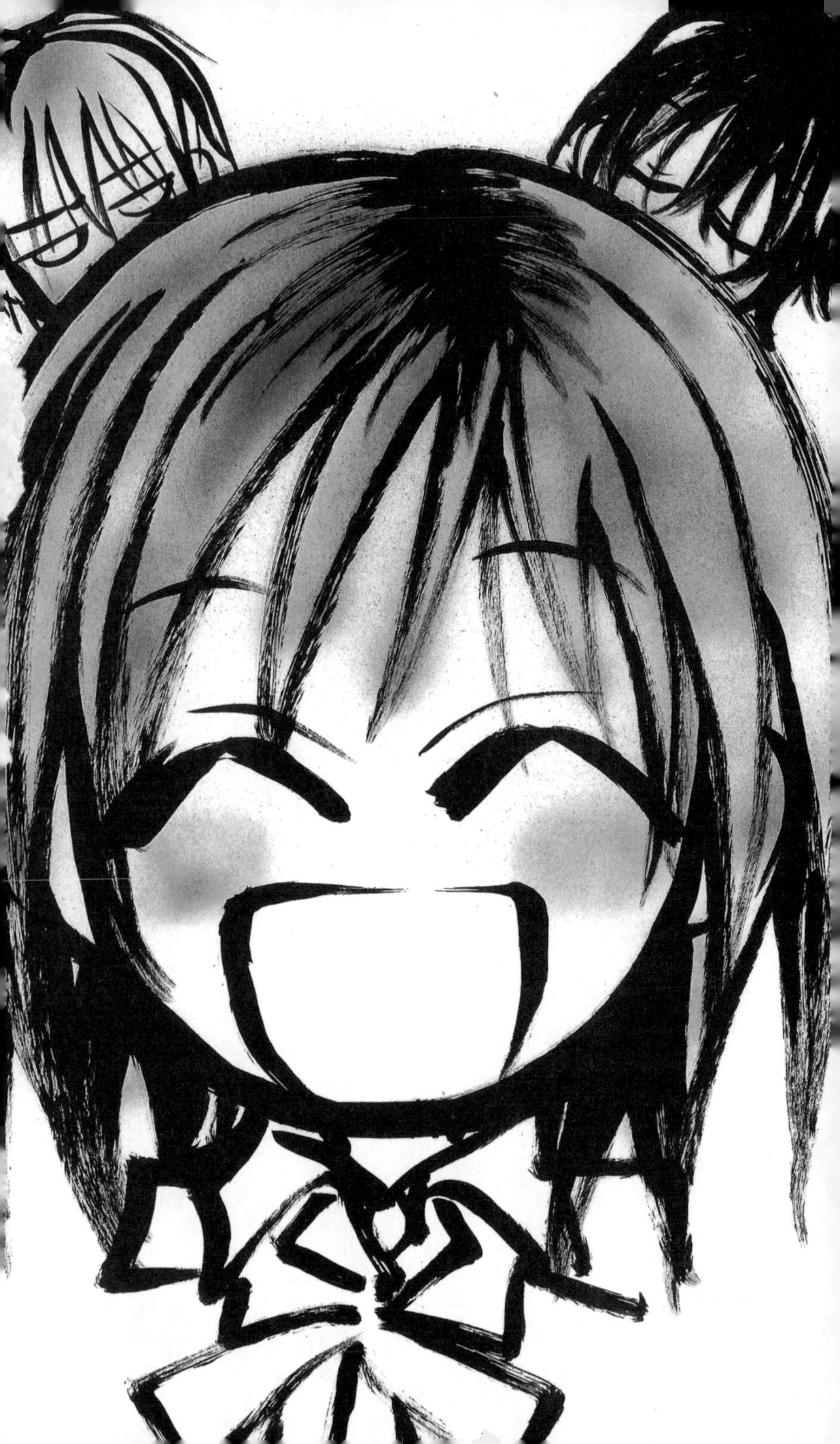